D0765565

Cooking for Today

Cooking for Today

250 imaginative recipes, from basic soups to elegant desserts

JG PRESS

First published in Great Britain in 1995
by Hamlyn
an imprint of Reed Consumer Books
Limited
Michelin House, 81 Fulham Road,
London SW3 6RB
and Auckland, Melbourne, Singapore
and Toronto

ISBN 1-57215-187-0

Library of Congress Cataloguing in
Publication Number is available on
request.

Published in the USA 1995 by J G Press
Distributed by World Publications, Inc.
The J G Press imprint is a trademark of
J G Press, Inc.
455 Somerset Avenue
North Dighton MA 02764

Produced by Mandarin Offset
Printed in Hong Kong

Art Editor: Mark Winwood
Designers: Margaret Sadler
        Louise Leffler
        Leigh Jones
Managing Editor: Anne Johnson
Editors: Janet Smy
        Maggie Ramsay
        Elsa Petersen-Schepelern
        Isobel Holland
Recipe contributors:
        Mary Cadogan
        Sally Mansfield
        Annie Nichols
        Louise Pickford
        Ingeborg Pertwee
        Lyn Rutherford
        Jeni Wright
Production Controller: Melanie Frantz
Nutritional Consultants:
        Michael van Straten
Indexer: Hilary Bird

All black and white line Illustrations
by Coral Mulla

Notes

Standard level spoon measurements
are used in all recipes.
1 tablespoon = one 15 ml spoon
1 teaspoon = one 5 ml spoon

Eggs should be medium unless otherwise stated. Some recipes contain raw
eggs. Readers are reminded that it
would be prudent, particularly those
who are more vulnerable, such as
pregnant women, invalids, the elderly,
babies, young children, to avoid eating
uncooked eggs.

Milk should be whole unless otherwise
stated.

Pepper should be freshly ground black
pepper unless otherwise stated.
Fresh herbs should be used unless
otherwise stated. If unavailable use
dried herbs as an alternative but halve
the quantities stated. Parsley should be
the flat leaf variety.

Ovens should be preheated to the
specified temperature–if using a
convection oven, follow the
manufacturer's instructions for
adjusting the time and temperature.

For barbecuing, cooking times are
approximate. They have been estimated using a charcoal-fired barbecue and
will vary according to the size and type
of broiler, weather conditions and the
intensity of heat.

When barbecuing food: before using
wooden skewers or string soak them in
water for 30 minutes to avoid burning.

Vegetarians should look for the 'V'
symbol on cheese to ensure it is made
with vegetarian rennet.

To test if poultry is cooked, pierce the
flesh through the thickest part with a
skewer or fork–the juices should run
clear, never pink or red.

Do not refreeze poultry which has
been previously frozen and thawed.
Do not refreeze a cooked dish which
has been previously frozen and
thawed.

Acknowledgments

Divertimenti, 45/47 Wigmore Street,
London W1H 9LE, ph: 0171-935
0689, 139/141 Fulham Road, London
SW3 6SD, ph: 0171-581 8065,
Divertimenti Mail Order ph: 0171-386
9911, fax: 0171-386 9393: 67 top
left, 67 bottom right, 67 center left,
67 top right, 72 top left, 72 bottom
left, 74 right center, 74 top right, 74
top left, 75 bottom left, 75 top right,
75 center, 75 left center, 76 left, 76
bottom right, 76 top right, 77 bottom
left, 77 top right, 77 center, 77 top
left, 77 top center, 77 bottom right,
78 center left, 79 bottom left, 79
right center bottom, 79 center, 79 top
center, 79 center left, 80 top right, 80
bottom right, 80 left

David Mellor 4 Sloane Square,
London SW1W 8EE, David Mellor
Country Shop, The Round Building,
Grindleford Road, Hathersage,
Sheffield S30 1BA : 6 bottom, 66 bottom center, 66 bottom right, 66 bottom left, 66 top right, 67 top left center, 68 top left, 68 center, 68 top
right, 68 bottom, 69 bottom right, 69
top right, 69 bottom left, 69 top left,
69 bottom center, 70 bottom left, 70
top, 70 bottom right, 71 top, 71 bottom, 72 left center, 72 center, 72
right, 72 top right, 73 bottom left, 73
top, 73 bottom, 74 bottom, 75 right
bottom, 75 right center, 75 top left,
78 center, 78 top left, 78 bottom
right, 78 top right, 79 top right, 79
bottom center left, 79 bottom right

Reed International Books Ltd /Bryce
Attwell 64 above right, 64 above left,
64 bottom left, 65, /Steve Baxter
114, 123 above, 130 /1, 148 below,
191 bottom right, 210 /1, /Mitchell
Beazley 6 above, 8, 9, 10, 11, 12, 13,
14 above right, 14 above left, 14
below right, 14 bottom right, 14 top
right, 14 below left, 15 above right,
15 center/bottom right, 15 above left,
15 top right, 15 top left, 15 bottom
left, 16 top left, 16 below right, 16
bottom right, 16 above left, 16 below
left, 16 top right, 16 bottom left, 17
above right, 17 below right, 17 above
right, 17 below left, 18 /19, 22 /3, 25
above, 27 center, 34 /5, 38 /9, 38
below center, 38 below left, 38 below
right, 40 above, 41 above, 53 below,
/Nick Carman 128, 201 above, 201
below, 212 /3, 230, /Joe Cornish 217,
/Mick Duff 11 bottom left, /Alan
Duns 232, /Laurie Evans 56, 58 /9,
82, 90, 96 below, 116 /7, 129 below,
130, 134 right, 134 left, 139, 175
left, 180 bottom, 196, 197, 210
below, 214, 216, 230 /1, /Gus Filgate
Gatefold 1 (5), Gatefold 1 (4),
Gatefold 3 (11), 57, 164 bottom, 164
/165, 195 above, 198 below, 198
above, 199, 200 below, 204 below,
208 below, 209, 212 below, 214 /5,
221, /GGS Photographics 36, 40
below, 42 left, 42 right, 46 right, 46
left, 47 below, 49, 50 left, 50 right,
51 top right, 51 left, 51 center, 110
left, 110 right, 188 top left, 188 top
right, /Hamlyn Group Picture Library

234 above, 234 below, 235, 236
above, /Norman Hollands 24, 226 /7,
/Jeremy Hopley 2, 7 below, 52, 81,
113 above, 125 below, 138 /9, 158,
169 top, 184, 193 bottom right, 202
/3, /Tim Imrie Gatefold 3 (7), Gatefold
3 (3), Gatefold 3 (6), Gatefold 3 (4),
Gatefold 3 (9), /James Jackson 220
above, /James Johnson 7 above center,
7 above right, 7 above left, 219 left,
219 center, 219 right, /Paul Kemp 242,
243, /Graham Kirk Gatefold 1 (1),
Gatefold 2 (5), 2 /3, 25 below left, 27
below, 47 above, 86 /7, 86 top, 86
below, 86 center, 92 below, 94, 95 left,
95 right, 96 above, 97, 102, 103, 104
/5, 109 above, 112 above, 113 below,
115 below, 115 above, 118 below, 129
above, 135, 143 below, 154 bottom,
155, 159 right, 169 bottom, 170 left,
172, 173 top, 173 bottom, 174 bottom, 176 bottom, 177 bottom, 178,
179 bottom, 180 top, 185 top, 188
/189, 190, 193 bottom right, 202, 208
above, 226 above, /Duncan McNicol
220 below, /James Merrell Gatefold 3
(2), Gatefold 3 (10), Gatefold 3 (1),
Gatefold 2 (4), Gatefold 2 (3), Gatefold
3 (8), Gatefold 2 (7), Gatefold 2 (2),
Gatefold 3 (5), Gatefold 2 (1), Gatefold
2 (6), 44, 142, 143 above, 144 /5,
144, 146 below, 148 above, 150 /1,
150, 151 below, 151 above, 152
below, 152 above, 153, 170 /171,
206, 215, /Diana Miller Gatefold 1 (3),
54, 55, 82 /3, 84 above, 84 below, 85
above, 88 below, 88 above, 236 /7,
/James Murphy Gatefold 1 (2), 5, 26,
37, 85 below, 98 center, 98 below, 98
top, 99, 100, 105, 110 /1, 112 below,
124, 125 above, 137, 140, 141 above,
141 below, 156, 157, 166 top, 166
bottom, 167, 174 top, 176 top, 177
top, 182 /183, 186 /187, 187 bottom,
191 top left, 200 above, 204 above,
205, 212 above, /Peter Myers 236
below, /Alan Newnham 13 bottom, 39
below, 41 below, 90 /1, 92 above,
101, 104 above, 116, 118 above, 119,
120, 120 /1, 122, 123 below, 133, 146
above, 147, 149, 154 top, 168, 175
right, 179 top, 181, 185 bottom, 186
top, 192, 194, 195 below, 222, 222 /3,
226 below, 228 /9, 233, /Roger
Phillips 62 bottom left, /John Sims 225,
/Charlie Stebbings 224 left, /Roger
Stowell Gatefold 1 (7), Gatefold 1 (6),
Gatefold 1 (8), 62 above right, 62
above left, 63, 89, 93, 108, 109 below,
126 /7, 127, 132 /3, 132, 159 left,
160 /161, 161 bottom, 162, 163 bottom, 163 top, 206 /7, 210 above, /Phil
Webb 106 /7, 106, 107, 136 right,
136 left, /Paul Williams 224 right,
/Trevor Wood 25 below right

Tesco Stores Ltd 228 top, 229 top

Waitrose, Food Shops of the John
Lewis Partnership 53 top right, 60
right, 60 left

Foreword

Over the past years I have written many cookery books for Hamlyn Publishing. These covered a wide range of subjects and gave up-to-date information on various foods, cooking techniques and carefully tested recipes. The hugely enjoyable years of working with Hamlyn Publishing made me appreciate the expertise with which their books are prepared and the time and effort spent in producing both colorful and inspiring photographs. That is why I am delighted to write this foreword to their new and very exciting Cooking for Today.

This comprehensive book offers a fresh approach to everyday cooking. It will give the user confidence to cook all kinds of dishes from pasta to an elaborate dinner party menu. It begins with an illustrated reference section and an introduction to kitchen skills, together with a detailed look at important ingredients. Basic cookery techniques are explained with step-by-step spreads and cook's tip boxes. Foods like stocks, sauces, pastry and breads are examined in detail. There is helpful information about cooking equipment with sections on the best use of your microwave and freezer. The detailed look at different wines will be invaluable.

The second part of the book contains an extensive collection of 250 beautifully illustrated easy-to-follow recipes, many with interesting variations. Each recipe includes an at a glance guide to nutritional content. You will find classic dishes such as Coq au Vin, Tournedos en Croûte, Lasagne and Crème Caramel, with many modern recipes for such things as Linguine with Mussels and Tomato Sauce, Roasted Fall Vegetables with Garlic Sauce, Baby Eggplants with Herbed Greek Yogurt and a delicious Peach, Apricot and Blueberry Gratin.

In an exciting design innovation, there are three self-contained editorial features that open out to two double page: The Great Outdoors – which looks at barbecues; Saturday Night Fever – featuring cocktails and drinks for those special occasions and That's Entertainment which describes the way to plan a meal successfully.

I am sure you will find this a most valuable book in your kitchen. If you are a beginner it will give you great confidence; if you are an experienced cook its clear, concise recipes and magnificent photographs will soon be a regular source of inspiration.

Marguerite Patten

Contents

Vegetables

Season by season, the range of vegetables available for consumption is always plentiful, not to mention colorful and delicious. Today's constantly improving marketing techniques insure they can be bought at the peak of freshness.

Asparagus
The tips should be tightly closed and the stalks firm. Cook the stalks in a tall pan with the tips in steam and the bottoms in water for 10 minutes.

Avocado
The avocado should yield to gentle pressure at the stalk end but should not be squashy. Eat raw or make into a dip. When cut, always brush with lemon juice to prevent discoloration.

Beets
Young beets can be eaten raw, peeled, grated, and mixed with a dressing. To avoid the vegetable bleeding into the water during cooking, choose beets that do not have damaged skins, and cut off the tops, leaving 2 inches above the root. Boil in lightly salted water for 30–40 minutes, cool and peel. Serve either hot or cold.

Eggplant
The skin should be firm and bright. Some people cube and salt the flesh, let it drain and then dry it before cooking; others say this is not necessary. Particularly suited to Mediterranean styles of cookery, the eggplant can be stewed, roasted, made into fritters or stuffed.

Fava bean
Early in the summer season, the young bean can be eaten lightly cooked, pods included. As it matures, the skin becomes tough and should be rubbed off halfway through cooking.

Buying

Choose vegetables that really are good enough to eat without needing much preparation. Look for the following qualities:
• Leafy varieties, such as spring cabbage, celery and lettuce, should have a fresh appearance, with no sign of browning, wilting or slime.
• Root vegetables, such as carrots, should be firm and have no sign of damp or shiny patches or any surface damage. Avoid potatoes with dry wrinkly skins or if they are turning green or sprouting.

Broccoli

Calabrese has densely packed heads; sprouting broccoli has smaller, looser heads and is leafier. It should look firm and healthy, with no sign of yellowing. It is best lightly steamed or microwaved. Before cooking, trim the stems and cut the florets into even-size pieces before boiling or steaming.

Cabbage

Use shredded red or white cabbage in salads, dressed with a well-flavored vinaigrette. To prepare hearted cabbage, halve and then quarter, cutting out and discarding the hard core, and shred finely. Rinse well and cook slowly in a covered pan with only the water that clings to the leaves, and some butter or olive oil, or stir-fry. Red cabbage is braised for 1–2 hours with sliced onion, apple, and a little red vinegar and stock.

Carrot

An inexpensive source of Vitamins A and C, mineral salts, trace elements and fiber, carrots can be eaten grated raw in salads or cooked. New carrots need only scrubbing, older ones should be lightly peeled. They can be boiled, braised, steamed, or used in soups or stews.

Cauliflower

Eat this all-year vegetable raw or lightly cooked. When cooked the florets should be just soft and the stem should be fairly crunchy.

Chinese cabbage

This has long, white, slightly ribbed stalks and is often called Chinese leaves. It is best cooked by steaming or stir-frying; it is also used for stuffing and in salads.

Celery

At its best during the winter months, celery may be used raw in salads or served with cheese at the end of a meal. It can also be made into soup, added to stews and casseroles, or braised.

Cucumber

Select one that is straight and firm with a slight bloom on the skin. It will be at its best when fresh and crisp, and lose these qualities after a few days. Use in salads or cube and fry quickly in butter to serve with chicken or fish.

Globe artichoke
Boil or steam for at least 30 minutes. It is ready when a leaf pulls away easily. Dip the bottom of each leaf into a sauce and scrape off the flesh with your teeth. Discard the hairy choke, and eat the heart with the sauce.

Storing

It is not a good idea to buy lots of vegetables which languish in the refrigerator for weeks before you get around to using them–the fresher they are, the more flavor and nutrition they have to offer. Any close-fitting packaging should be removed to prevent moisture from building up.

● Firm vegetables, such as cauliflower or cabbage, can be stored for up to a week in the refrigerator's salad drawer.

● Root vegetables will keep in a cool dark place for a couple of weeks. Remove from polythene bags and keep in strong brown paper bags with the top folded over.

● Leafy and salad vegetables will keep for several days at the bottom of the refrigerator.

Fennel
This bulb is white with overlapping leaves and has a mild rather sweet flavor similar to aniseed. Use it raw in salads, tossed in lemon juice to prevent the cut slices from browning; or steam, poach or boil and serve with cheese sauce.

French or green bean
At its best, this should be bright to darkish green in color and the skin should have a slight bloom. Boil or steam whole, or broken into even lengths, until just tender. Serve with fish, poultry or meat, or in salads.

Kohlrabi
When fresh and firm, this root vegetable has a crisp, delicate, turnip-like flavor. Choose small ones and do not peel; just scrape away any blemishes and drop into acidulated water. Steam or boil whole for about 15–20 minutes, or slice and stir-fry very small ones, or serve raw in salads.

Leek
Avoid older leeks with woody stems. Use the white part, reserving the green tops for soups. Leeks are best kept loosely wrapped in the bottom of the refrigerator. Lightly cook by boiling or steaming and serve with a sauce, or slice finely and stir-fry.

Lettuce

Varieties divide into three groups: round, like iceberg; long, like romaine; loose-leafed, like oak leaf or lollo. Wash and dry in a salad spinner or on a clean dishcloth. Use in salads, make into soups, or braise.

Mushroom

Button and flat mushrooms are widely available and other varieties appear on a seasonal basis. Simply wipe the stalk and cap with paper towels. Use raw in salads, cook in melted butter, or add to casseroles, soups and stews. Best eaten on day of purchase.

Squash

This is best eaten when about 12 inches in length, when it can be cooked quickly in a microwave oven, or sliced and cooked in butter or olive oil, steamed, boiled or stir-fried. When dealing with a bigger one, peel and halve it; remove the central pithy flesh and seeds, then stuff and bake.

Okra (ladies' fingers)

The five-sided pods of the okra give a silky finish to curries, soups or stews and can be sautéed in butter. To prepare for cooking, wash and dry, being careful not to break the seed pod.

Onion

A wide choice ranges from small pickling onions through to the large bulbous Spanish onion, with red and scallions in between, both essential in salads, and the pungent garlic-flavored shallot. Use in casseroles, soups, sauces, stews and also in savory tarts.

Pea

Pea pods should be round and full but not hard. When young, peas may be eaten raw in salads, but as they mature they should be steamed or boiled in lightly salted water. Older peas (the pods will no longer be bright green) can be made into soups or puréed.

Bell pepper

A brightly colored vegetable (red, green, black, white or yellow) which can be used raw in salads, or stuffed and baked, stewed or stir-fried. To prepare, remove the core and seeds. Bell peppers keep well in the refrigerator.

Potato

This is one of the most versatile of all vegetables and when plain boiled, steamed or baked is low in calories. Peel potatoes for French fries, cook the rest in their skins. There are many varieties that are well worth trying.

Pumpkin

This winter squash is a good source of Vitamin A, has dark yellow fibrous flesh and a sweet flavor. To prepare, remove the seeds and central pithy part, cut off and discard the skin and cube the flesh. Steam or boil until soft (allow about 20 minutes), drain and purée. Use for savory and sweet dishes.

Radish

The small, round, red and white variety is the most common. Others may be elongated or have white, black or violet skins, but all are eaten raw in salads. Choose those that are firm and glossy. Large ones have no flavor.

Sorrel

This midsummer vegetable has small, fleshy, light green rounded leaves. It looks like spinach and is prepared in the same way. Serve raw in salads, steam or cook in the water remaining on the leaves after washing.

Corn

This should be creamy yellow and firm. Remove husk and silk and boil in unsalted water for about 5 minutes until the kernels are soft. Drain and serve hot with melted butter, or use in salads, casseroles and soups. Baby corn can be stir-fried or lightly steamed for salads.

Spinach

Wash the dark green leaves very carefully in several changes of water to get rid of any grit or soil. Young spinach can be used raw in salads. For cooking, allow 8–10 ounces per person and steam or cook in the water remaining on the leaves after washing, drain and press out excess liquid.

Turnip

Small young turnips can be eaten raw in salads, or finely sliced and cooked in butter. Older ones should be peeled before they are added to soups and stews.

Tomato

Varieties range from the tasty sweet cherry to the large beef tomato, which can lack flavor. In summer, plum tomatoes are a great delight.

Fruit

Always refreshingly appetizing, fruit plays an essential part in a healthy balanced diet, providing energy in the form of sugar (fructose), dietary fiber, minerals and vitamins. The wonderful colors of fruit add brightness to savory dishes and fruit salads, and it is a perfect palate cleanser between courses.

Apple
A very good source of Vitamin C and water-soluble dietary fiber; apples are available in a wide variety. Always take the opportunity to savor home-grown varieties of eating apples when they are in season. Popular eating apples are Grimies, Jonathan and McIntosh. The best varieties for cooking include Granny Smith, Pippin and Spitzenberg.

Banana
Use unripe fruit with a pale skin for baking or frying. For eating, choose bananas with a rich yellow skin mottled with brown. Do not refrigerate, as the skins will blacken and the fruit will become squashy.

Apricot
Eat these raw; poach for pies, mousses and conserves; or add to meat dishes. Use the pit's kernel to add an almond flavor to the cooked fruit. Underripe apricots will be pale, or tinged with green. At their best the skin will have a warm golden color. Eat quickly after purchase.

Berries
Eat or cook on the day of purchase. Cultivated blackberries can be eaten raw, but the wild fruit is best cooked. Raspberries are best served with cream or in a fruit salad, pie, ice cream or in sauces. The elongated deep red loganberry is very juicy and has a tart flavor. Eat fresh with sugar and cream, puréed, or in sorbets, ice creams, mousses, pies and preserves.

Cherry
Sweet eating cherries are delicious raw. The sour cherries, like morello, are best cooked and served with poultry and game. Cooked sweet cherries can be used for tarts, pies, ice cream, preserves or made into soups.

Buying

- Fruit that is firm, plump and unwrinkled will be fresh and its juice content will be good.
- The fruit skins should not be split, broken or bruised in any way.
- There should be no insect damage.
- Fragrance is a good way of selecting fruit at its very best.
- Berries should look dry and full with no signs of mold or wetness. Always check the bottom of containers of berried fruit; there should be no sign of juice leakage.
- Buy soft berried fruit for immediate consumption.
- Store fruit in a cool place—at room temperature it will quickly deteriorate.

Coconut
Puncture 3 indentations at the top of the nut to pour out the colorless juice. Crack open the nut by hitting it with a hammer one-third of the way from the top. Use the flesh raw, or dry and shredded.

Currants–black, white, red
To strip the picked fruit off the stems, hold over a bowl and slide a fork down the length of the stem. Poach lightly in syrup and serve with ice cream, or use to make pies, tarts, ice cream, sorbets, preserves and also jellies.

Date
Fresh dates should have a shiny brown skin and soft, sweet flesh. Use with other fruit in pies, eat with cheese at the end of a meal; or pit and stuff with nuts, either chopped or whole.

Fig
Sold either fresh or dried. Figs range in color from pale green to deep purple. The skin is edible. Eat raw with cheese, ham or in fruit salads, or poach lightly in syrup.

Gooseberry
The eating variety has a red skin with sweet juicy flesh. The cooking types, which are green and hairy, are used for pies, mousses, ice creams and preserves. Gooseberry sauce is often served with broiled mackerel or roast pork.

Grape
Grapes are usually eaten raw. If they are used to make open tarts, they should be peeled and any seeds removed. Small seedless grapes are sometimes cooked with fish. The best flavor of all is that of the Muscat grape.

Grapefruit
Use either white- or pink-fleshed grapefruit for first-course salads with fish and seafood, squeeze for refreshing juices, or make into marmalade. Choose heavy fruit with plump skin and a sharp perfume.

Kiwifruit
Best eaten raw–either remove the peel and slice, or cut off the top and scoop out the flesh and seeds with a small spoon. The kiwifruit has a very high Vitamin C content and its high level of acidity will dissolve aspic and gelatin.

Lemon and lime
Use a few drops of lemon juice to enhance the flavor of smoked salmon and fish dishes, cooked green vegetables, mayonnaise and salad dressings, and fruit salads. To prevent discoloration, apply it to the cut surface of an avocado or banana, or to a bowl of water for apple slices. For plenty of juice, choose thin-skinned lemons; for peel and pith pick the knobbly ones. Add the grated zest to soufflés, sponges and tarts. Use limes as a substitute for lemons. You can use less juice because their flavor is stronger.

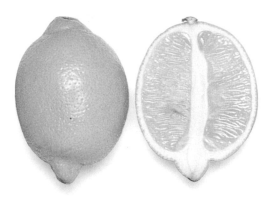

Mango

The inedible skin, which can be dark green, yellow, orange or red, should be shiny and the mango will yield slightly when held. The fruit should be pale orange, juicy and full of flavor. To pit, cut a thick slice lengthways down each side and scoop out the flesh with a spoon. Cut the flesh off the pit section. Slice and serve with ham, or add to fruit salads, purée for ice creams and mousses; cook in vegetable curry, tarts and pies. Use ripe or unripe for chutney.

Melon

There are many varieties but good ones for eating will feel dense and heavy for their size. The melony perfume should be detectable from the top end, and in some varieties the top end will yield when pressed. The water melon is the largest member of the family. Cover cut fruit in the refrigerator to contain its fragrance. Serve melon, chilled to intensify its flavor, for breakfast or at the end of a meal, and add to fruit or savory salads.

Orange and tangerine

Dessert oranges can be sliced and added to savory and fruit salads, the juice used for jellies, sorbets and ice creams, and the zest used to flavor cakes. The bitter Seville oranges are used to make

marmalade. Small "easy-peelers" include tangerines, clementines, satsumas and mandarin oranges. Sweet and juicy, they are best eaten raw. They can also be used in fruit salads and to make jams and preserves.

Peach

The furry peach skin conceals flesh that can be white, yellow or pink, depending on the variety. Peel the skin with a sharp knife for eating raw, or immerse in boiling water for 30 seconds. The smooth-skinned nectarine is very juicy and has fragrant yellow or white flesh. To pit, slice around the groove and twist the two halves against each other. Use cooked in pies, tarts and preserves.

Pear

There is a wonderful range of pears, and they are best eaten for dessert with cheeses such as Parmesan, Gruyère or Gorgonzola. Use cooked in tarts and puddings, and with game recipes.

Pineapple

When it is ripe, a leaf can easily be pulled from the center and the flesh will have the distinctive pineapple fragrance. It contains an enzyme that breaks down protein, so is good to serve at the end of a meal. Avoid using with gelatin because it will not set.

Pomegranate

The size of an apple, with a tough, brown, leathery skin. The flesh is bright reddish-pink, packed with seeds and very juicy. Slice in half and spoon out the flesh. Use as a dessert or add to sauce. Extract the juice with a lemon squeezer and use for water ices or jellies.

Rhubarb

This is really a vegetable, and only the stems are used. There are two types, the forced or early with pink thin stalks and yellow leaves, and maincrop with thick reddish green stems and dark green leaves. Steam, poach or stew with sugar, and use for pies, tarts, and preserves.

Strawberry

There are many different varieties, but for eating they should all be bright red and firm, with a bright green calyx. Are usually cultivated but can also be wild. Eat strawberries on the day of purchase. Wash gently before removing the calyx. Usually served simply with cream or yogurt, but also used to make pies, tarts, ice cream, and preserves.

Legumes

The edible seeds of peas, beans, and lentils are highly nutritious, and they can be used in soups, stews, curries, or as an accompanying vegetable. Their only drawback–long soaking and cooking times–is avoided by using canned beans.

Adzuki beans
Also known as aduki beans, these small red, shiny beans are popular in China and Japan. They have a sweetish flavor and are often made into "red bean paste" as a filling for crêpes and dumplings. The dried beans can be ground to a flour to make cakes and bread. Use in soups, salads, or with other vegetables, or grow as bean sprouts.

Black-eyed peas
Known as black-eyed beans or cow-peas, these cream-colored beans with a black spot are similar in shape to kidney beans, but smaller. Widely used in spicy African, Caribbean, and Indian cooking.

Borlotti beans
Kidney-shaped, speckled and ranging in color from creamy pink to deep brownish pink, these are the beans traditionally used in Italian cooking. Use in rustic salads, soups and pasta dishes, or substitute them in recipes using kidney beans.
Pinto beans look rather like borlotti beans, and are a typical Mexican ingredient.

Butter beans
Large, flattish, creamy white beans with a mild flavor and floury texture, which tend to turn mushy if overcooked. They are good added to mixed beans salads or used in rich stews, where they absorb other flavors.

Garbanzo beans
Also known as chick peas, these look rather like small hazelnuts, and have a nutty flavor. They are popular in the Mediterranean region, the Middle East, India, and many other countries. They are added whole to salads, chunky soups, curries, and stews; puréed in dips; toasted with spices as an appetizer; or ground and made into flour (sometimes called besan flour). Garbanzo beans need a long soaking and cooking time.

Navy beans
Pale green or white, very tender young beans with a delicate flavor. Add them to other beans for a salad, or serve in a creamy, garlicky sauce as an accompaniment to roast lamb.

Great Northern beans
Creamy white and oval-shaped, the familiar "baked beans" are ideal for dishes which need long slow cooking–with sausages, meat, tomatoes, or herbs–such as the cassoulet of France, because they readily absorb other flavors. They can be used in salads, soups or as purées. Cannellini are a type of navy beans.

Preparing and cooking

Store dry legumes in an airtight container in a cool, dark place. Do not keep them for too long, as they dry out during storage. After cooking they can be frozen or kept in a covered container in the refrigerator for 2–3 days.

All dry legumes, except lentils and split peas, need to be soaked before cooking. First, rinse them well to remove dust and grit. There are three soaking methods:

- Cover the beans with 2–3 times their volume of cold water and leave in a cool place for about 10 hours or overnight.
- Cover with plenty of boiling water and leave for 2–3 hours.
- Bring a pan of beans in water slowly to a boil, then boil fast for 2 minutes. Remove from the heat and leave for 1–2 hours.

After soaking, drain the legumes and rinse well in fresh water. Put them into a large saucepan and cover generously with stock or water. Bring to a boil, then reduce the heat and simmer until the beans are tender, allowing 20 minutes–1 hour for lentils and split peas; 1–4 hours for garbanzo and other beans, depending on their size and age. Add boiling water if necessary. When the beans are tender to the bite, drain and use. Some recipes require legumes to be cooked for a shorter time, and then added to the dish while it cooks, so they take on the flavor of herbs and other ingredients.

A pressure cooker will cook soaked legumes in a third of the time taken by conventional methods. To prevent froth clogging the pressure valve, add 2 tablespoons oil to the cooking water.

Bean sprouts

The most familiar bean sprouts are from the small green mung bean, but other beans and lentils can also be sprouted to become nutritious crisp vegetables to use in salads and stir-fries. You can buy a special sprouter, with two or more layers, but a large glass jar will do. Rinse the beans and place in the jar or sprouter, cover and keep in a light place (not direct sunlight) at a constant temperature of 50–70°F. Rinse the beans twice a day with fresh water; tip off excess water. After 3–6 days, pale green shoots will appear, which are best when about 1–2 inches long.

Lentils
Lentils need no soaking, just rinsing. Red and yellow lentils, often sold split, cook quickly to a purée. They are used in Indian cooking for soups, rissoles, and to thicken curries. Brown and green lentils keep their shape when cooked and have an earthy flavor, which goes well with ham and bacon, and makes a delicious winter vegetable.

Warnings

After soaking, kidney beans (black and red), adzuki beans and black-eyed peas must be put in a saucepan with plenty of cold water, brought a boil and then boiled fast for 15–20 minutes to destroy the toxins on the outer skin. Soybeans should be treated in the same way, but boiled fast for 1 hour to destroy a substance that prevents the body from absorbing protein.
Salt will toughen the outer skin of legumes, so add it only about 10 minutes before the end of cooking. Baking soda destroys some of the vitamin content if added to legumes during cooking.

Peas
Available as yellow or green split or whole peas, these need only 1–2 hours soaking, and cook in less than 1 hour. Split peas become a purée as they cook, and do not need to be mashed or blended. The large whole green marrowfat peas are used to make the traditional English dish, mushy peas.

Red kidney beans
The "meaty" flavor and texture of these beans makes them a popular choice for salads, soups, casseroles and hot, spicy dishes. They hold their shape well and should be boiled for at least 15 minutes at the beginning of their cooking time.
Black kidney beans are traditional in many South American soups and stews. They can be substituted for red kidney beans in most recipes—or use half and half for a stunning contrast.

Soybeans
Small, round and yellowish-brown, these have the highest protein content of all legumes and are used to make tofu (bean curd), soy milk, soy sauce and miso—a fermented bean paste used in Japanese cooking. Soybeans are also ground to make flour and play an important part in TVP (textured vegetable protein) foods. They are bland in flavor, so always use them in combination with strongly flavored herbs and spices.

Herbs

The colors and flavors of herbs will transform your cooking. Many are easy to grow in a garden or windowbox, but they are widely available from supermarkets, either in packages, growing in pots or freeze-dried in jars. Herbs are best when freshly picked, but will keep for a few days in a pitcher of water, or in the salad drawer of the refrigerator.

Basil
Its warm, spicy flavor goes well with tomatoes and pasta, and it is the main ingredient of pesto sauce. Shred–rather than chop–the leaves to retain maximum flavor and add toward the end of cooking.

Bay
Bay has a strong flavor, but usually needs long cooking to bring out its qualities. It is included in all kinds of savory dishes–casseroles, pâtés and stocks–and adds fragrance to white sauces.

Chervil
The mild flavor is similar to parsley, with a hint of aniseed. It goes well with egg and fish dishes and delicate sauces. The lacy leaves are used as garnishes, but they wilt soon after picking.

Chives
The mildest member of the onion family and best added to dishes just before serving. Snip chives to give color to potato salad, vichyssoise soup, and scrambled eggs, or sprinkle on salads. The purple flower-heads can also be added to salads.

Cilantro
An essential ingredient of curries and other spicy dishes, cilantro looks rather like flat leaf parsley and is very aromatic. It goes well with meat, fish and vegetable dishes and is added toward the end of cooking. Also good in salads.

Dill
The feathery leaves are often used with fish, such as the Scandinavian salmon dish gravad lax, but dill also goes well with cream or mustard sauces, chicken and vegetable soups. Use it also to garnish cucumber salads.

Garlic
Essential in Mediterranean dishes, garlic cloves are used to season sauces, soups, casseroles, and salads. The flavor becomes milder as it cooks, but if you fry it, do not let it brown as this tends to make it bitter. To remove the outer skin, squash a clove under a flat knife and chop the flesh very finely. Garlic can be white, pink or purple. The purple variety keeps for longer than the other two.

Fennel
It is easy to confuse this herb with dill, because both plants look similar, with fine feathery leaves, and both of them also have an aniseed flavor. The flavor is stronger in fennel. Chop the leaves and add to sauces and fish dishes. The stalks are often laid over barbecues to flavor fish while it cooks.

Horseradish
The root of this plant goes down deep into the soil, so it is not much liked by gardeners. The grated root is traditionally used with roast beef.

Marjoram and oregano

The traditional flavoring for pizza tomato sauces and Greek salads, marjoram also goes well with fish and lamb dishes, omelets and vegetables. Oregano is wild marjoram and has a more powerful flavor. The leaves retain their flavor during cooking.

Mint

Spearmint is the common variety, but mints such as apple, ginger, pineapple, and lemon are all worth trying. Use mint to flavor ice cream, fruit salads, summer drinks, salads, baby potatoes, and peas. Fresh mint is wonderful used with bulgar wheat in tabbouleh.

Parsley

There are two varieties of parsley, both of which are commonly available–curled and flat-leaf, which is becoming more popular. Use in salads, stocks and sauces, with vegetables and in fish dishes. It forms an effective part of a bouquet garni.

Rosemary

This bushy shrub has ever-green needles and a robust overpowering flavor. Chop and use sparingly in stuffings for meat dishes, or add sprigs to flavor lamb, pork or game. Remove the sprigs after use.

Sage

The leaves of this plant retain their powerful flavor even during long, slow cooking. Use sparingly with pork and game birds, or in a tomato sauce.

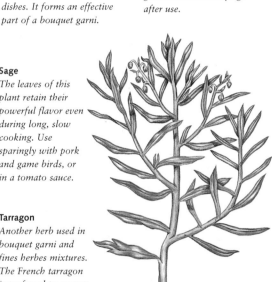

Tarragon

Another herb used in bouquet garni and fines herbes mixtures. The French tarragon is preferred to coarser flavored Russian. Chop the leaves and add to salads, or use in sauces, with chicken, fish and vegetables, or infuse in vinegar. It is best used fresh.

Arugula

This is traditionally used in salads and in pasta dishes. It is now widely available in the salad section of supermarkets and is increasing in popularity.

Thyme

This is used in bouquet garni, and to flavor meat casseroles. The lemon thyme combines particularly well with fish and chicken dishes.

Bouquet garni and fines herbes

The classic bouquet garni is made up of a bay leaf, a sprig of thyme, and 2–3 sprigs of parsley, which can either be bound together with string or tied into a small cheesecloth bag. It is used to flavor almost any savory dish that needs long cooking, and is removed before the dish is served. Celery, or other herbs such as fennel or dill, can be included.

The mixture known in French cooking as fines herbes–used in omelets and chilled butter to top fish and meat–is traditionally made from chopped fresh chervil, chives, parsley, and tarragon.

Spices

Spices come to us from the aromatic parts of plants, generally the seeds, pods, berries and bark. Their warm fragrant scents add a special aroma and flavor to all forms of cooking. For the best flavor, buy them whole, store them in tinted glass jars away from sunlight, and grind them with a pestle and mortar just before you use them.

Cardamom
An essential ingredient in Indian cooking, but also used in cakes and pastries in northern Europe, the pods come in green, white and black. The first two have a finer flavor than the black which has an earthy flavor best suited to long cooking. Use the small black seeds in the pods to flavor vegetable dishes, curries such as biryanis, pilaus and dhal, and as a flavoring for ice cream. It is delicious in spiced tea and espresso coffee.

Allspice
The berries are similar to large peppercorns and when ground the flavor has the taste of cloves, cinnamon and nutmeg. Grind it for cakes, biscuits and pies, use whole in marinades or add to casseroles.

Cayenne and chili
Cayenne has an affinity with fish and seafood, and goes particularly well with cheese and egg dishes. It comes from the hot chili pepper and appears in Indian, North African and Latin American food. Use sparingly. Chili can be mild or very hot, so use it in small amounts to begin with. It is ground from different kinds of chili pepper and is sometimes mixed with other herbs and spices. Use it as a flavoring for many meat, egg, poultry, and fish dishes.

Cinnamon
Use the stick form of cinnamon for meat and vegetable casseroles, for curries and rice dishes, and in syrup for poaching fruit, but buy it ready ground for cakes, pies and puddings.

Caraway
Seeds are small, oval, and ribbed, and are strongly aromatic. Their peppery undertone is used in German and Austrian cooking to flavor breads such as pumpernickel, and in goulashes, and cakes.

Cloves
These can be used in savory or sweet dishes, but with restraint because their aroma can swamp other tastes. Push cloves into an onion to flavor sauces and meat stews, stud a ham with them, and add to apple dishes or mulled wine.

Ginger
Familiar to us in Chinese and Indian dishes, fresh ginger root is very easy to use. Peel off the outer skin, and grate or finely slice. Add it to cakes, poultry and seafood dishes, vegetables and fruit pies.

Coriander
The small ridged seeds have a mild, slightly savory flavor and can be used whole or ground in quite large quantities. Used in chutneys and pickles, curries, meat and vegetable stews, and goes well with fish.

Cumin
The spicy cumin seeds are small, ridged and greenish brown in color. They have a pleasantly sweet, warm flavor. Use them in vegetable stews, in seafood dishes, and in mildly spiced curries.

Dill
Use the seeds with fish, potatoes, and in pickles, vinegars, marinades, and salad dressings, especially in the winter months when the fresh herb is not available. The flavor is similar to caraway seeds.

Fennel
Fennel is best known as a herb, salad ingredient and vegetable, but its seeds are also valuable in cooking. The seeds are sweet and can be used instead of aniseed in fish soups and stews, with broiled sardines or pork.

Other spices

There are several more exotic spices which are perhaps less commonly used but nevertheless deserve a place in the kitchen, particularly if you do a lot of Indian or Middle Eastern cooking.

Asafoetida, for example, has a very curious smell, but it is an essential ingredient of Indian and Middle Eastern cooking. Used in minute quantities, it has a remarkable ability to enhance the flavor of other foods, and goes well in vegetable, meat and fish stews. It is not easy to find, and is best bought in powder form.

Fenugreek is another spice that is used in Indian dishes, pickles and chutneys. Roast the seeds lightly to bring out their flavor, then grind to a powder.

Mustard seed comes as black, or yellow seeds. They have a strong flavor, and are used in Indian recipes where they are often added to hot oil at which point they pop, adding their taste to the oil. They are also used to prepare mustards and are included in pickles. Dry-fried, they lose their heat and have a warm nutty flavor.

Nigella seeds are important in Indian and Middle Eastern cookery. Ask for them in Indian food stores by their Indian name, kalonfi. They have an earthy, peppery flavor, and also give texture to bread doughs and cakes.

Juniper
The small black berries, with their spicy pine aroma, are generally used in marinades, casseroles and stuffings, or in robust meat dishes. Crush the berries before using.

Mace
This is the lacy cage that covers the nutmeg seed. The flavor is more delicate than nutmeg, and it is infused in milk and used to make sauces and milk puddings.

Nutmeg
The warm sweet flavor of nutmeg is quickly lost, so grate it as you need it. Use it to flavor sauces, cakes, pies and puddings, cheese dishes, meat, poultry, and vegetables.

Paprika
Milder than cayenne and chili, and is used in meat stews, with fish, and as a garnish. Traditional in Spanish seafood stews and is widely used in Hungary. Affected by light, so buy small amounts and store in airtight containers away from the light.

Pepper
Black peppercorns are stronger than white; red have a nutty flavor; and green have a mild, fresh taste. Use whole in marinades and stock, and grind as needed to preserve their aroma. An unusual use for black peppercorns is ground over strawberries.

Poppy seeds
The pretty opium poppy is not only the source of the highly narcotic drug, opium, but also of the delicious seeds used in cooking. The seeds are popular in Jewish baking, decorating many types of breads and rolls, including bagels and platzels.

Vanilla
Use two beans to flavor a jar of sugar. For milk puddings, infuse the bean in scalded milk. Wash, dry and reuse for sugar.

Saffron
This comes from the crocus and the filaments are generally infused in boiling water to extract the color. Use it in rice dishes, or with seafood stews.

Turmeric
The light, warm spicy taste and pungent aroma is best appreciated apart from ready-prepared curry powders. Learn to use its fragrance in Indian recipes such as pilau. Turmeric gives a golden glow to pickles.

Sesame seeds
The seeds have a strong nutty flavor and are best dry roasted until golden or fried in oil before use. In their ground form they are made into tahini paste. They are popular in Chinese, Japanese and Indian cookery.

Star anise
This has a spicy aniseed flavor, and is widely used in Chinese red-roasted dishes. It is an ingredient of the Chinese five-spice powder and is used to decorate finished dishes. The small gray-green ribbed seeds of aniseed have a spicy/sweet flavor and are used in sweet and savory dishes, and in pastry and bread. In India it is used to freshen the palate at the end of a meal. Also used in the drinks pastis, ouzo and anisette.

Pasta

Infinitely variable, quick and easy to cook, economical, satisfying, a staple standby, pasta is all these things and more. You can dress it up in an extravagant sauce, or toss it in a simple rustic sauce and make a meal in moments. Pasta is not a fattening food, although the sauces that go with it might be. In its home country of Italy, it is served as a first course but elsewhere it is frequently the main part of the meal, followed by salad, fruit or cheese.

Cooking methods

If you love pasta, it is worth investing in a big pan which will easily take at least 2½ quarts of rapidly boiling salted water. This is the amount you need to cook 1 pound pasta–it lets the pasta cook evenly and move about in the boiling water without sticking. Add the pasta to the boiling water, bring it up to a rolling boil, and occasionally stir the submerged pasta with a wooden fork. When adding long pasta, coil the strands around the sides of the saucepan as they soften until all the pasta is in the pan; do not break it. Do not cover the pan because the water may boil over. Test the pasta by nibbling a small piece from time to time and when it is elastic and firm, but not hard, turn off the heat and quickly drain it through a colander; tip it into a warmed serving bowl.

Cooking fresh pasta

This takes far less time, needing only 5 minutes, or just seconds in a microwave. A drawback of fresh pasta is that it can't be stored like dry pasta. Always buy good-quality fresh pasta: just because it is fresh, it does not always follow that it is good.

Homemade pasta dough

Few people make their own pasta dough, but it's essential for homemade ravioli.
Preparation: 1 hour

What you need:

- 2½ cups strong bread flour, sifted
- pinch of salt
- 3 eggs
- 1 tablespoon olive oil
- flour for dusting

1 Put the flour and salt on a work surface. Make a well in the center and add the eggs. Using your fingertips, gradually draw the flour in from the sides and mix well. Then add the olive oil and continue mixing until you have a soft dough. Alternatively, you can make the dough in a food processor.

2 Transfer the pasta dough to a lightly floured surface and knead well until it is really smooth and silky. Roll out the dough, giving it an occasional turn and stretching it out, until it resembles a thin sheet of cloth and is almost transparent.

3 Now you have to dry your pasta. Hang it over the back of a chair or a broom handle and leave for 10 minutes to dry. Alternatively, lay it out on a table with one-third overhanging the edge and keep turning it until it dries out completely.

Types of pasta

Bought pasta is factory-produced dry pasta. Made from durum (hard wheat) flour it is the familiar pale straw color, but it is brown if made from buckwheat or whole wheat flour. Coloring is added by spinach (green), tomato paste (red), beet juice (red or pink), saffron or turmeric (yellow), and squid or octopus ink (black).

Durum wheat can be difficult to work with and, to make it easier, it is sometimes mixed with soft wheat flour which reduces the protein content and makes the product more starchy. Look for pasta that is made from 100% durum wheat.

Egg pasta (*pasta all'uovo*) is the pasta of flour and eggs which originated from the Emilia-Romagna region of Italy and is available fresh or dry. This is often used for stuffed pasta.

Storage

- Freshly made pasta should be eaten preferably on the day it is made or purchased, but it can be refrigerated for up to 24 hours.
- Homemade pasta dough can be frozen for up to 3 months.
- Dry pasta is best stored in its original package, or in a dry, airtight container.
- Dry pasta will keep for up to 9 months.

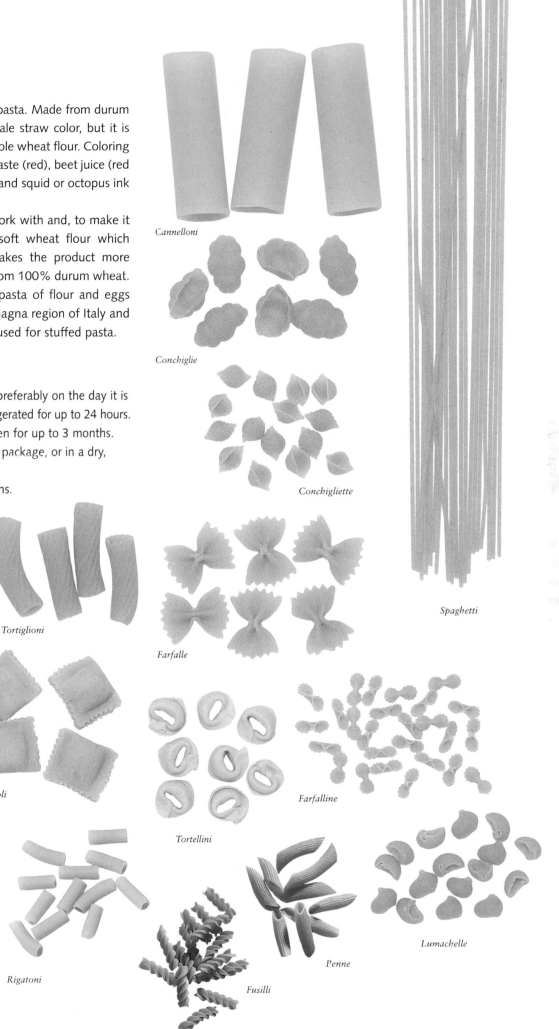

Cannelloni

Conchiglie

Conchigliette

Spaghetti

Whole wheat macaroni

Tortiglioni

Farfalle

Ruoti

Ravioli

Tortellini

Farfalline

Lumachelle

Lasagne verdi

Rigatoni

Fusilli

Penne

Rice

Along with pasta, rice is one of the most useful ingredients in the kitchen. It needs little advance preparation, cooks quickly, is adaptable, goes well with a variety of dishes, and is very nourishing. Rice is easy to cook, but there are different kinds of rice and ways of cooking it, so to achieve success every time, be sure that you match the method to the purpose.

Above right: fried rice with pork
Far right: green rice

Cooking methods

Absorption

For each cup of rice use 2 cups of water or stock, plus ½ teaspoon salt. Wash the rice under cold running water and stir well to separate the grains. Bring the measured water to a boil in a large saucepan. Add the salt and rice. Return to a boil, reduce the heat, and cover with a tight-fitting lid. Cook for 15 minutes (30 for brown), when the rice should be tender and fluffy, and the liquid completely absorbed.

Boiling

For ⅓ cup rice, use 2½ cups water and ½ teaspoon salt. Bring the water to a boil. Add the salt and sprinkle in the rice; return to a boil and simmer for 12–13 minutes (30–40 minutes for brown). A tablespoon of oil will help prevent it boiling over and the grains from sticking together. Rice is cooked when a grain squeezed between the fingers is soft on the outside but still retains its shape and some firmness in the center. Drain and then serve immediately.

Oven

To cook rice in the oven, preheat the oven to 350°F. Using 1 cup of washed rice to 2 cups water, put the washed rice in an ovenproof dish with a tight-fitting lid. Then cover with the measured boiling water or stock and ½ teaspoon salt. Stir, cover with foil and a lid. Cook for 30 minutes (1 hour for brown) until the liquid is absorbed and the rice is tender.

Steaming

This Chinese method lets the grains stay separate. Soak the rice in cold water for at least 1 hour, then drain. Add water to the bottom half of a steamer or large pan. Line the steamer, or a Chinese steamer basket, with cheesecloth. Spoon in rice and fold over the cheesecloth ends. Cover and steam for 25–30 minutes.

Fried rice

Preparation: 20 minutes

What you need:

- 2 tablespoons oil
- 1 garlic clove, chopped
- 1-inch piece of fresh ginger root, chopped
- 5 scallions, finely sliced
- 1½ cups shelled shrimp
- 1 tablespoon soy sauce
- 1½ cups frozen vegetables
- 2 beaten eggs
- 2 cups cooked rice
- salt and pepper

1 Heat the oil in a pan. Add garlic and ginger, fry for 30 seconds.
2 Add the scallions, toss for 30 seconds. Add the shrimp, stir for 1 minute. Add the soy sauce and vegetables, stir for 2 minutes.
3 Add the eggs, stir, let set, then mix into the shrimp and vegetables. Add the rice, toss with the other ingredients until hot, and season to taste.

Techniques for success

- When cooking rice by the absorption method, do not increase the amount of water or stock that you cook it in, or the rice will be soggy.
- Avoid removing the saucepan lid and letting steam escape when using the absorption method, as this would interfere with the process of absorption.
- Never stir the rice while it is cooking, as this tends to break the grains of rice.
- Rice is cooked when a grain squeezed between the fingers is soft on the outside but still retains its shape and some firmness in the center.
- Serve freshly cooked rice within 10 minutes of cooking to prevent it from sticking.
- If the rice is to be served cold, put it into a strainer, run warm water through it to separate the grains, and then let it drain and cool completely.
- Dress rice for salads while it is still warm so that all the flavors are absorbed.

Preparation

- Long-grained rice absorbs twice its volume in water.
- Brown rice absorbs twice its volume in water.
- 2½ tablespoons short-grained (pudding) rice will absorb 2½ cups whole milk.
- Soak Basmati rice in cold water for about 15 minutes and drain well before cooking.
- To prevent grains sticking together, wash white rice before cooking to remove the powdery loose starch.
- Allow ⅓ cup of uncooked rice per person.

The right rice for the job

- Curries: Basmati, Patna, American long-grained
- Puddings: American long-grained, Java, rice flakes, glutinous rice, pudding rice
- Stuffings: American long-grained
- Rice salads: Basmati, Patna, American long-grained
- Risottos: Arborio rice

Types of rice

American long-grained

It used to be called Carolina rice and was only grown there. It is now grown all over the world. The hulled and polished grains remain firm, fluffy and separate when cooked. Patna is also a long-grained rice.

Brown rice

Short-grained rice

Wild rice

Brown

The whole grain with only the outer husk removed, leaving the layers of bran. It is available long-, medium- and short-grained and it needs longer cooking, but it is far more nutritional, and has both a nutty flavor and a much chewier texture.

Basmati

Grown in the foothills of the Himalayas, this narrow long-grained rice has a distinctive flavor when it is cooked, especially evident when the absorption method is used.

Glutinous or sticky rice

This is actually a gluten-free rice, despite its name. It is a short- to medium-grained rice and when cooked the grains stick together slightly so that it becomes easy to eat with chopsticks. It is most easily obtained from stores selling ethnic products.

Ground rice or rice flour

This gluten-free flour is used as a thickening agent, sometimes mixed with other flours, to make cakes, puddings and cookies. In Chinese cookery, it is also sometimes used to make certain types of noodles.

Medium and short-grained

These tend to be stickier kinds of rice and are generally used for savory dishes where the rice needs to cling or to be molded or bound together, such as risottos and stuffings. Short-grained pudding rice is used for sweet dishes.

Pre-cooked rice

This only needs soaking in boiling water for 5 minutes following the manufacturer's instructions. It is useful for quick snacks and salads.

Parboiled or converted rice

Unlike other kinds of white rice, most of the nutrients and vitamins are left in the grains due to the steaming process that takes place before milling. It retains the nutritional value of brown rice without its chewy texture and longer cooking time. It produces plump, fluffy and separate grains.

Pudding

This short-grained polished rice absorbs a great deal of liquid during cooking and becomes soft and mushy. It is used only for puddings and rice desserts.

Rice flakes

These are produced by steaming and rolling and can be made from whole or white rice. They are used for puddings, baking, muesli, and cereals.

Risotto

The best results are achieved by using the Italian Arborio rice, which has a roundish grain. When it is cooked, it becomes creamy, while still retaining a slight bite. Costing more than other kinds of rice, it is worth the expense.

Wild rice

This is not actually a rice at all, but is in fact the seeds of a grass that is grown in the United States of America and the Far East. It is a highly nutritious, gluten-free grain, which absorbs about four times its volume of liquid. It has an interesting, slightly nutty flavor. It is often served, mixed with white rice, to accompany various game and poultry dishes and can be combined with other ingredients to make stuffings. Cook it in the same way as you would regular rice, allowing at least 35–45 minutes. Soaking it overnight will slightly reduce the cooking time needed.

Fish

The nutritional qualities, short cooking times, tenderness, and adaptability of fish and seafood make them a popular choice with people who lead busy lives. There are many different varieties of fish, from both sea and river, and there are many ways of cooking them. Unless you can get it at the quayside, always buy fish from a reputable store to insure it is perfectly fresh.

Buying and storing

Seafood perishes more quickly than meat and poultry, so take great care, when you buy it, that it is fresh. Look for all the following signs:

● Your supplier's store should be clean, have plenty of ice and display the fish well.

● Freshness is easily seen in a whole fish. It should be stiff and firm, not limp.

● Eyes should be full, shiny and bright, and never sunken or opaque.

● The skin should be shiny, not dry and gritty.

● The gills should be rosy pink, not brownish or dry.

● Fillets should be translucent, not milky-white, firm and spring to the touch with no sign of discoloration. The flesh should be intact.

● Smoked fish should have a bright, glossy surface, a firm texture and a pleasant smoky smell.

● Commercially frozen fish which has been thawed badly will be unpleasantly watery and wooly.

● Fish should be eaten as fresh as possible, at least within 24 hours of purchase. Otherwise it should be cleaned, gutted and frozen. Fish fillets and steaks can be prepared up to 12 hours ahead, loosely covered in foil and refrigerated.

● To keep fish overnight, wrap in several layers of newspaper and put in coldest part of the refrigerator.

● Fresh mackerel, herrings and sardines should be eaten on day of purchase or put in the freezer overnight.

Preparation

A good fish vendor will trim, scale, skin, gut, and fillet for you in a matter of seconds. Flat fish are gutted at sea.

● To remove fish scales from round seafish and some freshwater fish, use the back of a heavy knife. Work on paper to collect the scales, scraping from tail to head. Rinse and pat dry.

● To skin, cut through just above the tail and tear the skin toward the head. Flat fish can be skinned after filleting.

Gutting

● Round fish: slit the belly open, working from the head toward the vent with a knife or scissors. Place the flat of the blade behind the entrails and slide them out; then wrap in paper and discard. Now scrape out the black blood channel down the backbone. Cut off the head and gills.

● Round fish, served whole: gut through the gills by grasping the fish in one hand and twisting its head to one side. Push a finger inside the gills and hook it under the entrails. Draw them out and snip off. Cut off the gills. Rinse and pat dry.

Filleting

You will need a very sharp, flexible knife. Use the discarded head, bones and trimmings to make stock. Remove any tiny bones with tweezers or pliers.

● Round fish: scale, cut off the head, tail and fins, and gut through the belly. Place opened fish flesh down on board and press firmly along the backbone with your thumbs to loosen it. Turn the fish over, release the bone with a knife, and lift out carefully so rib bones are also removed. Cut along the center to divide into 2 fillets.

● For small round fish: cut off the heads and gut through the belly. Hold the fish open under running water so that the force of the water separates the fish into 2 fillets and washes out backbone.

● Flat fish: cut off the head and trim away the fins with scissors. Cut through the fish along the backbone. Slip the knife blade under the flesh on one side of the backbone. Then using a sawing motion with the flat of the blade against the rib bones, work the fillet away from the bones and detach. Remove the second fillet in the same way. Turn the fish over and repeat on the other side to divide into 4 fillets.

Marinades

Fish responds well to being marinated before cooking. It should soak in the marinade for anything between a few hours and overnight. Try to always use glass, china, plastic or stainless steel bowls for storing food in marinades. Do not use foil as a covering, as the acidic marinade will "burn" into it and taint the fish. The marinade can also be rubbed into the slashed flesh of the fish just before cooking, or even added to the accompanying sauce for extra flavor.

Soy sauce marinade

This marinade works especially well with any white fish.

What you need:

- 2 tablespoons oil
- 2 tablespoons light soy sauce
- 1 tablespoon lemon juice
- ½ teaspoon ground cumin
- 1 teaspoon chopped fresh chives

Mix all the ingredients together. Let the fish marinate for at least 30 minutes, or overnight.

Spicy marinade

This marinade works especially well with a strong-flavored fish such as halibut.

What you need:

- pinch of saffron
- 2 garlic cloves, crushed with salt
- pinch of ground coriander
- 1 tablespoon finely chopped fresh parsley
- ⅔ cup wine vinegar
- 2 tablespoons tomato ketchup
- 1 tablespoon lemon juice
- salt and pepper to taste

Soak the saffron for 30 minutes in 1 tablespoon boiling water. Mix all the marinade ingredients together, including the saffron. Marinate the fish for several hours; then drain, dry, and broil.

Herb marinade

This works particularly well with any fish that is going to be broiled or barbecued, such as tuna and mackerel.

What you need:

- 4 tablespoons olive oil
- 4 garlic cloves, crushed
- ½ cup dry white wine
- 1 small onion, finely chopped
- 1 sprig each of fresh rosemary, thyme and parsley

Mix all the ingredients together and then marinate the fish for up to 24 hours.

Court bouillon

This is the poaching liquid for whole fish, such as salmon.

What you need:

- 2–3 small onions, sliced
- 3 carrots, sliced
- 2 bay leaves
- small bunch of fresh parsley
- 2–3 slices lemon
- 1 tablespoon butter or 2 tablespoons olive oil
- 5–6 black peppercorns
- 4½ pints water
- 1¼ cups wine vinegar or 2½ cups white wine

Put all the ingredients in a large pan. Bring to a boil, cover and simmer for 20 minutes. Let cool slightly (95°F) before you add the fish.

Cook's Tip

When the fish is cooked, the cooking liquid can then be strained and used as a basis for sauces. The liquid will lend extra flavor to them.

Flatfish

Sole
Blunt-nosed body is dark brown on the back with white underside, flesh is firm, white and delicate. Can be used for most cooking methods, goes well with sauces. Best cooked whole and served with butter, parsley and lemon; serve poached fillets in a sauce.

Turbot
Commonly called window pane. Much smaller than European turbot. Round flatfish with a small head. Sandy or dark brown with small hard nodules but not scales and a white belly. Flesh is firm and delicate in flavor. Suits any cooking method, but best poached or broiled and then served with hollandaise sauce.

Plaice
Dark brown with russet spots on its back with white underside. Best deep-fried in batter or egg and bread crumbs, or poached and served with a parsley or cheese sauce.

Halibut
Largest of all the flatfish. Gray to olive-green back, and white underside. Good flavor, fresh better than frozen. Sold in steaks and fillets. Best poached or baked, served with sauce or melted butter.

Witch flounder
Oval shape with pale or medium-brown, slightly mottled back and a white underside. Good-quality white flesh which needs to be well seasoned. Best cooked using sole recipes.

Megrim
Sandy-brown body with faint spots, white underside. Can be dry, substitute for any flatfish. Best served in well-seasoned dishes.

Dab
Plump oval body, sandy-brown back with mottled markings, small head, white underside. At its best when very fresh.

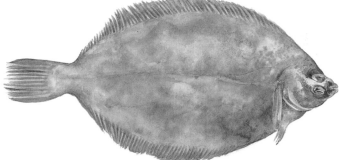

Haddock

Smaller than cod, with dark gray back, silver underside, and marked black lateral line. Usually sold in fillets. Best deep-fried and served with French fries, or use cod recipes.

Whiting

Slim, silver-gray fish, silver sides, and white belly. When very fresh, has sweet flaky flesh. Best poached, fried, or flaked and used in fish cakes.

Hake

Long, dark gray, tapering body with large head, black mouth. Flesh is white, soft, and creamy. Best deep-fried in batter, pan-fried, baked, or poached. Hake is best eaten very fresh since it can become tasteless after a few days.

Cod family

Cod

Greenish-gray back with mottling, paling to light gray on the sides, and a white belly. Firm white flesh with good flavor, sold as steaks and fillets. Combines well with other fish in pies and stews, can be used for fish cakes. Can be baked, poached, broiled, and fried.

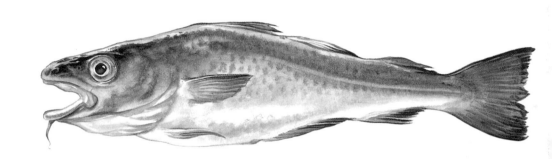

Bass, bream, grouper

Grouper

Large species, identified by deep body, large head and a mouth that looks upward. Flesh has a good flavor and texture. Cook as for bass.

Bream

Also called porgy. Small narrow fish with greenish-yellow, silver body, big eyes on a small head. Sardine-like flavor. Best barbecued, broiled, or baked.

Bass

Diverse fish with stream-lined body, steel gray through to silver. Good texture and flavor. Best cooked by steaming, poaching, or baked in salt; also good in salads.

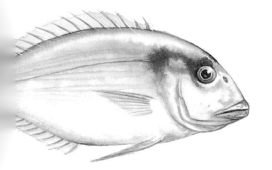

Oily fish

Mackerel
Glistening green-blue back with dark wavy lines and white underbelly. Buy very fresh, and do not buy if it looks dull. Rich flesh has good strong flavor and firm texture. Best broiled or barbecued and served with gooseberry sauce. Good stuffed, baked or poached. Roll fillets in oatmeal and fry.

Herring
Dark blue-green back becoming silver on sides and belly, reddish tint round eyes. Flesh is fragile, has strong flavor and creamy texture. Best cooked patted with seasoned oatmeal and fried in butter, or scored, brushed with fat, and broiled.

Sardine
Smaller than herrings, with blue-green back paling to silver. Best fried in olive oil or broiled over charcoal.

Whitebait
Also called silversides. Bright, silver, and slender. Very good flavor. Best dipped in milk, shaken in a bag of flour, and deep-fried.

Sprat
Name given to some species of herring. Good flavor, but small and bony. Best cooked tossed in well-seasoned flour and fried in bacon fat with fresh thyme.

Great fish

Tuna and bonito
Deep streamlined body, pointed snout, and fast-tapering tail. Flesh is not attractive but improves during cooking. Best cooked by broiling, barbecuing or baking.

Swordfish
Large fish with sword-like upper jaw. Creamy-beige flesh with sweet flavor. Best broiled, barbecued, or made into kabobs, having first been marinated.

Freshwater fish

Sea trout
Migratory form of trout. Flesh is pale pink, but not as rich as salmon. Best cooked as for salmon.

Trout, rainbow
Similar to salmon, but with a trim body, blunt head, olive green-blue back, finely spotted. Delicate flavor with white or pink flesh. Responds well to freezing. Best cooked by poaching, broiling, or frying.

Salmon
Streamlined silvery body with scattered black markings. When really fresh, has a creamy substance between the flakes of flesh which sets to a curd when cooked. Avoid steaks that look soft, gray, oily, or watery. Best cooked whole by poaching or baked wrapped in foil. Broil or bake steaks and cutlets.

Assorted fish

Skate and ray
Flat, kite-shaped body, pointed snout for skate, blunt for ray. Similar to dog fish. Any slight odor should disappear on cooking–if it doesn't, the fish is inedible. Best poached and served with browned butter. Also good broiled or deep-fried.

John Dory
Gray body, large ugly head. The firm white flesh is moist and sweet. Best cooked by steaming, baking or frying. Sold only in specialty stores.

Monkfish
Enormous horny head with huge mouth, tapering tail and mottled skin. Good flavor, dense firm flesh. Best broiled, poached, or roasted.

Red mullet
Deep rose, with faint golden bar along each side; not related to gray mullet. Best cooked with strong flavors such as garlic, rosemary, fennel. Good for broiling and barbecuing. Sold only in specialty stores.

Snapper
Very large species, some of which are now imported. Red snapper is the best known in the US. A very versatile fish with well-flavored juicy flesh. Best broiled, barbecued, baked, or poached.

Shellfish and crustacea

Squid
Long body sac has eight short tentacles and two long, the mottled skin is easily removed. Body, flaps and tentacles are eaten, the sac can be stuffed. Best cooked either very quickly, or for a long time.

Shrimp
Frozen shrimp in their shells have the best flavor and are good in salads, pasta dishes and risottos. When buying frozen shelled shrimp, choose the ones with the least glaze. Those that come from South-east Asia are cheap but have very little flavor so use in strongly flavored dishes such as curries.

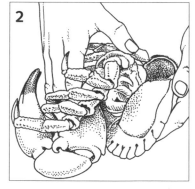

Crab
There are many different species of crab across the world. All have a hard shell and ten claws or legs, with both brown and white meat. Fresh crabs which you cook yourself will have better flavor than cooked crab meat.

Buying and storing shellfish

Shellfish deteriorates more quickly than fish; eat when very fresh and discard if they smell at all "high." Buy it live when possible, but if you buy it already cooked, it should smell fresh.

- Live shellfish should have all their claws intact and should be quite frisky. A lobster that looks tired is most probably dying.
- Mussels, clams, and oysters are all bought live and, if fresh, they should have tightly closed, uncracked shells. They should not be gaping open, but if slightly opened, give them a sharp tap against a hard surface and this should make them close. Discard any that don't close.
- Scallops may be sold gaping open.
- Cooked crabs and lobsters should have intact shells. If their shells are cracked, the texture of the meat may also have been damaged during the cooking process. They should also feel quite heavy in relation to their size. Cooked ones that feel light could indicate poor condition. They may contain water, so shake them close to your ear and listen. A strong smell of ammonia means that they are stale and old.

Preparing crab

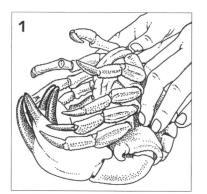

1 *Stand the crab on its head and lever away the back end of the shell with your fingers*

2 *Gently pull the body and legs away from the shell*

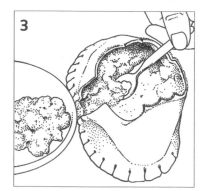

3 *Discard the intestines. Then scoop out the brown creamy meat and discard gills*

4 *Dig out white meat with skewer; crack open claws and legs and extract meat*

Crayfish
Shaped like a lobster with slender orange body, long claws. Mainly eaten as scampi (their tails). If raw, cook in their shells in gently boiling water for no more than 10 minutes and eat with melted butter. If preboiled, reheat slowly but do not recook as they easily toughen.

Mussels
Mussels can be found throughout the world most commonly having a blue-black shell with cream or orange meat. Mussels are commonly eaten cooked, but some varieties, like the date-shell can be eaten raw.

Lobster
When alive, dark blue, but then turns a vivid red when cooked. Best boiled, steamed or broiled. Eaten hot or cold.

Clam
There are several varieties including cherrystones or razorshell. Cook quickly in chowders or eat raw.

Preparing lobster

1 *Crack the legs and claws with the back of a knife, a hammer or a nutcracker*

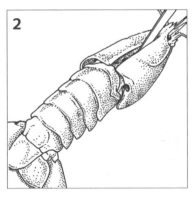

2 *To split lobster in half, draw a sharp knife up through head, then down through body*

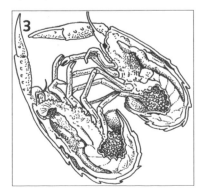

3 *Pull halves apart to expose flesh, which should include red coral and dark roe*

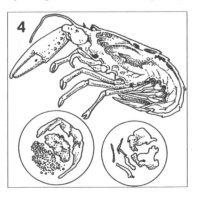

4 *Discard gills and intestines. Creamy green liver should be reserved to make a sauce*

Preparing shellfish

● Shelling cooked shrimp: pinch off the legs and take out any roe. Remove the shell by peeling it back from the underside and discard. Pull the meat away from the head and discard the head. Remove intestinal tracts from large shrimp, but not if pale and barely noticeable. To make a delicious shellfish stock, place shells and heads in a pan, cover with water, bring to a boil, and simmer for 30 minutes. Strain and reduce to a good flavor. The stock can then be frozen and used as required, to enrich sauces.

● To open an oyster: grip firmly using a coarse cloth. Push an oyster knife into the hinge and twist to lever open. Be careful not to cut your hands, which can easily happen if the knife slips.

● To prepare live lobsters: put them in the freezer for 5–10 minutes prior to cooking, where they will quietly fall asleep. They can then be killed quickly during the cooking process by boiling.

● To prepare mussels: scrub them, removing any protruding beards and barnacles. Tap them sharply against the work surface and discard any that don't close. Steam them quickly in a large saucepan, shaking the pan continuously, until they open up. Discard any that do not open.

Poultry

There are many different types of poultry and game that can be used by the enthusiastic cook. Chicken, duck, turkey, and goose are all available for the table all year round. Fall is the season to appreciate wild game, although some–to protect the species–is now farmed specially for the table.

Buying and storage

● Remove from the plastic covering, refrigerate and use within four days. For longer storage, freeze on purchase.

● Freezer-burn on a frozen chicken will make it dry and tasteless.

● Chunks of ice between the poultry and bottom of the wrapping indicates partial thawing and refreezing. The flesh will be poor quality.

● Thaw deep-frozen birds thoroughly. There should be no ice crystals on the inside or undue coldness before cooking begins.

● Thaw slowly in the refrigerator, at room temperature, or in a bath of cold water. Never use warm water, as this will spoil the texture of the meat.

● As soon as possible remove the giblet bag so that air can get to the cavity.

● To counteract hardening and drying out of poultry, spread a thin layer of margarine over the skin to form a seal and cover loosely with foil.

Right: sautéeing chicken pieces seals them and prepares them for the casserole
Far right: Stuffed chicken wings

Types of poultry

● Poulet: immature spring chicken. Allow 1 for 2 people.

● Poussin: baby chicken. Allow 1 per person. Fiddly and boney, eat with your fingers.

● Capon: neutered rooster fattened on corn. Very succulent because the flesh is marbled with fat. They are now illegal to produce in most countries.

● Boiling fowl: an old bird, tough and cheap. Use for dishes requiring a long gentle simmer.

● Roasting chickens: use for most chicken recipes. Allow 3½–4-pound bird to feed 4–6 people.

● Turkey: for best flavor, choose a hen, hung for 3 days, with moist skin tinted pearly white. Frozen turkey takes at least 48 hours to defrost; let it thaw gradually in the refrigerator

and finally at room temperature for a few hours. When thawed, cook as soon as possible. It must be cooked through to the center. Allow 1 pound dressed weight per person.

● Goose: choose a young bird, with pliable lower beak and breastbone and well-filled plump breast. A gosling weighs up to 5 pounds; at 8–9-months-old it becomes a goose and weighs 6–12 pounds. Thereafter it becomes much fatter and tougher, and therefore needs longer cooking.

● Duck: duckling describes birds aged up to 6 months. If too young, the bird will not have enough meat to be worth eating. Look for a breast that, when pinched, feels meaty. Duck freezes well because of its high fat content.

Preparing poultry and game

● Game birds are lean and need to be barded or protected by a cover before roasting.

● Feel game birds with your fingers and ease out any lead shot.

● Poultry is trussed to keep a stuffing inside or to give a good shape. When the strings are removed, the bird can then be easily carved.

● Before roasting, wipe poultry and game with a damp cloth. Pat dry with paper towels.

● Stuff large birds to provide a contrast flavor to the flesh and make them more interesting.

● Boned birds can be reshaped by careful stuffing and are then simple to carve.

● Tiny game birds can easily be flavored with a grape, a pinch of fresh herbs or with a clove-studded onion.

● Weigh poultry after stuffing and then calculate the cooking

Approximate cooking times for poultry

	Fast roasting	Combined high and low heat roasting	Slow roasting
		Sear at 425°F, then reduce the heat to 325°F	325°F for total roasting time
Chicken 2–3 pounds 3–5 pounds		Sear 30 mins, then 15–30 mins Sear 30 mins, then 30–60 mins	1¼ –2 hours
Goose 8–10 pounds 10–12 pounds		Sear 45 mins, then 1¾–2 hours Sear 45 mins, then 2–2½ hours	
		Sear at 425°F, then reduce the heat to 350°F	
Turkey 8–12 pounds 12–15 pounds 15–20 pounds		Sear 50 mins, then 1½–2 hours Sear 50 mins, then 2–2½ hours Sear 50 mins, then 2½–3 hours	3½–4 hours 4–4½ hours 4½–5 hours
Duck or duckling 3–6 pounds		Sear 30 mins, then 50 mins–1½ hours	
Guinea fowl 1½–3 pounds	425°F; 30 mins–1 hour		
Poussin 1–1½ pounds	425°F; 20–30 mins		
Squab 1–1½ pounds	425°F; 20–30 mins		
Quail	425°F; 15 mins		

time to be sure the stuffing will be cooked right through.

● Duck is seldom stuffed; it gives off too much fat. Add more flavor with a clove-studded apple or onion, and discard before serving.

Cooking poultry and game

● Steaming: suitable for chicken breast and for small whole quail. Place the poultry on a piece of cheesecloth, lower onto steamer bottom, and cook over just boiling water, allowing 8 minutes per 1 pound weight.

● Roasting: chicken, turkey and poussin should be draped with

fatty bacon, cheesecloth soaked in butter or oil, or rubbed with butter and basted frequently. Duck and goose need to be pricked all over so their fat can escape and baste the bird at the same time.

● Roasting: game birds are very lean and do not require a great deal of cooking. They do, however, need barding with a thin layer of bacon fat, tied in place and removed for the last 10 minutes so that the top of the bird can brown.

● Light-fleshed game birds are roasted until well done, those with darker flesh are usually served underdone.

● Cooking times depend on the size, type, weight, and age of the bird that is being cooked.

● Goose and duck give out a lot of fat during roasting so cook them on a rack.

● Birds for spit-roasting should be stuffed, trussed and secured on a roasting fork.

● Testing if cooked: a meat thermometer, placed in the thickest part of the muscle, is really the most accurate way of testing. Poultry is ready when a skewer in the thickest part of the thigh releases absolutely clear juices, tinged with gold, and without any trace of pink (uncooked meat) in them.

Internal temperatures

All poultry should be cooked to an internal temperature of not less than 155°F to eliminate the risks of bacterial and parasitic infection.

Above: *this assortment of poultry, already plucked, cleaned and ready for the pot, hangs from hooks in the butcher's shop. They offer the cook a wide choice for cooking. The birds, from left to right: poulet; roasting chicken; boiling fowl; turkey; goose; duck; and two guinea fowls*

Trussing a chicken

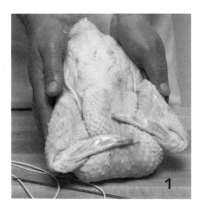

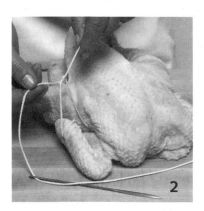

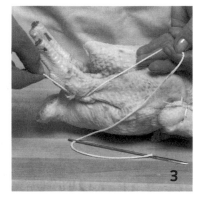

1. Stretch the neck flap firmly under the bird and fold back the wing tips to secure the flap firmly in place.

2. Push threaded trussing needle right through body just above the wings. Return it through the body, this time piercing wings. Tie and trim loose ends of string. Re-thread the trussing needle.

3. Push the needle through the skin just underneath the drumstick joint, then through the gristle on either side of the parson's nose and bring it out through the skin under the far drumstick. Return the needle through the bird, just to one side of the original path. Tie securely and trim the ends.

Below: *carving the bird is not particularly difficult but you do need to know something of the bird's anatomy to make sure you are doing it right, and it does require some practice. If in doubt, practice in the kitchen and bring it to the table when carved*

Carving a chicken

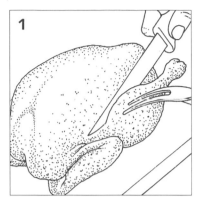

1. Place the bird breast-side up, remove the legs and wings on each side. If the chicken is large, separate drumsticks from thighs.

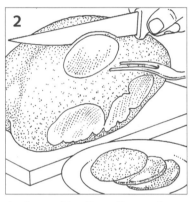

2. Carve thin slices diagonally from each side of the breast.

Resting a roast

A roast must be allowed to rest in a warm place for 10–15 minutes after it is cooked. Resting settles the meat so that it is easier to carve and loses less juice. A lot of people worry that the meat will get cold, but a cooked bird has a lot of heat stored in it and would take hours to get cold.

Carving

Use a sharp knife, which is much safer than a blunt one. If you are unsure about it, carve away from the table, keep the meat warm, and serve it all at once. Always use a fork fitted with a safety guard. At the table, keep the cut side toward you, presenting the uncut side toward the guests.

● Duck: difficult to carve, so use poultry shears. Insert shears into vent and cut through breast. Open up and cut along each side of backbone and remove. Place each half skin-side up on a board, cut between wing and leg to give 2 portions.
● Game birds: as for duck.
● Turkey and goose: carve as

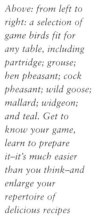

Above: from left to right: a selection of game birds fit for any table, including partridge; grouse; hen pheasant; cock pheasant; wild goose; mallard; widgeon; and teal. Get to know your game, learn to prepare it–it's much easier than you think–and enlarge your repertoire of delicious recipes

Buying game

- Young birds generally have pointed flight feathers at the tip and edge of wings, downy feathers on the breast and under the wing, soft pliable feet and short rounded spurs on the legs.
- The best test is to insert a matchstick into the small opening that young game birds in feather have just above the vent. This is smaller or may close in mature birds. In young pheasant it will open to a depth of 1 inch; in partridge or grouse it will be ½ inch.

Right: cooking a duck

Warnings

- **Wash your hands thoroughly before and after handling poultry. Also, wash all knives and utensils between handling raw and cooked food.**
- **Prepare raw poultry on white non-porous boards which can be washed in hot water with a little bleach.**

- **Avoid any contact between cooked and raw foods, during both storage and preparation.**
- **Cool poultry that you have cooked for eating later as quickly as possible, Cover it immediately and refrigerate it as soon as possible.**

- Ripeness is judged by smell and the condition of the bird round the vent. This becomes moist and fragile when the bird is well hung. A high bird smells gamy, a rotten one smells bad.
- Hanging tenderizes meat, retains moisture and develops the gamy flavor.
- If game is smelly when plucked, wipe with a cheesecloth dampened in diluted vinegar.
- After hanging, it is plucked, drawn and trussed.

Plucking and drawing game

After game has been hung, place on a newspaper-covered bowl or board. Pull out the body feathers first, then the remainder with fingers or tweezers.

When all the feathers are out and before drawing, singe any stubborn quills using a lighted candle, a taper or low gas flame. Cut off the head, roll back the neck skin and cut off the neck. Slit neck skin, loosen windpipe and gullet with the fingers. Make a slit above the vent to enlarge it, slide in your fingers and remove innards. Do not break the gall.

Types of game

- Grouse: this is the most popular game bird. The meat is dark red, rich and gamey, yet delicate. A young bird can be roasted for 15–20 minutes and served slightly

Below: Peking duck, served with wafer-thin pancakes, cucumber matchsticks and plum sauce, is one of the most most interesting and delicious ways of serving duck, popularized in Chinese restaurants the world over

underdone. Allow 1 per person. Older birds are best marinated and casseroled.

● Partridge: the gray-legged or common partridge is generally regarded as the best for eating; the red-legged is slightly larger. Best eaten when young, weighing about 1 pound and needing little hanging. Allow 1 per person. Use older birds in pâtés, pies, casseroles, and soups.

● Pheasant: the hen is often the plumper, juicier bird. Feel the width of the breast to see if it is plump, the legs should be smooth and feet soft. One bird will make 4 servings.

● Pigeon: wild woodpigeons are gamier than those bred for the table, squab are the young ones. The most tender bird will be a young one which has soft, supple feet without scales. Marinate older birds in red wine prior to cooking them.

● Quail: the smallest game bird, which is now usually farmed for the table. The gamy flavor is very faint. Allow 2 per person.

● Venison: the meat is fine textured, dense and dark red, with little marbling or fat. Roast young venison, and casserole or stew older venison.

● Wild duck: this is rated highly for its characteristic fishy flavor. Drakes tend to be tougher than ducks, and are therefore best marinated. Eat within 24 hours of killing.

Meat

Meat is an important source of food. In this chapter you can find out many ways of making the most of inexpensive cuts of meat, and achieving the best with those that cost a bit more. Enjoy creating different flavors from the same cuts of meat and explore the enormous versatility of the many cuts of meat.

Choosing

● All the cuts of meat, at a good store, should look appetizing, silky, but not wet. Boneless, rolled meat should be neatly tied; bones should be sawn smoothly; meat should be neatly trimmed with all the excess fat removed.

● The best meat of each animal comes from the hindquarter and loin, the tenderest comes from the parts that have had least exercise. Exercise develops muscle fiber and the connective tissue that holds muscles together. Connective tissue is mostly responsible for toughness.

Left: frying some tender fillet mignon
Far right: *marinating the meat before cooking*

● Tough meat can be prepared so that it arrives at the table full of flavor and juice by marinating in a marinade which includes wine, lemon juice, vinegar, yogurt, or pulped tomatoes. These acids break down connective tissue. Lengthy cooking completes the process.

● Oil used in marinades adds succulence to the meat.

● Pounding or cutting also breaks up any connective tissue, while flavorings such as chopped onions, garlic, herbs, spices, and seasonings add taste.

● Aging (the hanging of carcasses) tenderizes beef and lamb. Mature beef is a dark red color, its fat will be pale gold. White fat and bright red meat indicate that it is immature. Pork, veal and kosher meat are not aged.

Cooking beef

● Per person, allow about 4 ounces boneless lean meat; 8–12 ounces with the bone.

● Use dry heat–roasting, frying and broiling–for tender cuts; and moist heat–braising, pot roasting, stewing, and simmering–for tougher cuts.

● Broil small, reasonably thick pieces of best-quality meat. Brush the meat on both sides with oil to prevent it drying out,

sear the meat on both sides, and rest it after cooking for a few minutes to acquire an even texture.

● Fry good-quality flat cuts in a little hot oil or butter in a large shallow skillet, turning the meat once or twice. Do not pierce it while cooking; keep a fairly brisk heat going; do not overheat the fat or it will burn.

● Steak (per pound for a 1-inch steak): blue, inside almost rare: 5 minutes; rare, red inside with the juices running freely: 7 minutes; medium rare, fewer juices, paler center: 12 minutes; medium, pink in center, juices set: 14 minutes; well done, center beige, flesh still juicy: 15 minutes.

● Stir-fry both round steak and fillet mignon.

● Roast cuts from the back, ribs, fillet or sirloin. Small cuts shrink more than the large ones, choose a cut larger than you actually need and use the leftovers for other dishes, such as curries and salads. If roasting with the bone, allow 20 minutes per pound plus 20 minutes extra, at 400°F. If boneless, allow 25 minutes, plus 25 minutes extra.

● Boil brisket slowly with root vegetables. Allow 15–20 minutes per pound.

● Braise any small lean pieces of top chuck, flank steak or chuck steak.

● Stew or casserole the cheaper cuts such as shank, neck, heel of round, and flank.

Storing meat

- Store meat in a film-covered plastic tray on a plate in the refrigerator.
- Any meat not prepacked should be wrapped in foil or baking parchment and then refrigerated.
- Chops deteriorate faster than roasts.

Approximate maximum storage times for meat

Uncooked meat	In a refrigerator	In a freezer
Beef	3–5 days	12 months
Veal	3–5 days	12 months
Lamb	3–5 days	9 months
Pork	2–4 days	6 months
Ground beef	1–2 days	3 months

Internal temperatures of meat

This is extremely important and pork as well as all poultry should always be cooked to an internal temperature of at least 155°F. This eliminates all risks of both bacterial and parasite infection.

Internal temperatures of meat

	Rare	Medium	Well done
Beef	140°F	155°F	175°F
Veal		165°F	175°F
Lamb	140°F	147°F	175°F
Pork		155°F	175°F

Warnings

- Wash hands before and after handling meat. Wash knives and utensils between handling raw and cooked food.
- Prepare raw meat on white nonporous boards which can be washed in hot water with a little bleach.
- Carefully but loosely cover meat in a shallow container or if prepacked, leave in tray and refrigerate.
- Avoid contact between cooked and raw foods during storage and preparation.
- Cool meat cooked for eating later as quickly as possible, cover and refrigerate.
- Meat should be thoroughly cooked.

1 Shank
2 Heel of round
3 Round
4 Boneless rump
5 Top sirloin
6 Sirloin
7 Porterhouse
8 Flank
9 Navel
10 Thick plate
11 Corner piece
12 Prime rib (8 ribs)
   a: Prime rib roast (ribs)
   b: Blade roast (2 ribs)
13 Chuck
14 Neck
15 Top chuck
16 Cross rib
17 Brisket
18 Fore shank

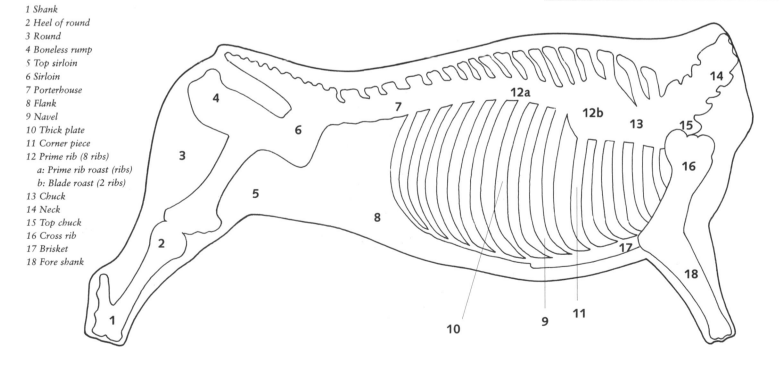

Approximate cooking times for meat *(minutes per 1 pound and temperatures)*

Meats and cuts	Roasting	Pot roasting/braising	Boiling
Beef Tender cuts: rare	15 minutes plus 15 minutes in a hot oven	30–40 minutes on stove top	
Tender cuts: medium	40 minutes in a warm oven		
coarser cuts	20 minutes in a fairly hot oven		1 hour at a steady simmer
Boneless/rolled	30 minutes in a fairly hot oven		
Veal Thin cuts and with the bone	25 minutes plus 20 minutes in a fairly hot oven		
Thick and boneless and rolled cuts	35 minutes in a warm oven	40–50 minutes in a warm oven	
Lamb Tender cuts	20 minutes in a fairly hot oven (plus 15 minutes for large cuts)		
Smaller cuts for casseroles and stews		Total of 2½ hours in a warm oven	30 minutes
Pork Small, thin cuts	30 minutes plus 20 minutes in a medium oven	60 minutes on stove top	
Thick cuts	30 minutes plus 20 minutes in a medium oven	60 minutes in a warm oven	
Pickled cuts			Your butcher will advise

Cooking veal

● Roast leg, loin, ribs and boneless and rolled shoulder. Use a medium oven, 325°F, allowing about 35 minutes per pound with the bone; about 40–45 minutes per pound boneless and rolled. Baste frequently and serve thoroughly cooked.

● Fry or broil chops, fillets and escalopes cut from the leg in butter or olive oil. If broiling, baste frequently to stop the meat from drying out.

● Braise, pot roast, stew or casserole fore and hind shanks, heel of round, breast, and neck.

Right: *Broiled lamb noisettes*

Carving a rib of beef

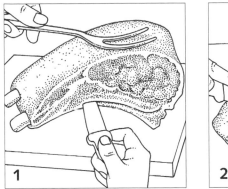 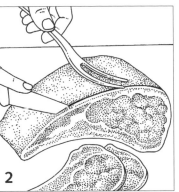

1. Remove the bones at the wide end of the rib before carving, then run the knife along between meat and contours of the ribs.

2. Steady the roast with the back of the carving fork, and then slice the meat vertically, with each slice falling free.

Basic roast beef

Serves 6–8

What you need:

- 4 pound sirloin or rib with the bone
- dry English mustard
- 1¼ cups stock
- ⅔ cup red wine
- salt and pepper

1 Preheat the oven to 425°F. Weigh the beef and allow 20 minutes per pound for medium rare meat and 15 minutes for rare.

2 Place the beef, with the fatty side uppermost, on a wire rack over a roasting pan and sprinkle with dry mustard and pepper but no salt.

3 Roast for 20 minutes. Turn the oven down to 325°F, and time the joint from now. Baste occasionally. Halfway through the cooking time, tip off the drippings and use for roasting potatoes and root vegetables such as parsnips.

4 When cooked, sprinkle with salt and let stand in a warm place for about 20–30 minutes.

Marinades

A marinade is a mixture of oil, wine and other flavorings which penetrates the outer layer of the meat when left in it overnight in the refrigerator. The acid in the marinade breaks down the tough fibers and the oil prevents moisture evaporation and adds richness.

Lamb kebabs

For 2 pounds boneless lamb for kebabs

What you need:

- ⅔ cup red wine
- 1 tablespoon lemon juice
- 1 tablespoon oil
- 8 whole allspice
- 1 heaped tablespoon cumin
- 1 sprig of fresh thyme
- ½ onion sliced
- 6 black peppercorns

Cut the meat into 2-inch lean cubes. Mix all the marinade ingredients together. Place the cubes of meat in a shallow dish, pour the marinade over, and leave for 8 hours, or overnight, turning the meat occasionally.

Broiled meat

For 1½ pounds meat for broiling or frying

What you need:

- 2 cups olive oil
- juice of 1 lime or lemon
- 1 onion, sliced
- pepper
- ⅔ cup white wine
- 2 crushed garlic cloves
- freshly chopped basil

Combine all the ingredients in a mixing bowl. Place the meat in a large dish, pour over the marinade, and leave for several hours.

Barbecue steaks

For 4 6-ounce barbecue steaks

What you need:

- 1 crushed garlic clove
- ½ cup brown sugar
- 1 teaspoon whole grain mustard
- 1 tablespoon wine vinegar
- 1¼ cups stout
- finely chopped onion
- pepper

Combine all the ingredients for the marinade in a pan and bring to a boil. Reduce the heat and simmer for 10 minutes. Cool before pouring over the steaks. Cover and refrigerate for at least 2 hours–overnight is ideal.

Cook's Tip

Roast meat should rest for 20–30 minutes before serving. This makes it easier to carve.

Buying pork

- Look for firm white fat, pink, smooth velvety flesh.
- Bones should be pale with a tinge of blue to them.
- Do not buy any pork that looks damp or clammy, or has oily, waxy-looking fat.

Far right: *brushing the pork shoulder with oil before cooking*
Right: *lightly frying the pork noisettes*

Cooking pork

- Roast the belly and foreloin (which can be rolled and stuffed), leg and loin.
- Roast with the bone at 400°F, allowing 25 minutes per 1 pound plus 25 minutes extra. Boneless, roast pork slowly at 350°F, allowing 35 minutes per 1 pound plus 35 minutes extra. Add about 10 more minutes for a stuffed roast.
- To get good crackling on pork, score the skin with several parallel lines right down through the fat. Do not baste or let it come in contact with any fat, liquid, or cooking juices in the roasting pan.
- Broil and fry the center loins , shoulder and rib-chops.
- Spare ribs come from the belly and can be roasted, barbecued or braised.
- Braise both tenderloin and end loin chops.

Bacon and ham

Cured meat from the pig's back or side, used for bacon, is called "green" or unsmoked and has a mild flavor. Smoking bacon preserves the meat for longer by retarding bacterial growth, adds flavor and improves color. Good-quality bacon will be firm and deep pink with white fat, a pleasant flavor and no yellow or greenish stains.

The pig's hind and shoulder, are used for ham and cured very much more slowly than bacon. Ham can be eaten in its cured "raw" state or used for boiling and braising. Hams sold ready for baking are milder cures and do not need soaking first. Other cuts should be soaked for up to 24 hours if traditionally cured. The rind is left on during cooking and keeps the meat in shape and flavors it.

A soaked ham is slowly simmered in water for just about 25 minutes per 1 pound. Keep it covered with water which should not boil. When it is cooked, remove from the heat. When cool enough to handle, remove the rind and score the fat. Baste with honey or syrup and bake in a hot oven for about 20 minutes. Small hams, after soaking, can be marinated in cider and braised, casseroled or steamed.

Cuts of bacon and ham

- Canadian bacon is prepared from the ham-end cut of pork loin. It is sometimes called English or Irish bacon.
- Regular bacon is prepared from belly strips below the spare ribs and is more fatty.

1 Hind feet
2 Hams
3 Loin butt
4 Fat back
5 Pork loins
6 Leaf fat
7 Clear bellies
8 Spare ribs
9 Brisket
10 Neck bones
11 Boston butt
12 Picnic butt
13 N.Y. style shoulder
14 Picnic
15 Jowl butts
16 Fore feet

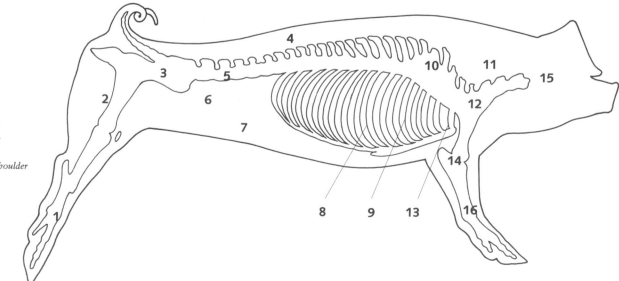

- Sliced ham from the center cut is more expensive than slices from the butt or shank ends, but there is little waste.
- Smoked butts are prepared from Boston butt without the blade bone.
- Smoked picnics cost less than ham and should be boiled. Sometimes the bottom or the shank end of the shoulder is cut off and then cured.
- Processed hams are sold ready to be baked. They do not need to be boiled first. Follow the directions on the wrapper.

Using bacon

Bacon can be used in various ways, in addition to serving broiled slices for breakfast or brunch.
- Line pans for pâtés with thin slices of fatty bacon.
- Cover the breasts of roasting chickens or pheasants with slices of fatty bacon.
- Wrap pitted prunes or pineapple wedges in slices of bacon. Secure well with a wooden toothpick and broil under a medium heat.
- Broil bacon slices until crisp, then crumble and mix with a green salad. Serve when the bacon is still warm.
- Dice bacon slices and sprinkle over cauliflower covered with a cheese sauce before baking.

Speciality hams

Most hams can be boiled or baked after curing and eaten either hot or cold. Some types are only available in speciality stores.

Bradenham

With its coal-black skin and deep red flesh, this is a famous British ham. It is cured with molasses and so has a sweet but robust flavor. If it is bought uncooked, it should be soaked for at least a week before it is cooked, otherwise it will tend to taste very salty.

Jambons de campagne

These are French country hams from the Dordogne area of France. They are farm-cured and often quite salty but are delicious sliced and served with unsalted butter and French bread.

Prague

This is traditionally salted and then mildly brined before being lightly smoked over beechwood embers, from which it emerges as perhaps the sweetest of all smoked boiling hams.

Prosciutto

This is dry-cured for part of the time under weights which gives it a flattened shape. After it has matured for about a year, it is soaked in tepid water to soften the rind. After drying and storing, it can be very thinly sliced and is often served with melon slices.

Suffolk

Traditionally cured in brine with spices and honey, this British ham is then smoked and hung to mature. It has a full delicate flavor.

Virginia

This is among the so-called "country-cured" hams of America. Pigs destined for this ham are fattened on peanuts and acorns, and the meat is usually smoked over scented hickory and applewood.

Westphalian

This German ham is smoked over juniper brush. Paper-thin slices are eaten raw as an hors d'œuvre.

Wiltshire

This British ham is cured as part of the whole pig. It is extremely mild and does not keep so well as most other hams. Like bacon, it is sold smoked or unsmoked.

York ham

Firm and tender, this is the best known of the British boiling hams. It is delicately pink, with fat that is white and translucent. This ham is cured by the dry-salt method. Green York ham is dry-cured, washed and placed in a calico bag to mature for about six months.

Above: *prosciutto and melon makes a simple but delicious summer salad*
Below: *broiled bacon gives flavor to a hearty casserole like Boeuf à la bourguignonne*

Crown roast of lamb

For a crown roast of lamb, curve two trimmed racks of lamb around into a ring, bones up and fat inside. Sew the ends together or tie with kitchen string.

For a guard of honor, interlace the bones of two trimmed racks, meat inside, and hold together with some string tied around between the bones.

Carving a shoulder of lamb

1. Place the shoulder, skin-side uppermost, on a board or platter and make a series of parallel cuts in the middle of the shoulder. Run the knife horizontally along the length of the bone to release these short slices.
2. Turn the shoulder over, remove all the fat, and then carve the meat in larger, horizontal slices.

Carving a leg of lamb

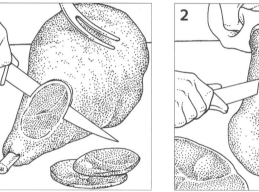

1. Holding the roast steady with the back of the fork, begin carving from the rounded side of the leg. Slice thinly away from yourself, gradually turning the knife to get large slices almost parallel to the bone.
2. Turn the leg over and, holding the bone in a clean cloth, carve long slices from the opposite side of the leg.

Buying lamb

● It should have a fine grain when cut across the muscle.
● Fat will be white, waxy, firm, yet brittle.

Cooking lamb

● Trim off fat before roasting.
● Roast a leg or loin at 350°F for 25 minutes per pound plus 25 minutes extra for well-done meat. For rarer meat, allow 15 minutes per pound and remove it from the oven and let it rest in a warm place for 25 minutes.
● Crown roast consists of 2 trimmed pieces of rack of lamb joined together.
● Roast breast of lamb after boning, trimming and stuffing.
● Stew and casserole shank, neck and flank.
● Spit roast or barbecue shoulder or leg of lamb.
● Broil or fry loin chops, rack of lamb chops, tenderloin, medallions cut from the loin.
● Casserole boneless shoulder and square chuck.

1 Leg
2 Loin
3 Flank
4 Breast
5 Rack
6 Brisket
7 Shank
8 Square chuck
9 Neck

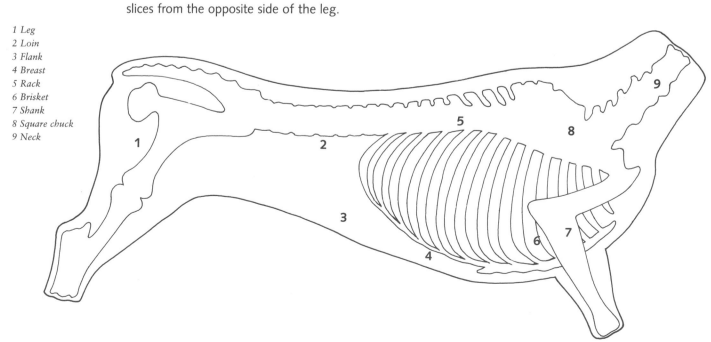

Sundries

The collective name for all the edible innards and heads and toes of animals, each type has different distinctive flavors and texture which respond well to careful cooking. They should be bought fresh and cooked as quickly as possible.

Sweetbreads

Veal (not on sale in the US) is the best, being whiter and larger than lamb's. Sweetbreads are two parts of the thymus gland; those that came from the pancreas gland are coarser. They need a lot of initial preparation before being finally cooked.

Brains

Calf's are better than lamb's. They are first soaked in water, then boiled in lightly salted water before being slowly fried or poached until cooked.

Liver

Liver is the most nutritious and widely eaten of all sundries. Sold either whole, when the membrane covering should be removed, or in slices. Strongly flavored pork or beef liver should be soaked in milk before cooking.
● Calf's: slice and cook quickly and lightly by broiling or frying and serve while still rosy pink inside. Overcooking will make the liver tough, dry and very leathery.
● Lamb's: deeper color than calf's and has a less good flavor but can be substituted for it in recipes using liver.
● Pork: use in pâtés, or braised in one large piece with wine and different vegetables.
● Beef: the coarsest and also the strongest flavored, best braised for 1–2 hours with onions.

Kidneys

These should be firm and smell sweet. Skin, halve, remove gristly core and either broil or sauté them briefly, or simmer slowly for a long time–anything in between and they will be very tough and rubbery.

● Calf's: large and pale from milk-fed veal, small and dark from grass-fed veal. Brown briskly in butter, then grill over charcoal or roast encased in their own fat.
● Lamb's: mild and delicious flavor, an essential part of a British "mixed grill."
● Pork: larger than lamb's and a stronger flavor. Broil or fry or cook slowly in wine.
● Beef: dark and strongly flavor, best braised. Used in steak and kidney pies.

Tongue

Available fresh, but more often salted or smoked. Choose one that is soft to the touch and soak overnight if salted. Simmer with vegetables and herbs until tender. Skin carefully and serve hot or cold. Beef is best.

Tripe

The lining of first and second stomachs and usually from beef and calf. It comes in a variety of textures–honeycombed (the best), slightly rough and smooth.

Tripe is usually sold prepared and partly cooked; it should always look white and fresh.

Heart

Beef is tough and best sliced and braised. Lamb's, pig's and calf's are more tender, and good blanched, stuffed, wrapped in bacon and roasted.

Heads, tails and feet

Long slow cooking is needed to tenderize and bring out their velvety, gelatinous qualities.

Heads: preparation is a lengthy business.

● Pig's: generally used for brawn, and eaten cold. Cheek is cooked until tender, then shaped and coated in egg and bread crumbs.
● Calf's: can be cooked, boned and chopped and eaten cold.
● Beef cheek: dark, dense flesh but good when very fresh. Marinate in wine and then braise slowly until cooked.
● Calf's and pig's ears: simmer, coat with egg and bread crumbs and fry.
● Tail (oxtail): needs long, slow, cooking and makes very good soup and stew. Make the day before serving, and remove the fat before reheating it.

Feet

● Pig's trotters: simmer until tender and serve hot or cold in their own jelly. When cooked, they can be coated with bread crumbs and then broiled slowly.
● Cow heel: when boiled and skinned and its meat cut into strips, can be added to beef stew to give a velvety texture.
● Calf's foot: cook in stews and casseroles to add richness and texture to the dish.

Left: *slowly frying sweetbreads*

Basic techniques

Cookery is an endlessly fascinating and rewarding art, but intensely disappointing when things go wrong. Disappointments are fewer and success more easily achieved if you understand how and why things happen. Mastering the basic techniques described below will insure that you soar more frequently to culinary heights.

Right: *boiling is one of the most commonly used methods of cooking food. Remember, though, that if food is boiled for too long in too much water, it will lose a lot of its nutrients into the cooking liquid*
Far right: *steaming is a healthier way of cooking than boiling because it retains a lot of the food's nutrients, as well as its texture, color and flavor. Steaming food in a special bamboo steaming basket is a popular way of cooking many foods in China*

Boiling

A form of cooking in liquid at a temperature of 212°F. The liquid used for this can be stock, salted water or flavored with wine, herbs or spices.

● Salt added to water raises the boiling point and makes food cook more quickly. It is added at the start of cooking to vegetables, but close to the end for stocks and stews.

● Simmering takes place over a low heat and small bubbles break just below the liquid's surface. Stocks and soups are covered so that as much as possible is extracted from the ingredients.

● Poaching: in which delicate food is cooked in liquid, is a gentler form of simmering.

● Fast boiling–a rolling boil–is used for cooking pasta, reducing liquid and jam making.

● Vegetables such as peas and greens, cooked in an open pan in fast-boiling, well-salted water.

● Root vegetables are simmered in a covered pan.

● Blanching: placing foods in boiling water to loosen skins or, for freezing, to prevent deterioration in color and flavor. Food is put into boiling water for a set time, then into ice-cold water for the same time.

● Reducing: the liquid is boiled, uncovered, over a high heat in a pan with a large surface area.

Steaming

Cooking food in hot vapor over boiling liquid retains a high proportion of flavor and nutrients. Direct steaming uses a tiered steamer, trivet or colander inside a saucepan, or a pressure cooker. Indirect steaming is when food in a covered pudding basin is set in a pan of water reaching halfway up the basin's side. Food such as fish can be placed on a lightly buttered covered plate over a pan of water.

Braising

This is a method of cooking meat on a bed of finely chopped vegetables over a low heat in a pan with a tight-fitting lid. It is used for meat that is past its prime, or which is low in natural fat (like venison), and for some vegetables. Casseroling cooks meat and vegetables in more liquid than is used for braising. Tight-lidded pots keep in condensation and keep food moist. To stop steam escaping, cover the pot first with foil and then the lid.

● Mirepoix: bed of diced vegetables on which meat or whole vegetables are braised.

Broiling

Select food that is tender, no more than 2 inches deep, and marinate drier and leaner cuts of meat, poultry, and thick-fleshed fish. Preheat the broiler (not the broiler pan) at its highest setting for at least 10 min-

utes. Lightly grease the broiler rack before placing the food on it. Regulate the intensity by lowering the pan rather than reducing the heat. The food to be broiled should be at room temperature.

● Gratin: dishes on which a thin golden brown crust is formed under a high heat from a broiler or in the oven.

● Searing: sealing the surface of the food, to retain juices, goodness, and flavor.

● Steaks: blue, inside almost rare; rare, red inside with juices running freely; medium rare, fewer juices and a paler center; medium, pink in center, juices set; well-done, center beige, flesh still juicy.

● Seasoning: add salt just before putting food under the broiler. Salting ahead draws juices out, leaving the inside dry.

Frying

A method of quickly cooking or browning food in hot fat or oil. This method is suitable for tender pieces of meat, fish, and certain vegetables. Always pay attention when frying, as deep fat will catch fire if it becomes too hot.

● Shallow frying is carried out over a medium heat using equal amounts of sizzling oil and butter, or just oil.

● Sautéeing uses very little fat, and the food is moved constantly throughout the process to prevent sticking and burning.

● Pan-frying or dry-frying uses a thick-bottomed heated pan and the food cooks in its own juices.

● Stir-frying uses little oil. The cooked foods are pushed to the side of the wok while fresh food is tossed and turned in the oil.

● Batting out: tenderizing by placing delicate meat between sheets of baking parchment and pressing with a rolling-pin, or using a specially designed bat.

● Deep-frying uses very hot oil which seals the outside of the food, preventing moisture escaping and fat soaking in.

● Deep-frying: fat should come only halfway up the pan to avoid overflowing; it should be strained after use and stored covered; if it foams with yellow bubbles and smells unpleasant, it should be discarded.

Eggs

Full of nutrition and an indispensable ingredient in all kinds of cooking, eggs deserve a place in every cook's kitchen. They are inexpensive and easy to prepare and cook. A lot of people claim that they are unable to cook an egg properly, but master the techniques of a few simple ways of cooking them and, in no time at all, you will be surprised to learn that you have acquired an enviable culinary reputation.

Cooking techniques

There are many different ways in which to prepare eggs. Most people have their favorites.

Boiling

● The eggs should not be cold, or the shell will crack when you lower it into boiling water.
● If they are to be peeled, they should be a couple of days old,

Below: making a successful soufflé is within everyone's reach

otherwise the white will stick to the shell when you peel it.
● The fresher the eggs, the longer they should be cooked.
● Soft-cooked eggs have a softly set white and a runny yolk. Lower eggs into boiling water and cook for 3 minutes.
● Medium-cooked have a firm white with a just soft yolk. Cook for 4 ½ minutes.
● Hard-cooked eggs are firm throughout. Lower into cold water, bring slowly to a boil, simmer and time from this point for 8–10 minutes. As soon as the eggs are cooked, place in a bowl under cold running water. When cool, peel and use at once.

Coddling

A coddler looks like an egg cup with a lid. Place a knob of butter in the bottom and drop in the egg. Add a little salt and pepper and screw on the lid. Place in simmering water, which should come three-quarters of the way up the coddler. Turn off the heat. Cover the pan and leave for 8–9 minutes. Remove the coddler from the pan, unscrew the lid and serve the egg in the coddler.

Poaching

Skillet method: pour water into the pan to a depth of 1½ inches and bring to simmering point. Break each egg into a saucer and carefully lower it into the water. Cook for about 3 minutes, either covering the pan or just basting the egg with hot water. Remove on a fish slice or perforated spoon.

Poacher method: half fill the pan with water, place the cups in position and add a knob of butter to each cup. Bring to a boil. Lower the heat, break the eggs into the cups, and simmer, covered, for 4–5 minutes. Loosen each egg with a knife and tip out.

Scrambling

For 2 people, break 3–4 eggs into a bowl and whisk lightly with a fork. Season with salt and pepper and stir in 2 tablespoons of milk or light cream. Melt about 2 tablespoons of butter in a pan over a low heat. Pour in the eggs and leave for about 30 seconds before lightly stirring with a wooden spoon. Cook for 30–60 seconds longer, stirring, until the eggs are just set. Serve at once.

Baking

The eggs are cooked in individual ramekin dishes. Lightly grease the dishes with butter. Place in a roasting pan with 1 inch warm water, break an egg into each dish and season well. Dot with a little butter or cream and cook in a preheated oven, 350°F, for about 8–10 minutes, until just set. Remove from the water at once.

Omelet

For 2 people, beat 3–4 eggs very lightly just before using, and season lightly with salt and pepper. Heat a knob of butter in a pan. When the butter has melted and is just turning in color, pour in the eggs. Tip the pan toward you and lift up a little of the mixture on the far side with a fork, tipping the pan so that the unset egg runs into the space. With a little unset egg on the top, fold the omelet in half and serve.

Beating egg whites

● Use egg whites at room temperature, and clean utensils, free of grease.
● Soufflés need the egg whites to be beaten until slightly translucent and holding soft peaks.
● Meringues require the whites to be beaten until they are opaque and hold in firm peaks.
● Use beaten egg white immediately as it may collapse if left for even a short time.

Folding in egg whites

● Stir in a big spoonful of egg white into the mixture to lighten it. Then scoop the rest of the egg whites on top.
● Using a metal spoon or a spatula, cut down into the center of the bowl.
● With a scooping action, bring the spoon up toward you, turning the mixture bottom to top. Continue, turning the bowl and working clockwise.

Uses

● The yolk acts as a binding agent for stuffings, fish cakes, and rissoles.
● The yolk emulsifies and will hold butter or oil in suspension (as in mayonnaise).
● Eggs act as a thickening agent for soups, sauces, and stews, as well as custards where the yolk coagulates as it is heated to hold the liquid in suspension.
● Egg whites aerate, having the ability to hold air and increase volume by many times (as in meringue).
● A whole egg, or egg yolk, is used for coating foods or glazing them.

Quail egg   *White hen egg*   *Brown hen egg*   *Duck egg*   *Goose egg*

Fresh test

● Break a fresh egg and the white should be translucent and cling to the yolk; if the white runs away from the yolk it is not very fresh.
● When placed in a glass of water, a fresh egg will sink to the bottom and lie completely flat on the bottom. If it tilts slightly, it is a little stale. If the egg floats to the top of the water, it is not suitable to use for boiling and should be cracked before use. If a pungent smell comes from the egg, it should be thrown away immediately.

Storage

● Buy date-stamped eggs in small quantities, and then use them as soon as possible.
● Store eggs, pointed end down, in the refrigerator and bring to room temperature about 30 minutes before using.
● Eggs are enclosed in porous shells so they will easily absorb smells; store them away from strong-smelling food.

Warnings

● Do not use cracked or dirty eggs.
● The egg's shell is porous and can absorb contamination from birds' feed, the laying process or through handling. Always buy where high standards of cleanliness are practiced and there is a rapid turnover.

● A certain amount of heat will kill the bacteria in eggs, but often eggs are used raw (in mayonnaise, for instance) or lightly cooked. Pasteurized eggs are available and can be used for most kinds of cooking, but not for mayonnaise or lemon curd.

Stocks

What's the point of making stock? It adds a depth of flavor to sauces and soups, and although it may take a while to cook, the results are well worthwhile and a lot better than the flavor achieved by a bouillon cube. The finished stock can be reduced by boiling uncovered over a high heat in a saucepan with a large surface and then frozen in an ice cube tray for later use.

Below: *a good brown stock will enrich many soups and stews*
Right: *ham stock adds flavor to lentil and bacon soup*

Basic techniques

● Do not add salt. When the stock is reduced, the flavor will be concentrated, so add salt only to the finished soups, casseroles, and sauces.

● Simmer the stock, partially covered, and remove the scum frequently; adding a cup of cold water to the ingredients will bring froth to the surface.

● Let cool in the pan and skim off as much fat as possible before removing the bones. Strain into a bowl and remove the remaining fat when cold.

● Raw bones, sometimes available free from a butcher, make a stronger-flavored stock than those that come from the remains of a roast.

● Raw meat, with a lot of blood in it, helps to make the liquid rich and clear.

● Veal bones make a stock that will set to a jelly, which will keep longer than liquid stock.

● Reboil stocks every two or three days if refrigerated to stop them going bad; every day if kept in a larder.

Fish

Fish stock

Strain and reduce this to use as the basis of a sauce, or to make into aspic to glaze fish that is to be served cold. Cod, flounder or salmon can be substituted for fish trimmings; the addition of crab legs and shrimp shells will add extra flavor; and 2 glasses of wine can be substituted for some of the water.
Makes about 6 cups

What you need:

● 2–3 stalks celery
● 2 onions
● 1 carrot
● 1 bay leaf
● bones and trimmings of 2–3 sole
● 2½ quarts water

Skin and slice the vegetables. Put all the ingredients in a large pan, bring to a boil and simmer, uncovered, for 30–45 minutes.

Meat

Brown stock

Use this for strongly flavored meat and vegetable soups; add to stews, casseroles, ground meat dishes and meat sauces. Fry the bones, meat scraps, vegetables until a dark even brown but never let them burn or scorch. Makes about 7½ cups

What you need:

● 3 pounds beef or veal knuckle bones
● 12 ounces shin of beef
● 3 quarts water
● 2 stalks celery, chopped
● 2–3 carrots, chopped
● 2 onions, chopped with the skins on
● 2 leeks, chopped
● 2 tomatoes

- 2 cloves
- 1 sprig fresh thyme or ¼ teaspoon dry
- 1 bay leaf
- 1 glass red wine (optional)

1 Brown the knuckle bones in the stockpot, pour off the fat and retain. Add cold water and bring slowly to a boil. Simmer for 2–3 hours, skimming frequently.

2 In a separate saucepan, fry the vegetables (including the onion skins) in some of the fat until brown. Drain off the fat and add the vegetables to the stockpot with the remaining ingredients. (Adding the onion skins gives the stock a good color.)

3 Simmer for 2 hours, then strain and let cool. Remove any fat when the stock is cold.

Chicken stock

Use this more delicate stock for risottos and those soups, stews and sauces that need substance but not a strong flavor.
Makes about 5 cups

What you need:

- 2 onions, peeled and chopped
- 1 carrot, chopped
- 2 stalks celery, chopped
- 1 leek, chopped
- handful of parsley stalks
- 1 bay leaf
- 5–6 peppercorns
- 2 chicken carcasses, jointed with skin but not fat
- 1 veal bone
- 1 sprig of fresh thyme or ¼ teaspoon dry
- about 2½ quarts water

1 Put all the ingredients into a large pan. Cover with the water and bring slowly to a boil.

2 Skim off any scum or fat. Simmer for 3 hours, skimming frequently. Strain, cool and take off any fat.

Ham stock

Use this as a basis for soups made with legumes.
Makes about 5 cups.

What you need:

- 1 ham bone
- 1 large onion, stuck with a clove
- 2 stalks celery, chopped
- 2 carrots, chopped
- 1 bay leaf

Cover the ham bone with cold water. Bring to a boil, add the vegetables and bay leaf, and simmer for 3 hours. Strain and cool.

Vegetables
Light vegetarian stock

Use for soups and sauces, risottos, and vegetarian dishes.
Makes about 5 cups

What you need:

- 2⅓ cups chopped onions
- 2 cups chopped carrots
- 2 stalks celery, chopped
- 1 clove garlic, crushed
- 1 small turnip, chopped
- cauliflower or broccoli stalks, chopped
- 7½ cups water
- handful of parsley stalks
- 2 sprigs fresh thyme or ½ teaspoon dry
- 1 bay leaf

Put all the ingredients into a saucepan. Bring to a boil and simmer slowly for 1 hour. Strain.

Sauces

The basic rule for sauces is that they should have a good flavor and texture, and be made from the best ingredients. Defined as "liquid seasoning for food," they should enhance or complement whatever you are serving. Success comes from knowing your way confidently round the simple methods that are used to make flour-based and butter- or oil-based sauces.

Above: *onions, garlic and different herbs for flavoring sauces*

Flour-based sauces

Most savory sauces thickened with flour incorporate it into the sauce in the form of a roux, a liaison of flour and butter. These are the white sauces like Béchamel (made with milk), the "blond" sauces like velouté (made with white stock) and the sauces made with brown stock.

Béchamel sauce

Makes about 1¼ cups

What you need:

- 1¼ cups milk
- 2 tablespoons butter
- ¼ cup all-purpose flour
For the infusion:
- ½ small onion, halved
- 1 small carrot, halved
- ½ stalk celery, cut into small pieces
- 1 small bay leaf
- 1 bouquet garni
- 4 black peppercorns
- pinch of grated nutmeg
- pinch of salt

1 Put the milk and all the infusion ingredients into a saucepan. Slowly bring to a boil. Remove from the heat, cover and leave until cold. Pour the milk through a fine strainer and discard the flavorings.

2 Melt the butter in a heavy-bottomed saucepan over a low heat. Add the flour and stir well with a wooden spoon to make the roux. Do not let it color. Gradually add one-third of the infused milk, blending well and stirring constantly.

3 Gradually blend in the rest of the milk. Bring to a boil, stirring well, and cook for 2 minutes longer. Season to taste.

Velouté sauce

Makes 300 ml/½ pint

What you need:

- 1 scant tablespoon butter
- 1 scant cup flour

Variations

- *Mornay: off the heat, stir in ½ cup grated Gruyere or Parmesan. Use with chicken, veal, eggs, fish, pasta and vegetables.*
- *Egg: stir in 1–2 finely chopped hard-cooked eggs and 1–2 tablespoons chopped fresh parsley or chives. Use with fish.*
- *Mushroom: gently fry 1⅓ cups mushrooms in 2 tablespoons butter, drain and stir into the sauce with a squeeze of lemon juice. Use with fish, meat and poultry.*
- *Parsley: stir in 2 tablespoons finely chopped fresh parsley, cook for 2 minutes. Use with bacon, fish, eggs and vegetables.*

- 1¼ cups chicken, veal or fish stock
- 1 egg yolk
- 2–3 tablespoons cream
- salt and white pepper

1 Melt the butter in a saucepan until foaming. Stir in the flour and cook for 5 minutes until the roux is straw-colored.

2 Bring the stock to a boil and gradually stir into the roux. Bring to a boil, season with salt and pepper, and simmer for 15 minutes, whisking, until the sauce is the correct consistency.

3 When the sauce is thick and smooth, enrich with egg and cream just before serving. To avoid it curdling, remove the pan from the heat, mix a little of the hot liquid with the egg and cream before stirring it into the sauce. The sauce may be returned to the heat to heat through, but do not let it boil.

Alternative method

An alternative way of making sauces is to use a wire whisk. Use the same ingedients for Béchamel and velouté sauces.

Put the liquid into a saucepan and whisk in the flour until thoroughly blended. Continuing to whisk, add the butter and bring slowly to a boil.

When just bubbling and thick, turn the heat down and whisk well. Season to taste.

Brown sauce

A brown roux is made from oil or clarified butter (melted butter strained through cheesecloth). If the butter is not clarified, it is likely to burn. It is important to use a well-flavored stock, and always use cold stock as this helps to clear the sauce by the rising of

scum. The sauce can be frozen unless you've used frozen stock. Makes about 2 cups

What you need:

- 3 tablespoons oil or clarified butter
- 1 small onion, finely diced
- 1 small carrot, finely diced
- ½ stalk celery, trimmed and finely diced
- 2 tablespoons all-purpose flour
- 1 teaspoon tomato paste
- 2½ cups brown stock
- 1 bouquet garni
- salt and pepper

1 Heat the oil in a saucepan. Add the onion, carrot, and celery, and cook for 5–7 minutes, stirring constantly, until they are on the point of changing color.

2 Stir in the flour, reduce the heat, and cook for 15 minutes until the roux is a rich brown, stirring constantly. Remove from the heat, cool slightly and stir in the tomato paste.

3 Return to the heat and gradually stir in two-thirds of the stock. Slowly bring to a boil, whisking constantly. Add the bouquet garni, salt and pepper, and half-cover with the lid. Simmer for 35–40 minutes, skimming the surface frequently. Add half the remaining stock, bring to a boil and skim again. Simmer the stock for 5 minutes, half covered. Whisk in the remaining stock, bring to a boil without stirring and skim again. Strain the sauce into a clean pan, bring back to a boil and then skim thoroughly until clear. Season with salt and pepper and use as required.

Variations

- *Aurore: whisk in 2 tablespoons tomato paste, season, remove from the heat and whisk in 1 tablespoon butter. Use with eggs, chicken, pork, fish, veal.*
- *Caper: stir in 1 tablespoon lemon juice and 1 tablespoon chopped capers. Use with fish.*
- *Tarragon: put ⅓ cup white wine, 3 tablespoons chopped tarragon and a finely chopped shallot into a pan, and heat to reduce to 1½ tablespoons. Strain into the sauce and simmer for 2–3 minutes. Off the heat, stir in 1 tablespoon butter and another 3 tablespoons of chopped fresh tarragon. Use this sauce with eggs, fish, chicken and vegetables.*

Above left: *Spinach pancake and asparagus in cheesy Béchamel sauce*

Butter- and oil-based sauces

Hollandaise, which uses egg yolk and butter and is served hot, and mayonnaise, served cold and made with egg yolk and oil, are thought to be tricky to make but a food processor or liquidizer makes them foolproof.

● The type of oil used determines the flavor. A vegetable oil will give a blander flavor than olive oil.
● Vinegar also varies the flavor.
● All the ingredients should be at room temperature.

Hollandaise sauce

Makes about 1¼ cups

What you need:

● 1 cup lightly salted butter
● 3 egg yolks
● 1 tablespoon water
● 1 tablespoon lemon juice
● ¼ teaspoon salt
● pinch of cayenne pepper

Melt the butter in a pan with a pouring lip until it begins to foam. Place the egg yolks, water, lemon juice and seasoning into the food processor or liquidizer and blend at high speed for a few seconds. With the motor running, pour the butter, except for the residue at the bottom of the pan, very slowly in a continuous stream onto the egg mixture. When all the butter is amalgamated, the sauce should be thick and creamy. Season to taste and serve with asparagus, broccoli or poached salmon. If you don't want to use butter, you can use yogurt or crème fraîche.

Mayonnaise

Makes about 2 cups

What you need:

● 1 egg
● ¼ teaspoon salt
● ½ teaspoon dry mustard
● 1 tablespoon wine vinegar
● 1¼ cups olive oil

1 Crack the egg into the liquidizer or processor, add salt and mustard. Process for 30 seconds, then add the wine vinegar and blend again.
2 With the motor still running, pour in the oil in a thin steady stream. The sauce will thicken after half the oil has been added. Continue to add the oil until it has all been absorbed.
3 Scrape the mayonnaise into a bowl with a rubber spatula and store, covered, in the refrigerator.

Using wine to deglaze the sediments in a pan

Remove the cooked meat or fish and keep warm. Pour off any unwanted fat from the pan, but keep the juices. Pour a little dry or medium wine into the pan and over heat scrape up the sediment, dissolving it into the liquid. Reduce the wine down until only a glaze is left on the pan's bottom. Then add 1 tablespoon butter, swirling it round the pan until incorporated. Add any residual juices from the meat or fish, season and serve. Or, instead of butter, use fresh heavy cream or crème fraîche.

Gravy

Skim off all the fat from the roasting pan without losing any of the juices. Use a paper towel to remove the last traces of fat.

Pour in 1¼ cups stock and bring to a boil, scraping the bottom of the pan to loosen any sediment.

Variations

● *Bearnaise: bring a tablespoon of vinegar to the boil with a teaspoonful each of chopped shallot and fresh tarragon. Strain and add the vinegar in place of the lemon juice. Serve with steaks and strong-flavored fish.*
● *Maltaise: substitute the juice of half an orange for the lemon juice.*
Use with fish, asparagus and other vegetables.

Variations

● *Aïoli: mix 3 cloves crushed garlic with the egg, and use equal quantities of olive and sunflower oils. Serve as a dip with vegetables.*
● *Verte: blanch ½ cup fresh herbs, ½ cup watercress and 1 cup spinach for 2 minutes in boiling water. Refresh under cold running water, dry and pound or liquidize to a purée. Press through a strainer and stir into ½ cup mayonnaise. Use with fish.*
● *Tartare: stir 1 tablespoon each chopped capers, gherkins, fresh herbs and 1 finely chopped hard-cooked egg into ½ cup mayonnaise. Serve with fish, deep-fried mushrooms and shellfish.*

Boil for a moment or two and season to taste. If a thicker gravy is needed, add a little arrowroot, slaked with water, or some mustard and whisk well. Strain the sauce into a warm gravy boat.

Left: *aïoli, garlic-flavored mayonnaise, is a traditional accompaniment to a plate of fish stew*

Tomato sauce

For a quick tomato-based sauce, make use of the ready-prepared passata sauces (strained tomatoes), or add whole or chopped plum tomatoes. To these, you can add all sorts of other ingredients to make a special sauce, such as fried ground beef (bolognese); slowly fried finely chopped small button mushrooms; clams (alle vongole); or shelled prawns. The addition of 1 tablespoon of tomato paste will thicken it slightly, while 2 tablespoons of cream or crème fraîche will make it richer.

Aids to success

- Use a heavy-bottomed pan to prevent scorching.
- Cook the roux thoroughly, stirring well, to prevent a "raw" taste in the finished sauce.
- Whisking helps to prevent lumps and gives the sauce a shiny glaze.
- Add seasonings during cooking, not at the end, so that maximum flavor is absorbed.
- If the sauce is too thick add, a tablespoonful at a time, milk, cream or stock.
- If you are enriching with egg, cream or butter, add off the heat and just before serving to prevent curdling or separation. Do not reboil.
- Always taste before serving.
- If the sauce is made ahead, cover the surface with plastic wrap to prevent a skin forming.
- Sauces can be kept covered in the refrigerator for about 3 days.
- To thicken sauces at the last minute, use cornstarch (which may taste floury), farina (potato starch) or arrowroot because they need to be cooked only very briefly. Mix 1 teaspoon with cold water to make a thin paste. Stir into the sauce a little at a time over heat. It will thicken at once.

Dressings

Salads are a wonderful way of providing the essential minerals or vitamins that are lost in the cooking process. The crunchy texture of raw vegetables, the subtle colors of mixed salad leaves, the contrast between flavor and texture of fruit in a spicy dressing, and the subtlety of marinated beans, rice or pasta all make for interesting meals. Prepare the dressings and store them in the refrigerator so that there is always an interesting one to hand.

Below: *keep a selection of good-quality oils and vinegars in your kitchen*

Oils

Salads are the best medium to appreciate the greenish-golden color and beautiful fruity flavor of extra virgin oil that comes from the first cold pressing of the olives. Virgin oil is the next grade down, followed by blended oils from subsequent pressings. Generally Spanish has a strong flavor, Provençal is fruity and Italian nutty, while Greek has a heavy texture.

● Sunflower oil, light, mild and thinly textured, can be used with more expensive oil when making delicate salad dressings and is the best oil for those recipes where a fairly neutral oil is required.

● Walnut oil, cold pressed from dried walnuts, has a deliciously nutty flavor and is expensive. It does not keep well when opened, so buy in small bottles, refrigerate and let it warm up before use.

● Hazelnut oil is delicately flavored, lighter than walnut and particularly good in salads containing fruit.

Vinegars

● Wine vinegar is ideal for salad dressings and can be red or white. If it is stronger than you like, dilute it with a little wine of the same color.

● Cider vinegar has a strong distinctive taste and in sharpness is midway between wine and malt vinegars. It is good used in dressings for tomato or potato salad.

● Sherry vinegar is made from sweet sherry. Use half and half with lemon juice in a vinaigrette to give a nutty taste, almost like walnut oil. Use in dressings if you don't want to add sugar.

● Herb vinegars are easy to make. Allow 1 tablespoon of fresh herbs to 2½ cups wine vinegar. Place the herbs–tarragon, mint, basil or thyme–in a jar, cover with vinegar and keep in a warmish place for a week, giving the jar an occasional shake. Decant into a bottle and add a sprig of the herb.

● Garlic vinegar is made by crushing cloves of garlic and leaving in vinegar for 24 hours. Use in salads with anchovies and capers.

Vinaigrette

This is the most commonly used dressing. It can be used with any type of salad.
Makes about 7 tablespoons

- 1 tablespoon white wine vinegar or tarragon vinegar
- 1 small teaspoon Dijon mustard
- 1 large clove garlic, sprinkled with salt and crushed
- 5 tablespoons extra virgin olive oil
- salt and pepper

Put the vinegar into a small bowl, and stir in the mustard and garlic. Add the oil, gradually beating it in with a teaspoon or fork. It should blend thoroughly with the other ingredients. Season with salt and pepper to taste.

Cider vinaigrette

Use with potato or tomato salad.
Makes about 1¼ cups

- 4 tablespoons cider vinegar
- 1 teaspoon Dijon mustard
- ½ teaspoon salt
- ½ teaspoon sugar
- 1 cup sunflower oil

Mix the vinegar, mustard, salt and sugar together until the salt and sugar are thoroughly dissolved. Add the oil and blend or shake until thoroughly mixed.

Herb vinaigrette

Use for green bean salads, or dress warm pasta or rice and leave to cool.
Makes about 1¼ cups

- ¼ cup lemon juice
- ¼ cup white wine or cider vinegar
- ½ teaspoon sugar
- 2 teaspoons finely chopped fresh parsley
- 2 teaspoons finely chopped fresh chives
- 2 teaspoons finely chopped fresh basil
- 1 cup sunflower oil

Put the lemon juice, vinegar, salt, sugar and herbs in a liquidizer or jar and process or shake to dissolve the sugar. Add the oil and process or shake again.

Yogurt dressing

Use for potato salad or coleslaw.
Makes about ¾ cup

- juice of 1 lemon
- ½ teaspoon sugar
- ½ teaspoon salt
- 3 tablespoons salad oil
- 6 tablespoons plain yogurt

Mix the lemon juice, sugar and salt until dissolved. Add the oil and whisk in the yogurt. Let this stand for at least 30 minutes before using.

Blue cheese dressing

Use on any mixed salad.
Makes about 1½ cups

- 1 cup crumbled blue cheese
- ½ cup milk
- 4 tablespoons salad oil
- 1 tablespoon white wine vinegar
- 1 teaspoon sugar
- salt and pepper

Put all the ingredients in a liquidizer or food processor and blend until smooth. If the dressing is too thick, add a little more milk until the mixture is the texture of very thick cream. Season to taste.

Honey and lemon dressing

Use this when making salads containing fruit. It is also good with white cabbage salads.
Makes about 1 cup

- ⅔ cup cottage cheese
- ⅔ cup low-fat yogurt
- juice of 1 lemon
- 4 tablespoons runny honey
- 1 teaspoon finely chopped onion
- 1 teaspoon paprika
- 1 teaspoon celery seed

Put all the ingredients in a liquidizer or food processor and blend until the dressing is smooth and creamy.

Salad hints

- Always tear salad leaves: if you cut them they go limp quickly.
- All salad stuff should be washed in cold water and then dried in a salad spinner, or with a clean dishcloth or paper towels.
- After washing, refresh in the refrigerator for about 15 minutes; the leaves will crisp up.
- Prepare salad dressing and toss the leaves in it just before serving otherwise they will go limp.
- Salads of tomato and scallion and red or white cabbage benefit from marinating in the dressing for an hour or so before serving.
- Add dressings to salads of beans, pasta and rice while still warm so that as they cool they absorb the full flavor.
- A food processor or liquidizer will mix the oil, vinegar and flavorings thoroughly and they won't separate easily.
- Dressings can be put in a screw-top jar and just shaken until well mixed.
- Make dressings and keep them in the refrigerator for a week or more, using as necessary.

Pastry

The different forms of pastry are given their distinctive texture and taste by the proportions of flour, fat, and water, and the method of making. The handling of the ingredients and the mixed dough is very important–lightness of touch, speed of work, and the coolest of conditions are all essential for successful pastry-making, combining to make rich yet light pastry.

Below: *Profiteroles*
Right: *Covering, sealing and edging a pie*
Far right: *Peach and honey pie*

Ingredients

● Fats: butter gives a crisp, rich pastry with a good flavor. Use cold, straight from the refrigerator, cut into tiny cubes or coarsely grate. Solid vegetable fat has good shortening qualities, works well used in equal quantities with butter. Low-fat spreads do not work well as they contain water. Oil makes the pastry soft to handle but gives it a crumbly texture.

● Flour: use all-purpose white flour; self-rising to give a soft, thicker crust; whole wheat will give a nutty flavor, but is more difficult to work with, so it is often mixed in equal quantity with white flour. Always sift before using.

● Liquid: the less the better. Water give crispness and firmness, too much makes the pastry easy to handle but cooks to a very hard crust. Add egg or egg white to give a firm, not hard crust, and egg yolk for a rich, soft, crumbly crust.

Techniques

● Rubbing in: keep everything as cool as possible, including your mixing bowl. Rub the fat into the flour using your fingertips until it is the texture of bread crumbs. Shake the bowl so that large pieces of fat come to the surface and rub again. Dough should be handled as little and lightly as possible as over-rubbing makes large oily crumbs and tough pastry.

● Adding liquid: make a well in the mixture, sprinkle in some liquid, and mix in using a fork. Add more liquid if necessary. Stop mixing when it holds together in lumps. Lightly flour your hands and quickly gather the pastry into a ball, rolling it around the bowl to pick up any remaining crumbs.

● Kneading: using a light touch, bring the outside edge of the dough into the center, rotate anti-clockwise until the bottom and sides are smooth. Turn the dough over, wrap, and rest.

● Resting: prevent pastry shrinking by covering it and chilling for at least 30 minutes before rolling out or baking.

● Rolling out: lightly dust the counter with flour. Roll in short strokes in one direction only, but not to the edge. Rotate the dough 90° after each rolling to stretch the dough evenly. Over-stretching causes shrinkage.

● Lining a pie pan: roll dough to a size that will cover the bottom and sides. Roll around a rolling pin, lift over the pan, and unroll. Ease into the bottom and up the sides.

● Baking blind: this stops the pastry bottom from rising. After lining the pie pan, prick the bottom with a fork to release trapped air. Cover the bottom with baking parchment, fill with ceramic or dried beans. Bake for 10 minutes, remove the beans, return to the oven for 5 minutes. Shells can be fully baked when a filling only requires reheating.

● Temperature: all pastry needs a hot oven. If the temperature is too low, the pastry will be tough and heavy. If too hot, the outside will brown while the inside stays soggy. The usual temperature is 400°F; puff pastry and filo needs an even hotter oven, 425°F.

Variations

- *Sweet pastry: add a tablespoon of confectioners' sugar to the flour mixture.*
- *Pâte brisée: this French pastry is crumbly and can be rolled really thinly: 1¼ cups all-purpose flour; 5 tablespoons butter; ½ teaspoon salt; 1 egg yolk; 1–2 tablespoons cold water. Mix all the ingredients together well.*
- *Pâte sablée: French sweet pastry, as above, use 1 cup all-purpose flour and add ¼ cup sugar.*

Types of pastry

Freshly made pastry can give the most wonderful results if you have the time, but many of the ready-made pastries now available, work just as well.

Plain

This is the easiest of all pastry doughs and a favorite for both savory and sweet pies. Preparation: 15 minutes, plus chilling time

What you need:

- 1½ cups all-purpose flour
- pinch of salt
- ⅓ cup butter
- 2–3 tablespoons water

Mix the flour, salt and butter together by hand or in a processor until the mixture resembles fine bread crumbs. Add the water a tablespoonful at a time until the dough binds together. Knead it carefully, wrap in plastic wrap and chill for 30 minutes.

Choux

Preparation: 30 minutes
Cooking: 25 minutes

What you need:

- 1 cup water
- ¼ cup butter
- 1¼ cups flour

1 Preheat the oven to 425°F. Grease a baking sheet.
2 Bring the water to a boil. Turn off the heat, add the butter, and let it melt. Put the flour in a food processor and, with the motor running, pour on the water/butter mixture, to form a paste. Return the paste to the pan and cook, stirring for 3–4 minutes. Return the paste to the processor bowl, start the motor and add the eggs one by one.
3 Place tablespoonfuls of the mixture on the baking sheet. Bake for 25 minutes or until golden. Remove the choux balls and prick each to let the steam out. Split, fill, and serve.

Food processor method for plain pastry dough

Cut the fat into small pieces. Add all the ingredients except the liquid and process for 10–15 seconds. Add the liquid and process until the mixture balls up around the knife. Do not over-process as the paste will become sticky and taste greasy.

Pastry to buy

- Filo: this gossamer-thin pastry, used for strudel, samosas, and other sweet and savory fillings can be bought in packages, either fresh or frozen. When using it, work with a few sheets at a time, making sure to keep the others covered to prevent drying out. Each sheet of pastry should be brushed with melted butter or oil. To fit a dish of a specific size, simply overlap by 1 inch. Filo can be deep-fried or baked. Frozen filo will defrost quickly, and can be refrozen.
- Flaky and puff: save time and buy these ready-made, either butter or vegetarian-based, fresh or frozen. Puff pastry is very similar to flaky pastry. Both pastries are time-consuming to make yourself with difficult techniques to master, plus some skill and patience are needed to achieve acceptable results.
- Pastry shells: these come in different sizes and flavors and are worth buying ready-made particularly if you are short of time or planning to feed a large number. Available fresh or frozen and are easy to use.

Bread

There is nothing quite like the warm fragrance of baking bread. Like riding a bicycle, bread-making once learned is never forgotten. The recipes given here are easy and when you have mastered them, you will find that they can be adapted for other breads. The secret is to practice and to understand how the dough reacts as you handle it. You do need time to prove bread, let it rise while you get on with other things. And while it is baking, savor the fragrance.

Below: *Flower pot loaves*
Right: *Unrisen and risen dough*
Far right (top to bottom): *Tin loaf, Bloomer, Short baton, Coburg, Cottage loaf*

Ingredients

● Yeast: compressed should be beige, crumbly-soft, and also be sweet smelling. Yeast will keep for 5 days loosely wrapped in the refrigerator. Dry yeast must be "sponged" in some liquid to reconstitute it.

● Flour: strong flour is best for bread-making. Whole wheat, flour produces a heavier loaf which will not keep as well as a white loaf. A mixture of whole wheat and white flour works well.

Techniques

● Kneading: dough must be pushed and pulled to develop the gluten. Place on a lightly floured surface and stretch the dough, using the heel of one hand to push away, and the knuckles of the other to pull towards you. Fold, then give the dough a quarter turn, and repeat. By hand, it takes up to 10 minutes for the dough to

become smooth and elastic. A food mixer with a dough hook takes less time.

● Punching down: risen dough is punched with the knuckles to push out air. Punched to its original size, it is then kneaded briefly before being shaped.

● Shaping: to make rolls knead pieces of dough, cup your hand over the dough and then rotate it, gradually straightening your fingers until the ball is smooth. Loaves can

be made in any shape–to secure a smaller roll on top, press a wooden spoon handle through to the work surface. Prove the dough on greased baking sheets or in pans and then glaze.

● Proving: this second rising is given after the dough has been punched down and shaped. It is placed in or on greased pans, covered with oiled polythene or a damp dishcloth and left until doubled in size–either in a warm place (not too hot or the yeast will be killed) or overnight in the refrigerator. The more

slowly dough rises, the more even the bread's texture.

● Glazing: beaten egg yolk gives a crusty finish and holds toppings in place. Sweetened milk gives a shiny, sticky surface.

● Baking: bread continues to rise in the oven for a short time. After 20 minutes the loaf's shape will be set and you can glaze this part with egg yolk and return to finish cooking.

● Testing: turn out of the pan, tap the bottom. If it sounds hollow, it is cooked; if not return to the pan to finish cooking.

Whole wheat rolls

Makes 8
Preparation: 45 minutes
Cooking: 20 minutes, plus rising and proving

What you need:

- ¾ cake compressed yeast, or ½ package fast-action dry
- 1¼ cups lukewarm milk
- 1 teaspoon superfine sugar
- 2 cups whole wheat flour
- 2 cups all-purpose flour
- 1 teaspoon salt
- ¼ cup butter

1 If using compressed yeast, dissolve the yeast with a little of the milk and the sugar in a small bowl. Warm a large mixing bowl and sift the flours, dry yeast if using, and salt into it.
2 Pour in the fresh yeast mixture, all the milk (this applies to both yeast methods) and the beaten egg, and mix to a fairly slack dough.
3 When the dough leaves the sides of the bowl, press it into a ball and tip out onto a lightly floured board.
4 Knead the dough for about 15 minutes until it is elastic, smooth, and shiny. Put the dough back in the bowl, cover with oiled polythene or a damp dishcloth, and leave in a warm place until doubled in size, for approximately 1 hour. Take the dough out of the bowl, punch down, and knead again for 10 minutes.
5 Preheat the oven to 425°F. Divide the dough into 8 pieces and shape them all into flattish ovals. Put the ovals on a floured baking sheet and let them prove for 15 minutes. Bake for about 20 minutes or until firm.

Ciabatta

This Italian-style bread is deservedly popular. You can use the dough for pizza by adding an extra tablespoon of oil at the second kneading. Then divide the dough in half and spread out with your hands on a baking sheet until ¼ inch thick all over. Add toppings, prove for 15–20 minutes, and bake in a pre-heated oven 425°, for 15–25 minutes.
Makes 2 loaves
Preparation: 15–20 minutes
Cooking: 40 minutes, plus rising and proving

What you need:

- ½ cake compressed yeast or ½ package fast-action dry
- pinch of sugar
- 1¼ cups warm water
- 4 tablespoons olive oil
- 1 teaspoon salt
- 4 cups strong white flour

1 Cream compressed yeast and sugar with a little warm water. Leave for 10 minutes until frothy.
2 Mix oil and salt into flour and dry yeast, if using. Add compressed yeast mixture, if using, and knead for 1–2 minutes. Gradually add remaining water, making sure dough does not become too moist.
3 Brush a tablespoonful of oil in the bowl, roll dough in it. Cover with a damp dishcloth or plastic wrap. Let rise for 45–50 minutes.
4 Punch down and knead again, making sure all the oil is incorporated. Divide into 2 for loaves. Roll out to 9 inches. Place on a baking sheet, flatten. Let rise for 35–40 minutes.
5 Bake in a preheated oven, 425°F, for 40 minutes.

Utensils

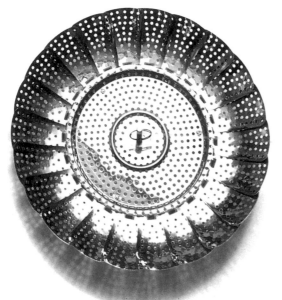

Left and above:
A stainless steel folding steaming platform which adjusts to fit most pan sizes is a very useful cookware item if you don't have a steamer unit in your saucepan range. Steaming lets you cook food quickly and retain a high proportion of flavor and nutrients.
This shallow saucepan is made from stainless steel and has a heat diffusing bottom— a thick layer of aluminum sealed in a stainless steel casing—which insures even cooking and cuts down on energy consumption. The rim is gently curved to prevent liquids boiling over.

Above:
Vitreous enameled cast iron cooking pots last a lifetime. Useful ones to have are gratin dishes and casseroles. If used on the stove top, heat the pan very slowly over low-to-medium heat.

Below:
Stainless steel deep casserole with a 5-layer bottom which lets food be steam-cooked without fats or oil. Evaporation is prevented by the heavy weight of the well-fitting lid.

Pots and pans

For long-term wear buy the best saucepans you can afford; stainless steel with a copper bottom, or a thick layer of aluminum, is a combination that is hard to beat and will give you a lifetime's service. Buying cheap pans is a false economy; they quickly burn and soon reach the throwing-away stage. Good pans should be well balanced, easy to hold, and have welded handles and lids that fit tightly. You will need about 3–4 in the range of 1–7 quarts.

Left:
Pans that do double duty, like this shallow casserole/sauté pan are a blessing to cooks with limited storage space. This comes from the same range as the casserole above, and can take a steamer insert or a second pan, which would turn it into a double boiler.

Dry-frying, using a cast-iron broiler pan is fast, direct and simple. The pan is heated until very hot and the seasoned food cooked directly on the ridged surface, producing extra flavor where food comes into contact with intense heat. It can be used with no fat or with food that has been marinated.

Above and below right:

Plain steel pans are best for making omelets and crêpes, and a lidded skillet with a heat-resistant handle can be used on the stove top or in the oven. If you want to use slightly less oil or butter, heat the pan for 2–3 minutes over a medium heat before adding the oil or butter. Do not heat an empty pan over a high heat because this simply makes the pan too hot too quickly and will mean your ingredients dry out and burn. To season steel pans, heat slightly and wash to remove the protective coating. Dry and reheat with cooking oil to a fairly high temperature. Run oil over the bottom and up the sides to cover the whole area. Cool and wipe out surplus. To prevent ingredients sticking to the pan, move them about the pan with a non-scratch implement; handle fragile ingredients with care.

Above:

If you love pasta, then you will need a pot that is large enough so that it can cook in plenty of boiling salted water with enough room for it to move without sticking. This 7-quart pot is large enough for 7–8 portions and is fitted with a stainless steel draining basket. Its thick bottom means this saucepan can also be used for making stock, soups, and stews.

Cleaning stained pans

- Burned pans: cover burned matter with water; add 2 tablespoons salt or vinegar, bring to a boil and leave overnight.
- Enamel pan stains: add 2½ cups water, add 1 teaspoon bleach and leave for 2 hours. Wash and rinse thoroughly.
- Discolored aluminum: boil a weak solution of rhubarb, tomatoes or lemon peel in the pan.
- Stainless steel: clean with a soft bristle brush and warm soapy water; polish when dry.

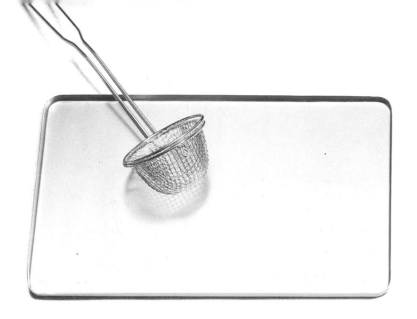

Above and far right:
The cookie/baking sheet has raised sides which prevents anything sliding off when it is removed from the oven. Resting on it is a deep-frying basket for use when you are making samosas, doughnuts or potato baskets. Use the rectangular pan for cakes or as a bain marie when you are baking custards.

Lining cake pans

Cut a long strip of baking parchment 2 inches wider than the pan's depth; fold one long edge in 1 inch; and snip at intervals. Place snipped edge down in greased pan and cover bottom of pan with parchment. Line jelly roll pans using one sheet of parchment, make 45° angle slits into corners, fold edges in 1 inch, then raise to make a 90° angle at corners. Secure with paper clips.

Below left:
A pan of individual pie shapes can be used for small quiches, fruit tarts or Yorkshire puddings. It has a hard-wearing nonstick finish, nevertheless it is always better to oil the surface lightly before use.

Above:
Roasting pans should be smooth and have no seams or crevices in which fat can collect or germs breed. Those with a rolled top edge or a generous rim are easy to lift. A roasting rack keeps meat or poultry from frying in fat.

Baking pans and sheets

When food is placed in the dry, hot atmosphere of the oven, it is cooked equally from all directions, and the containers do not have to withstand and conduct heat from an intense source as saucepans do. The function of a baking pan is to mold and contain, and to respond as fast as possible to the temperature of the oven. The shape of the pan you use depends entirely on what you are baking and what you want it to look like.

Some baking pans have bright shining surfaces, which deflect the heat away from the contents so that they will not scorch; others pans have dark finishes which absorb and hold the heat, and need a slight temperature reduction to achieve the same results.

Tin plate is most widely used for baking containers. Aluminum, a good conductor of heat, is more expensive than tin. Nonstick surfaces, applied to either tin or aluminum, are hard-wearing but can be easily damaged by metal implements. Clean by soaking in water, then wipe with a soapy cloth and rinse.

Choose pans that are sturdy, smooth inside with no crevices for trapping food; rolled edges will make the pans easier and safer to handle. Never use abrasives or steel wool on your bakeware, and make sure that it is washed, dried and aired thoroughly in a warm dry place and given a light coating of cooking oil before storing. You can expect a lifetime's wear from good quality pans and constant use will give them a dark protective patina.

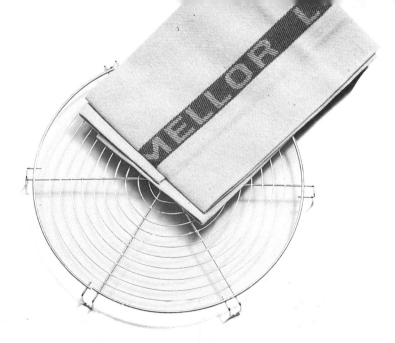

Above right:

Deep quiche pans, in three sizes, have loose bottoms which makes the job of removing the cooked quiche much easier, and also means that you can put the pan bottom onto a plate for serving. If you want to lift the quiche off the bottom for any reason, use two wide egg slices to support the bottom of the quiche.

Below:

These pans can be used for sponges or pies; some have fluted edges and a choice between removable or fixed bases, some are deep—like those shown here—others are shallow. Fluted pans can be difficult to clean because food sticks to them, so always soak them in hot water after use. Metal pans are preferable to porcelain dishes as they conduct heat very well which prevents soggy dough.

Above right:

Cooling racks are either circular, specifically for cakes, or rectangular for all types of baked food and are meshed to allow good circulation of air. They are used for cooling cakes and cookies without letting them sweat. It is better to buy one that is larger than you think you need, and it should stand fairly high. If leaving food, especially cakes, overnight, cover with a dishcloth to prevent it becoming crusty and dry. After baking leave the cakes or cookies in their pans for a little time before transferring them to a cooling rack. Cakes, cookies and pies can be very tender and are liable to crumble if handled too soon after removal from the oven. Letting them cool for about 20 minutes is usually sufficient, but these timings can vary depending on the size of the cake, pie or cookies and the length of time in the oven.

Below:

A 5-inch tart pan is very useful to have as a standby. Often extra pastry dough from a baking session can be used to line it, and it is also a good size to freeze as a shell, the larger ones take up more room and can be damaged more easily. Small pans are good for individual tarts, and can be ready when the cook needs it for a quick meal! Small pans are also useful when you want to present family or guests with individual portions, which can be attractively garnished or decorated, on the plate.

Right:

Cake pans can have loose bottoms or spring clips. When using the latter, make sure the bottom fits into the groove at the side and won't move or let the mixture escape; place the bottom rim-side up on the counter, place ring above it and close clips. Bottoms can then be greased and floured or bottom lined.

Above right:

Individual tart pans, 3½ inches in diameter are just right for baking blind and filling with delicious concoctions for stunning appetizers or with fruit for desserts. You can also use them as buffet party and picnic food pastry cases.

Below:
Wooden spatulas and spoons are the perfect tool to use in nonstick pans. The slanted straight end will fit against the sides of pans and bowls, making it easy to remove all the food.

Above:
A ladle for serving soups and sauces and for jam-making. The kitchen spoon has a pouring lip which can be helpful for pouring batter. The disc skimmer will move over the surface removing fat from liquid and scum from jam and stock.

Metal turners must be able to slide under food without causing damage and be wide and firm enough to support it as it is turned or lifted from the pan. Perforations in the turner will let excess fat or oil escape.

A metal fork with long tines will hold meat firmly while it is being lifted from a roasting pan or casserole. A carving fork should have a guard.

Mesh skimmers are better than solid perforated disk ones for scooping food that is being deep-fried because the oil can drain freely through the mesh and such skimmers will not lower the temperature of the oil.

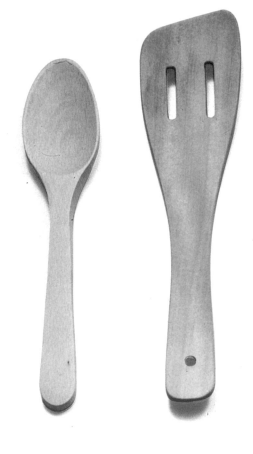

Spoons and stirrers

The wooden spoon is one of the most useful tools in the kitchen. It is invaluable for beating, mixing and stirring; it will never burn your hand because wood is a very bad conductor of heat; it will not scratch or wear away saucepans, and it is quiet and strong in use. The best ones to use are those made of a close-grained wood which is not likely to split. The design of wooden spoons has been honed by cooks over the centuries, and you will find shapes for all sorts of purposes but especially useful are those with a bowl that has a fairly thin edge which can get right to the bottom corner of steep-sided saucepans.

Metal spoons are used for transferring food quickly from pan to dish, gently folding together delicate mixtures and last-minute taste checks on soups and sauces. Wood should not be used for this because it can retain the flavor of its last use.

Whisks introduce air, emulsify and blend ingredients, or thicken those substances containing fat, and they are wonderful for rescuing lumpy sauces. Metal skimmers, ladles, slices and perforated spoons, all have their own particular roles to play, and these are the items that you are likely to buy as your needs arise.

Keep all these items close to your stove top. Many of them have hooks or loops for hanging and can be kept on racks, but wooden spoons are most usefully kept in a jar where they will be ready for immediate use.

Below, left to right:

Olive wood deep server; tasting spoon; kitchen spatulas; and a selection of stirrers, long-handled ones make the best beaters, use those with short handles for mixing as well as stirring.

Above left to right:

A large, heavy-duty balloon whisk is the chef's answer to dealing with egg whites, but you need a very strong arm to use it; the classic size whisk, is the one most often used for making sauces, but many people prefer to use the flat one next to it. This can be used in jugs and will also beat egg whites on a plate.

Cut a flourish with this swizzle stick which, used in an up and down movement, will froth liquids, but can also be used to mix dressings for salads as well as whisking up cocktails.

The round balloon and the small egg whisks are good for sauces if you are using a small saucepan, but the larger one is better for mayonnaise and for beating egg whites—it does not need the strength required by the large balloon whisk. When beating whites, start beating from the bottom of the bowl, lifting the whisk high in a round to incorporate as much air as possible.

You want to take air into the egg whites as you beat so that they are really light to taste. This will mean the dish you add the beaten egg whites to will be light also. When the whites start foaming, increase the size of the rounds, using the whole bowl, and beat as fast as you can. When stiff, beat down in the whites to stiffen, rather than incorporate air, and continue until a shallow peak holds its shape.

Above:
Poultry shears make light work of cutting through gristle and bone, either during preparation or serving at the table. The pointed tips enable the shears to reach and operate effectively in small, awkward places.

Below left and right:
Almost a classic piece of equipment, this small rotary grater makes quick work of cheese and herbs. Hand-held graters need to be chosen carefully, they should rest firmly on a flat surface or sit in a bowl without slipping or sliding. The different kinds of surfaces should be able to grasp tough or brittle foods, and cut smooth slices or slivers from softer cheeses and vegetables. The grated food texture is controlled by the size of the cutting holes. Use them carefully to avoid grating your knuckles.

Below:
Kitchen scissors should be very sharp, strong and made of stainless steel. The lower handle should be large enough to take the last three fingers of the cutting hand. A serrated edge will give an extra bite to the first cut and blades should cut evenly right down to the tips. Have them professionally sharpened when they become blunt.

Left:
Herbs can be finely chopped in this wooden bowl. It is a version of the pestle and mortar, still the most effective method for pulverizing nuts, garlic, berries, seeds, and herbs. Use a wooden bowl for crushing dry food but not for anything that exudes moisture because the pungent juices will impregnate the wood.

Cutting and carving

Essential tools in the kitchen are good sharp knives that are comfortable to hold; they take the hard work out of food preparation, making it a pleasure rather than a troublesome chore. Six or seven knives will provide you with a good selection that will enable you to deal easily and swiftly with various tasks. They should be stored where you can see them, get at them swiftly, and return them after use ready for the next time, so a knife block (see illustration) or a wall-fixed rack, inaccessible to children, is ideal. Keeping knives in drawers will damage their blades and you may also cut your hand.

Choose a knife that feels comfortable in the hand, heavy and well balanced. The part of the blade that extends into the handle should run the whole length and be securely riveted in place. Although expensive, high-carbon stainless steel knives are good buys; they last a long time, hold a very fine edge, and can be easily cleaned. Carbon-steel knives are quite easy to sharpen but rust and discolor.

Knives should always be kept in razor-sharp condition. A blunt knife is frustrating and dangerous to use–it performs badly, needing a great deal of force, and it can easily slip out of control. One of the best methods for sharpening knives is to use a hand-held steel and draw the blade lightly down it at a shallow angle, between 18–20°. Put the knife first to the front of the steel, then the back. The steel should have a small guard or hilt to protect the hand. A few strokes every time you use the knife will keep it well sharpened. (See illustration opposite.)

Cutting boards

It is best to have at least two cutting boards, one made from a hard wood, such as maple, which you can use for most tasks, and the other to be kept for the preparation of raw meat. The latter should be made from a white non-porous material which can be cleaned with hot water and a little bleach. Always remembers to wash boards and knives between handling raw and cooked food.

Choose wooden boards at least 1½ inches thick; ideally the grain on the main part of the board should run in the opposite direction to that on the reinforced ends. Melamine boards may look attractive when new, but their hard surfaces soon blunt knife blades and may cause knives to slip. Apart from your basic cutting boards, other useful ones are a round board specially for bread, a rectangular cheese board with a slot for a knife, and a small board for cutting lemons.

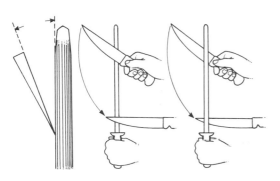

Below, left to right:
Steel: *The traditional way of sharpening knives. Keep a knife sharpener in the kitchen and use it often.*

Bread knife: *Choose one with a fairly long blade with deep serrations as this will be most efficient.*
Carving fork: *This is used to lift roast meat and keep it steady while carving. It should have a guard to prevent the knife slipping. The long, straight tines are essential for bigger roasts.*
Carving knife: *Used together with the carving fork for cutting thin slices from roast and cooked meat.*
General kitchen knife: *A general-purpose knife usually 6–10 inches long. Use for chopping, slicing, paring, and cutting.*
Cleaver or chopper: *This is the heaviest knife, which comes in various sizes. It is used for chopping through*

bone. It has a very broad rectangular blade, which can be used for crushing garlic– place the garlic under the cleaver on a board and hit the blade. It may also be used to flatten sliced meat.
Paring knife: *Designed to peel fruit and vegetables. They usually have stainless steel blades 3 inches long, plain or serrated.*
Other specialty knives
Other knives have very specific purposes.
Palette knife: *A knife with a very flexible, round-ended blade in different sizes; it is used for spreading jam, butter-cream and frosting over cakes.*
Filleting knife: *This has a flexible, pointed blade to follow the contours of the*

fish, lifting flesh off the bones.
Grapefruit knife: *This is a small knife with a double-serrated curved edge for loosening grapefruit flesh.*
Canelle knife: *This has a short flat blade with a U-shaped indentation, used to cut strips of lemon or orange rind, or to create patterns in the peel of cucumbers and other vegetables.*
Oyster knife: *This has a very short, broad, pointed blade and usually has a guard. It is used for opening oysters and other shellfish.*

Straining, sifting, and measuring

At first glance there seems little difference between one kind of strainer or colander or another, but it is only through use in the kitchen that the cook can discover just how well designed and useful the various types can be. As with other kitchen tools, these items can sometimes double up in function– a colander can be used as a steamer, the asparagus slice (below) for fish and handsome shakers and pitchers will go from kitchen to table.

However casual the addition of ingredients to a recipe might seem, cookery is in fact an exact science, so care taken in measuring is repaid by the taste and appearance of the cooked product. In these days of international recipe exchange it is only too easy to become confused by the different ways of measuring ingredients (see opposite page). Scales and pictures marked with imperial and metric measurements are invaluable to anyone using recipes published in European cookbooks.

Below left and below:
stainless steel, long-handled colander has a stable bottom and can be held firmly while draining items. This stainless steel wire colander will look good on the table, but its shape also lets it be used as a steamer.

Above:
Garlic is an essential addition to many recipes but is very fiddly to prepare. This press makes it an easy job: you don't need to peel the clove and when the hammer is released the debris clings to it.

Below:

Lemon squeezers are often flimsy little things, with room for the juice of one lemon only. This one, in stoneware, has a nice capacious bowl, is sturdy so you can really apply pressure to the lemon, and looks good enough to be taken from the kitchen to the table.

Right:

Storing things in the kitchen can be a real problem. It has recently been fashionable to hang things from the ceiling, but if the items are low enough to be easy to reach, they are dangerous for the unwary heads of tall people! It is probably most practical to have a secure rail fitted close to your stove top on which things can be hung from sturdy butcher's hooks. Securely attached to a wall, this iron bar is strong enough to take heavy pans.

Below:

Simple traditional French stoneware pitchers in two sizes fulfil a useful function in storing liquids prior to refrigeration. The glaze will not craze or fade because of the high temperature they are fired at.

Opposite page below left and this page right below:

Round, fine mesh stainless steel strainers can be used for sifting as well as straining and puréeing. For sifting, never fill too full and tap the side of the frame gently against the palm of your hand. If you cook asparagus in a shallow pan rather than up-right in a steamer, a slice will lift it out and drain off liquid. Use it for fish, too. A funnel is good for transferring liquids from one container to another.

Below left:

A light dredging of fine sugar or cocoa powder is often the only finish a cake needs. To add interest, sift confectioners' or superfine sugar over a paper doily and then carefully lift it off.

Right:

A heatproof glass measuring pitcher is a most useful item to have. The toughened glass will withstand boiling liquids and you can see very clearly exactly how much is in the pitcher, and because this type of glass is a poor conductor of heat, the handle remains cool. However, it is also necessary to have plastic cups in which you can measure ingredients accurately.

Measuring

In the US cooks use cups of standard sizes to measure most ingredients. The metric system of measurement is now used in many other countries, but in Britain the old imperial mea-surements are also still used. It must be remembered that an imperial pint is 20 fluid ounces whereas an American pint is 16 fluid ounces.

Barbecue equipment

Come the first warm day of spring or summer and out comes the barbecue attended by all its accessories. This most popular form of outdoor entertaining is great for everyone except the cook who spends much of the time getting hot and bothered and spattered with fat. Nevertheless, barbecued food tastes marvelous and gives everyone a healthy appetite.

There is no other option than to go about it with good humor and see if there are ways of making it an efficient operation, the result of which is to be showered with praise and eager requests that you give another barbecue party soon.

Barbecuing is a healthy and exciting way of cooking with many inspiring accompaniments and a taste not achieved from any other cooking method.

Left:
A stainless steel barbecue designed to eliminate the need for firelighters and starter fluids. The combination of the chimney, which concentrates the heat, and the ventilation holes, which create a powerful draw present a fail-safe method of igniting charcoal. Simply put crushed newspaper in the chimney, spread charcoal on the hearth, light the paper and start cooking 20–25 minutes later. Slots on the wind-shield make it possible to raise or lower the grid as needed.

Barbecue preparation

Buy good quality charcoal and store it in a dry place. Charcoal absorbs moisture readily and won't burn well if damp. Line the barbecue with foil to reflect heat and make it easy to clean later. Pile the charcoal in a pyramid and light (never use gas and never lean over the grid when lighting). Light the fire in plenty of time, to get hot. Leave until covered with white ash and then spread the embers. If you can hold your hand over the heat for 10 seconds, it isn't warm enough for cooking.

Above:
Well made turner, fork, knife and tongs, with exceptionally long handles, keep your hands safely away from heat. Other useful items would be long flat skewers for kebabs, then food will not be able to skid round them; a bristle brush for basting food (manmade fibers can melt or burn) and a meat grid.

Right:
Fish can fall apart or, if small, can be difficult to turn over on the barbecue. A double-sided grid, like this 26-inch long one, has folding legs for standing on the barbecue and easily holds a large fish or several smaller ones, carefully placed within.

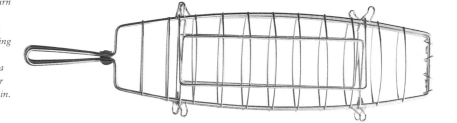

Above:

Care needs to be taken with table ware taken outdoors, because it is usually placed on the ground and accidents can only too easily happen, so keep an eye on the safety factor when you are choosing tumblers. These, for instance, are made of tough, chip-resistant glass.

Above right:

When you are eating outdoors, cheese, butter, meat, and anything sweet or creamy needs to be protected from flies and wasps. This food cover, an old-fashioned idea but up-to-date in its hygiene applications, is made of fine, tinned wire mesh.

Food tips

Marinades tenderize, prevents undue drying up, and adds flavor. Precook food when you can, and finish off on the barbecue. Salt draws out moisture, save it for last-minute seasoning. Cook beef rare or medium rare; veal and lamb, medium to well done; pork thoroughly; poultry thoroughly, the juices should run clear when pierced with a skewer; sausages thoroughly; fish is cooked when opaque and the flesh comes easily from the bone. Be sure to keep raw and cooked food apart and prepare on different work surfaces.

Above:

Grape-decorated earthenware wine cooler with glazed rim, lends a suitable rustic look to outdoor drinking. Soak the cooler in cold water before placing the bottle inside to keep cool. Excellent, too, for riverside picnics.

Right:

When you are cooking outdoors, you need a work surface for preparation and serving; this foldaway table solves the problem admirably. The reversible top is made of hardwood—one side is smooth, the other, which has a groove running around it, becomes a large carving board.

Left:

The enjoyment in eating steak goes if you have to battle with a less-than-sharp knife and a fork with unsatisfactory tines. Look for serrated stainless steel blades, resin-impregnated wooden handles which are smooth and well-balanced and a fork with sturdy tines.

Right:

Hurricane lamps, like this one made of tin-coated steel, provide a safe, easily adjusted flame for hours on one filling of paraffin. Although at night the light might attract the moths, it is generally believed the paraffin smell keeps mosquitoes at bay.

Oriental cooking

A Chinese cook has described stir-frying as being like a conjurer, magically changing–in the twinkling of an eye–raw pieces of food into a succulent and fragrant dish. She said there was nothing more therapeutic than stirring away in the wok to get rid of any pent-up emotions or tensions, nor was there anything more gratifying than to have a wokful of goodies to share and enjoy with family and friends.

Oriental techniques appear simple, but they actually require great mastery in order to get them just right. The practise, though–as in so many things that are worth doing right–is sheer delight.

Another advantage of stir-frying is that it is one of the healthiest of all cooking methods, requiring very little oil. Food is cooked until it is still crisp–never mushy–and therefore retains a great deal of its delicious flavor, texture and color.

On this page are some of the tools that you need for this particular form of cookery.

Above and top:
A nonstick, substantial wok with two handles with a draining rack and chopsticks, and a heavy natural steel one with handles, drainer and bamboo rice paddle. Both measure about 14 inches in diameter which is wide and deep enough for all wok cookery techniques.

A new steel wok has a protective film of grease. Remove the film by filling the wok with water and boiling for 30 minutes. Scrub the wok with an abrasive, rinse and dry over heat for 5 minutes. When cool, wipe both sides thoroughly with vegetable oil. Clean after each use; wash with water, using a mild detergent if necessary, and a clean cloth or soft brush. Dry and rub with oil.

Above:
A tava, skillet, used for cooking Indian chapati. These are made from whole wheat flour and water, rolled out very evenly, then cooked on the smoking hot steel pan and finished over an open fire to make them puff up.

Left:
A wok-turner, based on a classic oriental design, is a cross between scoop and stirrer. A cleaver is used to slice, cut, shred, and grind vegetables, meat, and bones. A porcelain grater is traditionally used for ginger root.

Above left:
A terracotta baking brick for Indian breads or pizzas retains heat for serving. Use a chinese scouring brush for cleaning a wok, an oriental ladle for serving soups and a noodle spoon to serve.

Above:
A bamboo steamer with slatted steaming basket. Stand the steamer in the wok, and add the basket with food wrapped in leaves or on a plate. Add boiling water to within 1 inch of the bottom and cover with the wok lid. Turn up the heat; fish should cook very quickly.

Gadgets

Every cook has a collection of tools, bought because they seemed a good idea at the time, but in fact are rarely used. On this page, we share with you some of the "good ideas" that *are* in everyday use.

A good collection of kitchen tools is invaluable and will save you both time and money. It is worth spending as much as you can afford on good-quality equipment which will perform the necessary tasks quickly and easily at the times you need them most.

There are numerous gadgets to perform every imaginable kitchen task. Before you buy any new equipment, do think about what you will be using it for; some of the tools are versatile enough to be used for a number of tasks. Also, the more often you think you will be using it, the stronger it needs to be. If you are thinking about buying a big piece of equipment, do consider where and how you can store it to prevent it from being damaged when not in use.

Above:
A citrus squeezer with ample room for pith and pips to prevent overflowing. The bottom has a lip on both sides.

Right:
Wooden lemon squeezer is just the thing to keep by the stove. Lemon juice is indispensable, just a few drops of juice will bring out the flavor of mayonnaise and salad dressings, smoked salmon, fruit dishes, various kinds of sauces, and fish and poultry.

Left:
If you cannot afford a food processor, the next best kitchen aid is the stainless steel mouli. A classic design, it has been available for generations of French cooks. It will purée baby food and vegetables for soups, make fresh sauces from tomatoes and acid fruit, and makes the very best potato purée. It comes with coarse, medium and fine discs.

Below:
This mill for peppercorns has hardened steel grinders that can be adjusted from very fine to coarse. It is simplicity itself to refill and is made of metal alloy. Black peppercorns are mild and aromatic; white are hot and less fragrant. A few allspice berries added to your grinder along with black peppercorns will give an extra spicy flavor.

Above:
For good presentation of an apple tart, the fruit should be cut into neat slices, which can be quite tricky. So welcome to this little gadget which really does deserve a home. Simply push the slicer which has stainless steel blades through the apple and it will divide it into 14 segments. It also cores the apple.

Below:
Can openers are essential kitchen equipment, and this design has a butterfly action, and is also fitted with a useful piercer. This makes it possible to drain juices or liquids from cans without losing any of the contents, or having to tip them into a strainer.

Below:
Two fruit utensils: the lemon zester, on the left, cuts slivers from all citrus fruit in a matter of seconds; the orange peeler removes the pith, cuts strips and also peels. The two tools make the preparation of dishes such as caramelized oranges and lemon meringue pie very much simpler.

Below:
Even the design of the humble potato peeler, has variations; here are three of them. Left, swivel-blade for left- or right-handed use. Center, traditional steel blade. Right, stainless steel blade for left- or right-handed use.

Food processors

These remarkably versatile machines are only worthwhile having if kept on a counter, with accessories easily to hand. When you buy one, make a point of using it in some different way every couple of days. That is the best means of building up your understanding of how it works and just how time-saving and helpful it can be. This will also mean that when there is a real rush on in the kitchen, you will be able to use the food processor to advantage and be fully in charge of the situation. And there is only a bowl, lid and blade to clean which takes no time at all.

Liquidizers can be bought as attachments to a food processor, but it is useful to have one as a separate machine, because it is actually easier to deal with small quantities in them. Food for a baby, for instance, is more easily puréed in a goblet rather than in a bowl which can leave a ring of ingredients round the edge.

Safety points

The double-bladed knife, the food processor's basic tool, is very sharp. It is important that you remove it from the bowl before you tip out the food inside it, to prevent the blade falling out and giving you a nasty cut.

Above left:
The Magimix 2100 will cover all your basic everyday cooking activities. It comes with shatterproof bowl and stainless steel blades; it will chop, grate, knead dough, liquidize, purée, and slice. Included as accessories are the master and dough blades, slicing/grating disk, and egg whisk. There are other extra tools which you can buy.

Above right:
The Magimix 4000 is for the larger family, but one of its accessories is a mini processor for small quantities. The bowl has the capacity to make dough for a 2-pound loaf or a seven-egg sponge, and an extra julienne disk for vegetables, a slicer, coarse grater, and citrus press are included.

Above and below right:
Two classic American designs, the Waring Professional Blender with a heavy-duty motor and a thick glass jar holds 2 pints and is heat-resistant. Full marks for its ability to crush ice. The Kitchen Aid Mixer has a stainless steel bowl, heavy stable bottom, ten mixing speeds, beater attachment, dough hook, and wire whisk.

Soups

Soups come in all manner of guises. They can be thin and light, they can be thick and chunky, they can be hot or cold, they can be vegetarian, meaty or fishy, they can be no more than a taster to sharpen your appetite at the beginning of a meal or they can be a hearty meal in themselves. Whatever your taste and whatever the occasion, there is bound to be something here to suit you.

Red bell pepper soup

Serves 4–6
Preparation: 15 minutes
Cooking: 25–35 minutes
Carbohydrate: 17 g, Protein: 4 g, Fat: 4 g, Fiber 3 g, Calories: 119 kcal, Sodium: 529 mg (per portion)

What you need:

- 1 tablespoon sunflower oil
- 1 large onion, chopped
- 2 garlic cloves, finely chopped
- 2 tablespoons dry sherry
- 3–4 red bell peppers, deseeded and chopped
- 1 potato, diced
- 2 tablespoons tomato paste
- 2 large tomatoes, peeled and sliced
- 4½ cups stock
- salt and pepper

To garnish:

- 2–3 tablespoons plain yogurt
- cracked black peppercorns
- sprigs of chervil

1 Heat the oil in a large saucepan and fry the onion for 4–5 minutes, stirring occasionally. Stir in the remaining ingredients and seasoning.

2 Bring to a boil, cover, and then simmer for 20–30 minutes. Purée the soup in a blender or food processor, or press through a strainer. Reheat slowly and adjust the seasoning if necessary. Garnish each bowl of soup with swirls of yogurt, a sprinkling of cracked peppercorns and a few sprigs of chervil. Serve piping hot.

Cook's Tip

For carrot soup, replace the bell peppers with 3–4 carrots. Use chicken or vegetable stock in this recipe.

Left: *Red bell pepper soup*

Split pea and ham soup

Serves 8
Preparation: 10–15 minutes
Cooking: 40–45 minutes
Carbohydrate: 58 g, Protein: 24 g, Fat: 22 g, Fiber: 6 g, Calories: 507 kcal, Sodium: 560 mg (per portion)

What you need:

- 2 tablespoons butter
- 1 onion, chopped
- 1 carrot, diced
- 2½ cups yellow split peas, rinsed
- 8 ounces cooked ham, cut into chunks
- 2 bay leaves
- 1 celery stalk
- 1 garlic clove, crushed
- ½ cup heavy cream
- salt and pepper

To garnish:
- croûtons (see Cook's Tip)
- heavy cream

1 Melt the butter in a large saucepan and fry the onion and carrot for 2–3 minutes, stirring occasionally. Add 4½ pints water and the split peas, and bring to a boil. Add the ham, bay leaves, celery, garlic and seasoning. Cover and simmer slowly for 40–45 minutes.

2 Discard the bay leaves, then purée the soup in a blender or food processor –you will have to do this in batches. Return the puréed soup to the cleaned pan. Stir in the cream and reheat slowly, without boiling, stirring constantly. Taste and adjust the seasoning if necessary. Garnish with a few croûtons and a swirl of heavy cream.

Pumpkin soup

Serves 6
Preparation: 20 minutes
Cooking: 40–50 minutes
Carbohydrate: 27 g, Protein: 14 g, Fat: 26 g, Fiber: 2 g, Calories: 385 kcal, Sodium: 498 mg (per portion)

What you need:

- ¼ cup butter
- 1½ pounds pumpkin, deseeded and cut into chunks
- ½ teaspoon grated nutmeg
- ½ teaspoon dry thyme
- 6 cups milk
- ⅓ cup long grain rice
- salt and pepper

1 Melt the butter in a large saucepan. Add the pumpkin and cook for 10 minutes, stirring occasionally. Add the nutmeg, thyme, and salt and pepper to taste; then add ⅔ cup water, cover and cook over a high heat until the pumpkin is tender.

2 Purée the pumpkin mixture in a blender or food processor, or press through a strainer.

3 Return the pumpkin purée to the cleaned pan. Add the milk and rice, and cook, covered, for 20–30 minutes until the rice is cooked, stirring occasionally.

Cook's Tip

To make croûtons for 4–6 people, cut the crusts from 2 slices of bread and cut into ½–inch cubes. Heat 2 tablespoons butter and 2 tablespoons oil in a skillet; when it is hot, add the bread and fry for 1–2 minutes, stirring frequently, until the bread is crisp and golden. Drain well on paper towels. For garlic croûtons, crush 1–2 garlic cloves with 1 teaspoon salt and add to the skillet when the bread is nearly cooked.

Left: *Split pea and ham soup*
Right: *Pumpkin soup*

Variation

Curried pumpkin soup

Cook the pumpkin in 2 tablespoons oil with 1 onion, 1 green bell pepper and 2 garlic cloves (all chopped), until softened. Add a little chopped fresh ginger, 2 teaspoons chili powder, and 2 teaspoons turmeric, and cook for 2–3 minutes, stirring frequently. Add ⅔ cup water, cook until the pumpkin is tender, then purée. Simmer the pumpkin purée with 1¾ cups coconut milk, 3¾ cups water and the rice.

Haddock and fennel soup

Serves 4
Preparation: 15 minutes
Cooking: 25–30 minutes
Carbohydrate: 13 g, Protein: 16 g,
Fat: 14 g, Fiber: 2 g, Calories: 236 kcal,
Sodium: 384 mg (per portion)

What you need:

- 8 ounces fennel bulbs, sliced finely, leaves reserved
- 1 leek, white part only, sliced
- ¼ cup butter
- 2½ cups fish stock
- 1 bay leaf
- 2–3 potatoes, finely sliced
- 8 ounces skinned haddock fillet
- 1¼ cups milk
- salt and pepper

1 Fry the fennel and leek in the butter for 5 minutes, or until soft. Add the stock, bay leaf and potatoes. Bring to a boil, then lower the heat and simmer, covered, for 10–15 minutes.

2 In a separate pan, simmer the fish with the milk and pepper for 5 minutes. Remove from the heat, let stand with the lid on for 5 minutes, then flake.

3 Discard the bay leaf and purée 1¼ cups of the fennel mixture in a food processor. Return the purée to the pan and add the fish and milk mixture. Reheat slowly, without boiling. Taste and adjust the seasoning. Garnish with fennel leaves.

Below: Provençal fish soup
Above right: Haddock and fennel soup

Provençal fish soup

Serves 6–8
Preparation: 20 minutes
Cooking: 15–20 minutes
Carbohydrate: 28 g, Protein: 23 g,
Fat: 29 g, Fiber: 2 g, Calories: 522 kcal,
Sodium: 494 mg (per portion)

What you need:

- 1 leek, chopped
- 2 onions, chopped
- 2 garlic cloves, crushed
- 5 tablespoons olive oil
- 3 tomatoes, peeled and chopped
- 2 potatoes, diced
- 1 large red snapper or 2 medium red mullet, scaled and cleaned
- 1 monkfish tail, skinless and filleted, bone reserved
- 2½ cups dry white wine
- 2 strips of orange peel
- 1 bay leaf
- a few sprigs of fresh fennel
- large pinch of saffron threads, soaked in 1 tablespoon hot water
- 2 tablespoons chopped fresh parsley
- salt and pepper

To garnish:
- French bread, sliced and toasted
- rouille (see Cook's Tip)
- ¾–1 cup grated Gruyère cheese

1 Fry the leek, onions and garlic in the olive oil until soft. Add the tomatoes and potatoes, and cook slowly for 2–3 minutes.

2 Remove the fish heads and add to the pan with the monkfish bone. Add 3 cups water, the wine, orange peel, bay leaf, fennel, and seasoning, and bring to a boil. Reduce the heat, and add the fish, roughly chopped. Simmer for 15–20 minutes.

3 Remove and discard the fish heads and bones, the bay leaf, orange rind, and herbs. Purée the soup and return to the cleaned pan with the soaked saffron and parsley, and reheat slowly.

4 To garnish, spread the toasted bread with a little rouille, then sprinkle with the cheese. Float on the soup.

Cook's Tip

To make rouille, mix together ⅔ cup mayonnaise with 1 red bell pepper which has been peeled, deseeded, and puréed, a pinch of chili powder and seasoning.

Spanish garbanzo bean soup

Serves 8–10
Preparation: 15 minutes
Cooking: 2 hours
Carbohydrate: 18 g, Protein: 22 g, Fat: 8 g, Fiber: 4 g, Calories: 227 kcal, Sodium: 1491 mg (per portion)

What you need:

- 1 small, boneless piece of smoked ham, about 1–1½ pounds
- 1 onion, studded with 4 cloves
- 2 garlic cloves, crushed
- 1 bay leaf
- 1 sprig of fresh thyme, or ¼ teaspoon dry thyme
- 1 sprig of fresh marjoram
- 1 sprig of fresh parsley
- 7½ cups chicken stock
- 14-ounce can garbanzo beans, drained
- 2–2½ cups diced potatoes
- 3½ cups shredded Savoy cabbage
- salt and pepper

1 Place the boneless piece of smoked ham in a deep saucepan and cover with cold water. Bring to a boil, then drain the ham, discarding the water.

2 Return the ham to the cleaned pan. Then add the onion, garlic, herbs and 7½ cups water. Bring to a boil; then reduce the heat and simmer, partially covered, for about 1½ hours. Discard the onion and herbs. Lift the ham out and cut it into small pieces. Then set aside.

3 Add the garbanzo beans, potatoes and cabbage to the stock, and simmer for 15 minutes. Add the ham pieces and cook for 10 minutes longer. Add salt and pepper to taste. Ladle into bowls and serve piping hot.

Thai chicken and coconut soup

Serves 4–6
Preparation: 15 minutes
Cooking: 40–45 minutes
Carbohydrate: 11 g, Protein: 26 g, Fat: 5 g, Fiber: 1 g, Calories: 189 kcal, Sodium: 764 mg (per portion)

What you need:

- 5 cups chicken stock
- 3 chicken breasts
- 1 onion, finely chopped
- 3 stalks lemon grass, cut into 3 pieces and crushed
- 3 kaffir lime leaves
- 8 slices fresh ginger root
- 1¾ cups coconut milk
- juice of 1 lime
- 2 teaspoons brown sugar

To garnish:

- 2 fresh red chilies, deseeded and chopped
- fresh basil leaves

1 Put the stock, chicken breasts, onion and flavorings into a pan. Bring to a boil then reduce the heat, cover and simmer for about 30 minutes.

2 Strain the stock into a clean saucepan. Add the coconut milk, bring to a boil, then simmer gently over a low heat for 10 minutes longer.

3 Meanwhile, cut the chicken breasts into thin slices.

4 Stir the lime juice, brown sugar and chicken into the soup. Simmer for 3 minutes. Serve garnished with chilies and basil leaves.

Above left: Spanish garbanzo bean soup
Below: Thai chicken and coconut soup

Soupe au pistou

Serves 8
Preparation: 15 minutes
Cooking: 1 hour 5 minutes
Carbohydrate: 50 g, Protein: 25g,
Fat: 14 g, Fiber: 8 g, Calories: 408 kcal,
Sodium: 460 mg (per portion)

What you need:

- 2½ cups sliced green beans
- 1½ cups dry navy beans
- 1 onion, finely chopped
- 3 zucchini, sliced
- 4 potatoes, peeled
- 4 tomatoes, peeled, deseeded and chopped
- 4½ pints hot water
- 8 ounces shell pasta
- salt and pepper

For the pistou:
- 3–4 garlic cloves, peeled
- 15–20 fresh basil leaves
- 2 tablespoons olive oil
- 2 cups grated Parmesan cheese

1 Put all the beans, onion, zucchini, potatoes, and most of the chopped tomatoes in a saucepan. Cover with the hot water and season. Bring to a boil, reduce the heat and simmer for 45 minutes.

2 Meanwhile, make the pistou. Place the garlic, basil leaves and remaining tomato in a mortar and crush with a pestle. Add the olive oil, half the Parmesan, and salt and pepper. Make a smooth paste. After 45 minutes, add the pasta to the soup and continue cooking over a low heat for 15–20 minutes longer.

3 To serve, stir half the pistou into the hot soup. Ladle the soup into individual bowls and top with grated cheese and more pistou.

Right: *Soupe au pistou*

Vichyssoise

Serves 6
Preparation: 15 minutes, plus
3 hours chilling
Cooking: 35 minutes
*Carbohydrate: 36 g, Protein: 11 g,
Fat: 34 g, Fiber: 6 g, Calories: 482 kcal,
Sodium: 675 mg (per portion)*

What you need:

- 2 pounds leeks
- ¼ cup butter
- 1 onion, chopped
- 4½ cups chicken or vegetable
  stock
- 5 cups diced potatoes
- pinch of grated nutmeg
- 2½ cups milk
- 1¼ cups light cream
- ⅔ cup heavy cream, chilled
- salt and white pepper
- small bunch of fresh chives,
  to garnish

1 Cut off the green tops of the leeks and discard. Slice the white parts thinly. Melt the butter in a large saucepan. Add the leeks and the onion, and fry over a medium-low heat for 5 minutes, stirring constantly, until soft.

Below: Vichyssoise
Above right: Tomato and zucchini soup

2 Add the stock and potatoes, nutmeg and seasoning to taste.

Bring to a boil; reduce the heat and simmer, partially covered, for 25 minutes. Add the milk and then simmer for about 5–8 minutes longer.

3 Purée the soup in a food processor—you will have to do this in several batches—then press through a strainer into a bowl. Add the light cream, then cover and chill in the refrigerator for at least 3 hours.

4 To serve, swirl in the heavy cream, taste and adjust the seasoning. Garnish with chives.

Tomato and zucchini soup

Serves 4
Preparation: 15 minutes, plus
3 hours chilling
Cooking: 15 minutes
*Carbohydrate: 11 g, Protein: 4 g,
Fat: 8 g, Fiber: 3 g, Calories: 124 kcal,
Sodium: 533 mg (per portion)*

What you need:

- 3 tablespoons olive oil
- 1 garlic clove, crushed

- 2 pounds ripe tomatoes,
  peeled, deseeded and
  chopped
- 2 tablespoons tomato paste
- 1 tablespoon chopped fresh
  basil
- 3 cups chicken stock
- 2 zucchini, coarsely shredded
- salt and pepper

To garnish:

- 4 ice cubes
- 3 tablespoons plain yogurt
- fresh basil leaves

1 Heat the oil in a saucepan. Add the garlic, tomatoes, and tomato paste and cook over a low heat for 10 minutes. Stir in the basil, stock, and seasoning.

2 Bring to a boil then reduce the heat, cover and simmer for 5 minutes.

3 Purée the soup in a food processor, then let cool. Stir in the zucchini, cover and chill in the refrigerator for at least 3 hours, or overnight.

4 To serve, place an ice cube in each bowl, then pour in the soup, and add a swirl of yogurt and a few basil leaves.

Black bean chili

Serves 8
Preparation: 20 minutes, plus
soaking overnight
Cooking: 1 hour 20 minutes

What you need:

- 1⅓ cups dry black kidney
  beans, soaked overnight
- 8 ounces small mushrooms
- 4 tablespoons olive oil
- 1 large onion, chopped
- 2 garlic cloves, crushed
- 2 large potatoes, cubed
- 1 red or green bell pepper,
  seeded and diced
- 2 teaspoons ground
  coriander
- 1 teaspoon ground cumin
- 2 teaspoons hot chili
  powder
- 1 14-ounce can of chopped
  tomatoes
- 1 tablespoon lime juice
- 1 square dark chocolate,
  chopped
- 2 tablespoons chopped fresh
  cilantro
- Avocado salsa (see Cook's
  Tip), to serve

1 Drain the kidney beans, place
in a pan with 6¼ cups water.
Bring to a boil, boil rapidly for
15 minutes. Reduce the heat,
cover the pan, and then simmer
for 45 minutes.
2 Stir-fry the mushrooms in
half the oil. Remove from the

Cook's Tip

To make avocado salsa, dice
1 ripe avocado and mix with
4 finely chopped scallions,
1 tablespoon lemon juice,
1 tablespoon chopped
fresh cilantro, and salt
and pepper.

French onion soup

Serves 6
Preparation: 10 minutes
Cooking: about 35 minutes

What you need:

- ¼ cup butter
- 1 pound Spanish onions, thickly sliced
- ¼ cup all-purpose flour
- 5 cups beef stock
- 1 tablespoon Cognac (optional)
- ½ teaspoon Dijon mustard
- salt and pepper
- 6 slices French bread
- ¾ cup grated Gruyère cheese

1 Melt the butter in a heavy-bottomed saucepan. Add the onions and cook over a medium heat, stirring constantly until soft and pale gold. Sprinkle in the flour, stir for 1 minute, then gradually pour in the stock. Bring to a boil, stirring constantly. Season to taste.

2 Reduce the heat and simmer for 20–25 minutes. Add the Cognac, if using.

3 Lightly toast the bread, then sprinkle with grated Gruyère. Pour the soup into flameproof bowls and float a slice of cheese-topped bread in each bowl. Put the bowls under a hot broiler until the cheese begins to bubble. Serve immediately.

Cook's Tip

The soup can be prepared ahead of time. It can then be reheated before pouring it into bowls, topping with slices of cheesy bread and broiling until the cheese begins to bubble.

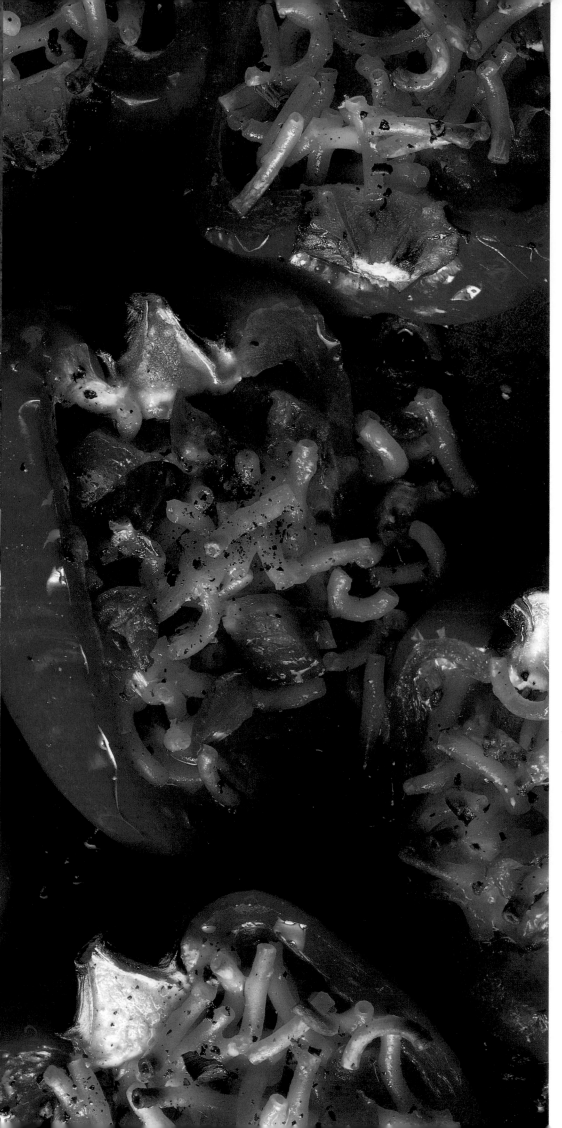

Planning a menu

When you have invited people to share a meal with you, it is important to plan the menu carefully. It need not be complicated – often the simplest things are the best, especially if you make the most of seasonal produce: asparagus and strawberries in early summer, for example, and ripe pears or rich game in the fall.

First decide on the main course and build the rest of the menu around it. Is it a summer lunch or a winter dinner? Do any of your guests have certain preferences or dislikes? Do you want a rich warming casserole, a light fish dish or a vegetarian main course? Will the predominant color be red, green, or brown?

Think about textures and flavors: a menu loaded with smooth creamy sauces would be dull, but too many crunchy or spicy hot dishes might feel like an assault on the taste buds.

Be sure that any side dishes and vegetables complement the rest of the meal. When a menu includes a variety of colors and textures, it is probably quite well balanced nutritionally–but avoid butter or cream sauces in more than one course. Do not be over-ambitious and prepare as much as possible ahead, in order to avoid any possible awkward last-minute panic.

The dishes that follow show just how easy it is to create a successful menu, which is both delicious and satisfying.

Far left: *Colorful salads are easy to prepare and incredibly versatile. Serve them as a first course or as a side dish. Vary the colors by using green, red or bronze salad leaves, fresh herbs, and edible flowers. Add texture with croûtons, or toasted nuts*
Left: *Pasta-packed red bell peppers have instant eye-appeal. They make a good appetizer, but they could also be served as a vegetarian main course or as a side dish*

pan and reserve. Add the remaining oil to the pan, along with the onion, garlic, potatoes, bell pepper and spices, and fry over a medium heat for 10 minutes.

3 Drain the beans, reserving the liquid. Boil the liquid until reduced to 2 cups. Stir the beans into the pan with the vegetables, then add the bean stock, tomatoes and mushrooms. Bring to a boil, cover and simmer for about 30 minutes.

4 Stir in the lime juice, chocolate, and cilantro and cook for just 5 minutes longer. Serve hot, with avocado salsa.

Leeks with blue cheese and hazelnuts

Serves 4–6
Preparation: 5 minutes
Cooking: 35–40 minutes

What you need:

- 1½ pounds baby leeks, halved lengthways
- 2 tablespoons hazelnut oil
- 4 tablespoons vegetable stock
- 1 tablespoon butter
- 1 cup crumbled dolcelatte cheese
- 2 tablespoons chopped hazelnuts
- 2 tablespoons chopped fresh chervil
- salt and pepper

1 Toss the leeks with the oil and place in a large roasting pan with the stock. Place in a preheated oven, 400°F, for 15 minutes.

2 Dot the leeks with the butter, cheese, nuts, and chervil. Then return them to the oven and cook for 15–20 minutes longer, until the leeks are tender and the cheese is melted and golden. Season the dish to taste and serve it immediately.

Pasta-packed red bell peppers

Serves 4
Preparation: 20 minutes
Cooking: 45 minutes

What you need:

- 4 red bell peppers, halved and deseeded
- 4 ounces mini macaroni or small pasta shapes, already cooked
- 2 plum tomatoes, chopped
- 1 cup grated Cheddar cheese
- 2 scallions, finely chopped
- 2 tablespoons chopped fresh parsley
- 3 tablespoons olive oil
- salt and pepper

1 Place the bell peppers on a baking sheet. Mix the macaroni or the pasta shapes, tomatoes, cheese, scallions and parsley in a bowl. Spoon the mixture into the bell peppers. Drizzle with plenty of olive oil and season with salt and plenty of pepper.

2 Place the bell peppers in a preheated oven, at 350°F, for 35–45 minutes, until the filling is golden and bubbling. Serve the stuffed bell peppers at once, accompanied with fresh crusty bread to mop up all the juices.

Far left: *French onion soup is a warming, comforting dish with an easy yet impressive last-minute topping of toast and melted cheese. This is the perfect start to a dinner party in winter weather, when you want something warm and hearty that is bound to satisfy your guests*
Center: *Black bean chili is an unusual dish, which includes a little dark chocolate in its ingredients. It can be garnished with fresh cilantro or with fresh parsley and should be served with rice*
Left: *Leeks with blue cheese and hazelnuts are a delicious combination, which can be served either as an interesting side dish, or as a light first course*

Chocolate crumb tart with exotic fruit

Serves 6
Preparation: 20 minutes, plus chilling

What you need:

- ⅓ cup butter
- 1 tablespoon golden syrup
- 1½ cups crushed chocolate coated cookies
- 1¼ cups crème fraîche
- selection of exotic fruits, such as papaya, pineapple, star fruit, and pomegranate
- 2 tablespoons redcurrant jelly
- 1 tablespoon lime juice

1 Melt the butter with the syrup. Add the cookies and mix well. Press the mixture onto the bottom and sides of a greased loose-bottomed 8-inch round quiche pan. Then chill until firm.
2 Carefully remove the crumb shell from the pan and place on a serving plate. Fill with the crème fraîche. Prepare the fruit and arrange over the crème fraîche.
3 Warm the redcurrant jelly with the lime juice and drizzle over the fruit.

Strawberry crumble tart

Serves 6
Preparation: 20 minutes, plus chilling

What you need:

- ⅓ cup butter
- 1½ cups crushed ginger cookies
- 1 cup softened cream cheese
- ⅓ cup superfine sugar
- 1 teaspoon grated lemon rind
- 4 tablespoons light cream
- 3 cups strawberries
- confectioners' sugar, for dusting

1 Melt the butter. Add the cookie crumbs and mix well. Press the mixture on to the bottom and sides of a loose-bottomed 8-inch round quiche pan. Chill the cookie shell in the refrigerator until firm.
2 Beat together the cream cheese, sugar, lemon rind, and light cream.
3 Carefully remove the chilled ginger cookie shell from the quiche pan and place on a serving plate. Fill with the cream cheese mixture. Arrange the strawberries over the filling and dust with confectioners' sugar.

French apple tart

Serves 8
Preparation: 30 minutes
Cooking: 40–45 minutes

What you need:

- 10-inch quiche pan lined with sweet plain pastry dough

For the filling:

- 750 g/1½ lb eating apples
- 3 tablespoons lemon juice
- 4 tablespoons warmed, strained apricot jam
- ¾ cup light cream
- 2 eggs, beaten
- ¼ cup superfine sugar

1 Chill the pastry shell in the refrigerator for 30 minutes.
2 Make the filling: peel and core the apples, slice thinly into a bowl, and toss with lemon juice. Drain and arrange in concentric ring over the pastry shell. Brush with apricot jam. Bake in a pre-heated oven, at 375°F, for 10 minutes. Then lower the oven temperature to 375°F.
3 Whisk the cream, beaten eggs and sugar in a bowl. Pour this mixture carefully over the slices of apple. Return the flan to the oven for 30–35 minutes, until the pastry is golden and the filling is cooked.

Left: *French apple tart*
Above: *Chocolate crumb tart with exotic fruit*
Right: *Strawberry crumble tart*
These stunning fruit tarts are easy to vary, depending on what fresh fruits are available. Use fruit singly or in combinations, such as raspberries, blackberries, and sliced ripe peaches, glazed with redcurrant jelly, or bananas, kiwifruit, pineapple, and mango, dusted with coconut

Appetizers

Appetizers are just that: they are only the opening paragraph, the introduction to the meal, not the main part of it. As such, they should arouse interest while not providing the complete answer, they should whet the appetite rather than satisfy it. You and your guests should still be hungry and eager for the delights that the meal will have to offer next. Ideally, appetizers should also be quick and easy to serve, so that you are free to concentrate on the next course. Many of these recipes can be prepared ahead.

Goat cheese and cherry tomato puff tartlets

Makes 4–6
Preparation: 15 minutes
Cooking:10–15 minutes
Carbohydrate: 13 g, Protein: 6 g, Fat: 14 g, Fiber: 1 g, Calories: 201 kcal, Sodium: 347 mg (per portion)

What you need:

- 8 ounces puff pastry dough, thawed if frozen
- 2 tablespoons olive oil
- 8 ounces cherry tomatoes, preferably a mixture of red and yellow, halved
- 8 ounces firm goat cheese, sliced
- 2 teaspoons chopped fresh thyme
- salt and pepper

1 Roll out the dough on a lightly floured surface and cut into 3-inch rounds. Place on a greased baking sheet and brush lightly with olive oil.
2 Arrange half the cherry tomatoes over each dough round to within 1 inch of the edge. Place the goat cheese on top and finally arrange the remaining tomatoes. Season with a little salt and pepper to taste. Sprinkle with the fresh thyme and then drizzle 1–2 tablespoons of olive oil over the top.
3 Bake in a preheated oven, 425°F for 10–15 minutes, until the pastry is risen, crisp and golden brown. Serve hot, accompanied by a salad of bitter leaves.

Cook's Tip

To make one big tart, cut the dough into a 9-inch round and place on a lightly greased baking sheet. Top as in the main recipe above and bake in the oven for 20–25 minutes. Serve piping hot either as an appetizer or as a light lunch.

Left: *Goat cheese and cherry tomato puff tartlets*

French country pâté

Serves 8
Preparation: 30 minutes, plus
cooling and chilling overnight
Cooking: 1½ hours
*Carbohydrate: 4 g, Protein: 33 g,
Fat: 29g, Fiber: 1 g, Calories: 405 kcal,
Sodium: 785 mg (per portion)*

What you need:

- ¼ cup butter, plus extra for greasing
- 2 onions, finely chopped
- 4 garlic cloves, crushed
- 1 pound pork liver, carefully trimmed
- 10–12 bacon slices, rind removed
- 4½ cups ground or chopped lean pork
- 2 tablespoons chopped fresh parsley
- ½ teaspoon dry sage
- ¼ teaspoon ground mace
- ¼ teaspoon ground nutmeg
- 2 egg whites
- 2 tablespoons brandy
- 2 bay leaves
- salt and pepper

1 Melt the butter in a skillet and cook the onions and garlic slowly for a few minutes until tender and golden. Transfer to a large bowl. Add the pork liver to the pan and fry until just lightly browned. Remove and grind or chop finely.

2 Chop 8 of the bacon slices and add to the bowl, along with the trimmed liver, chopped pork, chopped parsley, sage, ground mace, ground nutmeg, salt, pepper, egg whites, and brandy. Mix well together until all the ingredients are thoroughly combined.

3 Line a lightly greased 1-pound terrine or loaf pan with the remaining bacon slices so that they hang over the sides. Fill with the pâté mixture and fold the bacon over the top. Put the 2 bay leaves on top and place in a roasting pan of hot water. Cook in a preheated oven at 375°F, for 1½ hours, or until the juices run clear and the pâté has shrunk slightly from the sides of the pan.

4 Let the pâté cool for 30 minutes, then cover with a piece of baking parchment or foil and weight lightly. Leave until completely cold and set. If you wish, replace the bay leaves with fresh ones. Cover and refrigerate for about 36 hours. Serve sliced with toast or crusty bread.

Chicken liver pâté

Serves 4–6
Preparation: 20 minutes, plus cooling and chilling
Cooking: about 10 minutes

Carbohydrate: 1 g, Protein: 16 g, Fat: 57 g, Fiber: 0 g, Calories: 614 kcal, Sodium: 209 mg (per portion)

What you need:

- 1½ cups unsalted butter
- 2 garlic cloves, crushed
- 1 pound chicken livers, trimmed, chopped roughly
- 6–8 tablespoons brandy, according to taste
- salt and pepper
- parsley sprigs, to garnish

1 Melt ¼ cup of the butter in a large skillet over a medium heat until foaming. Lower the heat; add the garlic and stir for 2–3 minutes until softened but not colored.

2 Add the chicken livers to the skillet, increase the heat to medium again, and toss vigorously for about 5–8 minutes until the livers are browned on the outside but still tinged with pink in the center.

3 Pour in the brandy and stir well to mix. Let the mixture bubble in the skillet for about 1–2 minutes, then transfer to a food processor or blender. Cut 1 cup of the remaining butter into pieces and add to the machine. Work the mixture to a smooth purée, and add salt and pepper to taste.

4 Turn the mixture into individual ramekins or a large serving bowl and smooth the surface. Melt the remaining butter in a clean pan, then pour over the surface of the pâté. Leave until cold, then cover and chill in the refrigerator overnight. Serve chilled, garnished with sprigs of parsley and accompanied by triangles of hot whole wheat toast.

Left: *French country pâté*
Right: *Chicken liver pâté*

Guacamole

Serves 6
Preparation: 15 minutes, plus
1 hour chilling
Carbohydrate: 2 g, Protein: 2 g,
Fat: 11 g, Fiber: 2 g, Calories: 110 kcal,
Sodium: 138 mg (per portion)

What you need:

- 2 large, ready-to-eat ripe avocados
- 3 tablespoons lemon or lime juice
- 2 garlic cloves, crushed
- ⅓ cup chopped scallions
- 1–2 tablespoons chopped mild green chilies or jalapeños
- 2 tablespoons chopped fresh cilantro
- 4 ounces tomatoes, peeled, deseeded and chopped
- salt and pepper

Above right: Potato
skins with soured
cream dip
Below: *Guacamole*

1 Cut the avocados in half and remove the pits. Scoop out the flesh and sprinkle with a little of the lemon or lime juice to prevent discoloration.

2 Put the avocado flesh in a mixing bowl with the remaining lemon or lime juice, and mash coarsely. Add the garlic, scallions, chilies, cilantros and some seasoning to taste. Mix in the chopped tomatoes. Cover the bowl and place in the refrigerator for at least 1 hour. Serve with tortilla chips or toast.

Potato skins with sour cream dip

Serves 4–8
Preparation: 20 minutes
Cooking: 1¼ hours
Carbohydrate: 15 g, Protein: 3 g,
Fat: 11 g, Fiber: 1 g, Calories: 169 kcal,
Sodium: 217 mg (per portion)

What you need:

- 4 large baking potatoes, scrubbed and dried
- ⅔ cup sour cream
- 1 teaspoon snipped fresh chives
- sunflower oil, for frying
- coarse sea salt and pepper
- snipped fresh chives, to garnish

1 Prick the potatoes with a fork. Bake in a preheated oven, 400°F for about 1¼ hours until they are tender.

2 Meanwhile, prepare the dip. In a bowl, mix the sour cream with the chives. Season to taste. Cover the bowl and chill.

3 When all the potatoes are cooked, cool for a few minutes, then cut each one into quarters lengthways. Scoop out most of the potato flesh, leaving a thin layer next to the skin. (The scooped-out potato may be reserved and used to top a pie.)

4 Pour the oil into a skillet to a depth of 3-inches. Heat the oil to 350–375°F or until a cube of bread browns in 30 seconds. Add the potato skins carefully to the hot oil. Fry for about 2 minutes until brown and crisp. Remove and drain on paper towels. To serve, arrange the potato skins on a plate with the dip, sprinkled with chives, in the center.

Wild mushrooms in crispy bread cases

Serves 8
Preparation: 15 minutes
Cooking: 10–15 minutes
Carbohydrate: 10 g, Protein: 3 g, Fat: 12 g, Fiber: 1 g, Calories: 157 kcal, Sodium: 291 mg (per portion)

What you need:

For the bread cases:
- 8 thin slices bread, crusts removed
- ¼ cup melted butter

For the filling:
- 2 tablespoons butter
- 1 shallot, chopped
- 2 cups sliced mushrooms (crimini, shiitake, oyster)
- 1 tablespoon Madeira

- 4 tablespoons heavy cream
- 1 tablespoon chopped fresh parsley
- salt and pepper
- assorted salad greens, to serve

Variation

Chicken tartlets

Prepare eight bread cases as in the main recipe. For the filling, melt 1 tablespoon butter, add 1 chopped celery stalk and fry for about 3–4 minutes until softened. Then add 2 chopped rindless smoked bacon slices and ¾ cup chopped skinless chicken breast and cook for 10–12 minutes longer until the bacon is crispy and the chicken thoroughly cooked. Remove from the heat and stir in 1 tablespoon sherry and let the mixture bubble in the pan briefly. Stir in 4 tablespoons heavy cream and 1 tablespoon chopped fresh parsley or 2 teaspoons chopped fresh cilantro. Add seasoning. Cook over a medium heat for a few minutes until the mixture thickens to a sauce. Serve as in the main recipe.

1 Brush both sides of the bread with the butter. Press firmly into 8 tartlet or muffin pans. Bake in a preheated oven, 400°F, for 10–15 minutes, until the bread cases are crisp and golden brown.

2 Meanwhile, make the filling. Melt the butter in a small saucepan. Add the shallot and fry for about 5 minutes until softened. Add the mushrooms and cook for 5 minutes longer until the mushrooms are tender. Stir in the Madeira and let the mixture bubble briefly; then stir in the cream and chopped parsley, and season with salt and pepper to taste. Cook over a medium heat for a few minutes more, until the mixture thickens slightly and forms a sauce.

3 Arrange the assorted salad greens on 8 small serving plates and place a bread case on each. Fill with the mushroom mixture and serve warm.

Above: *Wild mushrooms in crispy bread cases*

Beefsteak tomato salad

Serves 4
Preparation: 15 minutes, plus 15 minutes standing
Carbohydrate: 3 g, Protein: 1 g, Fat: 11 g, Fiber: 1 g, Calories: 113 kcal, Sodium: 525 mg (per portion)

What you need:

- 4 beefsteak tomatoes, sliced
- 5 tablespoons extra-virgin olive oil
- 2 scallions, chopped
- 2 tablespoons chopped fresh oregano or marjoram
- a few leaves of fresh basil, roughly torn
- ½ cup black olives
- coarse sea salt and pepper

1 Arrange the tomatoes, overlapping slightly, in concentric rings on a large platter. Drizzle the olive oil carefully over the top of the tomatoes, and add salt and pepper to taste.

2 Sprinkle the scallions over the tomatoes, together with the oregano or marjoram and the basil. Scatter the olives over the top. Let the salad stand for about 15 minutes before serving, to let the flavors mingle.

Cook's Tip

Black olives are preserved in a number of ways. The most appropriate for salads are those preserved in olive oil. However, olives in brine would be just as good.

Right: *Beefsteak tomato salad*
Center: *Spinach and goat cheese salad*
Far right: *Wild rice, orange and walnut salad*

Spinach and goat cheese salad

Serves 4
Preparation: 15 minutes
Carbohydrate: 9 g, Protein: 10 g,
Fat: 24 g, Fiber: 3 g, Calories: 289 kcal,
Sodium: 472 mg (per portion)

What you need:

- 6 ounces young spinach leaves
- 2 oranges, peeled and segmented
- 1½ cups diced goat cheese
- 5 tablespoons olive oil
- ½ cup roughly chopped hazelnuts
- 1 garlic clove, crushed
- juice of 1 large orange
- 1 bunch of watercress, leaves stripped from the stalks, very finely chopped
- 2 tablespoons chopped fresh mixed herbs (e.g. parsley, tarragon, mint, dill, basil)
- salt and pepper

1 Combine the spinach leaves, orange segments and goat cheese in a large salad bowl.
2 Heat the olive oil in a small skillet. Add the hazelnuts and garlic and cook for 1–2 minutes. Stir in the orange juice, water-cress and herbs. Heat through, then quickly pour the hot dress-ing onto the spinach, orange and goat cheese. Add salt and pepper to taste, toss well and serve immediately.

Wild rice, orange and walnut salad

Serves 4
Preparation: 25 minutes
Cooking: 30 minutes
Carbohydrate: 26 g, Protein: 5 g,
Fat: 41 g, Fiber: 3 g, Calories: 483 kcal,
Sodium: 205 mg (per portion)

What you need:

- 1½ cups wild rice
- 2 small oranges
- 1 small fennel bulb, trimmed and thinly sliced
- 3 scallions, finely chopped
- ½ cup walnut pieces
- ½ cup vinaigrette made with walnut oil
- salt and pepper
- chopped fennel tops, to garnish

1 Bring a large saucepan of water to a boil. Add the rice. Lower the heat and simmer for 30 minutes, or until tender. Drain the rice in a colander, refresh under cold running water, then drain. Transfer the rice to a large salad bowl.
2 Using a small, sharp knife, peel away the skin and all the pith from the oranges. Slice them as thinly as possible, and then add to the rice together with the sliced fennel and scallions.
3 Spread the walnuts on a bak-ing sheet and toast under a pre-heated hot broiler for 1–2 minutes, until they are lightly browned. Add to the salad, with salt and pepper to taste.
4 Pour over the dressing and toss lightly. Sprinkle with chop-ped fennel tops to garnish.

a day. When it is ready for cooking, wash the cod thoroughly and cut it into large pieces. Place in a wide-bottomed pan, cover with water, and bring to a boil slowly. Cover the pan and simmer for 8 minutes. If using fresh cod, poach in salted water in the same way.

2 Remove the cod from the pan and discard all the skin and bones. Roughly flake the fish and place in a mixing bowl with the crushed garlic. Mix all the ingredients together thoroughly.

3 Gradually add the oil in a thin stream, stirring all the time, until the mixture is rich and creamy. Alternatively, you can do this in a food processor.

4 Transfer the mixture to a saucepan and heat very slowly. Add the cream, stirring continuously, and then add the black pepper and lemon juice. Turn into 4 individual ramekins or a

5 cup soufflé dish and let cool. Serve cold, garnished with black olives and parsley, with slices of fried bread.

Seafood coquilles

Serves 4
Preparation: 30 minutes
Cooking: 15 minutes
Carbohydrate: 103 g, Protein: 18 g, Fat: 12 g, Fiber: 1 g, Calories: 253 kcal, Sodium: 588 mg (per portion)

What you need:

- 2½ cups mussels in shells
- 6 ounces small scallops
- ¼ cup butter
- 1 tablespoon finely chopped onion
- 1 garlic clove, crushed
- ⅔ cup sliced mushrooms
- 1 cup fresh white bread crumbs
- ⅔ cup dry white wine

Above: Cod mousse
Below right: Seafood coquilles

Cod mousse

Serves 4
Preparation: 30 minutes, plus 24–48 hours soaking and cooling
Carbohydrate: 35 g, Protein: 30 g, Fat: 17 g, Fiber: 1 g, Calories: 403 kcal, Sodium: 766 mg (per portion)

What you need:

- 8 ounces dry salt cod or 1 pound fresh cod fillet, seasoned with salt and pepper
- 2 garlic cloves, crushed
- 6 tablespoons olive oil
- ⅓ cup light cream
- freshly ground black pepper
- juice of 1 lemon

To garnish:
- black olives
- chopped fresh parsley
- ½ French bread stick, sliced and fried

1 If using salt cod, cover it with water and let soak for 24–48 hours, changing the water twice

- 1 tablespoon lemon juice
- 1 tablespoon chopped fresh parsley
- salt and pepper

1 Wash and scrub the mussels and place them in an ovenproof dish with a little water. Put in a preheated oven at 350°F until they open. Remove the mussels from the shells. Separate the white parts and corals of the scallops.

2 Melt half the butter in a skillet and sauté the onion, garlic and mushrooms until they are lightly colored. Mix in the mussels and the scallops, and heat through slowly.

3 Butter 4 deep scallop shells and sprinkle in half the breadcrumbs. Divide the seafood mixture between the shells. Boil 4 tablespoons of water with the wine and lemon juice until reduced, and then spoon over the mixture in the shells.

4 Combine the remaining bread crumbs with the chopped parsley and seasoning, and scatter over the shells. Melt the remaining butter and pour over the top. Place the shells on a baking sheet and bake in a preheated oven at 350°F for 15 minutes until golden brown.

Cook's Tip

When cooking with live mussels, it is important to insure that they are thoroughly cleaned before use. Scrub under cold running water until cleaned of all filaments attached to the shells. Throw out any shells that do not close tightly when tapped sharply against the work surface.

Butterfly shrimp with basil

Serves 2–4
Preparation: 35 minutes, plus 1 hour marinating
Carbohydrate: 2 g, Protein: 23 g, Fat: 18 g, Fiber: 1 g, Calories: 263 kcal, Sodium: 574 mg (per portion)

What you need:

- 1 pound uncooked large shrimp in their shells
- about 6 ounces salad greens (e.g. frisé, corn salad, aragula, batavia)
- 4 ounces cherry tomatoes, halved
- a few sprigs of fresh basil, leaves removed from stems and roughly torn
- mayonnaise, to serve

For the marinade:
- 3 tablespoons lemon juice
- 3 tablespoons light olive oil
- ½ garlic clove, crushed
- 1 tablespoon chopped fresh basil
- salt and pepper

1 Remove the heads from the shrimp. Using sharp kitchen scissors or a small knife, carefully cut the shrimp lengthways, almost in half, leaving the tail end intact. Place them in a single layer in a large shallow dish.

2 To make the marinade, place the lemon juice, light olive oil, crushed garlic, fresh basil and salt and pepper into a small bowl. Pour over the shrimp, cover the dish and leave for about 1 hour, turning the shrimp just occasionally.

3 Arrange the shrimp in a single layer on a rack over a broiler pan. Place under a preheated hot broiler and cook for about 3–4 minutes, or until the shrimp have curled or 'butterflied' and are bright pink in color.

4 Meanwhile, arrange the salad greens and cherry tomatoes on a serving platter or individual plates. Scatter over the torn basil leaves, to garnish.

5 Arrange the hot butterfly shrimp on the salad. Serve at once, with mayonnaise.

Above: *Butterfly shrimp with basil*

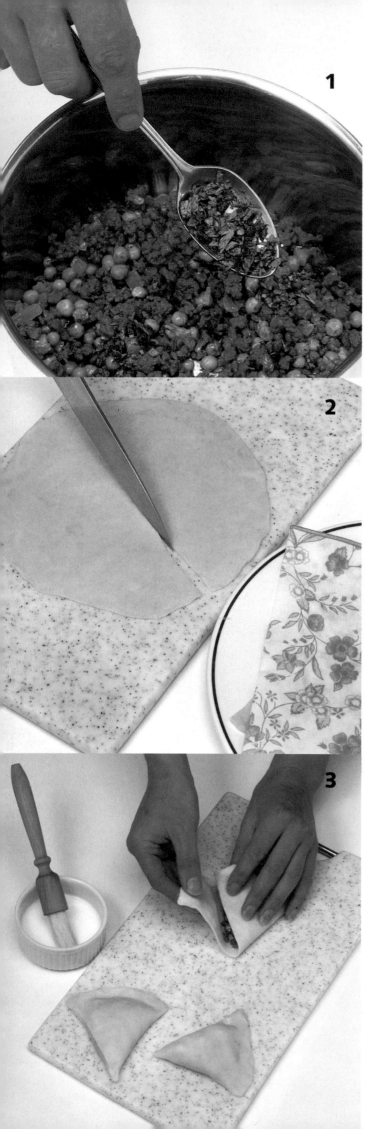

Ground meat samosas

Makes 12
Preparation: 1 hour
Cooking: 10 minutes
Carbohydrate: 36 g, Protein: 9 g,
Fat: 7 g, Fiber: 2 g, Calories: 234 kcal,
Sodium: 290 mg (per portion)

What you need:

For the dough:
- 4 cups all-purpose flour
- ½ teaspoon baking powder
- 1 teaspoon salt
- 2 tablespoons melted butter
- 4 tablespoons plain yogurt
- about 8 tablespoons tepid water

For the filling:
- 1 tablespoon butter
- 1 small onion, chopped
- ½ teaspoon cumin seeds
- 2 cups ground beef or lamb
- 1 green chili, finely chopped
- 1 teaspoon salt
- ¾ cup cooked peas
- black pepper
- 1 teaspoon chopped cilantro leaves

To assemble:
- 2 tablespoons milk
- oil for deep-frying
- chutney, to serve

1 Make the samosa dough. Sift the flour with the baking powder and salt into a mixing bowl. Make a well in the center and add the melted butter and yogurt. Draw the flour into the liquid, using a wooden spoon, adding water as necessary to make a smooth dough. Knead until free from cracks. Set aside.

2 Make the filling: melt the butter in a saucepan, and fry the onion and cumin seeds over medium heat, stirring occasionally, for 5–7 minutes. Add the ground beef or lamb, chili and salt. Mix thoroughly. Reduce the heat and simmer for 10 minutes.

3 Stir in the peas and continue cooking over moderate heat for 5 minutes, or until the liquid has evaporated. Remove the pan from the heat and mix in the pepper and cilantro. Let cool before using to stuff the samosas.

4 Divide the samosa dough into 12 equal portions, and roll out each one to a thin 7-inch diameter round. Cut each round in half with a sharp knife, and then cover the semicircles with a damp cloth while you fill them, one at a time.

5 Brush the edges of each semicircle with a little milk and spoon some filling onto the center. Fold in the corners, overlapping them to form a cone. Fold over and seal the top to make a triangle. Deep-fry in hot oil, in batches, until crisp and golden. Drain on paper towels. Serve hot with chutney.

Cook's Tip

Samosas are a tasty traditional Indian snack. Indian doughs generally require much more kneading than is usual. This helps to break down the gluten in the flour and changes a sticky unmanageable dough into one that can be rolled out smoothly and thinly. Before rolling out the dough in this recipe, shape each of the 12 portions into a small ball between the palms of your hands and flatten slightly to form a disc shape.

Right: *Ground meat samosas*

Satay

Serves 4
Preparation: 5 minutes, plus
2 hours marinating
Cooking: 45 minutes
Carbohydrate: 18 g, Protein: 30 g,
Fat: 17 g, Fiber: 1 g, Calories: 332 kcal,
Sodium: 1299 mg (per portion)

What you need:

- 1 pound pork tenderloin
- 1 teaspoon salt
- 2 teaspoons brown sugar
- 1 teaspoon ground turmeric
- 1 teaspoon ground coriander
- 1 teaspoon ground cumin
- ¾ cup coconut milk

For the peanut sauce:
- ½ cup roasted peanuts
- 1 teaspoon salt
- 1¼ cups coconut milk
- 2 teaspoons red curry paste
- 2 tablespoons sugar
- ½ teaspoon lemon juice

1 Cut the pork into 2-inch long strips and place in a large bowl. Add the salt, sugar, turmeric, coriander, cumin, and 4 table-spoons of the coconut milk. Mix thoroughly, using clean hands to knead the spices into the meat. Cover and let marinate for at least 2 hours.

2 Make the peanut sauce: grind the peanuts together with the salt in a mortar until the mixture has the consistency of thick cream. Set aside.

3 Put half the coconut milk in a saucepan with the curry paste. Heat slowly for 3 minutes, stir-ring constantly. Stir in the creamed peanuts with the sugar, lemon juice and the remaining coconut milk. Simmer slowly for 20–30 minutes, stirring occa-sionally, to prevent it sticking to the pan. Transfer to a bowl.

4 Thread the marinated pork onto oiled bamboo skewers. Cook on a barbecue or under a hot broiler for 12–15 minutes, turning the kebabs several times and brushing frequently with the reserved coconut milk. Serve the kebabs with the peanut sauce.

Vegetable terrine with chicken mousseline

Serves 8
Preparation: about 1 hour, plus cooling and chilling
Cooking: 1¼ hours
Carbohydrate: 7 g, Protein: 19 g,
Fat: 15 g, Fiber: 3 g, Calories: 232 kcal,
Sodium: 359 mg (per portion)

What you need:

- 3½ cups roughly chopped, skinless chicken breast fillets
- 2 eggs, lightly beaten
- ¾ cup heavy cream
- ¼–½ teaspoon Tabasco sauce
- about 30 young spinach leaves, with any tough stalks removed
- 6 ounces green beans, topped and tailed
- 3 large carrots, cut into very thin matchstick strips
- 1½ cups frozen peas
- salt and pepper

1 To make the mousseline, purée the chicken in a food processor. Add the eggs, cream, Tabasco, salt and pepper to taste, and purée again.

2 Blanch the spinach leaves for 10 seconds in a large saucepan of lightly salted boiling water. Cool the leaves quickly under running cold water. Then sepa-rate them carefully and let dry on a clean dishcloth.

3 Blanch the beans, carrots and peas separately in the spinach

blanching water, allowing only 2 minutes for each vegetable. Remove as before, refresh them under cold running water and dry them thoroughly on a clean dish cloth.

4 Line the bottom and sides of a 2-pound pan with three-quarters of the spinach leaves.

5 Spoon one-quarter of the mousseline into the pan and smooth the surface. Place the beans closely, lengthways, over the mousseline.

6 Spoon in another quarter of the mousseline and arrange the carrot sticks lengthways on top. Repeat with more mousseline and the peas, then top with all the remaining mousseline. Cover with the remainder of the spin-ach leaves.

7 Cover the loaf pan with foil and place in a roasting pan. Pour in enough hot water to come halfway up the sides of the loaf pan. Place in a preheated oven, 375°F, for 1¼ hours.

8 Remove the loaf pan from the water and let the terrine cool. Chill for at least 4 hours before turning out onto a platter.

Left: *Satay*
Below: *Vegetable terrine with chicken mousseline*

Fish

There are innumerable reasons for putting fish on your menu. It is not only delicious, it's also excellent value for money, and it's highly nutritious. It's a good source of vitamins, particularly A and D, and minerals, particularly iodine; it's also very low in calories! There are an enormous number of varieties of fish, many of which are available all year round.

Fish is a highly versatile ingredient which features in many delicious recipes, from the simplest to the most elaborate. And then there's shellfish which falls into two groups: jointed shells such as crab and prawns, and hinged shells like mussels and scallops. Shellfish is a gastronomic treat.

Below: *Red mullet with Ricard*
Right: *Tuna with tomatoes*

Red mullet with Ricard

Serves 4
Preparation: 10 minutes, plus
10 minutes marinating
Cooking: 12 minutes
Carbohydrate: 2 g, Protein: 33 g,
Fat: 56 g, Fiber: 0 g, Calories: 662 kcal,
Sodium: 408 mg (per portion)

What you need:

- 4 medium or 8 small red mullet, scaled and cleaned
- 3 tablespoons Ricard
- 1 tablespoon fines herbes
- ½ cup butter
- scant 1 cup heavy cream

1 Sprinkle the red mullet with 2 tablespoons of the Ricard and the fines herbes. Set aside for at least 10 minutes to marinate.
2 Preheat the broiler to medium. Place the mullet on a rack, and broil for 6 minutes on each side.
3 Meanwhile, make the sauce. Melt the butter in a pan. Warm the remaining Ricard and pour over the melted butter. Set alight.
4 Cook for a few minutes to reduce the sauce, then add the cream and reduce again. Arrange the fish on a large serving dish and pour the sauce over the top.

Tuna with tomatoes

Serves 4
Preparation: 15 minutes
Cooking: 30 minutes
Carbohydrate: 15 g, Protein: 40 g,
Fat: 14 g, Fiber: 4 g, Calories: 338 kcal,
Sodium: 527 mg (per portion)

Variation

Swordfish with tomatoes

This recipe also works well using swordfish steaks. You can use green olives instead of black ones if you prefer. If you like your fish to taste strongly of garlic, fry 2 garlic cloves, peeled but whole, in olive oil until golden. Then discard the garlic and brown the fish steaks in the same oil.

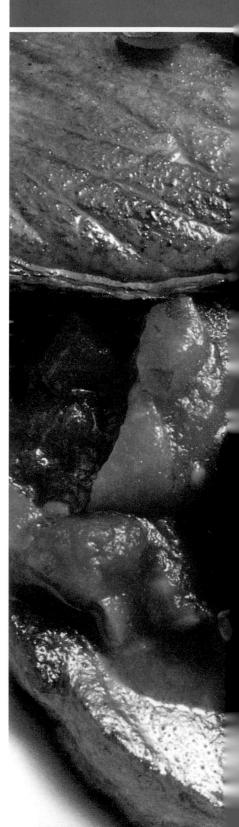

What you need:

- 4 fresh tuna steaks, about 5 ounces each
- flour for dusting
- 3 tablespoons olive oil
- 1 onion, chopped
- 2 garlic cloves, crushed
- 2 pounds tomatoes, peeled and chopped
- 2 tablespoons chopped fresh parsley
- a few basil leaves, chopped
- 1 bay leaf
- 4 anchovy fillets, mashed
- 8 black olives
- salt and pepper

1 Wash the tuna steaks thoroughly and pat dry with paper towels. Season with salt and plenty of freshly ground black pepper, and then dust the steaks lightly with flour.

2 Heat half the olive oil in a large shallow skillet. Sauté the tuna steaks until golden on one side. Flip the steaks over and cook the other side until golden. Carefully remove the tuna steaks from the pan; transfer to a large dish and keep warm while making the sauce.

3 Add the remaining oil to the pan and sauté the onion and garlic for about 5 minutes, until both are golden and soft. Then add the tomatoes, parsley, basil, bay leaf, and mashed anchovies, and stir well. Bring the mixture to a boil and continue boiling until it reduces and thickens.

4 Return the tuna steaks to the pan, season to taste and simmer slowly for 15 minutes, turning once during that time. Turn the heat off. Add the olives and let stand for 5 minutes. Remove and discard the bay leaf; then transfer the tuna steaks in their sauce to a warm serving dish.

Above: *Baked red snapper with potatoes and olives*
Below right: *Stuffed sardines*

Baked red snapper with potatoes and olives

Serves 4
Preparation: 15 minutes
Cooking: 30–40 minutes
Carbohydrate: 24 g, Protein: 28 g,
Fat: 28 g, Fiber: 3 g, Calories: 459 kcal,
Sodium: 1431 mg (per portion)

What you need:

- 1 pound potatoes, peeled and very thinly sliced
- 2 lemons, sliced
- ⅓ cup butter
- 1 large or 4 small red snapper, cleaned
- 1½ cups pitted black and green olives
- olive oil, for sprinkling
- salt and pepper
- dill sprigs, to garnish

1 Arrange the sliced potatoes and lemons in a layer in the bottom of a large greased shallow baking dish or roasting pan and dot generously with butter.

2 Place the fish on top of the potatoes. Season with salt and pepper and scatter the olives over the snapper. Sprinkle the fish generously with olive oil. Bake in a preheated oven, 375°F, for 30–40 minutes depending on the size of the fish, or until the flesh flakes easily and is tender. Serve at once, sprinkled with dill.

Stuffed sardines

Serves 4
Preparation: 35 minutes
Cooking: 10 minutes
Carbohydrate: 40 g, Protein: 70 g,
Fat: 37 g, Fiber: 8 g, Calories: 768 kcal,
Sodium: 831 mg (per portion)

What you need:

- 20 sardines
- 1 pound spinach
- 2 shallots, finely chopped
- 2 tablespoons olive oil
- 1 garlic clove, crushed
- 1 teaspoon chopped fresh thyme
- ½ cup ricotta or soft cheese
- 1 cup fresh bread crumbs
- olive oil for sprinkling
- salt and pepper

1 Prepare the sardines: wash and scale them, and remove the heads. Slit them open underneath and carefully remove all the backbones. Sprinkle lightly with salt and pepper to taste; then set the fish aside while you prepare the stuffing.

2 Wash the spinach, removing any thick stems, and put into a large saucepan–do not add any water. Cook, covered, over a low heat for about 5 minutes, or until cooked. Drain well.

3 Meanwhile, sweat the shallots in the olive oil until tender. Add the garlic and cook slowly for 2–3 minutes. Remove from the heat and mix with the cooked

spinach, thyme and ricotta. Season with salt and pepper.

4 Fill the sardines with this mixture, and press them into the bread crumbs. Arrange in a large oiled ovenproof dish and then sprinkle with olive oil. Bake in a preheated oven, 425°F, for 10 minutes. Serve immediately.

Variation

Fish tandoori

If you prefer, you can just as well use any other firm white fish steaks, such as monkfish, haddock or cod. Leave your decision until you are at the fish counter and there be guided by availability and price.

Halibut tandoori

Serves 4
Preparation: 15 minutes, plus
4–5 hours marinating
Cooking: 30 minutes
Carbohydrate: 3 g, Protein: 39 g,
Fat: 7 g, Fiber: 1 g, Calories: 236 kcal,
Sodium: 332 mg (Per portion)

What you need:

- 4 halibut steaks, about
  6 ounces each
- ¼ cup plain yogurt
- 2 tablespoons oil
- 2 tablespoons paprika
- 1 tablespoons ground
  cumin
- 1 teaspoon ground fennel
  seeds
- 1 teaspoon chili powder
- salt

To garnish:

- 1 small lettuce,
  shredded
- 1 fennel bulb, sliced

1 Wash the halibut steaks thoroughly under cold running water, and then lightly pat them dry with paper towels. Set the steaks aside while you prepare the tandoori mixture.

2 Put the yogurt in a bowl with the oil, paprika, cumin, fennel seeds, chili powder and a little salt. Mix well.

3 Place the halibut steaks in the bowl and rub well with the tandoori mixture. Cover and leave in a cool place to marinate for 4–5 hours.

4 Transfer the marinated fish to a shallow, ovenproof baking dish. Bake in a preheated oven, at 350°F, for 20–25 minutes. Arrange the lettuce on a warm serving dish; place the fish on top. Spoon over the juices and serve garnished with fennel.

Above: *Halibut tandoori*

Squid and green bell peppers

Serves 2–4
Preparation: 15 minutes
Cooking: 5 minutes
Carbohydrate: 3 g, Protein: 10 g,
Fat: 8 g, Fiber: 1 g, Calories: 118 kcal,
Sodium: 411 mg (per portion)

What you need:

- 8 ounces squid
- 1 green bell pepper, cored, deseeded and thinly sliced
- oil for deep-frying
- 2 slices fresh ginger root, peeled and shredded
- 1 tablespoon soy sauce
- 1 teaspoon vinegar
- 1 teaspoon sesame oil
- salt and pepper

1 Clean the squid, discarding the head and transparent backbone as well as the ink bag. Wash well under cold running water and pat dry with paper towels.
2 Peel off the thin skin of the squid and cut the flesh into small pieces–about the size of a matchbox.

3 Heat the oil in a wok or deep skillet until it is fairly hot. Deep-fry the prepared squid for about 30 seconds and then remove from the wok or skillet with a slotted spoon. Carefully pour off the excess oil, leaving about 1 tablespoon of oil in the bottom of the pan. Add the ginger, pepper and squid.
4 Stir-fry for a few seconds and then stir in the salt, soy sauce, vinegar and pepper. Cook for about 1 minute; then add the sesame oil and serve.

Steamed sea bass

Serves 2
Preparation: 10 minutes, plus soaking
Cooking: 15 minutes
Carbohydrate: 13 g, Protein: 56 g,
Fat: 8 g, Fiber: 1 g, Calories: 358 kcal,
Sodium: 2048 mg (per portion)

What you need:

- 2 Chinese dried mushrooms
- 1 pound sea bass, cleaned and scaled
- 2 slices fresh ginger root, peeled and shredded
- 2 scallions, shredded
- ½ cup shredded, cooked ham
- ⅓ cup shredded, bamboo shoots
- 3 tablespoons dry sherry
- 2 tablespoons soy sauce
- 1 teaspoon sugar
- 1 teaspoon salt

1 Cover the mushrooms with warm water and let soak for 10 minutes. Squeeze the mushrooms dry and discard the stalks. Then thinly shred the stalks.
2 Slash both sides of the fish diagonally, as deep as the bone, at intervals of ½ inch. Dry and place the fish on a plate.

Above: *Squid and green bell peppers*
Right: *Steamed sea bass*
Far right: *Seafood with vegetables*

3 Neatly arrange the shredded mushrooms, ginger root, scallions, ham, and bamboo shoots on top of the sea bass.

4 Mix together the sherry, soy sauce, sugar and salt in a small bowl, and pour over the fish. Place the fish on the plate in the top of a steamer set over simmering water. Cover and steam vigorously for about 15 minutes. Serve hot.

Cook's Tip

Slashing both sides of the fish as described in this recipe prevents the skin from bursting during cooking. It also lets the heat penetrate more quickly and more evenly.

Seafood with vegetables

Serves 3–4
Preparation: 20 minutes
Cooking: 5 minutes
Carbohydrate: 12 g, Protein: 25 g, Fat: 6 g, Fiber: 2 g, Calories: 207 kcal, Sodium: 655 mg (per portion)

What you need:

- 4–6 fresh scallops
- 1½ cups headless uncooked shrimp
- 1 egg white
- 1 tablespoon cornstarch
- vegetable oil for deep-frying
- 3 celery stalks, sliced
- 1 red bell pepper, deseeded and sliced
- 1–2 carrots, sliced
- 2 slices fresh ginger root, peeled and shredded
- 2–3 scallions, chopped
- 2 tablespoons sherry
- 1 tablespoon light soy sauce
- 2 teaspoons chili bean paste
- 1 teaspoon salt
- 1 teaspoon sesame oil, to finish

1 Cut each scallop into 3 or 4 pieces. Shell the shrimp and remove the black vein running along the back. Leave whole if small, or cut into 2 or 3 pieces if large. Put all the scallops and shrimp in a bowl together with the egg white and half the cornstarch, and mix well.

2 Heat the vegetable oil in a deep wok, and then deep-fry both the scallops and the shrimp for 1 minute, stirring all the time to keep the pieces separate. Remove with a slotted spoon and then drain well on paper towels.

3 Pour off all but 2 tablespoons of oil from the wok. Increase the heat to high and add the celery, sliced red bell pepper, carrots, ginger root and scallions. Stir-fry for about 1 minute. Add the scallops and prawns and then stir in the sherry, soy sauce, chili bean paste, and salt.

4 Mix the remaining cornstarch to a smooth paste with just a little water, and then add this mixture to the wok. Stir well until thickened and thoroughly mixed in with the seafood and vegetables. Sprinkle over the sesame oil and serve immediately.

Salmon in puff pastry

Serves 6–8
Preparation: 30 minutes
Cooking: 35–40 minutes
Carbohydrate: 32 g, Protein: 43 g,
Fat: 49 g, Fiber: 0 g, Calories: 726 kcal,
Sodium: 628 mg (per portion)

What you need:

- 2 pounds salmon, skinned and filleted, cut into 2 pieces
- 2 tablespoons butter
- 2 slices bacon, chopped
- 1⅓ cups chopped mushrooms
- ½ cup soft cheese with garlic and herbs
- 2 tablespoons milk
- 1 pound puff pastry dough, thawed if frozen
- beaten egg, to glaze
- salt and pepper

Below: Salmon in puff pastry

1 Season the salmon fillets on both sides. Melt the butter in a skillet, add the bacon, and fry for about 5 minutes, until crisp. Add the mushrooms and fry for about 2 minutes, until softened, stirring all the time. Stir in the soft cheese and milk with salt and pepper to taste. Cook slowly, stirring until well mixed. Remove from the heat and let cool.

2 Roll out half the dough to measure 1 inch larger all round than the fish. Transfer the dough to a greased baking sheet and place one fish fillet, skinned side down, in the center. Spread with the cheese mixture and then cover with the second fillet, skinned side up.

3 Brush the edges of the dough with a little of the egg. Roll out the remaining dough and cover the fish. Trim the edges, then pinch them together to seal. Roll out the dough trimmings and cut them into strips. Brush the top of the pie with beaten egg and arrange the strips in a lattice design over the top. Brush again with beaten egg.

4 Bake in a preheated oven, 400°F, for 35–40 minutes, until the pastry is crisp and golden. Serve the pie hot with asparagus or zucchini, or cold with a fresh green salad.

Provençal-style salt cod

Serves 4
Preparation: 15 minutes, plus soaking overnight
Cooking: 1¼–1½ hours
Carbohydrate: 27 g, Protein: 77 g,
Fat: 9 g, Fiber: 4 g, Calories: 610 kcal,
Sodium: 721 mg (per portion)

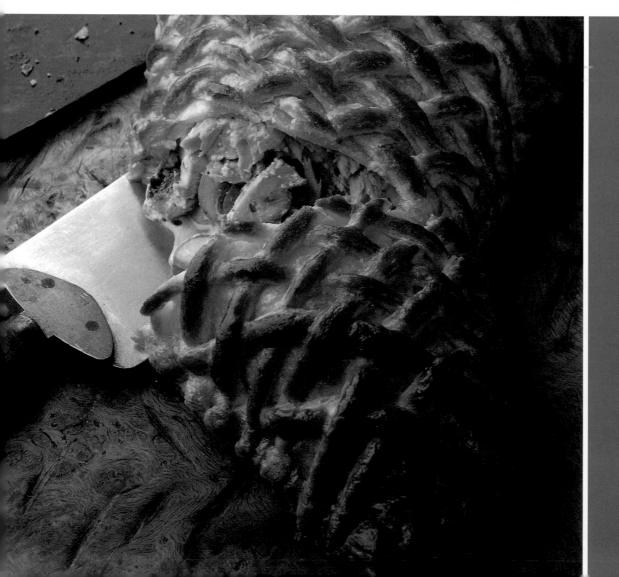

Variation

Bass in puff pastry

For this, you need a 2 pound bass, skinned and filleted. Season the bass fillets. Trim off any tough stalks from a bunch of watercress, and wash and dry it. Plunge the watercress into a pan of salted, boiling water, cook for 1 minute, then drain and cool quickly under cold running water. Drain again and then dry well, chop finely. Beat 2 tablespoons butter, 1 garlic clove and 1 tablespoon of lemon juice in a bowl. Season to taste. Beat in the watercress. Then continue from Step 2 of the salmon recipe, substituting the watercress butter for the cheese mixture. Bake as for the main recipe.

What you need:

- 2 pounds salt cod
- 2 onions, sliced
- 1 pound potatoes, peeled and thickly sliced
- 4 large tomatoes, peeled, deseeded, and quartered
- 3 garlic cloves, crushed
- ½ cup capers
- 1 cup pitted black olives
- 2½ cups dry white wine
- 1 tablespoon chopped fresh basil
- 1 bay leaf
- 2 tablespoons olive oil
- pepper
- 1 tablespoon chopped fresh parsley, to garnish

1 Put all the salt cod in a large bowl and cover it with water. Let soak overnight, and then rinse well and drain before using.

2 Cut the cod into large chunks and place them in a large earthenware casserole. Cover the cod with a layer of the sliced onions.

3 Next add a layer of sliced potatoes, to cover the onions, and then add a layer of the quartered tomatoes. Continue making these layers, in the same order, until all the onions, potatoes and tomatoes are used up. Sprinkle the garlic over the top with the capers and olives, and then pour over the white wine. Try to pour the white wine over the whole dish so that its flavor is taken into all the ingredients.

4 Sprinkle with the chopped basil and add the bay leaf. Lastly, drizzle the olive oil over the top and add a good grinding of pepper. Bake in a preheated oven, 400°F, for 1¼–1½ hours, or until tender. Sprinkle with the chopped parsley just before serving.

Scalloped fish pie

Serves 4
Preparation: 25 minutes
Cooking: 15 minutes
Carbohydrate: 44 g, Protein: 42 g, Fat: 16 g, Fiber: 4 g, Calories: 481 kcal, Sodium: 480 mg (per portion)

What you need:

- 1½ pounds haddock or cod fillet
- 2 bay leaves
- 6 peppercorns
- 2 cups milk
- 5 tablespoons butter
- 1 leek, trimmed, cleaned and sliced
- ⅓ cup all-purpose flour
- 2 tomatoes, peeled, and quartered
- 2 tablespoons chopped fresh parsley
- 1½ pounds potatoes, cooked, and thinly sliced
- salt and pepper

1 Place the fish in a skillet with bay leaves, peppercorns, and milk. Add just a little salt and pepper, to taste. Gradually bring the contents of the pan to a boil, then cover the pan, lower the heat, and simmer slowly for about 10 minutes, until the fish is tender and flakes easily when tested with the tip of a knife. Using a slotted spoon, remove the fish from the skillet, leaving the cooking liquid in the pan; remove the skin from the fish and flake the fish flesh. Strain the cooking liquid left in the skillet into a pitcher.

2 Melt 3 tablespoons of the butter in a saucepan. Add the sliced leek and fry for about 5 minutes until softened and tender. Stir in the flour and cook for

1 minute. Gradually add the reserved milk/cooking liquid to the pan, stirring continuously until the sauce is both thickened and smooth.

3 Remove the saucepan from the heat and then stir in the fish, tomatoes and parsley with salt and pepper to taste. Melt the remaining butter in a small saucepan. Turn the fish mixture into a greased 5-cup ovenproof dish. Arrange the potatoes over the top of the fish mixture in overlapping rows. Brush the potatoes generously with the melted butter.

4 Carefully place the pie in a preheated oven, 400°F, and bake for about 25 minutes, until the topping is golden brown. Serve hot with a green vegetable such as green beans.

Above: *Provençal-style cod*
Below left: *Scalloped fish pie*

Mussels with Thai herbs

Serves 4
Preparation: 20 minutes
Cooking: 20 minutes
Carbohydrate: 6 g, Protein: 28 g,
Fat: 4 g, Fiber: 1 g, Calories: 171 kcal,
Sodium: 2134 mg (per portion)

What you need:

- 2½ quarts fresh mussels in shell
- 5 cups water
- 6 kaffir lime leaves
- rind of 1 lemon
- 2 blades lemon grass
- 1 tablespoon salt
- 3 fresh red chilies, sliced
- 3 scallions, chopped
- a few cilantro leaves, torn

1 Wash the mussels under cold running water and scrape away any barnacles. Remove the beards, discarding any mussels that do not close tightly when tapped sharply against the work surface.
2 Put the water in a pan and bring to a boil. Add the kaffir lime leaves, lemon rind, lemon grass and salt. Add the mussels, cover and bring back to a boil.
3 Cook the mussels, shaking the pan occasionally, until the mussels open. Then drain them, reserving half the cooking liquor. Transfer the mussels to a deep serving dish, discarding any that have not opened.

4 Drain the reserved cooking stock, discarding the lime leaves, lemon rind and lemon grass. Bring to a boil, add the red chilies and scallions. Boil vigorously for 2 minutes. Pour over the mussels and sprinkle with the torn cilantro leaves.

Cook's Tip

Thai food takes quite a long time to prepare but the actual cooking is very simple and quick. It is therefore an extremely healthy fast food.

This recipe uses two ingredients that help to give Thai food its distinctive flavor. Strongly citrus-flavored kaffir lime (makrut) leaves are used in many dishes including curries and soups. If you cannot find them, you can substitute bay leaves but the flavor will be different. Lemon grass (takrai) is an aromatic root which looks rather like a small, slim leek. It has a strong lemon fragrance and flavor and is used sliced, crushed or chopped in a wide range of Thai dishes, especially curries, soups and salads.

Right: *Mussels with Thai herbs*

Shrimp in coconut sauce

Serves 4
Preparation: 10 minutes
Cooking: 17–20 minutes
Carbohydrate: 25 g, Protein: 68 g,
Fat: 38 g, Fiber: 2 g, Calories: 393
kcal, Sodium: 695 mg (per portion)

What you need:

- 16 large uncooked shrimp
- 2 tablespoons oil
- 1 large onion, finely chopped
- 2 stalks lemon grass, chopped
- 2 fresh red chilies, sliced
- 1-inch piece fresh ginger root, shredded
- 1 tablespoon ground cumin
- 1 tablespoon ground coriander
- 2 tablespoons fish sauce
- 1 cup coconut milk
- 3 tablespoons roasted peanuts, coarsely ground
- 2 tomatoes, peeled, and chopped
- 1 teaspoon sugar
- juice of ½ lime
- fresh cilantro leaves, chopped

Below: *Shrimp in coconut sauce*
Right: *Mexican garlic shrimp*

1 Remove the shrimp from their shells, leaving the tails intact. Remove the dark veins running along the back of the shrimp and then slit them right down the underside.

2 Heat the oil in a wok or heavy skillet. Add the onion and fry until soft and golden. Add the lemon grass, sliced red chilies, ginger, cumin, and coriander, and sauté for 2 minutes.

3 Add the fish sauce and coconut milk to the wok. Stir well and then add the peanuts and chopped tomatoes. Cook over a low heat until the tomato is soft and the flavors of the sauce are well developed.

4 Stir in the prepared shrimp and simmer slowly for 5 minutes, or until the shrimp are pink and tender. Add the sugar and transfer to a serving dish. Serve hot sprinkled with the lime juice and chopped cilantro leaves.

Mexican garlic shrimp

Serves 4–6
Preparation: 15 minutes, plus
1 hour marinating
Cooking: 5 minutes
Carbohydrate: 1 g, Protein: 61 g,
Fat: 22 g, Fiber: 1 g, Calories: 449 kcal,
Sodium: 941 mg (per portion)

What you need:

- 24 uncooked large shrimp
- 6 garlic cloves, crushed
- 2 red chilies, deseeded, and chopped
- 3 tablespoons olive oil
- ¼ cup butter
- juice of 2 limes
- 3 tablespoons chopped fresh cilantro
- sea salt and whole black peppercorns

To serve:
- lime wedges
- sliced avocado

1 Prepare the shrimp: remove the heads and, leaving them in their shells, split them carefully down the middle toward the tail end without separating them. Remove the dark vein running along the back of the shrimp.

2 Mix the garlic with sea salt, peppercorns and chilies in a pestle and mortar, to make a thick aromatic paste.

3 Coat the shrimp with this mixture and place in a bowl. Cover the bowl and leave in a cool place to marinate for at least 1 hour.

Above left: *Smoky chilied prawns*
Below: *Fried mixed seafood*

4 Heat the olive oil and butter in a large heavy-bottomed skillet. Add the shrimp and garlic paste. Quickly sauté them over a medium heat for 2–3 minutes, until they turn pink. Remove from the pan and keep warm. Add the lime juice to the pan and stir into the pan juices. Boil vigorously for a couple of minutes and then pour this liquid over the shrimp. Sprinkle with cilantro, and serve with lime wedges and sliced avocado.

Smoky skewered shrimp

Serves 4
Preparation: 10 minutes, plus 30 minutes marinating
Cooking: 6 minutes
Carbohydrate:01 g, Protein: 50 g, Fat: 12 g, Fiber:0 g, Calories: 309 kcal, Sodium: 1032 mg (per portion)

What you need:

- 10 green chilies, deseeded and halved lengthways
- 20 raw large shrimp, peeled, with tails left intact
- 5 tablespoons olive oil
- coarsely ground sea salt
- lemon wedges, to serve

1 Wrap one half of each chili round the middle of each large shrimp and thread 5 shrimps onto each of 4 metal or soaked bamboo skewers.
2 Place the skewers in a long shallow dish and sprinkle over the oil and the salt. Cover the dish and let marinate in a cool place for about 30 minutes.
3 Cook the shrimp on an oiled preheated barbecue, or under a preheated broiler, for 3 minutes on each side, basting with any remaining marinade. Serve the shrimp hot with lemon wedges.

Fried mixed seafood

Serves 4
Preparation: 15 minutes, plus 2 hours chilling
Cooking: 3–6 minutes
Carbohydrate: 29 g, Protein: 98 g, Fat: 14 g, Fiber: 1 g, Calories: 630 kcal, Sodium: 1097 mg (per portion)

What you need:

- 1 cup all-purpose flour
- pinch of salt
- 2 tablespoons olive oil
- ⅔ cup tepid water
- 1 egg white
- 2 pounds mixed seafood (e.g. scallops, white fish fillets, large shrimp)
- oil for deep-frying
- sea salt

For the garnish:

- lemon wedges
- sprigs of fresh parsley

1 Make the batter: sift the flour and salt into a mixing bowl and make a well in the center. Pour in the olive oil and gradually beat in the tepid water to make a smooth, thick batter. Cover the bowl and put in the refrigerator to rest for 2 hours.
2 Immediately before using, beat the egg white until it forms stiff peaks; then lightly fold, but do not beat, the egg white into the batter with a metal spoon.
3 Meanwhile, prepare the seafood: wash all the fish and shellfish under cold running water and pat dry. Clean the scallops. Cut the white fish into smallish pieces, and remove any remaining skin and bones. Shell all the shrimp, leaving the tails intact and removing the black vein running along the back. Dip them in the prepared batter and shake off any excess batter.
4 Heat the oil for deep-frying to 375°F. Cook the batter-coated fish, scallops, and shrimp for 3–6 minutes, until crisp and golden. Lift out and drain on crumpled paper towels. Sprinkle with sea salt and pile up on a warm serving dish. Garnish with lemon wedges and parsley, and serve immediately.

Crab Creole

Serves 4
Preparation: 15 minutes
Cooking: 30 minutes
Carbohydrate: 18 g, Protein: 37 g,
Fat: 14 g, Fiber: 1 g, Calories: 353 kcal,
Sodium: 1122 mg (per portion)

What you need:

- 4 medium-sized cooked crabs
- 1½ cups fresh bread crumbs
- 2 red bell peppers, deseeded, and finely chopped
- 1 garlic clove, crushed
- 1 fresh red chili, deseeded, and finely chopped
- pinch of ground mace
- ½ teaspoon ground allspice berries
- 2 tablespoons chopped fresh parsley
- juice of 1 lime
- 2 tablespoons rum (optional)
- 1 tablespoon butter
- salt and pepper

1 Remove the crab claws and legs, and crack them to extract the meat. Open the crabs by pressing with your thumbs on the edge of the section of the shell to which the legs were attached. Pull out the central section.

2 Discard the stomach sac and feathery gills. Scoop out the meat from inside the shell and put in a bowl with the meat from the claws and legs. Remove the meat from the leg sockets with a skewer and mash well with the other crab meat.

3 Add 1 cup of the fresh bread crumbs to the crab meat, with the red bell peppers, garlic, chili, mace, allspice, and parsley. Add the lime juice and rum (if using), with salt and pepper.

4 Scrub and wash all the empty crab shells. Fill with the crab

meat mixture. Sprinkle with the remaining bread crumbs and dot with butter. Bake in a preheated oven, 350°F, for 30 minutes.

Fried scallop salad

Serves 4
Preparation: 25 minutes
Cooking: about 6 minutes
Carbohydrate: 3 g, Protein: 10 g, Fat: 7 g, Fiber: 1 g, Calories: 114 kcal, Sodium: 276 mg (per portion)

What you need:

- 3 large fresh scallops
- 3 tablespoons light olive oil
- ½ small red bell pepper, cored, deseeded and cut into matchstick strips
- ⅔ cup vinaigrette
- 1 tablespoon chopped parsley
- 2 cups arugula
- ½ small head curly chicory, leaves roughly torn
- 2 scallions, finely shredded
- salt and pepper

1 Remove the corals from the scallops and set aside. Trim the white parts of the scallops and cut each one in half horizontally. Using a very sharp knife, lightly score each scallop piece in a small lattice pattern.

2 Heat the oil in a large skillet. Add the scallops, including the corals. Cook, stirring frequently, for 3–4 minutes or until opaque. Using a slotted spoon, transfer the scallops to a plate.

3 Add the red bell pepper strips to the pan and cook, stirring, for 1 minute. Pour the dressing into the pan and heat through. Stir in the parsley, then remove the skillet from the heat. Return the scallops to the pan and add salt and pepper to taste.

4 Arrange a bed of arugula and curly chicory on individual serving plates. Scatter over the shredded scallions. Spoon the warm scallop mixture onto the plates and serve at once.

Red snapper in cilantro

Serves 4
Preparation: 10 minutes
Cooking: 20 minutes
Carbohydrate: 39 g, Protein: 54 g, Fat: 11 g, Fiber: 2 g, Calories: 462 kcal, Sodium: 1581 mg (per portion)

What you need:

- 2 pounds red snapper or other white fish fillets
- 4 tablespoons lime or lemon juice
- 2 teaspoons salt
- 4 tablespoons olive oil
- ½ cup fresh bread crumbs
- 1 garlic clove, crushed
- 6 tablespoons crushed fresh cilantro leaves
- 1 teaspoon grated lime or lemon rind
- salt and pepper
- warmed tortillas, to serve

1 Rinse the fish under cold running water and pat dry with absorbent paper towels. Rub with half of the lime or lemon juice and 1 teaspoon of the salt. Place skin side down in a lightly oiled heavy skillet.

2 Add sufficient cold water to cover the fish and then simmer slowly for 5 minutes, turning twice during the cooking time.

3 In another pan, heat half the olive oil. Add the bread crumbs, garlic, remaining salt and 4 tablespoons of the cilantro. Cook over a low heat, stirring, until golden brown. Spread over the fish and simmer for 7–10 minutes, until the fish flakes easily.

4 Blend the remaining juice and oil together and pour over the fish. Cook for 2–3 minutes. Mix the remaining cilantro with the lime or lemon rind and sprinkle over the fish. Serve with tortillas.

Far left: *Crab creole*
Below left: *Fried scallop salad*
Above: *Red snapper in coriander*

Poultry

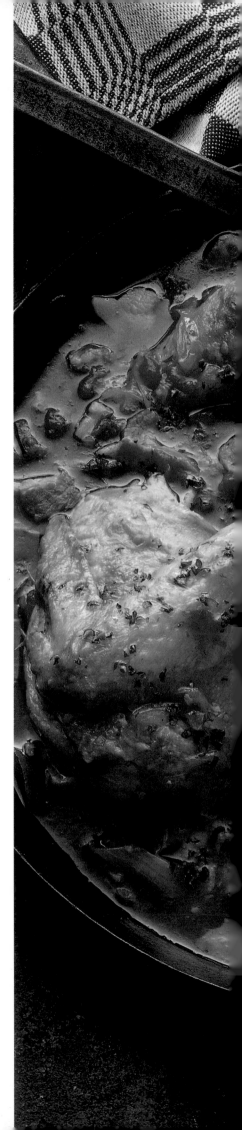

Chicken, turkey, duck and other farmyard birds, as well as game birds such as pheasant, are all incredibly versatile. They can be successfully combined with a great variety of other ingredients, including fruit, vegetables, herbs and spices, and cooked in hundreds of different ways. Most poultry is low in fat compared with other meats, and, especially if it is cut into pieces and baked, poached or stir-fried, can make a simple, healthy meal in next to no time. Dressed up with a classic, rich or elaborate sauce, poultry lends itself to many splendid dishes from around the world.

Coq au vin

Serves 4
Preparation: 30 minutes
Cooking: 50 minutes

Carbohydrate: 15 g, Protein: 36 g, Fat: 34 g, Fiber: 3 g, Calories: 576 kcal, Sodium: 967 mg (per portion)

What you need:

- 1 chicken, cut into 8 pieces
- 3 tablespoons sunflower oil
- 1½ cups chopped smoked bacon
- 16 small onions, peeled
- 8 ounces button mushrooms
- 3 garlic cloves, crushed
- 3 tablespoons brandy
- 1½ cups red wine
- 2 tablespoons all-purpose flour
- 1 tablespoon butter
- salt and pepper

1 Fry the chicken in the oil in a flameproof casserole until golden brown. Remove with a slotted spoon. Add the bacon and onions, fry for 5 minutes. Add the mushrooms and garlic.

2 Pour in the brandy and wine, and bring to a boil. Return the chicken to the casserole, and add salt and pepper. Cover and simmer for about 40 minutes, until the chicken is cooked.

3 Remove the chicken and vegetables and keep hot.

4 Mash the flour into the butter to form a smooth paste. Whisk into the sauce and simmer, stirring, for 2–3 minutes, until thick. Season to taste. Spoon over the chicken and vegetables.

Basque-style chicken

Serves 4
Preparation: 20 minutes
Cooking: 1 hour
Carbohydrate: 15 g, Protein: 38 g,
Fat: 17 g, Fiber: 4 g, Calories: 360 kcal,
Sodium: 1165 mg (per portion)

What you need:

- 1½ cups diced smoked ham or bacon
- 4 tablespoons olive oil
- 4 large chicken pieces
- 4 onions, sliced
- 3 garlic cloves, crushed
- 2 green bell peppers, deseeded and diced
- ½ teaspoon dried marjoram
- 14 ounces fresh or canned tomatoes
- ⅔–1¼ cups chicken stock
- salt and pepper
- 2 tablespoons chopped fresh parsley, to garnish

1 Fry the diced ham or bacon in the oil in a sauté pan until lightly browned, then remove with a slotted spoon. Add the chicken to the pan and cook until brown all over. Remove the chicken. Add the onions and garlic, and cook gently until soft and golden. Add the peppers and marjoram, cover and cook slowly for 10 minutes.

2 Add the tomatoes, seasoning and stock (1¼ cups if using fresh tomatoes; ⅔ cup if canned). Return the chicken and ham to the pan, cover and simmer for 40–45 minutes, until the chicken is cooked and tender.

3 Transfer the chicken to a serving dish. Boil the sauce to thicken slightly, and pour over the chicken. Sprinkle with parsley.

Far left: *Coq au vin*
Left: *Basque-style chicken*

Chicken in tarragon cream

Serves 4
Preparation: 10 minutes
Cooking: 30 minutes
Carbohydrate: 2 g, Protein: 33 g,
Fat: 35 g, Fiber: 0 g, Calories: 485 kcal,
Sodium: 609 mg (per portion)

What you need:

- 2½ cups well-flavored chicken stock
- scant 1 cup dry white wine
- 8 fresh tarragon sprigs
- 4 boneless, skinless chicken breasts
- 1 cup heavy cream
- pinch of dry mustard
- salt and pepper

Below: *Stuffed chicken breasts*

1 Pour the stock and wine into a flameproof casserole. Add 2 tarragon sprigs, season, and bring to a simmer.

2 Add the chicken, cover and simmer over a low heat for 20–25 minutes, or until just tender, turning occasionally.
3 Remove the chicken with a slotted spoon and set aside. Pour the cream into the casserole and bring to a boil, stirring constantly; then reduce the heat and simmer, stirring frequently, for about 15 minutes, until the cream sauce is reduced by one-third and is slightly thickened.
4 Remove the leaves from 2 of the remaining tarragon sprigs and chop finely. Add the chopped tarragon and mustard powder to the casserole; then add the chicken, together with any of the cooking juices that have

collected on the plate. Heat through slowly for 5 minutes, basting the chicken frequently with the sauce. Adjust the seasoning to taste and serve hot, garnished with the remaining tarragon sprigs.

Stuffed chicken breasts

Serves 4
Preparation: 10 minutes
Cooking: 20 minutes
Carbohydrate: 5 g, Protein: 39 g,
Fat: 21 g, Fiber: 1 g, Calories: 371 kcal,
Sodium: 1155 mg (per portion)

What you need:

- 4 boneless, skinless chicken breasts
- 4 small, thin slices prosciutto
- 4 thin slices Bel Paese cheese
- 4 cooked or canned asparagus stalks, plus extra to garnish
- flour for dusting
- ¼ cup butter

Chicken with Champagne

Sauté the chicken in 1¼ cups butter for 7–10 minutes. Flambé (see page 219) with 4 tablespoons Cognac, then add scant 1 cup stock and 2 tarragon sprigs, season and simmer for 20 minutes, until the chicken is tender, turning often.

Remove the chicken to a warm plate. Add scant 1 cup Champagne, 1 tablespoon tomato paste and 1½ cups heavy cream. Bring to a boil, then simmer for about 5 minutes, until thickened. Pour over the chicken and serve at once.

- 1 tablespoon olive oil
- 6 tablespoons Marsala or dry white wine
- 2 tablespoons chicken stock
- salt and pepper

1 Place each chicken breast between 2 sheets of plastic wrap or damp baking parchment and beat with a rolling pin until thin. Season lightly.

2 Place a slice of ham on top of each beaten chicken breast, then a slice of cheese and, finally, an asparagus stalk. Carefully roll up each chicken breast and wind a piece of cotton around it to hold the stuffing in place. Tie securely and dust with flour.

3 Heat 2 tablespoons of the butter with the oil in a skillet. Sauté the chicken rolls over a very low heat, turning them frequently, for about 15 minutes, or until they are golden brown and cooked through. Remove the cotton, transfer the chicken to warm serving plates and keep warm while you make the sauce.

4 Add the Marsala or wine, stock and remaining butter to the juices in the pan. Bring to a boil and simmer for 3–4 minutes, stirring and scraping the bottom of the pan with a wooden spoon. Spoon the sauce over the chicken and garnish with asparagus stalks.

Chicken with white wine, Gruyère and mushrooms

Serves 4
Preparation: 30 minutes
Cooking: about 35 minutes
Carbohydrate: 10 g, Protein: 42 g, Fat: 41 g, Fiber: 1 g, Calories: 595 kcal, Sodium: 575 mg (per portion)

What you need:

- 4 boneless, skinless chicken breasts
- ¼ cup unsalted butter
- ½ teaspoon dry mixed herbs
- ½ teaspoon dry tarragon
- 2¾ cups thinly sliced button mushrooms
- ¼ cup all-purpose flour
- 1¼ cups milk
- ⅔ cup dry white wine
- ⅓ cup heavy cream
- 1 cup grated Gruyère cheese
- good pinch of grated nutmeg
- salt and pepper

1 Put the chicken in a single layer in an ovenproof dish, dot with half the butter and sprinkle with the herbs, salt and pepper. Cover with foil and place in a preheated oven, 350°F, for 30 minutes, or until just tender.

2 Meanwhile, melt the remaining butter in a saucepan. Add the mushrooms and sauté over a medium heat, stirring frequently, for about 5 minutes.

3 Sprinkle in the flour and cook, stirring constantly, for 1–2 minutes. Remove the pan from the heat and add the milk, a little at a time, beating vigorously with a balloon whisk or wooden spoon after each addition. Add the wine in the same way.

4 Return the pan to the heat and bring to a boil, stirring all the time. Reduce the heat and simmer, stirring, for about 5 minutes, until thickened.

5 Add the cream, two-thirds of the Gruyère, the nutmeg and salt and pepper to taste, and simmer slowly for 5 minutes longer.

6 When the chicken is tender, remove from the oven and increase the oven temperature to maximum. Carefully tip any cooking juices from the chicken into the sauce and stir well to mix. Pour the sauce over the chicken in the dish and sprinkle with the remaining Gruyère.

7 Return the chicken to the oven and bake for 5 minutes, until golden and bubbling.

Above left: *Chicken in tarragon cream*
Above: *Chicken with white wine, Gruyère and mushrooms*

Chicken with 40 garlic cloves

Serves 4
Preparation: 15 minutes
Cooking: 2–2¼ hours
Carbohydrate: 17 g, Protein: 73 g,
Fat: 23 g, Fiber: 2 g, Calories: 565 kcal,
Sodium: 431 mg (per portion)

What you need:

- 1 4-pound oven-ready chicken
- 1 bouquet garni
- 4 tablespoons olive oil
- 1 celery stalk, chopped
- 40 garlic cloves, separated, but not peeled
- salt and pepper
- a few sprigs each of fresh rosemary, sage and thyme, to garnish

To seal:

- 4 tablespoons all-purpose flour
- 4 teaspoons water

1 Wash and dry the chicken cavity. Insert the bouquet garni and some seasoning, then truss the chicken with string.

2 Heat the oil in a large flame-proof casserole into which the chicken just fits. Add the celery and all the garlic; then add the trussed chicken, and cook over a medium heat until it is lightly colored on all sides.

3 Cover the casserole with its lid. Make a paste with the flour and water and seal the edge.

4 Place in a preheated oven, 350°F, for 2–2¼ hours, without opening the oven door.

5 Break the flour and water seal; then lift out the chicken and place on a warmed serving platter. Arrange the garlic cloves around the chicken and garnish with sprigs of fresh herbs.

Chicken in a brick

Serves 4
Preparation: 10 minutes
Cooking: 2 hours
Carbohydrate: 12 g, Protein: 71 g,
Fat: 16 g, Fiber: 3 g, Calories: 472 kcal,
Sodium: 442 mg (per portion)

What you need:

- 1 4-pound oven-ready chicken

- 2 onions, quartered
- 2 garlic cloves, quartered
- 4 small carrots, cut into strips
- 1 teaspoon dry tarragon
- 2 teaspoons chopped fresh tarragon
- salt and pepper

1 Soak the chicken brick in cold water for 30 minutes.

2 Wash and dry the chicken cavity; then put half the onion and garlic quarters inside the bird, with some salt and pepper.

3 Put the chicken in the bottom half of the soaked brick, surrounded by the carrots and the remaining onion and garlic. Sprinkle with the dried tarragon, salt and pepper. Cover with the top half of the brick and place in a cold oven. Set the oven to 450°F, and cook for exactly 2 hours, without opening the oven door.

4 Carefully lift the chicken out of the brick and place on a warmed serving platter. Discard the onion and garlic from the chicken cavity. Drain off most of the juices from the vegetables in the brick, then stir the fresh tarragon into the vegetables. Serve the chicken surrounded by the vegetables.

Cook's Tip

Chicken bricks must always be soaked in cold water for about 30 minutes before use. They provide a healthy way of cooking, because no extra fat is required. None of the natural juices is lost, so the food retains its flavor, moisture and tenderness.

Left: *Chicken with 40 garlic cloves*
Right: *Chicken in a brick*

Variation

Turkey in a brick with cranberries and orange

Mix 2½ cups fresh or thawed frozen cranberries with the grated rind and juice of 1 orange, 2 tablespoons soft brown sugar and a little thyme. Put them in the bottom half of the soaked chicken brick.

Soften ¼ cup butter with the grated rind of 1 orange and salt and pepper to taste. Lift the skin away from a bone-in turkey breast, weighing about 4 pounds, and spread the butter over the flesh. Press the skin back into place.

Put the turkey, skin-side up, on the cranberries in the brick. Cover and cook as in the main recipe.

Lift the turkey out of the brick and place on a warmed serving platter. Remove the cranberries with a slotted spoon and arrange around the turkey. Garnish with fresh thyme. Serve the juices separately.

Above: *Stir-fried duck with pineapple*

Variation

Five-spice chicken with cashew nuts

Heat 1 tablespoon oil and stir-fry ¼ cup shelled unsalted cashews and 4–6 sliced scallions for 1 minute. Remove and drain on paper towels.

Add 2 tablespoons oil and stir-fry 1 pound chicken, cut into strips, and 1 crushed garlic clove for 5 minutes.

Mix 1 teaspoon cornstarch with 2 tablespoons each of water, sherry and soy sauce, and ½ teaspoon five-spice powder. Pour into the wok and continue stir-frying until the sauce thickens.

Return the nuts and scallions to the wok and stir-fry for 30 seconds. Taste for seasoning and add more soy sauce if liked.

Stir-fried duck with pineapple

Serves 3–4
Preparation: 10 minutes
Cooking: 10 minutes
Carbohydrate: 9 g, Protein: 35 g, Fat: 13 g, Fiber: 1 g, Calories: 286 kcal, Sodium: 607 mg (per portion)

What you need:

- 2 tablespoons sunflower oil
- 4 duck breast fillets, about 6 ounces each, skin and fat removed, cut into thin strips
- ¼–½ teaspoon chili powder
- 2 tablespoons soy sauce
- 2 tablespoons sweet sherry
- 2 cups canned pineapple chunks in natural juice,

drained, with juice reserved
- 4–6 scallions, cut diagonally into 2-inch lengths
- salt and pepper

1 Heat a wok or a large, deep skillet over a medium heat until hot. Add the oil and heat until hot but not smoking. Add the duck strips and stir-fry for about 5 minutes, until it changes color on all sides.

2 Sprinkle in the chili powder, according to taste, and stir-fry for 1 minute. Add the soy sauce, sherry, pineapple juice, and salt and pepper to taste.

3 Stir-fry for about 5 minutes or until the duck is tender, adding the pineapple chunks and scallions for the last minute or so to heat through.

Duck breasts with spicy mango relish

Serves 6
Preparation: 30 minutes, plus 1 hour chilling or overnight
Cooking: 25 minutes
Carbohydrate: 15 g, Protein: 24 g, Fat: 8 g, Fiber: 2 g, Calories: 220 kcal, Sodium: 464 mg (per portion)

What you need:

- 6 duck breast fillets, about 6 ounces each
- salt

For the mango relish:
- 3 ripe mangoes
- 1 tablespoon sunflower oil
- 1 small onion, finely chopped
- 1-inch piece of fresh ginger root, finely chopped

- 1 garlic clove, crushed
- 2 teaspoons dark brown sugar
- ¼ teaspoon chili powder
- 2 tablespoons chopped fresh cilantro

1 First make the mango relish. (It can be made the day before.) Slice each mango on either side of the pit. Cut the flesh in these pieces into a criss-cross pattern; then push the skin inside out and slice off the flesh in neat dice. Cut the remaining mango flesh away from the pits and dice neatly.

2 Heat the oil in a saucepan. Add the onion, ginger root and garlic, and fry gently, stirring frequently, for about 5 minutes, until soft but not colored.

3 Add the diced mango, sugar, chilli and a pinch of salt. Sauté for a few minutes or until the mango softens slightly. Transfer to a bowl and let cool. Add the cilantro, cover and chill for at least 1 hour or overnight.

4 Put the duck breasts, skin-side down, between 2 sheets of plastic wrap or baking parchment and flatten them slightly by beating with a rolling pin.

5 Score the duck skin in a criss-cross pattern with a sharp knife and rub all over with salt.

6 Put the duck, skin-side up, on a rack in a roasting pan. Place in a preheated oven, 400°F, for 20–25 minutes, until the duck is tender.

7 Slice the breasts on the diagonal, removing the skin if preferred. Serve on warmed plates, with the chilled mango relish.

Jamaican jerked chicken

Serves 6
Preparation: 20 minutes, plus 1–2 hours marinating
Cooking: 20–30 minutes
Carbohydrate: 61 g, Protein: 33 g, Fat: 6 g, Fiber: 2 g, Calories: 411 kcal, Sodium: 244 mg (per portion)

What you need:

- 3 tablespoons allspice berries
- 2-inch piece cinnamon stick
- 1 teaspoon grated nutmeg
- 1 fresh red chili, deseeded and finely chopped
- 4 scallions, thinly sliced
- 1 bay leaf, crumbled
- 1 tablespoon dark rum
- 6 chicken pieces
- salt and pepper

For the pineapple chutney:
- 2 fresh pineapples, peeled and chopped
- 1-inch piece of fresh ginger root, finely chopped
- 1 onion, finely chopped
- 1 fresh red chili, deseeded and finely chopped
- ½ cup vinegar
- 1⅓ cups dark brown sugar

1 Pound the allspice, cinnamon and nutmeg in a mortar, or grind them to a powder in an electric grinder. Add the chili, scallions, bay leaf and seasoning, and pound to a thick paste.

2 Stir the rum into the paste and mix well. Make 2 or 3 deep cuts in each chicken piece and rub the paste all over the chicken. Leave to marinate in the refrigerator or a cool place for 1–2 hours.

3 For the pineapple chutney, put all the ingredients in a saucepan over medium heat and stir until the sugar has dissolved. Bring to a boil; then reduce the heat a little and cook vigorously, stirring occasionally, until thick. Pour into sterilized jars and seal. It can be kept for 2–3 weeks in the refrigerator.

4 Roast the jerked chicken at 400°F, for 20–30 minutes, or cook under a hot broiler. Serve with rice.

Below: *Duck breasts with spicy mango relish*
Above: *Jamaican jerked chicken*

Above:
Chicken biryani

Chicken biryani

Serves 4
Preparation: 30 minutes, plus
30 minutes marinating
Cooking: 50 minutes
Carbohydrate: 103 g, Protein: 40 g,
Fat: 28 g, Fiber: 2 g, Calories: 790 kcal,
Sodium: 422 mg (per portion)

What you need:

- 8 chicken drumsticks
- ¼ cup ghee or butter
- ¼ cup chopped almonds
- ¼ cup chopped cashew nuts
- 1 large onion, finely chopped
- 4 bay leaves
- biryani spice mixture (see Cook's Tip)
- 2¼ cups long-grain rice
- ½ teaspoon saffron threads
- salt

For the paste:

- 1 teaspoon garam masala
- 1 small onion, chopped
- 2 garlic cloves, crushed
- 2-inch piece of fresh ginger root, peeled
- ⅔ cup plain yogurt
- 1 teaspoon salt

To garnish:

- fresh cilantro
- slivers of red chili

1 Grind all the paste ingredients together with a pestle and mortar until smooth. Rub the paste over the chicken and leave to marinate for 30 minutes.

2 Heat the ghee in a skillet. Fry the almonds and cashews until golden brown. Remove with a slotted spoon and drain on paper towels. Set aside for the garnish. Add the onion to the pan and fry until golden. Remove half and reserve for the garnish.

3 Add the bay leaves and biryani spices to the onion in the pan, stir well; then add the chicken. Cook over a medium heat for 20 minutes. Stir in the rice, then add 3¾ cups warm water and some salt. Cover and cook for 15–20 minutes, until the rice is tender and all the water absorbed.

4 Steep the saffron in a little hot water for 5 minutes; stir into the rice. Garnish with the fried nuts and onions, cilantro and chili.

Cook's Tip

To make a biryani spice mixture, mix together 4 whole cloves, 8 black peppercorns, 4 green cardamom pods, 1 crushed black cardamom, 2-inch piece cinnamon stick and ½ teaspoon turmeric.

Chicken vindaloo

Serves 6
Preparation: 15 minutes, plus
1 hour marinating
Cooking: 55 minutes
Carbohydrate: 7 g, Protein: 42 g,
Fat: 16 g, Fiber: 2 g, Calories: 338 kcal,
Sodium: 798 mg (per portion)

What you need:

- 2 tablespoons hot curry powder
- 4 tablespoons vinegar
- 6 large chicken pieces
- 6 tablespoons mustard oil
- 4 bay leaves
- 1 teaspoon green cardamom seeds
- 1 large onion, thinly sliced
- 2 teaspoons turmeric
- 1 teaspoon chili powder
- 10 garlic cloves, crushed
- 1-inch piece of fresh ginger root, thinly sliced
- 2 tomatoes, peeled and quartered
- 2 teaspoons shredded coconut
- salt

1 Put the curry powder, 2 teaspoons of the vinegar and 2 teaspoons salt in a bowl, and mix until smooth.

2 Make 2 or 3 deep cuts in each chicken piece and rub the paste over the chicken. Leave to marinate in the refrigerator or a cool place for 1 hour.

3 Heat the oil in a large saucepan and stir in the bay leaves and cardamom seeds. Add the onion and fry until light brown. Stir in the turmeric and chili, then add the chicken. Cook, stirring occasionally, for 15 minutes. Add the garlic, ginger root, tomatoes, and 1 teaspoon salt, and cook for 10 minutes.

4 When the fat starts to separate, add the remaining vinegar and ⅓ cup water and stir well. Cover the pan and simmer slowly for 20–25 minutes, until the chicken is tender. Sprinkle with coconut and serve.

Cook's Tip

Mustard oil is a pungent yellow oil that is widely used in Indian cooking. It is available from many Asian stores, but if you cannot obtain it, groundnut oil can be substituted.

Chili chicken with pine nuts

Serves 4
Preparation: 30 minutes
Cooking: 15 minutes
Carbohydrate: 15 g, Protein: 35 g, Fat: 21 g, Fiber: 1 g, Calories: 391 kcal, Sodium: 1101 mg (per portion)

What you need:

- 4 boneless, skinless chicken breasts
- 4 tablespoons sunflower oil
- 1 red bell pepper, deseeded and cut into thin strips
- 1 green bell pepper, deseeded and cut into thin strips
- 1 fresh red chili, deseeded and finely chopped
- 1 fresh green chili, deseeded and finely chopped
- ½ cup pine nuts
- 1 garlic clove, finely chopped
- 4 tablespoons dry white wine
- 2 tablespoons lemon juice
- 3 tablespoons oyster sauce
- 2 teaspoons superfine sugar
- 1 teaspoon chili sauce
- 4 tablespoons light soy sauce

- 1 tablespoon cornstarch
- salt and pepper
- 2 scallions, sliced diagonally, to garnish

1 Cut the chicken into 2- by ¼-inch strips. Sprinkle with salt and pepper. Heat 2 tablespoons of the oil in a wok or large skillet. Add the chicken strips and cook, stirring constantly, for 5 minutes, or until tender. Remove the chicken and reserve.

2 Heat the remaining oil in the wok or skillet. Stir-fry the red and green bell pepper strips for 2 minutes, until just cooked. Lift out and reserve.

3 Add the chilies, pine nuts and garlic to the pan, and stir-fry for 1 minute. Drain off and discard any excess fat; then add the white wine, lemon juice, oyster sauce, sugar and chili sauce.

Cook, stirring frequently, for 1 minute.

4 Blend the soy sauce and cornstarch together; then add to the chili mixture and bring to a boil. Return the cooked chicken and bell pepper strips to the wok or skillet, then cover and cook over a medium heat until the chicken has warmed through.

5 Serve at once, sprinkled with the sliced scallions.

Above: *Chicken vindaloo*
Below: *Chili chicken with pine nuts*

Turkey, spinach and Brie filo pie

Serves 6–8
Preparation: 25 minutes
Cooking: 25 minutes
Carbohydrate: 26 g, Protein: 25 g,
Fat: 28 g, Fiber: 2 g, Calories: 446 kcal,
Sodium: 332 mg (per portion)

What you need:

- 1 cup frozen leaf spinach, thawed
- ⅓ cup butter
- 1 tablespoon olive oil
- ¼ cup pine nuts
- 12 ounces boneless turkey breast, cut into strips
- 6 ounces Brie cheese, rind removed, cut into chunks
- 4 scallions, chopped
- 1 teaspoon dry oregano
- grated rind and juice of 1 lemon
- 8 ounces filo pastry, thawed if frozen
- salt and pepper

1 Squeeze the spinach to re-move excess water; chop roughly.
2 Melt 2 tablespoons of the butter with the oil in a skillet. Fry the pine nuts for 1–2 minutes then add the turkey and fry until browned. Lower the heat and fry for 5 minutes, or until cooked. Mix the contents of the pan with the spinach, Brie, scallions, oregano, lemon rind and juice, and seasoning.
3 Grease a baking sheet and have the filo pastry ready, keep-ing it covered while you work. Melt the remaining butter.
4 Cover the baking sheet with 3 layers of filo pastry, brushing each layer with melted butter. Put the spinach filling on the center third of the pastry, about 1 inch from the top and bottom edges.

Layer the remaining pastry over the filling, brushing with butter. Fold in the sides of the pastry to enclose the filling, then scrunch the pastry on top.

5 Place in a preheated oven, 400°F, for 25 minutes, until the pastry is golden and crisp.

Chicken pie

Serves 4–6
Preparation: 30 minutes
Cooking: 1¼ hours
Carbohydrate: 40 g, Protein: 16 g, Fat: 47 g, Fiber: 3 g, Calories: 637 kcal, Sodium: 850 mg (per portion)

What you need:

- 1 tablespoon all-purpose flour
- 4 skinless chicken pieces, halved
- 2 tablespoons butter
- 1 tablespoon olive oil
- 2 onions, chopped
- 1¼ cups chicken stock
- 2 tablespoons lemon juice
- ⅔ cup heavy cream
- 1 bunch of parsley, chopped
- plain pastry dough (see Step 5)
- beaten egg, or milk, to glaze
- 1 tablespoon sesame seeds
- salt and pepper

1 Put the flour in a polythene bag and season. Add the chicken pieces and toss until coated.
2 Heat the butter and oil in a skillet, and fry the onions for 5 minutes, until soft. Remove the onions with a slotted spoon.

Left: *Turkey, spinach and Brie filo pie*
Above right: *Chicken pie*

3 Add the chicken to the pan and fry for 10 minutes, until evenly browned. Transfer the chicken to a 6-cup pie dish. Sprinkle the onions over the top.
4 Stir any remaining flour into the pan and cook for 1 minute. Gradually add the stock, stirring until the sauce is thick and smooth, scraping the bottom of the pan to incorporate any sediment. Stir in the lemon juice, then the cream, parsley and seasoning to taste. Bring to a boil, then pour the sauce over the chicken in the pie dish.
5 Roll out the dough to measure 2 inches larger than the pie dish. Cut off a 1-inch strip all round. Dampen the edge of the dish and attach the dough strip. Brush the strip with water and cover the pie with the remaining dough. Press the edges to seal, and make a hole in the center to let steam escape.
6 Brush with milk or beaten egg and sprinkle with sesame seeds. Place the pie in a preheated oven, 400°F, for 30 minutes, then reduce to 350°F, and bake for 45 minutes longer. Cover the top over with foil, if it becomes too brown. Serve the pie hot with new potatoes and green beans.

Roast pheasant flambéed with Calvados

Serves 4
Preparation: 30 minutes
Cooking: 45 minutes
Carbohydrate: 21 g, Protein: 53 g, Fat: 36 g, Fiber: 3 g, Calories: 665 kcal, Sodium: 473 mg (per portion)

What you need:

- 2 pheasants, preferably hen birds, plucked and cleaned, ready for the oven
- 1 large onion, quartered
- ¼ cup butter
- 4 tart eating apples, peeled, cored and thickly sliced
- ¼ cup all-purpose flour
- 300 ml/½ pint dry white wine
- 4 tablespoons Calvados
- ⅓ cup heavy cream
- 2 tablespoons chopped fresh parsley
- salt and pepper

1 Place the prepared pheasants in a roasting pan. Tuck the onion quarters under the birds and sprinkle with a little salt and pepper. Dot with the butter and place in a preheated oven, 375°F. Roast for about 45 minutes, or until the pheasants are cooked and tender.

2 Add the apples to the pan 15–20 minutes before the end of the cooking time.

3 Have ready a warmed serving dish. Remove the pheasants from the roasting pan and transfer them to the dish. Place the apple slices in a separate dish and keep them hot while making the sauce.

4 Stir the flour into the pan juices and cook over a medium heat for 1 minute. Stir in the dry white wine and bring to a boil, stirring all the time. Remove from the heat.

5 Heat the Calvados in a small saucepan until it is just warm. Carefully set it alight and when the flames die down, add it to the sauce. Stir in the cream and chopped parsley and adjust the seasoning to taste, then reheat the sauce slowly without boiling.

6 Cut the pheasants in half or carve the meat neatly. Serve the pheasants with the apple slices and a little of the sauce; serve the remaining sauce separately.

Cook's Tip

It is best to use young pheasants for roasting, as older birds can be dry. Adapt the recipe for older pheasants by cooking them in a covered casserole with the wine. Remove them and keep warm while you finish the sauce. Whisk in a little beurre manié (see Cook's Tip, right), then finish the sauce as in Step 5.

Below:
Roast pheasant flambéed with Calvados

Canard à la niçoise

Serves 4
Preparation: 15 minutes
Cooking: 1¾ hours
Carbohydrate: 21 g, Protein: 53 g, Fat: 83 g, Fiber: 7 g, Calories: 1103 kcal, Sodium: 1558 mg (per portion)

What you need:

- 4½–5½ pound duck
- 2 tablespoons olive oil
- 1 onion, finely chopped
- 2 pounds tomatoes, peeled and chopped
- 2 red bell peppers, deseeded and diced
- 1 celery stalk, chopped
- 2 carrots, finely diced
- 4 garlic cloves, crushed
- 1¾ cups dry white wine
- 1 bay leaf
- 2 teaspoons fresh thyme
- 1¾ cups small black olives
- salt and pepper

1 Season the inside of the duck with salt and pepper. Place the duck in a lightly oiled roasting pan and cook in a preheated oven, 400°F, for 30 minutes.

2 Meanwhile, heat the remaining oil in a skillet, and add the onion, tomatoes, bell peppers, celery and carrots. Cook slowly until the vegetables are soft, and then stir in the garlic.

3 Add 1 cup of the wine, the bay leaf and thyme, and cook slowly for 15–20 minutes. Stir in the olives.

4 Remove the duck from the oven and carefully pour the sauce over the top. Reduce the oven temperature to 350°F, and continue to roast the duck for about 1¼ hours, or until it is cooked and tender.

5 Remove the duck and keep it warm. Stir the remaining wine into the sauce in the roasting pan and cook over a high heat for a few minutes, stirring constantly, until reduced and thickened. Carve the duck and serve with the sauce.

Duck with oranges

Serves 6
Preparation: 20 minutes
Cooking: 1½ hours
Carbohydrate: 11 g, Protein: 56 g,
Fat: 99 g, Fiber: 1 g, Calories: 1247
kcal, Sodium: 1244 mg (per portion)

What you need:

- ¼ cup butter
- 2 tablespoons olive oil
- 1 4-pound duck, trussed
- 4 garlic cloves, crushed
- bacon slices, cut into thin strips
- 2½ cups dry white wine
- scant 1 cup chicken stock
- 1 bouquet garni
- pared rind and juice of 2 oranges
- 1 tablespoon flour
- 1 tablespoon wine vinegar
- salt and pepper
- 2 oranges, cut into thin rings, to garnish

1 Heat 2 tablespoons of the butter with the oil in a deep flameproof casserole. Add the duck and fry over medium heat until it is golden brown all over.
2 Add the garlic and strips of bacon to the casserole and fry for 1–2 minutes. Pour in the wine and stock. Bring to a boil and then simmer for a few minutes, until slightly reduced. Add the bouquet garni, salt and pepper and orange juice, and cover the casserole. Reduce the heat and

simmer slowly for 1½ hours, or until the duck is cooked. Baste occasionally during cooking.
3 Using a sharp knife, cut the pared orange rind into fine strips and plunge them into a small saucepan of boiling water. Boil for 5 minutes, then remove and drain. Dry thoroughly on paper towels and set aside.
4 Mash the remaining butter with a fork to soften, then beat in the flour until smooth.
5 Remove the cooked duck from the casserole, cut into serving pieces and keep warm. Boil the cooking liquid for about 10 minutes, until reduced and well flavored. Add the vinegar, strips of orange rind and little pieces of the butter and flour paste, stirring all the time, until the sauce thickens. Carve the duck and serve with the orange sauce, garnished with orange rings.

Cook's Tip

Add the butter and flour paste (beurre manié) at the end of cooking to thicken and enrich sauces and stews.

Above: *Canard à la niçoise*
Below: *Duck with oranges*

Meat

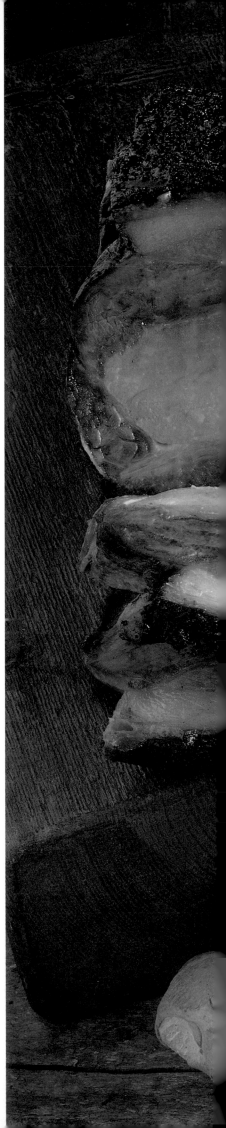

When it comes to meat dishes, we are spoiled for choice. Choose from lamb, beef, pork, veal or venison, and then choose your favorite method of cooking it. Whether it's leek and ham pie for a family meal, tournedos en croûte for a special celebratory dinner, paupiettes de veau for a party with friends or gigot au pistou for a grand weekend lunch, there's something here to suit every taste and every occasion. None of the recipes are difficult and all are absolutely delicious.

Below: *Leg of lamb à l'ail*
Right: *Spiced roast pork*

Lamb with garlic

Serves 6
Preparation: 25 minutes
Cooking: 2–2½ hours
Carbohydrate:68 g, Protein: 67 g, Fat: 53 g, Fiber: 0.5 g, Calories: 749 kcal, Sodium: 645 mg (per portion)

What you need:

- 1 cup chopped bacon
- 3 garlic cloves, crushed
- 2 teaspoons finely chopped fresh basil
- 1 tablespoon finely chopped fresh parsley
- 1 4-pound leg of lamb
- 2 tablespoons butter
- salt and pepper
- sprigs of fresh rosemary, to garnish

1 In a small bowl mix the bacon, garlic, basil and parsley.
2 Make a cut in the leg of lamb, through to the bone, and place the bacon mixture inside. Sew up the meat, enclosing the stuffing.
3 Put the lamb in a roasting pan, and spread with the butter. Place in a preheated oven, 350°F, for 2–2½ hours, depending on how well done you like your lamb to be.
4 Remove the string from the lamb and serve garnished with the sprigs of rosemary.

Spiced roast pork

Serves 6
Preparation: 10 minutes
Cooking: 2 hours

Carbohydrate: 3.5 g, Protein: 66 g, Fat: 53 g, Fiber: 0 g, Calories: 810 kcal, Sodium: 450 mg (per portion)

What you need:

- 1 4-pound pork loin
- ½ teaspoon ground cloves
- ½ teaspoon ground allspice
- 1 teaspoon ground ginger
- 2 garlic cloves, crushed
- 1 bay leaf, crumbled
- ¾ cup dark rum
- 2½ cups meat stock
- ½ cup soft brown sugar
- juice of 1 lime
- 2 teaspoons arrowroot
- salt and pepper

1 Using a very sharp knife, cut through the fat on the pork loin making a diamond pattern. Mix together the cloves, allspice, ginger, garlic, bay leaf, and salt and pepper, in a small bowl. Rub this over the scored pork fat.

2 Place the pork in a roasting pan. Pour ½ cup of the rum and ½ cup of the meat stock over the pork. Place the pork in a preheated oven, 350°F, and roast for 1¾–2 hours.

3 After 1 hour, blend the remaining rum with the sugar and lime juice, and use to baste the pork, adding more stock and a little water if necessary to moisten the meat a little.

4 When the meat is cooked, transfer it to a serving plate and keep warm. Discard most of the fat and add the remaining basting sauce and stock. Stir well to scrape up any meat residues. Place the pan over a medium heat and bring to a boil, stirring constantly. Mix the arrowroot with 1 tablespoon of water and stir into the gravy until thickened. Serve this gravy with the roast pork.

2 Put one-third of the mixture into a casserole. Cover with a layer of potatoes. Repeat the layering twice more, and pour over the stock. Dot with butter.

3 Cover and place in a preheated oven, 350°F, for 1½ hours. Remove the lid and bake for 15 minutes longer to brown the top layer of potatoes.

Pork and potato bake

Serves 4–6
Preparation: 30 minutes
Cooking: 1¾ hours
Carbohydrate: 20 g, Protein: 22 g, Fat: 15 g, Fiber: 2 g, Calories: 295 kcal, Sodium: 549 mg (per portion)

What you need:

- 1 tablespoon vegetable oil
- ½ cup chopped, rindless bacon
- 1 large onion, chopped
- 4 ounces mushrooms, quartered
- 1 teaspoon chopped fresh sage, or ½ teaspoon dry
- 1 teaspoon chopped fresh thyme, or ½ teaspoon dry
- 1 pound lean pork, cubed and tossed in 2 tablespoons seasoned flour
- 1 pound potatoes, sliced
- 1¼ cups chicken stock
- 2 tablespoons butter
- salt and pepper

1 Heat the oil in a skillet over a low heat. Add the bacon and fry for 3 minutes. Add the onion and cook until soft. Add the mushrooms, herbs and seasoning, and cook for 1 minute. Using a slotted spoon, remove the bacon and mushrooms from the pan and set aside. Brown the pork gently in the pan, then mix with the bacon and mushrooms.

Biscuit-topped lamb

Serves 4–6
Preparation: 40 minutes
Cooking: 25 minutes
Carbohydrate: 36 g, Protein: 26 g, Fat: 27 g, Fiber: 2 g, Calories: 502 kcal, Sodium: 663 mg (per portion)

What you need:

- 1 tablespoon olive oil
- ½ cup chopped rindless smoked bacon
- 1 onion, chopped
- 5 cups ground lamb
- 1 teaspoon dry oregano
- 2 tablespoons chopped fresh parsley
- ⅔ cup red wine
- 1¾ cups canned chopped tomatoes
- salt and pepper

For the topping:
- 2 cups self-rising flour
- ¼ cup diced chilled butter
- ¾ cup grated, sharp Cheddar cheese
- 2 teaspoons whole-grain mustard
- ½ cup milk

1 Heat the olive oil in a skillet. Add the chopped bacon and onion, and fry for 5 minutes, until softened. Add the lamb and fry, stirring, until evenly browned.

Above: *Pork and potato bake*
Right: *Biscuit-topped lamb*
Far right: *Leek and ham pie with cheese crust*

Shepherd's pie

Replace the biscuit topping with mashed potatoes. Boil 1½ pounds potatoes, then drain well and mash with 2 tablespoons butter, 3 tablespoons milk and salt and pepper to taste. Spread over the pie, sprinkle with ¼ cups grated cheese and bake as for the main recipe.

2 Stir in the herbs, wine and tomatoes, with salt and pepper to taste. Bring to a boil; then lower the heat and simmer, uncovered, for just about 25 minutes, until the lamb is cooked and the sauce is thickened.

3 For the biscuit topping, place the flour in a bowl with a little salt and pepper. Rub in the butter until the mixture resembles fine bread crumbs. Stir in ½ cup of the cheese, then add the mustard and enough of the milk to mix to a soft dough.

4 Knead the dough briefly on a lightly floured surface, then roll out to a thickness of ½ inch. Stamp into 2-inch rounds. Reroll the trimmings and stamp out more rounds.

5 Transfer the meat mixture to a large ovenproof dish. Arrange the biscuits over the top. Brush with milk and sprinkle with the remaining cheese. Place in a preheated oven, 400°F, for about 25 minutes, until golden brown. Serve hot.

Leek and ham pie with cheese crust

Serves 4
Preparation: 25 minutes
Cooking: 25–30 minutes
Carbohydrate: 61 g, Protein: 23 g, Fat: 34 g, Fiber: 4 g, Calories: 628 kcal, Sodium: 1427 mg (per portion)

What you need:

- ¼ cup butter
- 3 leeks, sliced
- ⅓ cup all-purpose flour
- 1¼ cups milk
- ⅔ cup vegetable stock
- 6 ounces cooked ham, cut into chunks

For the cheese crust:

- 2 cups self-rising flour
- ¼ cup diced chilled butter
- ¾ cup grated, sharp Cheddar cheese
- 6–8 tablespoons milk, plus extra to glaze

1 Melt the butter in a saucepan. Add the leeks and fry slowly until softened. Stir in the flour and cook for just 1 minute. Gradually add the milk and vegetable stock, stirring continuously until the sauce is thickened and smooth. Simmer for 5 minutes longer. Remove from the heat and stir in the ham, cut into chunks, with salt and pepper to taste.

2 For the cheese crust, place the flour in a bowl with a little salt and pepper, and rub in the butter until the mixture resembles fine bread crumbs. Stir in the cheese, then add enough of the milk to form a soft dough.

3 Transfer the leek mixture to a large ovenproof dish. On a lightly floured surface, press out the dough to a round, which should be the same size as the dish holding the leek mixture. Score into the dough wedges with a sharp knife, then place on top of the pie. Brush with milk.

4 Place the pie in a preheated oven, 400°F, for 25–30 minutes, until golden brown. Serve piping hot with a green vegetable or a fresh green salad.

Tournedos en croûte

Serves 4
Preparation: 30 minutes
Cooking: 30–35 minutes
Carbohydrate: 24 g, Protein: 49 g,
Fat: 49 g, Fiber: 1 g, Calories: 721 kcal,
Sodium: 937 mg (per portion)

What you need:

- 1 tablespoon oil
- 3 tablespoons butter
- 2 small onions, finely chopped
- 1 garlic clove, crushed
- 1⅓ cups finely chopped mushrooms
- pinch of grated nutmeg
- 4 fillet steaks, about 6 ounces each, trimmed
- 8 ounces puff pastry, thawed if frozen
- 1 egg, beaten
- 8 thin slices ham
- salt and pepper

Below: Tournedos en croûte
Below right: Porc aux pruneaux

1 Heat the oil and 2 tablespoons of the butter in a skillet. Cook the onions and garlic slowly until soft. Add the mushrooms, nutmeg, salt and pepper, and stir over a low heat until the mushrooms are cooked through and the moisture has evaporated. Remove the mushrooms from the pan and let cool; then divide into 8 portions.

2 Heat the remaining butter in a clean skillet Add the steaks and sear quickly on both sides. Remove the steaks from the pan, let cool, then chill until required.

3 Roll out the puff pastry dough on a lightly floured surface and cut into 4 rounds, 3 inches larger than the steaks; then brush a 1-inch border along the edge of each round with a little beaten egg. Then cut the thin ham slices into 8 rounds, about the same size as the steaks.

4 Place one piece of ham on each pastry round. Cover the ham with a portion of the mushroom mixture, a steak, another portion of mushrooms and then another round of ham. Bring the edges of the dough over to enclose the filling and press together to seal. Roll out the dough trimmings and cut out long thin strips. Brush the strips with water and wrap around the pastry packages. Place the packages, with the join underneath, on a damp baking sheet. Cut any remaining dough into decorative shapes and place on the packages. Brush with the remaining beaten egg, and place in a

preheated oven, 425°F, for 20 minutes, until golden brown in color.

Porc aux pruneaux

Serves 4
Preparation: 15 minutes, plus 4 hours soaking, or overnight
Cooking: 1¼ hours
Carbohydrate: 37 g, Protein: 31 g,
Fat: 17 g, Fiber: 6 g, Calories: 444 kcal,
Sodium: 191 mg (per portion)

What you need:

- 10 ounces large prunes
- 2 cups dry white wine
- 4 pork noisettes
- 2 tablespoons all-purpose flour, seasoned with salt and pepper
- 2 tablespoons butter
- 5 ounces button mushrooms
- 2 tablespoons redcurrant jelly
- scant 1 cup crème fraîche
- 3 tablespoons chopped fresh parsley

1 Soak the prunes in the white wine for several hours or overnight if more convenient.

2 Put the soaked prunes in an ovenproof dish together with 1¼ cups of the soaking liquid. Reserve the remaining liquid. Cover the dish and place in a preheated oven, 300°F, for just about 1 hour.

3 While the prunes are cooking, coat the pork noisettes lightly with the seasoned flour. Then melt the butter in a large sauté pan and fry the noisettes until they are lightly browned on both sides. Add the mushrooms to the pan, together with the reserved liquid from the prunes. Cover the pan and cook over low heat at a bare simmer for about 30 minutes. Turn the noisettes halfway through the cooking time.

4 Drain the prunes, reserving the cooking liquid, and keep them warm. Remove the noisettes from the pan with a slotted spoon and keep warm. Add the prune cooking liquid to the pan together with the redcurrant jelly, and boil until the sauce thickens slightly. Reduce the heat

to a simmer and then stir in the crème fraîche. Heat through without boiling, and adjust the seasoning to taste. Serve the pork and prunes with the warm sauce, sprinkled with parsley.

Paupiettes de veau aux olives

Serves 4
Preparation: 30 minutes
Cooking: 1 hour
Carbohydrate: 10 g, Protein: 49 g, Fat: 21 g, Fiber: 4 g, Calories: 448 kcal, Sodium: 2517 mg (per portion)

What you need:

- 8 thin slices veal escalopes
- 8 thin slices prosciutto or Bayonne ham
- 3 tablespoons olive oil
- 8 ounces small pickling onions, peeled
- 1 pound tomatoes, peeled, deseeded and quartered
- 1 teaspoon chopped fresh thyme
- 2 bay leaves
- ⅔ cup dry white wine
- 1 cup green olives
- 1 cup black olives
- salt and pepper
- 1 tablespoon chopped fresh parsley

1 Place each veal escalope on a slice of prosciutto or Bayonne ham. Roll up and tie each one securely with fine string.

2 Heat the oil in a large sauté pan. Add the pickling onions and fry slowly until they are golden brown color all over, turning occasionally.

3 Add the veal paupiettes to the pan together with the tomatoes, thyme, bay leaves, salt and pepper to taste. Pour the white wine over. Cover the pan and simmer slowly for 45 minutes.

4 Add the green and black olives to the pan and cook slowly for 15 minutes longer. To serve, remove the string from the paupiettes. Serve on a bed of freshly cooked spaghetti, with the tomato sauce poured over, sprinkled with parsley.

Above: Paupiettes de veau aux olives

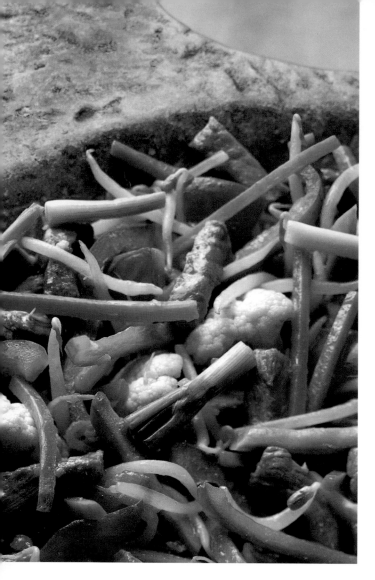

Pork chop suey

Serves 3–4
Preparation: 15 minutes
Cooking: 8–10 minutes
Carbohydrate: 15 g, Protein:17 g, Fat: 7 g, Fiber: 3 g, Calories: 194 kcal, Sodium: 1412 mg (per portion)

What you need:

- 2 tablespoons soy sauce
- 1 tablespoon dry sherry
- 2 teaspoon cornstarch
- 8 ounces pork tenderloin, sliced thinly and cut into strips
- 2 scallions
- 2 cups fresh bean sprouts
- 1 tablespoon oil
- 1 slice fresh ginger root, peeled and finely chopped
- 1 small green bell pepper, deseeded and cut into strips
- a few small cauliflower or broccoli florets
- 2–3 tomatoes, cut into pieces
- 2 carrots, cut into matchsticks
- 2 ounces green beans, trimmed
- 2 teaspoons salt
- 1 tablespoon sugar
- 3 tablespoons stock or water

1 Mix together the soy sauce, sherry and cornstarch. Add the pork strips. Stir well to coat the pork completely in the soy sauce/cornstarch mixture.

2 Cut the scallions into1-inch lengths. Wash the bean sprouts in a bowl of cold water and discard any husks that float to the surface of the water.

3 Heat half the oil in a wok or large, heavy skillet. Stir-fry the pork for 1 minute; then remove with a slotted spoon and set aside for a few minutes.

4 Add the remaining oil to the wok or skillet and heat. Add the scallions and ginger root, followed by the remaining vegetables and the salt and sugar. Stir-fry all of the vegetables for just 1–2 minutes, until they have heated through and have picked up the other flavors from the wok or skillet. Return the pork strips to the wok or skillet. Add the stock or water and stir-fry until the all vegetables are tender but still crisp to the bite. Serve immediately, with rice.

Ginger beef with bell peppers

Serves 3–4
Preparation: 10 minutes, plus 30 minutes marinating
Cooking: 5 minutes
Carbohydrate: 4 g, Protein: 28 g, Fat: 15 g, Fiber: 1 g, Calories: 258 kcal, Sodium: 702 mg (per portion)

What you need:

- 1 pound lean fillet steak, thinly sliced
- 2 teaspoons soy sauce
- 2 teaspoons sesame oil
- 1-inch piece fresh ginger root, peeled and sliced
- 2 teaspoons vinegar
- 1 tablespoon water
- 1 teaspoon salt
- 1 teaspoon cornstarch
- 1 garlic clove, crushed
- pinch of five-spice powder
- 1 red bell pepper, deseeded and cut into chunks
- 1 green bell pepper, deseeded and cut into chunks

To garnish:
- sliced scallions
- slivers of fresh red chili

1 Put the steak in a bowl and add the soy sauce, 1 teaspoon of the sesame oil, the ginger root, vinegar, water, salt and cornstarch. Stir well to mix until the steak slices are thoroughly coated in the mixture. Cover the bowl and leave in the refrigerator to marinate for at least 20 minutes.

2 Heat the remaining sesame oil in a wok or large, heavy skillet. Add the garlic and the five-spice powder. Stir-fry for 30 seconds and then quickly add the marinated steaks. Stir-fry over a high heat until the meat is browned on the outside yet still pink and tender on the inside. Remove and set aside.

3 Add the red and green bell peppers to the wok or skillet and stir-fry them briskly, over a high heat for 2–3 minutes, tossing them continuously to coat in the oil.

4 Return the strips of steak and any remaining marinade to the pan. Stir-fry for 1 minute, until the meat is heated through. Transfer to a serving dish and serve garnished with the scallions and chili.

Beef pasanda

Serves 4
Preparation: 15 minutes, plus marinating overnight
Cooking: 1¾ hours
Carbohydrate: 11 g, Protein: 33 g, Fat: 13 g, Fiber: 1 g, Calories: 280 kcal, Sodium: 662 mg (per portion)

What you need:

- 1 pound braising or stewing steak, finely sliced
- 1 teaspoon salt
- 1¼ cups plain yogurt
- 2 tablespoons ghee or butter
- 1 large onion, sliced
- 3 garlic cloves, sliced
- 1½ teaspoons ground ginger
- 2 teaspoons ground coriander
- 2 teaspoons chili powder
- ½ teaspoon ground cumin
- 1½ teaspoons turmeric
- 1 teaspoon garam masala

1 Place the finely sliced beef between 2 sheets of baking parchment and beat with a rolling pin or mallet until thin. Rub the beef with the salt, and then cut into serving pieces. Place in a large bowl. Add the yogurt, cover and let marinate overnight in the refrigerator.

2 Melt the ghee or butter in a heavy-bottomed saucepan. Fry the onion and garlic slowly for 4–5 minutes, until soft. Add the ground ginger, ground coriander, chili powder, ground cumin, turmeric, and garam masala, and then fry for 3 minutes longer, stirring constantly.

3 Add the beef together with its marinade, to the saucepan and stir. Cover the pan and simmer for 1½ hours, or until the meat is tender. Serve hot with rice.

Below: *Beef Pasanda*

Navarin of lamb printanier

Serves 4–6
Preparation: 30 minutes
Cooking: 1¾ hours
Carbohydrate: 37 g, Protein: 54 g,
Fat: 61 g, Fiber: 7 g, Calories: 905 kcal,
Sodium: 1047 mg (per portion)

What you need:

- 1 2-pound boneless lamb shoulder, or lamb tenderloin, trimmed of excess fat and cut into 2-inch cubes
- ½ cup all-purpose flour, seasoned with salt and pepper
- 2 tablespoons sunflower oil
- ¼ cup butter
- 8 ounces baby carrots, scrubbed
- 8 ounces baby turnips, peeled
- 8 ounces small pickling onions, peeled
- 1 garlic clove, crushed
- 2 cups chicken stock
- 2 teaspoons tomato paste
- small sprig of fresh rosemary
- ¾ cup frozen peas
- salt and pepper

1 Toss the meat in the seasoned flour, shake off and reserve any excess flour. Heat the sunflower oil in a flameproof casserole or heavy saucepan large enough to hold all the lamb, vegetables and the stock. Add the meat and fry briskly on all sides. Using a slotted spoon, remove from the pan and reserve.

2 Add the butter, baby carrots, baby turnips, onions and crushed garlic to the pan, and fry slowly until lightly browned all over. Then sprinkle in the reserved seasoned flour and cook slowly, stirring constantly, for about 1 minute.

3 Gradually stir in the chicken stock, tomato paste and rosemary. Bring to a boil, stirring constantly until the sauce has thickened and is smooth; then return the meat to the pan.

4 Cover the pan, reduce the heat and simmer, stirring just occasionally, for about 1 hour. Add the frozen peas and continue cooking for another 30 minutes, or until the meat is tender. Serve the navarin of lamb immediately with a fresh green vegetable or a mixed salad.

Boeuf à la bourguignonne

Serves 4–6
Preparation: 30 minutes, plus
4 hours marinating
Cooking: 2½ hours
Carbohydrate: 13 g, Protein: 63 g,
Fat: 54 g, Fiber: 3 g, Calories: 862 kcal,
Sodium:1166 mg (per portion)

What you need:

- 2 pounds chuck or round steak, cut into chunks
- few sprigs of fresh parsley
- few sprigs of fresh thyme
- 1 bay leaf, crushed
- 2 tablespoons brandy
- 1¾ cups red wine (preferably burgundy)
- 2 tablespoons olive oil
- ¼ cup butter
- 1¼ cups roughly chopped lean bacon
- 24 small onions, peeled
- 1 pound button mushrooms, halved
- ¼ cup all-purpose flour
- 1¼ cups beef stock
- 1 garlic clove, crushed
- 1 bouquet garni
- salt and pepper

1 Put the beef into a large bowl together with the parsley, thyme and the bay leaf. Add the brandy, red wine and oil, and stir once or twice; then cover the bowl and leave the beef to marinate for at least 4 hours.

2 Melt the butter in a flame-proof casserole. Add the roughly chopped bacon and fry over a medium heat until golden brown all over. Remove the bacon from the pan with a slotted spoon and set aside. Add the onions to the pan and fry until golden on all sides. Remove and set aside. Add the button mushrooms and fry, stirring, for 1 minute. Remove and set aside. Add the mushrooms and fry, stirring, for 1 minute. Remove and set aside.

3 Remove the beef from the marinade, strain and reserve. Add the beef to the casserole and fry briskly until browned on all sides. Sprinkle in the flour and cook, stirring, for 1 minute. Gradually stir in the strained marinade, then add the beef stock, garlic, bouquet garni, and the seasoning, to taste. Cover and simmer slowly for 2 hours.

4 Skim off any fat from the surface and add the bacon, onions and mushrooms to the casserole. Then cover and simmer for 30 minutes, or until tender. Discard the bouquet garni and serve.

Left: *Navarin of lamb printanier*
Right: *Bœuf à la bourguignonne*

Above: *Mexican chili shell bake*
Below right: *Parmesan meatballs*

Mexican chili shell bake

Serves 4
Preparation: 45 minutes
Cooking: 20 minutes
Carbohydrate: 45 g, Protein: 40 g,
Fat: 32 g, Fiber: 6 g, Calories: 609 kcal,
Sodium: 781 mg (per portion)

What you need:

- 1 tablespoon olive oil
- 2 garlic cloves, crushed
- 1 onion, finely chopped
- 1 green chili, deseeded and chopped
- 2 cups lean ground beef
- 2 teaspoons mild chili powder
- 3 tablespoons tomato paste
- 8 ounces dry wholewheat pasta shells
- 150 g/5 oz mozzarella cheese, grated
- 1¼ cups grated Cheddar cheese,
- 2 eggs, beaten
- salt and pepper

1 Heat the oil in a heavy saucepan. Add the crushed garlic and chopped onion, and fry for 5 minutes, stirring occasionally, until softened.
2 Add the chopped green chili and ground beef. Fry for 5 minutes, stirring constantly. Stir in the chili powder, tomato paste, with salt and pepper to taste. Simmer quite vigorously, par-

tially covered for 25 minutes, until the sauce is really quite dry and thick.
3 Meanwhile, bring at least 2 quarts water to a boil in a large saucepan. Add a dash of oil and a generous pinch of salt. Cook the pasta in the pan for 8–12 minutes, until tender. Drain the pasta and transfer it to a large oven-proof dish. Pour the sauce over the pasta and mix.
4 Mix the two cheeses with the beaten eggs and pour over the beef, chili and tomato paste mixture. Place the chili bake in a preheated oven, 375°F, for 20 minutes.

Parmesan meatballs

Serves 4
Preparation: 20 minutes
Cooking: 20 minutes
Carbohydrate: 8 g, Protein: 33 g,
Fat: 25 g, Fiber: 1 g, Calories: 385 kcal,
Sodium: 352 mg (per portion)

What you need:

- 1 onion, grated
- ½ cup grated Parmesan cheese
- 5 cups lean ground lamb
- 1 tablespoon tomato paste
- 1 teaspoon chili sauce
- 1 tablespoon mixed dry herbs
- 4 tablespoons olive oil
- salt and pepper

For the sauce:
- 1 onion, finely chopped
- 2 garlic cloves, crushed
- 1 tablespoon olive oil
- 1 14-ounce can chopped tomatoes
- 2 tablespoons tomato paste
- 2 tablespoons chopped fresh oregano
- oregano leaves, to garnish

1 In a large bowl combine the onion, Parmesan, ground lamb, tomato paste, chili sauce and herbs with seasoning to taste, and mix thoroughly.
2 Then using dampened hands, divide and shape the mixture into 30 small balls. Heat the olive oil in a large skillet. Fry the meatballs in 2 batches, for 10 minutes for each batch. Transfer the meatballs to a baking dish and keep hot.
3 For the sauce, fry the finely chopped onion and the crushed garlic together in the olive oil for 3-5 minutes, until softened. Stir in the chopped tomatoes, tomato paste and the oregano and simmer for 8 minutes.
4 Taste the sauce and adjust the seasoning if necessary; then toss the sauce thoroughly with some freshly cooked spaghetti. Serve the coated spaghetti with the hot meatballs and garnish the whole dish with oregano.

Lamb and pasta bake

Serves 4
Preparation: 20 minutes
Cooking: 45 minutes
Carbohydrate: 75 g, Protein: 31 g,
Fat: 16 g, Fiber: 9 g, Calories: 559 kcal,
Sodium: 992 mg (per portion)

Variation

Cilantro and chive meatballs

Replace the dry herbs in the recipe above with a bunch of chopped cilantro and a bunch of snipped chives. Add 1½ cups of finely chopped mushrooms to the meatball mixture. Continue as above.

What you need:

- 1 onion, sliced thinly in rings
- 1 tablespoon vegetable oil
- 8 ounces cooked lean lamb, cubed
- 1 14-ounce can chopped tomatoes
- 4 tablespoons tomato paste
- 2 tablespoons mixed dry herbs
- 1 14-ounce can red kidney beans, drained
- 1 teaspoon cornstarch
- 1 tablespoon water
- 6 ounces dry macaroni, cooked
- ¾ cup Cheddar cheese, grated
- 1½ cups fresh wholewheat bread crumbs
- salt and pepper

1 Fry the onion rings in the oil for 3 minutes, or until softened. Mix the softened onions with the lamb, tomatoes, tomato paste, herbs and kidney beans.

2 Mix the cornstarch with the water to form a smooth paste. Stir into the meat mixture, with the cooked pasta. Then season the mixture to taste.

3 Spoon the lamb mixture into a large ovenproof dish. Mix the cheese with the bread crumbs and sprinkle over the lamb mixture. Place in a preheated oven, 400°F, for about 45 minutes. You might need to cover the dish with foil after 30 minutes if the topping starts to over-brown.

Above: *Lamb and pasta bake*

Cook's Tip

Fresh herbs rather than dry herbs can add a lot of flavor and freshness to your dish. Thyme, sage and mint are all herbs which will go particularly well with lamb.
If you want to replace dry herbs with fresh herbs, use half the quantity given in the recipe.

Marinated veal with watercress sauce

Serves 4
Preparation: 30 minutes, plus
1–2 hours marinating
Cooking: 10–12 minutes
*Carbohydrate: 26 g, Protein: 59 g,
Fat: 24 g, Fiber: 6 g, Calories: 546 kcal,
Sodium: 678 mg (per portion)*

What you need:

- 4 veal loin chops, about
  8 ounces each
- finely grated rind and juice of
  2 oranges
- 1–2 garlic cloves, crushed
- 3 tablespoons olive oil

For the watercress sauce:

- ⅔ cups vegetable or meat
  stock
- 1 bunch watercress, leaves
  stripped from the stalks
- ¼ cup heavy cream
- salt and pepper

For the beet chips:

- 4 small whole raw beets,
  9–10 ounces each,
  peeled
- vegetable oil for deep-frying

1 Place the veal chops in a single layer in a shallow dish. Mix the orange rind and juice with the garlic and olive oil. Pour over the chops, and turn to coat; then cover the dish and leave to marinate for 1–2 hours.
2 For the watercress sauce, place the stock in a saucepan, bring to a boil. Add the watercress leaves and then simmer for 1–2 minutes. Tip the contents of the pan into a blender or food processor and then blend until just smooth.
3 For the beet chips, cut the beet into wafer-thin slices. Pat dry on paper towels and leave for 30 minutes. Heat the oil in a

deep-fat fryer or a deep pan to 375°F, or until a cube of bread browns in 30 seconds. Fry the beet slices in batches for just about 20–30 seconds each batch, until crisp and curly. Drain well on paper towels to absorb some of the oil.
4 Remove the veal chops from the marinade and place under a preheated hot broiler for 5–6 minutes on each side, basting often with the remaining marinade.
5 To serve, bring the watercress sauce to a boil in a small pan, stir in the cream and simmer for about 2 minutes. Season to taste. Serve the sauce with the veal chops and the beet chips.

Venison cutlets with red juniper berries

Serves 4
Preparation: 20 minutes
Cooking: 6–8 minutes
*Carbohydrate: 12 g, Protein: 43 g,
Fat: 10 g, Fiber: 0 g, Calories: 357 kcal,
Sodium: 114 mg (per portion)*

What you need:

- 4 eating pears
- 2 tablespoons lemon juice
- 1¼ cups red wine
- 6 juniper berries, crushed
- pared rind of 1 lemon, cut
  into fine julienne strips
- 1 cinnamon stick
- 3 tablespoons redcurrant jelly
- 8 venison cutlets
- oil or melted butter, for
  brushing
- a bunch of watercress, to
  garnish

1 Peel the pears; then halve them lengthways and remove the cores with a melon baller. Brush the flesh with the lemon juice to prevent discoloration.
2 Place the red wine, juniper berries, lemon rind and cinnamon stick in a pan. Bring to a boil. Add the pears, cover and simmer for 10 minutes.
3 Using a slotted spoon, transfer the pears to a bowl and set aside. Stir the redcurrant jelly into the liquid remaining in the

Left: *Venison cutlets with red juniper berries*
Below: *Fillet steaks with anchovy butter*

anchovies until well blended. Add the lemon juice, parsley and plenty of pepper, and mix well. (The easiest way to do this is in a blender or a food processor. If you have a pulse button on your processor then use it, to make sure all the ingredients are evenly incorporated; otherwise turn your blender or food processor on and off whilst mixing to achieve the same result.) Mold the anchovy butter into a fat sausage shape and wrap in foil. Place in the refrigerator for at least 30 minutes, until chilled and firm.

2 Heat the butter and olive oil in a heavy skillet. Season the steaks on both sides with salt and pepper, then fry until they are done to your liking; turning once, 2–3 minutes on each side for rare steaks, 6–8 minutes (over a slightly lower heat) for medium to well-done.

3 Serve each steak topped with a slice of the anchovy butter sprinkled with chopped parsley. Let the butter melt from the heat of the steak as you serve it.

saucepan. Boil the mixture until reduced by half. Pour the reduced liquid over the pears and leave to cool.

4 Brush the venison cutlets with a little oil or butter and place under a hot broiler for 2–3 minutes on each side. To serve, place 2 cutlets on each plate and add a portion of pears. Garnish with the watercress and serve the remaining pears separately.

Fillet steaks with anchovy butter

Serves 4
Preparation: 5 minutes, plus 30 minutes chiling
Cooking: 5–10 minutes
Carbohydrate: 0 g, Protein: 33 g, Fat: 34 g, Fiber: 0 g, Calories: 437 kcal, Sodium: 530 mg (per portion)

What you need:

- 2 tablespoons butter
- 1 tablespoon olive oil
- 4 fillet steaks, about 5 ounces each

- salt and pepper
- 2 tablespoons finely chopped fresh parsley, to garnish

For the anchovy butter:

- ¼ cup unsalted butter
- 4 canned anchovies, drained and chopped
- squeeze of lemon juice
- 2 tablespoons finely chopped fresh parsley

1 First make the anchovy butter: mix all the butter with the

Barbecues

As soon as the good weather comes round again, it's out with the charcoal, on with the pot holders or thick gloves, matches at the ready, and it's barbecue time again! Barbecues have become even more popular in recent times, and outdoor eating can now be a much more sophisticated affair than it used to be. Barbecues are the perfect way of entertaining family and friends. Relaxed and informal, they do much to heighten the exhilaration of summer. There's nothing quite like the smell of charcoal-cooked food wafting in the balmy night air to make any occasion seem like a special one.

Grilled sardines in chili oil

Serves 4
Preparation: 15 minutes, plus 8–12 hours infusing
Cooking: 6–8 minutes
Carbohydrate: 0 g, Protein: 35 g, Fat: 23 g, Fiber: 0 g, Calories: 347 kcal, Sodium: 697 mg (per portion)

What you need:

- ½ cup olive oil
- 2 tablespoons chopped dried red chilies
- 12 small sardines, cleaned and scaled
- coarse sea salt

1 Place the oil and chilies in a small saucepan and heat very slowly for 10 minutes. Remove the pan from the heat. Cover and let cool and infuse for about 8–12 hours.
2 Strain the oil through a strainer lined with cheesecloth or a clean towel, then pour into a sterilized jar or bottle.
3 Brush the prepared sardines with a little of the chili oil, then sprinkle with coarse sea salt. Cook the fish on an oiled barbecue grid over hot coals for about 6–8 minutes, or until the sardines are just cooked, turning once. Serve immediately, with lemon wedges, hot crusty bread, and a mixed salad, if liked.

Left: *Grilled sardines in chilli oil*
Right: *Monkfish with rosemary*

Monkfish with rosemary

Serves 4
Preparation: 30 minutes, plus
1 hour marinating
Cooking: 25–30 minutes
*Carbohydrate: 5 g, Protein: 28 g, Fat:
10 g, Fiber: 1 g, Calories: 219 kcal,
Sodium: 338 mg (per portion)*

What you need:

- 1 pound ripe tomatoes, peeled
- 1 tablespoon balsamic vinegar
- 2 monkfish fillets, about 12 ounces each, skinned
- 4 garlic cloves, cut into thin slivers
- 2 long fresh sprigs of rosemary
- 5 tablespoons olive oil
- 1 tablespoon lemon juice
- salt and pepper

1 Put the tomatoes into a liquidizer or food processor and purée until smooth. Press through a strainer into a bowl. Season with the vinegar, salt and pepper, then cover and set aside.
2 Slice each fillet lengthways, almost but not quite all the way through, making a pocket. Lay the garlic down the pocket lengths. Top with a rosemary sprig and season to taste. Re-form both fillets and tie with string at ¾-inch intervals.
3 Mix the oil and lemon juice in a large shallow dish. Add the fillets, spoon the marinade over the top and cover. Leave for 1 hour, turning occasionally.
4 Drain the fish and cook on an oiled barbecue grid over fairly hot coals for 20 minutes, basting frequently, until just cooked.
5 Remove the string. Slice the fish thinly. Serve with the tomato sauce, warmed through.

3 Put the drumsticks on oiled grid over hot charcoal on the barbecue. Cook, turning frequently, for about 20 minutes until the chicken is charred on the outside and no longer pink on the inside.

4 Meanwhile, pour the marinade into a small saucepan. Add the stock and bring to a boil over a medium heat, stirring. Simmer, stirring occasionally, until the sauce has reduced and thickened very slightly.

5 Serve the drumsticks hot, with the barbecue sauce. A rice pilaf and a mixed bell pepper salad are ideal accompaniments.

Turkey, tomato and tarragon burgers

Serves 4
Preparation: 20 minutes
Cooking: 20–25 minutes
Carbohydrate: 26 g, Protein: 38 g,
Fat: 26 g, Fiber: 1 g, Calories: 484 kcal,
Sodium: 1128 mg (per portion)

What you need:

- 8 sun-dried tomato halves in oil, drained and chopped
- 5 cups ground turkey
- 1 tablespoon chopped fresh tarragon
- ½ red onion, finely chopped
- ¼ teaspoon paprika
- ¼ teaspoon salt

Above: Barbecued chicken drumsticks
Below right: *Turkey, tomato and tarragon burgers*

Barbecued chicken drumsticks

Serves 8
Preparation: 15 minutes, plus 4 hours marinating, or overnight
Cooking: about 20 minutes
Carbohydrate: 6 g, Protein: 18 g,
Fat: 4 g, Fiber: 0 g, Calories: 131 kcal,
Sodium: 458 mg (per portion)

What you need:

- 16 chicken drumsticks
- 1¼ cups chicken stock

For the marinade:

- 4 tablespoons tomato ketchup
- 2 tablespoons Worcestershire sauce
- 2 tablespoons wine vinegar
- 2 tablespoons soft brown sugar
- 2 teaspoons chili powder
- 1 teaspoon celery salt

1 Score the drumsticks deeply with a sharp pointed knife, cutting down as far as the bone.

2 Whisk together all the marinade ingredients in a shallow dish. Add the drumsticks and turn to coat; then cover and leave in the refrigerator for at least 4 hours or preferably overnight, turning the drumsticks in the marinade occasionally.

Variation

Chicken tikka

Replace the chicken portions with 4 large skinned and boned chicken breasts, cut into cubes, and proceed as in the main recipe. After marinating, thread the cubes of chicken onto kebab skewers. Place the skewers on the oiled grid over hot charcoal on the barbecue (or under the broiler) and cook turning the skewers often, for about 10–15 minutes until the chicken juices run clear.

- 4 slices of smoked pancetta or rindless bacon, cut in half
- 4 ciabatta rolls
- shredded radicchio and cos lettuce

1 Place the sun-dried tomatoes, turkey and tarragon in a liquidizer or food processor and purée until smooth. Spoon the mixture into a bowl and stir in the onion. Season with the paprika and salt. Mix well, divide into 4 and shape into burgers. Stretch 2 strips of pancetta or bacon over each burger and secure with toothpicks soaked in water for at least 30 minutes.

2 Cook on an oiled barbecue grid over hot coals for 20–25 minutes turning frequently. Serve at once in the ciabatta rolls with shredded salad greens.

Tandoori chicken

Serves 4
Preparation: 20 minutes, plus 4 hours marinating, or overnight
Cooking: 40 minutes
Carbohydrate: 4 g, Protein: 29 g, Fat: 8 g, Fiber: 0 g, Calories: 186 kcal, Sodium: 116 mg (per portion)

What you need:

- 1 fresh hot red chili, deseeded and roughly chopped
- 2 garlic cloves, roughly chopped
- 1-inch piece of fresh ginger root, roughly chopped
- 2 tablespoons lemon juice
- 1 tablespoon coriander seeds
- 1 tablespoon cumin seeds
- 2 teaspoons garam masala
- 6 tablespoons plain yogurt
- 2 teaspoons tumeric
- 1 teaspoon paprika
- 4 skinless chicken pieces

To garnish:
- lemon wedges
- cilantro sprigs

1 Put the chili, garlic, ginger roots and lemon juice in an electric spice mill with the whole spices and the garam masala, and work to a paste.

2 Transfer the spice paste to a shallow dish in which the chicken pieces will fit in a single layer. Add the yogurt, tumeric, paprika and ½ teaspoon salt. Stir well to mix. Set aside.

3 Score the flesh of the chicken deeply with a sharp pointed knife, cutting right down as far as the bone. Put the chicken in a single layer in the dish. Spoon the marinade over the chicken and brush it into the cuts in the flesh. Cover and marinate in the refrigerator for at least 4 hours, but preferably overnight.

4 Place the chicken on an oiled grid over hot charcoal on the barbecue. Cook, turning often, for about 30 minutes or until the juices run clear when pierced with a skewer or fork. Serve hot, garnished with lemon wedges and cilantro sprigs, and accompanied by a salad of lettuce, white cabbage and raw onion slices, a sauce made of yogurt and chopped mint, and plain or garlic naan bread.

Above: *Tandoori chicken*

Cook's Tip

Lamb would make a great substitute for chicken. Lamb cutlets are the best for barbecuing. Before cooking, the meat should be marinated, preferably overnight, then grilled to your liking.

Above: *Pork kebabs with prunes and chestnuts*
Below right: *Beef and pineapple kebabs*

Pork kebabs with prunes and chestnuts

Serves 4
Preparation: 15–25 minutes, plus
12 hours marinating
Cooking: 10–12 minutes
Carbohydrate: 56 g, Protein: 29 g,
Fat:19 g, Fiber: 8 g, Calories: 514 kcal,
Sodium: 309 mg (per portion)

What you need:

- 1 pound pork tenderloin, trimmed
- 24 pitted prunes
- 4 tablespoons Cognac
- 4 tablespoons olive oil
- 2 sprigs of fresh rosemary, leaves stripped from the stalks, then chopped
- 24 chestnuts, roasted, dried or vacuum-packed
- salt and pepper

1 Cut the pork into ¾-inch pieces. Place in a bowl with the prunes. Mix the Cognac, oil and rosemary in a pitcher and pour over the meat. Toss to coat, then cover and leave to marinate overnight in the refrigerator. If using dried chestnuts, soak them in cold water overnight, then drain and treat as fresh.

2 Place the chestnuts in a small pan, and cover with cold water. Bring to a boil, lower the heat, and simmer for 15–20 minutes, until just tender. Drain, rinse well in cold water, and drain again.

3 Using a big slotted spoon, remove the meat and prunes from the marinade. Thread onto skewers, alternating with the chestnuts (if the chestnuts are too soft to skewer, stuff one into each prune). Pour the marinade into a small pitcher and set aside.

4 Cook the skewers on an oiled barbecue grid over hot coals for about 10–12 minutes, turning frequently and basting with the marinade. Season and serve.

Beef and pineapple kebabs

Serves 4
Preparation: 20 minutes, plus
1 hour marinating
Cooking: 10 minutes
Carbohydrate: 26 g, Protein: 29 g,
Fat:17 g, Fiber: 2 g, Calories: 367 kcal,
Sodium: 277 mg (per portion)

What you need:

- 1 pound round steak
- 3 tomatoes
- 2 onions

- 1 green bell pepper
- 12 pineapple cubes, fresh or canned
- boiled rice, to serve

For the marinade:
- 1 tablespoon molasses
- 4 tablespoons pineapple juice
- 2 tablespoons vinegar
- 1 tablespoon oil
- salt and pepper

1 First make the marinade: put the molasses, pineapple juice, vinegar, and oil in a bowl, and mix together well. Add a little salt and some pepper.

2 Cut the steak into 1-inch cubes and add to the marinade. Cover and leave in a cool place for at least 1 hour. Remove the steak. Pour the marinade into a small pitcher and set aside for basting the kebabs.

3 Cut the tomatoes into quarters. Peel the onions and cut them into small chunks. Remove the core and seeds from the green bell pepper, and then cut it into squares.

4 Thread the steak, tomatoes, onions, bell pepper and pineapple chunks alternately onto 4 long or 8 short skewers. Brush with the reserved marinade. Cook on an oiled barbecue grid over hot coals for 10 minutes, turning frequently and basting with the marinade. Serve with plain boiled rice with the remaining marinade on top.

Chicken and bell pepper kebabs

Serves 4
Preparation: 15 minutes, plus 30-60 minutes marinating
Cooking: 20 minutes
Carbohydrate: 8 g, Protein: 39 g, Fat: 12 g, Fiber: 1 g, Calories: 288 kcal, Sodium: 669 mg (per portion)

Variation

Japanese chicken kebabs

Crush a 2-inch piece of ginger root to a paste with 4 garlic cloves and 8 black peppercorns.

Place ⅔ cup Japanese soy sauce (shoyu), ⅔ cup rice wine (sake), 2 tablespoons soft brown sugar, and 1 tablespoon oil in a large shallow dish. Add the ginger root and garlic paste, and whisk to combine.

Cut 1 pound skinless chicken breast fillets diagonally into thick strips. Add to the marinade, cover and marinate at room temperature for at least 30 minutes. Meanwhile, soak 16–18 bamboo skewers in warm water.

Drain the skewers, then thread the chicken strips onto them. Cook on an oiled barbecue grid over hot coals for 8–10 minutes until the chicken is tender. Turn the skewers and baste the chicken with the marinade frequently during cooking. Serve hot, garnished with scallion tassels.

What you need:

- ⅔ cup plain yogurt
- 2 tablespoons extra-virgin olive oil
- 2 garlic cloves, crushed
- 2 tablespoons chopped fresh cilantro
- 2 teaspoons ground cumin
- 8 skinless and boneless chicken thighs, cut into large cubes
- 1 onion, cut into chunks
- 1 red bell pepper, cored, deseeded and cut into chunks
- salt and pepper

1 Mix the yogurt, oil, garlic, cilantro and cumin together in a large shallow dish with salt and pepper to taste. Add the cubes of chicken and stir well to mix. Cover and leave to marinate at room temperature for at least 30–60 minutes.

2 Thread the chicken cubes onto kebab skewers, alternating with the onion and bell pepper.

3 Cook the kebabs on an oiled barbecue grid over hot coals, turning frequently, for 20 minutes or until the chicken is tender when pierced with a skewer or fork. Serve hot, on a bed of saffron rice with a raita of yogurt, cucumber and chopped fresh cilantro.

Above: *Chicken and sweet pepper kebabs*

Baby eggplants with Greek-style yogurt

Serves 4
Preparation: 20 minutes
Cooking: 6 minutes
Carbohydrate: 7 g, Protein: 6 g,
Fat: 12 g, Fiber: 5 g, Calories: 153 kcal,
Sodium: 1038 mg (per portion)

What you need:

- 12 baby eggplants
- 3 tablespoons olive oil
- salt and pepper

For the Greek-style yogurt:

- 2 tablespoons chopped fresh parsley
- 2 tablespoons chopped fresh dill
- 2 tablespoons chopped fresh mint
- 1 small red onion, finely chopped
- 2 garlic cloves, crushed
- ¾ cup Kalamata olives, pitted and sliced
- 2 teaspoons fennel seeds, crushed
- 1 tablespoon capers, chopped

Cook's Tip

Baby vegetables are perfect for cooking whole on the barbecue as they are usually sweet and tender, so cook speedily. Little eggplants are usually available in ethnic markets.

Left: *Baby eggplant with herbed Greek-style yogurt*
Right: *Black bean kebabs*

- ½ ounce finely chopped gherkins
- finely grated rind and juice of 1 lime
- ⅔ cup strained Greek-style yogurt
- salt and pepper

1 First make the Greek-style yogurt. Mix all the ingredients together in a bowl and set aside.
2 Slice all the baby eggplants in half lengthways, leaving them attached to their stalks.
3 Using a small brush, coat the eggplants with olive oil. Cook on an oiled barbecue grid over moderately hot coals for about 2–3 minutes on each side.
4 To serve, place the eggplants on a serving dish or plate and spoon over the yogurt mixture.

Black bean kebabs

Serves 4
Preparation: 1 hour 20 minutes, plus soaking overnight
Cooking: 1 hour
Carbohydrate: 18 g, Protein: 10 g,
Fat: 6 g, Fiber: 2 g, Calories: 163 kcal,
Sodium: 28 mg (per portion)

What you need:

- ⅔ cup black beans
- 3 tablespoons olive oil
- 1 onion, very finely chopped
- 1 garlic clove, crushed
- 1 red chili, deseeded and finely chopped
- ½ teaspoon ground cumin
- ½ teaspoon ground coriander
- 1 tablespoon chopped fresh cilantro
- 2 medium zucchini
- 24 mixed red and yellow cherry tomatoes

1 Place the beans in a large bowl and cover with cold water. Soak overnight, then tip them into a colander, and rinse well under cold running water. Transfer the beans to a large saucepan and cover with fresh water. Bring to a boil and boil vigorously for about 10 minutes; then lower the heat and simmer for 40–50 minutes, or until the beans are tender. Drain well.

2 Heat 2 tablespoons of the olive oil in a skillet. Add the onion, garlic, and chili. Cook slowly for 5–10 minutes, until the onion is softened but not colored. Stir in the cumin and ground coriander, and cook for about 1–2 minutes longer.

3 Transfer the onion and spice mixture to a bowl. Add the drained beans and fresh cilantro and mash well. Divide the mixture into 24 and roll into balls.

4 Using a potato peeler, cut the zucchini lengthways into thin strips. Brush with the remaining olive oil. Thread the bean balls on to metal skewers, alternating with the cherry tomatoes and weaving the zucchini strips in between them.

5 Cook the black bean kebabs on a well-oiled barbecue grid over moderately hot coals for about 4 minutes on each side. Serve with rice.

Stuffed baby bell peppers

Serves 4
Preparation: 15 minutes
Cooking: 10–15 minutes
Carbohydrate: 7 g, Protein: 9 g, Fat: 11 g, Fiber: 2 g, Calories: 160 kcal, Sodium: 391 mg (per portion)

What you need:

- 8 baby bell peppers
- tomato sauce, preferably homemade
- Greek-style yogurt, to serve

For the stuffing:
- 4 ounces soft fresh goat cheese
- 2 ounces ricotta cheese
- 1½ tablespoons chopped fresh mint
- 1 red or green chili, deseeded and finely chopped (optional)
- salt and pepper

1 First make the stuffing, combine the goat cheese, ricotta cheese, and mint in a large bowl. Stir in the chili, if using, and season with salt and pepper to taste.

2 Make a small slit in the side of each bell pepper; carefully scrape out the seeds and core with a teaspoon, keeping the shells intact. Half fill each bell pepper with stuffing–do not be tempted to fill them completely, or they may burst during cooking.

3 Cook the filled bell peppers on an oiled barbecue grid over moderately hot coals for about 10–15 minutes, turning the peppers occasionally, until softened.

4 Place 2 of the filled bell peppers on each plate and serve with a tomato sauce and a spoonful of Greek-style yogurt.

Grilled sweet potatoes

Serves 4
Preparation: 15 minutes
Cooking: 10 minutes
Carbohydrate: 27 g, Protein: 2 g, Fat: 7 g, Fiber: 3 g, Calories: 172 kcal, Sodium: 50 mg (per portion)

What you need:

- 1 pound sweet potatoes, scrubbed
- 4 tablespoons olive oil

1 Cut each sweet potato into ¼-inch slices.

2 Brush with the oil and place on an oiled barbecue grid over moderately hot coals. Cook for about 5 minutes on each side until tender. Serve with garlic-flavored mayonnaise.

Above: *Grilled sweet potatoes*
Left: *Stuffed baby bell peppers.*

Above: *Baked bananas with cinnamon and rum mascarpone cream*
Below right: *Rum-flambéed pineapple parcels*

Variation

Baked bananas with chocolate ricotta cream

Mix 8 ounces ricotta cheese and 1–2 tablespoons of maple syrup in a large bowl. Stir in 2 tablespoons hazelnuts and beat in 2 squares melted chocolate. Prepare the baked bananas as in the main recipe. Serve with the ricotta cream and a few more hazelnuts sprinkled over the top

Baked bananas with cinnamon and rum mascarpone cream

Serves 4
Preparation: 5 minutes
Cooking: 10–12 minutes
Carbohydrate: 49 g, Protein: 6 g, Fat: 5 g, Fiber: 2 g, Calories: 258 kcal, Sodium: 21 mg (per portion)

What you need:

- 1–2 tablespoons superfine sugar
- ½ teaspoon ground cinnamon
- 2 teaspoons rum
- 1 cup mascarpone cheese
- 8 small bananas

1 Mix the sugar, cinnamon and rum together in a large bowl. Stir in the mascarpone, mix well and then set aside.
2 Place the whole unpeeled bananas on a barbecue grid over hot coals. Cook for about 10–12 minutes, turning as the skins darken, until they are black all over and the flesh is very tender.
3 To serve, carefully split the bananas open and spread the flesh with the mascarpone mixture.

Rum-flambéed pineapple packages

Serves 4
Preparation: 15 minutes
Cooking: 10–15 minutes
Carbohydrate: 45 g, Protein: 4 g, Fat: 21 g, Fiber: 3 g, Calories: 396 kcal, Sodium: 107 mg (per portion)

What you need:

- 1 ripe pineapple, peeled
- ¼ cup butter
- ½ cup light muscovado sugar
- 4 tablespoons dark rum (optional)
- ½ cup roasted and coarsely chopped pecan nuts
- crème fraîche or fromage blanc, to serve

1 Cut the pineapple into 8 even slices, then carefully remove the cores with a small cookie cutter to make rings.
2 Using doubled foil, cut out 4 foil squares, each large enough to hold 2 pineapple rings on each square.
3 Melt the butter in a small saucepan. Stir in the sugar and cook slowly until the sugar has dissolved completely. Divide the mixture evenly between the packages, then bring the edges of the foil together and press lightly to seal.
4 Cook on a barbecue grid over moderately hot coals for about 10–15 minutes.
5 When the pineapple is cooked, carefully open each package. Spoon 1 tablespoon of rum into each and carefully ignite with a match. Top with the chopped pecans and serve the packages at once with either crème fraîche or fromage blanc.

Cajun-style cod

Serves 4
Preparation: 10 minutes
Cooking: 4–6 minutes

What you need:

- 4 garlic cloves, crushed
- 1 teaspoon salt
- 2 tablespoons chopped fresh oregano
- 2 tablespoons chopped fresh thyme
- 1 teaspoon cumin seeds
- 1–2 teaspoons chili powder
- 4 green cardamom pods, seeds removed
- 12 whole allspice berries
- 2 teaspoons whole mixed peppercorns
- 2 teaspoons paprika
- ¼ cup all-purpose flour
- ½ cup melted butter
- 4 cod fillets, 7–8 ounces each
- 2 ripe plantains, unpeeled
- juice of ½ lime
- guacamole and lime wedges, to serve

1 Place the garlic, salt and all the herbs and spices in a mortar, then grind with a pestle until smooth. Tip the mixture into a shallow dish and stir in the flour.

2 Pour the melted butter into a second shallow dish. Dip the pieces of fish into the butter and then dust evenly with the spiced flour. Place the fish on an oiled barbecue grid over medium hot coals and cook for 2–3 minutes, then turn over and cook for 2–3 minutes on the other side.

3 Cut the plantains in half lengthways and brush with lime juice. Place on the grid, skin-side down. Cook for 2 minutes, until the skin is well blackened, then turn and grill for 1 minute more, or until the flesh is just cooked.

4 Serve the fish with the grilled plantains, guacamole and lime.

Baked beets with walnut and mustard sauce

Serves 4
Preparation: 15 minutes
Cooking: 40–50 minutes

What you need:

- ¾ cup walnut halves
- ¾ cup crème fraîche
- 1½ tablespoons whole grain mustard
- 3 tablespoons snipped chives, plus extra for garnish
- 8 raw beets
- salt and pepper

1 Roast the walnuts on a baking sheet in a preheated oven at 350°F, for about 8–10 minutes, until golden. Let cool, then chop roughly. Reserve 3 tablespoons of the nuts for the garnish, and put the rest in a bowl.

2 Stir in the crème fraîche, mustard and snipped chives. Season with salt and pepper to taste.

3 Wrap each beet in a double thickness of foil. Place in the embers of the hot barbecue and cook for about 40–50 minutes, or until tender.

4 Carefully unwrap the foil. Split open the beet and top with the sauce, the reserved walnuts and the extra chives.

Cook's Tip

Potatoes can be cooked in the same way as the beets. Scrub well, so the skins can be eaten. Do not use large potatoes, or they will not cook through. Sour cream can be used instead of crème fraîche in this recipe.

Planning a barbecue

A simple barbecue of sausages, steaks or burgers can make an easy informal meal but with a little planning you can include some unusual dishes.

● A marinade of flavored oil, wine and herbs can transform a piece of chicken or pork, and also helps to keep the meat tender and moist.

● Vegetables such as mushrooms, bell peppers, eggplants and zucchini do not need long cooking–thread onto skewers and marinate in seasoned oil for ½–1 hour before barbecuing for 10–15 minutes.

● Corn on the cob in its husk cooks perfectly on the barbecue: peel back the husks and remove silky threads; brush the corn with melted butter, then replace husks. Barbecue for ¾–1 hour.

● Pocket bread is ideal for filling with salad and barbecued meat. Sprinkle the bread with water and place on the barbecue for 5–10 minutes, turning once.

● Besides food and drink, you will also need some heavy-duty foil; tongs; large paper napkins; and enough charcoal to keep the barbecue going.

Countdown to barbecue time

● The day before–prepare the desserts. As an alternative to barbecued fruit, serve a simple fruit salad or ice cream. Marinate your meat or fish and leave in the refrigerator.

● Earlier in the day–chill the wine, beer, sodas and juices. Marinate the vegetables. Prepare salads and dressings–but only toss them together at the very last minute.

● 2 hours ahead–nominate a chef to take charge. Light coals.

● 1 hour ahead–start cooking the baked potatoes in coals.

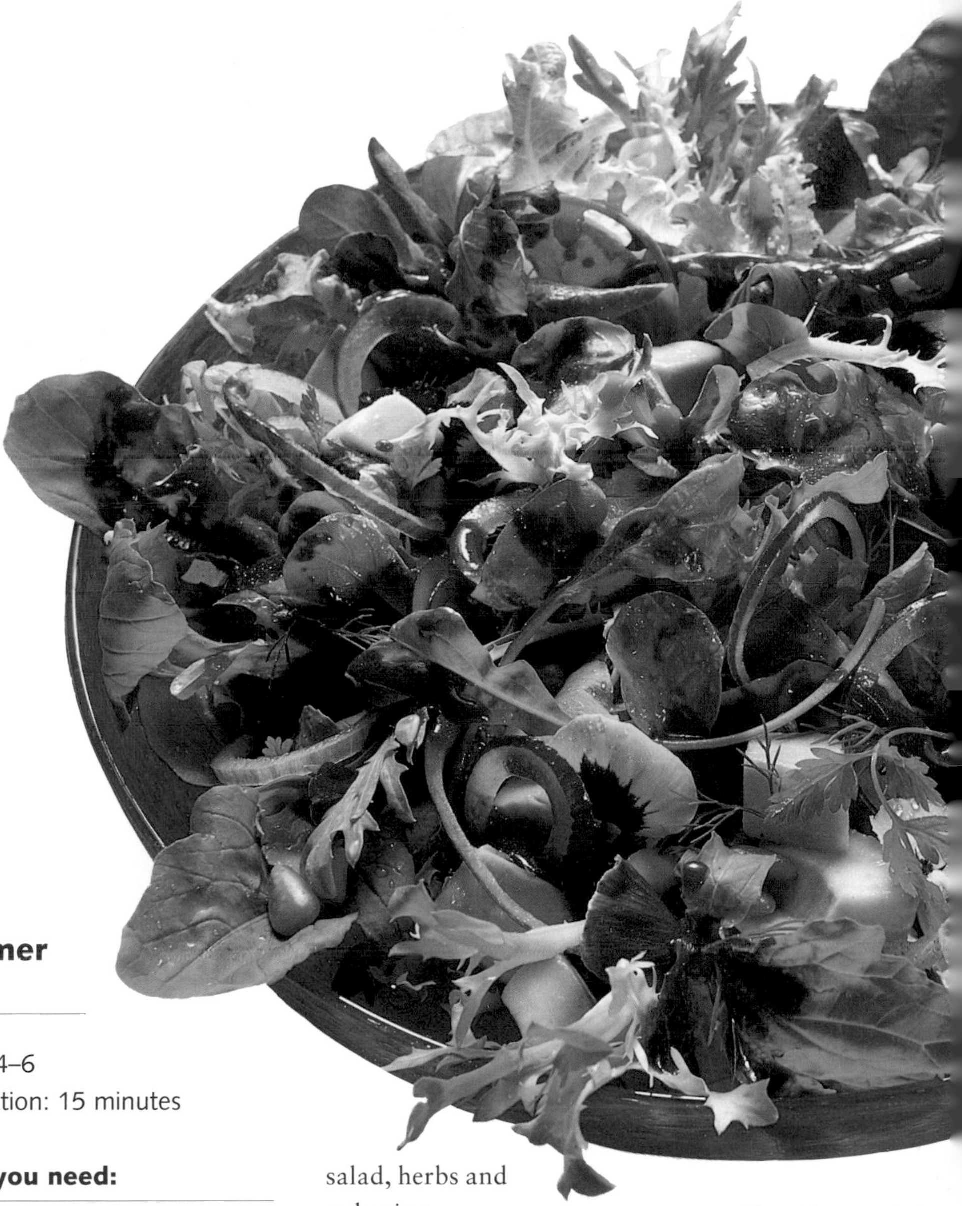

Summer salad

Serves 4–6
Preparation: 15 minutes

What you need:

- 1 red oak leaf lettuce
- ½ head of curly chicory
- about 1 cup arugula
- about 1 cup corn salad
- small handful of fresh herb sprigs
- 1 red onion, thinly sliced
- 1 large ripe avocado
- 1 tablespoon lemon juice
- ¼ cup toasted pine nuts
- French dressing or raspberry vinaigrette (see Cook's Tip)
- small handful of edible flowers (e.g. French marigolds, nasturtiums, pansies), optional, to garnish

1 Tear the oak leaf lettuce leaves and curly chicory into bite-size pieces. Place in a salad bowl with the arugula, corn salad, herbs and red onion.

2 Peel, halve and pit the avocado. Chop and toss in the lemon juice.

3 Just before serving, add the avocado and pine nuts to the salad. Spoon over the chosen dressing and toss lightly until all the ingredients are mixed. Finally, garnish with edible flowers.

Above: Summer salad, a colorful mixture of leaves, herbs, and flowers. If you don't want to use flowers, add sliced strawberries for color
Left: *Cajun-style Cod, an impressive yet easy to prepare barbecue dish*
Far left: *Baked beets with walnut and mustard sauce, an unusual alternative to baked potatoes*

Cook's Tip

To make a fresh raspberry vinaigrette, mash 1 cup raspberries with 1 teaspoon sugar, 2 tablespoons wine vinegar and ½ teaspoon Dijon mustard. Press through a strainer, Whisk in 5 table-spoons olive oil and season.

Figs and blackberries on toast

Serves 4
Preparation: 5–10 minutes
Cooking: 8–10 minutes

What you need:

- 12 ripe figs
- 1 cup blackberries
- pared rind and juice of 2 oranges
- 2 tablespoons crème de cassis (blackcurrant liqueur)
- 1 tablespoon superfine sugar
- ½ teaspoon cinnamon
- 2 tablespoons melted butter
- 4 slices white bread

1 Cut the figs into quarters, slicing almost through to the bottom. Cut 4 squares of double-thickness foil and place 3 figs and ¼ cup blackberries on each.
2 Cut the orange rind into thin strips. Mix with the orange juice and crème de cassis and divide between the fig packages. Bring up the edges of the foil and then press to seal.
3 Mix the sugar, cinnamon and melted butter in a bowl and brush over one side of each of the 4 slices of bread.
4 Cook the fig packages on a barbecue grid over medium hot coals for 8–10 minutes. After 5–6 minutes, place the bread on the grid, buttered side up, and toast until golden.
5 Serve the cinnamon toast on individual plates, topped with the figs and blackberries.

Grilled fruit skewers

Serves 4
Preparation: 20 minutes
Cooking: 4–6 minutes

What you need:

- 2 pounds assorted exotic fruits
- ⅓ cup butter
- 2 tablespoons muscovado sugar
- 1 tablespoon rum

1 If using wooden skewers, soak them in cold water for 30 minutes. Prepare the fruit according to type and cut it into even-size pieces. Thread onto 8 skewers.
2 Melt the butter and sugar in a small pan over a low heat, then stir in the rum.
3 Brush the fruit skewers with some of the rum butter. Cook on a barbecue grid over medium hot coals for about 2–3 minutes on each side, brushing the skewers with more rum and butter as they cook. Serve the hot fruit skewers at once.

Two delicious fruity puddings that can be prepared ahead, and then cooked on the barbecue for a few minutes.
Above: *Figs and blackberries on toast*
Right: *Grilled fruit skewers*

Cook's Tip

Try using strawberries, mango, cherries, papaya, oranges or pears.

Picnics

The great steak sandwich

Serves 4
Preparation: 35 minutes
Cooking:
4–6 minutes (very rare)
6–8 minutes (rare)
8–10 minutes (medium rare)
10–12 minutes (medium)
Carbohydrate: 36 g, Protein: 48 g,
Fat: 22 g, Fiber:3 g, Calories: 513 kcal,
Sodium: 906 mg (per portion)

What you need:

- 6 tablespoons olive oil
- 2 teaspoons mustard seeds
- 2 large red onions, thinly sliced
- 2 garlic cloves, crushed
- 3 tablespoons chopped fresh flat leaf parsley
- 1 tablespoon balsamic vinegar
- 2 round or sirloin steaks, about 8 ounces each
- 8 slices of olive bread or crusty bread
- 3 ounces fontina cheese, thinly sliced
- 2 ripe beefsteak tomatoes, sliced
- 2 cups arugula
- sea salt flakes and crushed black peppercorns

1 Heat 4 tablespoons of the oil in a skillet. Add the mustard seeds, cover and let them pop for 30 seconds over a medium heat – do not burn. Add the onions and garlic, cover and cook over a very low heat for 30 minutes until very soft but not colored.

2 Purée the softened onion mixture in a liquidizer or food processor, then spoon into a bowl. Stir in the parsley and vinegar, with salt and pepper to taste. Cover and set aside.

3 Brush the steaks with a little of the remaining oil and season with crushed black peppercorns. Cook on an oiled barbecue grid over hot coals for 2–3 minutes on each side for very rare, up to 5–6 minutes each side for medium (see cooking times, left).

4 Toast the bread slices on both sides until lightly golden. Spread with the onion purée. Slice the steaks thinly and divide between 4 of the bread slices. Top with the fontina, tomato and arugula. Season with the sea salt flakes and black pepper. Top with the remaining bread slices and then serve immediately.

Picnics conjure up an idyllic picture of long, hazy days spent basking in the sunshine, or perhaps cooling off in the shade of a tree, while nibbling delicate morsels of delicious food and sipping long cool drinks. The three most important essentials for the perfect picnic are good weather, good food, and a corkscrew. It is not, unfortunately, within our power to dictate the weather, but all the other ingredients are up to us. With the help of these delicious recipes, the food should be no problem. As for the corkscrew—you're on your own!

Below: *The great steak sandwich*

Club sandwich

Serves 2
Preparation: about 20 minutes
Carbohydrate: 54 g, Protein: 50 g, Fat: 62 g, Fiber: 3 g, Calories: 960 kcal, Sodium: 2297 mg (per portion)

What you need:

- 6 rindless bacon slices
- 6 slices white bread
- 6 tablespoons mayonnaise
- 8 small lettuce leaves
- 2 large slices of cooked turkey
- 2 tomatoes, thinly sliced
- salt and pepper

1 Cook the bacon in a heavy-bottomed skillet or under a pre-heated hot broiler for 5–7 minutes, turning once, until crisp on both sides. Remove and drain on paper towels.

2 Toast the bread slices lightly on both sides, then cut off and discard the crusts.

3 Arrange the toasted bread slices on a large board or work surface and spread one side of each slice with mayonnaise.

4 Arrange 2 of the lettuce leaves on each of 2 slices of toast and sprinkle with salt and pepper.

5 Arrange 1 slice of turkey on top of the lettuce on each sandwich, then top with another slice of toast, with the mayonnaise-side up. Arrange the remaining lettuce on top and add the tomato, then bacon, cutting the slices to fit wherever necessary.

6 Cover with the remaining 2 slices of bread, mayonnaise-side down. Leave the sandwiches whole, or cut into 4 triangles and serve. Ice-cold beer is the true traditional accompaniment.

Cook's Tip

This famous American sandwich always has three layers of white bread, but you can use granary or whole wheat if you like. Turkey is traditional, but chicken makes a good substitute.

Leafy salad with cheese and sun-dried tomatoes

Serves 4
Preparation: 20 minutes
Carbohydrate: 3 g, Protein: 11 g, Fat: 31 g, Fiber: 1 g, Calories: 335 kcal, Sodium: 559 mg (per portion)

What you need:

- 1 small romaine, separated into leaves
- about 1 cup arugula
- ½ head radicchio, separated into leaves
- 4 ounces cheese (such as Gruyère, Emmental or hard goat cheese)
- 5 tablespoons olive oil
- 1 garlic clove, chopped
- 4 scallions, chopped
- 6 sun-dried tomatoes preserved in oil, drained and sliced
- 2 tablespoons balsamic vinegar
- salt and pepper
- 2 tablespoons pine nuts, toasted (optional)

1 Tear the salad leaves into bite-size pieces and place in a shallow serving bowl. Using a cheese slicer or vegetable peeler, shave the cheese into wafer-thin slices and scatter over the salad.

2 Heat the oil in a skillet. Add the garlic and cook over a medium-high heat for 1 minute. Do not let the garlic brown. Stir in the scallions and sun-dried tomatoes; cook for about 1–2 minutes to heat through, then remove from the heat.

3 Stir the balsamic vinegar into the pan and season to taste. Spoon over the salad and serve, sprinkled with pine nuts, if using.

Cook's Tip

Take dressings separately in a sealed container, such as a jelly jar. Then you can dress and toss your salad once you have set up your picnic and just before serving.

Smoked chicken and citrus salad

Serves 4
Preparation: 30 minutes
Carbohydrate: 11 g, Protein: 29 g, Fat: 5 g, Fiber: 3 g, Calories: 196 kcal, Sodium: 112 mg (per portion)

What you need:

- 12 ounces smoked chicken, off the bone
- 1 pink grapefruit
- 2 small oranges
- ½ cucumber, thinly sliced
- 1 small fennel bulb, trimmed and thinly sliced (optional)
- 1 Boston lettuce, separated into leaves
- about 1 cup curly chicory
- about 1 cup corn salad or watercress
- pink peppercorns (optional)
- ⅔ cup yogurt dressing
- salt and pepper

1 Remove the skin from the chicken. Cut the flesh into even bite-size pieces and place in a large bowl.

2 Using a small sharp knife, peel the grapefruit and oranges, taking care to remove all the white pith. Working over a small bowl to catch the juices, segment and roughly chop the flesh, discarding any seeds. Pour the juice into a small pitcher and set aside. Add the citrus fruit to the chicken with the cucumber and fennel, if using, and toss the mixture lightly.

3 Arrange the chicken mixture and the salad leaves neatly on individual plates.

4 Stir the reserved citrus juices and the pink peppercorns, if using, into the yogurt dressing, and pour over the salad. Serve with crusty bread.

Vegetarian

If you think that a meal is not a proper meal without meat or fish, think again. You don't have to be a vegetarian to enjoy vegetarian food, as the dishes in this chapter will prove to even the most committed meat-eaters. Both delicious and nutritious, these recipes make full use of the flavor and color of the ingredients to create interesting and unusual combinations. Most of us could do with cutting down on meat, and this chapter should succeed in convincing you that you should try.

Below: *Garlic bread cassoulet*
Right: *Spicy eggplants*

Garlic bread cassoulet

Serves 6
Preparation: 40 minutes
Cooking: 1½ hours
Carbohydrate: 32 g, Protein: 11 g, Fat: 12 g, Fiber: 6 g, Calories: 283 kcal, Sodium: 677 mg (per portion)

What you need:

- 6 tablespoons olive oil
- 8 ounces shallots
- 2 garlic cloves, chopped
- 2 carrots, diced
- 2 celery stalks, sliced
- 1 red bell pepper, diced
- ⅔ cup red wine
- 14-ounce can navy beans, drained
- 4 tablespoons tomato paste
- 2 cups sliced mushrooms
- 3 tablespoons fresh mixed herbs
- salt and pepper

For the crust:

- ½ French stick, thinly sliced
- 2 tablespoons olive oil
- 1 garlic clove, crushed
- 2 tablespoons chopped fresh thyme
- ¼ cup Parmesan cheese

1 Heat half the oil in a pan and fry the shallots and garlic for about 5 minutes.

2 Heat the remaining oil and fry the carrots, celery, and bell pepper for 5 minutes. Add the wine and boil for 3 minutes. Add the beans, tomato paste, shallots and garlic mixture, mushrooms, and herbs. Season and spoon into a shallow ovenproof dish.

3 Layer the bread on top. Mix the oil, garlic, and thyme. Brush over the bread and sprinkle with the Parmesan. Cover and place in a preheated oven, 375°F, for 30 minutes. Uncover and bake for 20 minutes longer until golden.

Spicy eggplants

Serves 4–6
Preparation: 20 minutes
Cooking: 30 minutes
Carbohydrate: 8 g, Protein: 3 g, Fat: 9 g, Fiber: 4 g, Calories: 111 kcal, Sodium: 500 mg (per portion)

What you need:

- 4–6 eggplants, halved
- 1 bay leaf
- 1 large onion, finely chopped
- 2 garlic cloves, chopped
- 2 tablespoons ghee or butter
- 2 teaspoons coriander seeds
- 1 teaspoon cumin seeds
- 2–4 dried red chilies, chopped
- 1 teaspoon salt

1 Put the eggplants in a roasting pan, cut sides up. Add the bay leaf and ⅔ cup water, cover. Place in a preheated oven, 325°F, for 25 minutes.

2 Fry the onion and garlic in the ghee or butter for 5 minutes. Add the coriander, cumin, chilies, and salt and fry for 3 minutes.

3 Pat the eggplants dry with paper towels. Scrape out the flesh, mash, and add to the spice mixture. Fry for 2–3 minutes.

4 Put the skins under a medium hot broiler for 5 minutes until dried out, and then fill with the fried mixture and serve.

Right: Bell pepper and tomato pancakes

Bell pepper and tomato pancakes

Serves 4
Preparation: 10 minutes
Cooking: 30–40 minutes
Carbohydrate: 50 g, Protein: 15 g, Fat: 32 g, Fiber: 10 g, Calories: 540 kcal, Sodium: 378 mg (per portion)

What you need:

- 1 cup whole wheat flour
- 1 large egg, beaten
- 1 egg yolk
- ⅔ cup milk
- ⅔ cup water
- 2 tablespoons melted butter
- extra butter, for frying

For the filling:
- 1½ pounds red bell peppers
- 2 tablespoons olive oil
- 1 onion, chopped
- 3 pounds tomatoes, peeled, deseeded and chopped
- 2 tablespoons chopped fresh parsley
- salt and pepper

To serve:
- 1¼ cups sour cream or Greek-style yogurt
- paprika

1 First make the filling, place the bell peppers under a hot broiler, turning frequently, until the skins blacken and blister. Peel off the skins under cold running water. Remove the seeds and cut the bell peppers into small pieces.
2 Heat the olive oil in a large pan and fry the onion until soft. Add the bell peppers and tomatoes, and cook, uncovered, for 30 minutes, until the mixture is thick and dry. Stir frequently toward the end of cooking to prevent burning. Add the parsley and season to taste.
3 Make the pancakes. Put all the ingredients and ½ teaspoon of salt into a blender or food processor and blend well until smooth. Heat 1 teaspoon of butter in a small skillet; when it sizzles, pour off the excess butter, so that the pan is just glistening. Keeping the pan over a high heat, give the batter a stir; then put 2 tablespoons into the pan, tipping it so the batter covers the bottom of the pan. Cook for 30 seconds, or until the top is set and the underside is tinged golden. Flip over and cook the other side. Place the cooked pancake on a warmed plate. Make 12 more pancakes, piling them up on top of each other, interleaved with baking parchment paper. Keep warm.
4 To serve, put a spoonful of the filling on each pancake and roll up neatly. Spoon the cream or yogurt over the pancakes, and sprinkle with paprika. Serve at once, with salad.

Spanakopita

Serves 6
Preparation: 30 minutes
Cooking: 45–50 minutes
Carbohydrate: 33 g, Protein: 20 g, Fat: 51 g, Fiber: 5 g, Calories: 662 kcal, Sodium: 1372 mg (per portion)

What you need:

- 2 tablespoons olive oil
- 1 onion, chopped
- 2 pounds fresh spinach
- 1 teaspoon dry oregano
- 8 ounces feta cheese, crumbled
- 4 eggs, beaten
- grated nutmeg
- 12 ounces filo pastry dough, thawed if frozen
- ¼ cup melted butter
- salt and pepper

1 Wash the spinach in several

changes of water, then place in a large pan with only the water that clings to the leaves. Cover and cook for 8 minutes, shaking occasionally, until tender. Drain well, pressing out as much water as possible, then chop finely.

2 Heat the oil and fry the onion for 4–5 minutes, until soft. Add the spinach, oregano, feta cheese, and eggs, with the nutmeg. Season to taste and mix well.

3 Butter a shallow ovenproof dish, about 10 by 7 inches. Layer the filo dough in the dish, brushing each layer with melted butter. Continue until you have 3 sheets of filo dough left.

4 Fill the pie with the spinach mixture. Fold over the dough edges, covering the filling. Cover with the remaining filo sheets, tucking them in to fit the top, and brush with more melted butter.

4 Place in a preheated oven, 375°F, for 45–50 minutes until the dough is crisp and golden.

Vegetable fritters

Serves 6
Preparation: 15 minutes
Cooking: 1¾ hours
Carbohydrate: 34 g, Protein: 6 g, Fat: 4 g, Fiber: 2 g, Calories: 191 kcal, Sodium: 145 g (per portion)

What you need:

- oil for deep-frying
- 3 small zucchini, peeled
- 1 fennel bulb, thinly sliced
- 1 eggplant, thinly sliced

For the batter:

- 2 cups all-purpose flour
- pinch of salt
- 1 tablespoon vegetable oil
- ½ cake compressed yeast, creamed with 2 tablespoons warm water
- 1–1¼ cups warm water
- 1 egg white, lightly beaten

1 First make the batter, sift the flour and salt into a bowl, and make a well in the center. Pour the oil and the yeast mixture into the well, and gradually stir in the flour. Add the warm water and mix. Fold in the egg white and leave for 2 hours.

2 Heat the oil in a heavy pan or deep-fat fryer. Dip the sliced vegetables into the prepared batter and fry in batches until crisp and golden, turning as necessary. Drain on paper towels. Keep warm while cooking the rest of the vegetables. Serve the fritters at once, with garlic-flavored mayonnaise (aïoli).

Left: *Spanakopita*
Above: *Vegetable fritters*

Onion tart Tatin

Serves 4–6
Preparation: 30 minutes
Cooking: 20-25 minutes
Carbohydrate: 37 g, Protein: 9 g,
Fat: 26 g, Fiber: 7 g, Calories: 402 kcal,
Sodium: 410 mg (per portion)

What you need:

- 1½ cups self-rising wholewheat flour
- ⅓ cup diced chilled butter,
- 2 tablespoons chopped fresh parsley
- 2 teaspoons chopped fresh thyme
- 2–3 tablespoons lemon juice

For the topping:

- 1 pound shallots
- ¼ cup butter
- 2 tablespoons olive oil
- 2 teaspoons muscovado sugar
- salt and pepper

1 Place the flour in a bowl and rub in the butter until the mixture resembles bread crumbs. Stir in the parsley, thyme, and lemon juice, and mix to a firm dough. Knead briefly, then wrap and chill while preparing the topping.

2 Boil the shallots in a pan of water for 10 minutes, then drain. Heat the butter and oil, and fry the shallots stirring, for 10 minutes, until they start to brown. Sprinkle over the sugar, and season to taste. Cook for 5 minutes longer, until the shallots are well colored. Remove from the heat.

3 Roll out the dough on a lightly floured surface to form a round, a little larger than the pan. Support the dough over the rolling pin and place it over the shallots, tucking the dough edges down the side of the pan. Place in

Variation

Garden vegetable tart

Bake a dough case as in the main recipe. Prepare a selection of vegetables–such as asparagus, snow peas, baking carrots, sliced leeks, and fava beans, and cook until tender. Cut 4 ounces cherry tomatoes in half. Arrange all the vegetables in the pie shell.

For the filling, put ½ cup soft cheese with garlic and herbs in a blender or food processor with ⅓ cup milk and 2 eggs. Blend until the mixture is smooth, adding salt and pepper to taste. Pour over the vegetables in the pie shell. Sprinkle with Parmesan and bake for 20–25 minutes.

crumbs. Add about 2 table-spoons of water and mix to a firm dough. Roll out the dough on a lightly floured surface and line an 8-inch pan. Chill for 30 minutes, if time permits.

2 Fill the pie shell with crumpled foil and place in a preheated oven, 400°F, for 15 minutes; then remove the foil and return the pie shell to the oven for 10 minutes longer. Reduce the oven temperature to 350°F.

3 Cook the asparagus stalks in a wide skillet in boiling water for about 7–10 minutes, until tender. Drain well and refresh under cold running water, then drain again thoroughly.

4 Beat 1 egg with the cream. Season with salt and pepper to taste. Arrange the asparagus neatly in the pie shell. Break each of the 4 remaining eggs in turn into a saucer, then slide them carefully into the pie shell. Pour over the cream mixture and top with the grated Parmesan.

5 Return the tart to the oven for about 15–20 minutes, until the eggs have just set. Serve the tart warm with salad and bread.

a preheated oven, 400°F, for about 20–25 minutes, until the dough is crisp.

4 Let cool in the pan for 5 minutes; then place a plate over the pan and invert the tart on it. Serve warm or cold.

Asparagus, Parmesan and egg tart

Serves 4
Preparation: 35 minutes
Cooking: 40–45 minutes
Carbohydrate: 36 g, Protein: 19 g, Fat: 34 g, Fiber: 2 g, Calories: 513 kcal, Sodium: 541 mg (per portion)

What you need:

- 1½ cups all-purpose flour
- ⅓ cup diced, chilled butter

For the filling:

- 6 ounces thin asparagus stalks, trimmed
- 5 eggs
- ⅔ cup light cream
- ¼ cup grated Parmesan cheese
- salt and pepper

1 Place the flour in a bowl and rub in the butter until the mixture resembles very fine bread

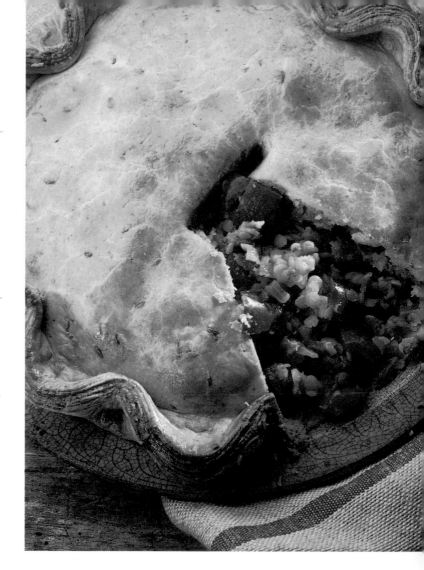

Right: *Spiced lentil pie*

Spiced lentil pie

Serves 6
Preparation: 40 minutes
Cooking: 35–40 minutes
Carbohydrate: 65 g, Protein: 14 g,
Fat: 30 g, Fiber: 4 g, Calories: 557 kcal,
Sodium: 596 mg (per portion)

What you need:

- 3 cups all-purpose flour
- ¾ cup diced, chilled butter
- 2 teaspoons cumin seeds
- 2 teaspoons ground coriander
- 3 tablespoons lemon juice

For the filling:

- 1 onion, chopped
- 2 garlic cloves, crushed
- 2 tablespoons sunflower oil
- 2 celery stalks, chopped
- 1 red bell pepper, deseeded and chopped
- ⅔ cup red lentils
- 3 ripe tomatoes, peeled and chopped
- ¾ teaspoon chili powder
- 2 cups vegetable stock
- 3 tablespoons chopped fresh cilantro
- 2 tablespoons lemon juice
- salt and pepper
- beaten egg, to glaze

1 Place the flour in a bowl and rub in the butter until the mixture resembles fine bread crumbs. Stir in the spices and salt; then add the lemon juice and 1–2 tablespoons water, and mix to a firm dough. Wrap and let rest at room temperature.

2 Fry the onion and garlic in the oil for 5 minutes until soft. Add the celery and bell pepper, and cook for 2 minutes. Stir in the lentils, tomatoes, chili powder, and stock, and simmer stirring occasionally, for 25–30 minutes, until the stock has been absorbed. Add the cilantro, lemon juice, and salt and pepper. Let cool.

3 Roll out just over half the dough and line a 9-inch pie dish. Add the filling and brush the dough edges with water.

4 Roll out the remaining dough and use to cover the pie. Pinch the edges together to seal. Brush the top with beaten egg and place in a preheated oven, 400°F, for 35–40 minutes, until golden. Cover with foil if it starts to over-brown. Serve hot.

> ### Cook's Tip
>
> For an even quicker pie, replace the lentils with a 10-ounce can of red kidney beans or black-eyed peas and omit the vegetable stock.

Spiced cauliflower crumble pie

Serves 4
Preparation: 25 minutes
Cooking: 25 minutes
Carbohydrate: 42 g, Protein: 17 g,
Fat: 20 g, Fiber: 9 g, Calories: 395 kcal,
Sodium: 625 mg (per portion)

What you need:

- 1 onion, chopped
- 1 garlic clove, chopped
- 1 teaspoon chopped fresh ginger root
- 1 teaspoon cumin seeds
- 1 teaspoon mustard seeds
- 2 tablespoons oil
- 12 ounces cauliflower, cut into small florets
- 1 tablespoon curry paste
- 1 14-ounce can chopped tomatoes
- 1 14-ounce can garbanzo

beans, drained
- salt and pepper

For the crumble:
- 2 garlic cloves, chopped
- 3 tablespoons olive oil
- 1 cup fresh brown bread crumbs
- ¼ cup slivered almonds, toasted
- 2 tablespoons chopped fresh cilantro

1 Fry the onion, garlic, ginger, cumin, and mustard seeds in the oil for 5 minutes, until the onion is soft. Add the cauliflower and coat in the spices.

2 Add the curry paste and tomatoes, and season to taste. Bring to a boil; then cover the pan and cook slowly for 10–12 minutes or until the cauliflower is tender. Stir in the garbanzo beans and heat through.

3 For the crumble, fry the garlic in the oil for 2 minutes. Add the bread crumbs, almonds, cilantro, salt and pepper, and mix. Transfer the vegetable mixture to an ovenproof dish and sprinkle the crumble over the top.

4 Place in a preheated oven, 400°F, for 25 minutes, until the topping is crisp and golden. Serve the pie piping hot.

Chestnut, celery, and mushroom pie

Serves 6
Preparation: 30 minutes
Cooking: 40–45 minutes
Carbohydrate: 57 g, Protein: 11 g, Fat: 16 g, Fiber: 3 g, Calories. 405 kcal, Sodium: 802 mg (per portion)

What you need:

- 3 cups all-purpose flour
- 1 teaspoon salt
- ⅓ cup butter
- beaten egg, to glaze

For the filling:
- 1 onion, chopped
- 1 carrot, chopped
- 2 tablespoons olive oil
- 3 celery stalks, chopped
- 1 garlic clove, chopped
- 14-ounces canned or vacuum-packed cooked chestnuts, drained and chopped
- 2½ cups chopped mushrooms
- ½ cup ground almonds
- ⅔ cup vegetable stock
- 1 tablespoon chopped fresh herbs
- 2 eggs, beaten
- salt and pepper

1 Make the filling. Fry the onion and carrot in the oil for 5 minutes, until soft. Add the celery and garlic, and cook for 2–3 minutes, stirring occasionally. Mix in the chestnuts, mushrooms, almonds, stock, herbs, and seasoning. Bring to a boil, stirring, until heated through. Let cool, stir in the eggs, and let cool again.

2 For the dough, mix the flour and salt together. Melt the butter with ¾ cup water. Add to the flour and mix to a soft dough. Wrap and let rest at room temperature for 15 minutes.

3 Roll out two-thirds of the dough on a lightly floured surface and line a greased 2-pound loaf pan. Spread the filling over the dough and dampen the dough edges.

4 Roll out the remaining dough and cover the pie, pinching the edges to seal. Make a hole in the center. Roll out the dough trimmings, and cut into leaves to decorate. Fix in place, then brush the top of the pie with egg.

5 Place in a preheated oven, 400°F, for 40–50 minutes, until crisp and golden. Let cool in the pan for 10 minutes. Remove the pie from the pan and serve hot.

Above: *Chestnut, celery and mushroom pie*
Below left: *Spiced cauliflower crumble pie*

Right: *Vegetable biryani*
Below: *Nut and fig pilaf*

Nut and fig pilaf

Serves 4–6
Preparation: 25 minutes
Cooking: 50 minutes
Carbohydrate: 41 g, Protein: 8 g,
Fat: 13 g, Fiber: 5 g, Calories: 288 kcal,
Sodium: 653 mg (per portion)

What you need:

- 2 tablespoons olive oil
- 1 onion, chopped
- 2 garlic cloves, chopped
- 1 teaspoon roasted coriander seeds, crushed
- 1 teaspoon roasted cumin seeds, crushed
- 2 dried red chilies, crushed
- 1 teaspoon ground cinnamon
- 2 large carrots, sliced
- 2 celery stalks, sliced
- 2 cups brown rice
- 3¾ cups vegetable stock
- 4 ounces green beans, halved
- ½ cup peas, thawed if frozen
- ⅓ cup chopped, dry figs
- ½ cup toasted cashew nuts
- 2 tablespoons chopped fresh cilantro or parsley
- salt and pepper

Variation

Carrot and ginger pilaf

Follow the main recipe, but omit the onions and sweet potato and double the amount of carrots and ginger. After frying the carrots, garlic, and ginger root for 10 minutes, add the tomatoes, ⅓ cup toasted slivered almonds, and cook for 5 minutes longer. Stir in the rice, 1 tablespoon lemon juice, salt and pepper, and stir-fry for 3–4 minutes until the rice is heated through. Serve at once.

1 Heat the oil in a large skillet. Add the chopped onion, garlic, coriander and cumin seeds, dried chilies, and ground cinnamon. Fry slowly for about 5 minutes, or until the onion starts to soften. Add the carrots and celery, and fry for 5 minutes longer. Season with salt and pepper to taste.

2 Add the rice to the pan and stir-fry for about 1 minute, then pour in the vegetable stock. Bring to a boil, cover the pan, and simmer over a low heat for about 20 minutes. Add all the remaining ingredients to the pan and cook for 10–15 minutes longer, until the rice is cooked and all the vegetables are tender. Serve the pilaf at once.

Vegetable biryani

Serves 4
Preparation: 25 minutes
Cooking: 50–55 minutes
Carbohydrate: 84 g, Protein: 18 g, Fat: 26 g, Fiber: 8 g, Calories: 625 kcal, Sodium: 680 mg (per portion)

What you need:

- 1⅓ cups Basmati rice, rinsed
- 6 tablespoons sunflower oil
- 2 large onions, thinly sliced
- 2 large carrots, diced
- 2 garlic cloves, crushed
- 2 teaspoons grated fresh ginger root
- 1¾ cups diced sweet potato
- 1 tablespoon curry paste
- 2 teaspoons ground turmeric
- 1 teaspoon ground cinnamon
- 1 teaspoon chili powder
- 1¼ cups vegetable stock
- 4 ripe tomatoes, peeled, deseeded and diced
- 6 ounces cauliflower florets
- ⅔ cup green peas, thawed if frozen
- ½ cup toasted cashew nuts
- 2 tablespoons chopped fresh cilantro
- salt and pepper
- 2 hard eggs, quartered, to serve

1 Add all the rice to a large saucepan of boiling salted water. Bring the water back to a simmer and cook the rice for about 5 minutes. Drain, refresh under cold running water, and drain again thoroughly. Spread the rice out on a large baking sheet and set aside to dry.

2 Heat 2 tablespoons of the oil in a large skillet and fry half the sliced onion for 10 minutes, until very crisp and golden brown. Remove from the pan and drain on paper towels. Reserve the remaining uncooked onion slices for garnish.

3 Add the remaining oil to the pan and fry the remaining onion with the carrots, garlic, and grated ginger root for 4–5 minutes. Add the sweet potato and spices, and fry for 10 minutes longer, until light golden.

4 Add the vegetable stock and diced tomatoes. Bring to a boil, cover the pan, and simmer slowly for about 20 minutes. Add the cauliflower and peas, and cook for 8–10 minutes longer, until all the vegetables are tender.

5 Add the rice, cashew nuts, and freshly chopped cilantro. Continue to cook, stirring constantly, for about 3 minutes. Cover the pan, remove from the heat, and let stand for about 5 minutes before serving. Garnish the biryani with the crispy onion slices and serve with the hard egg quarters.

Right: *Vegetable bolognese*
Below: *Deep-fried Camembert with fettuccine*
Far right: *Saffron barley with sun-dried tomatoes*

Deep-fried Camembert with fettuccine

Serves 4
Preparation: 10 minutes, plus 30 minutes chilling
Cooking: 12 minutes
Carbohydrate: 30 g, Protein: 34 g, Fat: 38 g, Fiber: 3 g, Calories: 585 kcal, Sodium: 1150 mg (per portion)

What you need:

- 8 Camembert wedges, chilled
- 2 eggs, beaten
- 2 cups fresh whole wheat bread crumbs
- 1 teaspoon paprika
- 10 ounces fresh fettuccine
- oil for deep-frying
- 1 tablespoon olive oil
- 1 tablespoon raspberry vinegar
- salt and pepper
- fresh raspberries, with leaves to garnish

1 Dip the Camembert wedges in beaten egg, then coat in bread crumbs. Sprinkle with paprika and chill for 30 minutes.
2 Cook the pasta in boiling salted water for 4–6 minutes, until the pasta is just tender.

3 Heat the oil to 350–375F°, or until a cube of bread browns in 30 seconds. Fry the Camembert for 1 minute, turning. Drain and keep hot.
4 Drain the pasta and return to the pan. Add the olive oil, vinegar and seasoning. Toss, twirl into 4 nests and put on plates. Add 2 Camembert wedges to each plate and serve with the fresh raspberries.

Vegetable bolognese

Serves 4
Preparation: 15 minutes

Cooking: 12 minutes
Carbohydrate: 66 g, Protein: 12 g, Fat: 4 g, Fiber: 6 g, Calories: 334 kcal, Sodium: 470 mg (per portion)

What you need:

- 10 ounces dry spaghetti
- 1 onion, chopped
- 1½ cups diced carrots
- 1 tablespoon olive oil
- 1 leek, sliced
- 2 celery stalks, sliced
- 1 14-ounce can plum tomatoes, drained and roughly chopped
- 1 tablespoon tomato paste
- 1 teaspoon cayenne pepper
- 1⅓ cups sliced mushrooms
- salt and pepper
- fresh basil leaves, to garnish

1 Cook the pasta in boiling salted water for 8–12 minutes, until just tender.
2 Fry the onion and carrots in the oil for 3–5 minutes. Add the leek, celery, tomatoes, tomato paste, cayenne, mushrooms, and seasoning. Cook for 10 minutes.
3 Drain the pasta, twist into 4 nests, and put on plates. Spoon some sauce into each nest. Season, garnish with basil and serve.

Saffron barley with sun-dried tomatoes

Serves 4
Preparation: 15–20 minutes
Cooking: about 30 minutes
*Carbohydrate: 54 g, Protein: 8 g,
Fat: 29 g, Fiber: 0 g, Calories: 494 kcal,
Sodium: 850 mg (per portion)*

What you need:

- 1¼ cups pearl barley
- 3 cups chicken or vegetable stock
- ¼ teaspoon saffron threads
- 1 shallot, finely chopped
- 6 tablespoons olive oil
- 1 garlic clove, crushed
- 12 ounces oyster mushrooms, halved if large
- 8–12 sun-dried tomatoes preserved in oil, drained and chopped
- fresh basil leaves, shredded
- 2 tablespoons wine vinegar
- salt and pepper

1 Put the pearl barley in a pan with the stock. Crumble in the saffron. Bring to a boil, cover, and simmer for 20–25 minutes, until the liquid has absorbed. Let cool in a bowl.

2 Fry the shallot in 3 tablespoons of the oil for 3 minutes, until soft. Add the garlic and mushrooms, and cook for 3 minutes, until tender. Remove from the heat and stir in the tomatoes and basil. Pile the mixture on top of the barley.

3 Add the remaining oil and the vinegar to the pan, and season. Spoon over the barley and serve.

Variation

Saffron couscous with tomatoes and thyme

Follow the main recipe, but substitute couscous for the barley, 3 ripe fresh tomatoes, peeled, deseeded and chopped for the sun-dried tomatoes, and a few sprigs of fresh thyme for the basil.

Above: *Tomato, spinach and ricotta casserole*
Right: *Carrot and almond loaf with tomato sauce*
Far right: *Zucchini tian*

saucepan. Add the onion and garlic, and cook until soft; then mix with the spinach.

3 Layer half the sliced tomatoes and half the ricotta cheese in an oiled casserole. Repeat the layers, seasoning each layer with salt and pepper. Sprinkle the Parmesan over the top.

4 Cover and place in a preheated oven, 350°F for 30 minutes. Remove the lid and cook for 10 minutes longer to brown the top.

Zucchini tian

Serves 4–6
Preparation: 25 minutes
Cooking: 20–30 minutes
Carbohydrate: 23 g, Protein: 16 g, Fat: 21 g, Fiber: 3 g, Calories: 341 kcal, Sodium: 494 mg

What you need:

- 1½ pounds zucchini, roughly chopped
- 1 onion, chopped
- 2 garlic cloves, crushed
- 5 tablespoons olive oil
- ½ cup long-grain rice
- 2 eggs
- salt and pepper
- ½ cup grated Gruyère cheese
- 3–4 tablespoons fresh bread crumbs
- 2 tablespoons grated Parmesan cheese

1 Fry the zucchini, onion, and garlic slowly in 3 tablespoons of the olive oil in a large skillet for 8–10 minutes, until soft and slightly golden.

2 Meanwhile, cook the rice in a large saucepan of boiling salted water until tender, but not sticky. Drain well.

3 Beat the eggs with salt and

pepper in a large bowl, and then stir in the cooked zucchini mixture, grated Gruyère cheese, and drained rice. Transfer to an oiled shallow ovenproof dish.

4 Sprinkle with the bread crumbs and Parmesan, and drizzle the remaining olive oil over the top. Place in a preheated oven at 350°F, for 20–30 minutes, until crisp and golden brown. Serve hot, warm or cold.

Cook's Tip

Tian is Provençal name for a wide, shallow baking dish or gratin dish, and also for the food cooked in it.

Variation

Neapolitan zucchini

Fry the zucchini separately in a little butter, then fry 1 pound tomatoes (peeled, deseeded and chopped) with the onion and garlic. Replace the rice with macaroni. Place the zucchini in a shallow baking dish, and cover with 1 cup grated or sliced mozzarella cheese, then the macaroni, the tomato mixture and the remaining mozzarella. Sprinkle over the bread crumbs, Parmesan, and olive oil and bake as in the main recipe.

Tomato, spinach and ricotta casserole

Serves 4
Preparation: 15 minutes
Cooking: 30 minutes
Carbohydrate: 11 g, Protein: 18 g, Fat: 20 g, Fiber: 5 g, Calories: 292 kcal, Sodium: 691 mg (per portion)

What you need:

- 1½ pounds spinach, shredded
- 2 tablespoons butter
- 1 onion, chopped
- 1 garlic clove, crushed
- 2 beefsteak tomatoes, peeled and sliced
- 12 ounces ricotta cheese
- 2 tablespoons grated Parmesan cheese
- salt and pepper

1 Put the spinach in a large saucepan with 1 tablespoon of water and a little salt. Cook for 2–3 minutes until soft, then drain the spinach well.

2 Melt the remaining butter in a

Carrot and almond loaf with tomato sauce

Serves 6–8
Preparation: 15 minutes
Cooking: 50 minutes
*Carbohydrate: 28 g, Protein: 12 g,
Fat: 23 g, Fiber: 6 g, Calories: 354 kcal,
Sodium: 511 g (per portion)*

What you need:

- ¼ cup butter
- 1 onion, thinly sliced
- 2 garlic cloves, chopped
- fresh whole wheat bread crumbs
- 8 ounces grated carrots
- 1 cup toasted, slivered almonds
- 2 eggs, beaten
- 4 tablespoons lemon juice
- 1 tablespoon chopped fresh parsley
- 1 teaspoon grated nutmeg
- salt and pepper

1 Melt the butter in a large skillet over a low heat. Fry the onion and garlic slowly for about 5 minutes, or until the onion is just translucent.

2 Mix the bread crumbs, carrots and almonds together in a large bowl. Add the onion and garlic, and stir well. Add the beaten eggs, lemon juice, parsley, and nutmeg. Season with salt and pepper to taste and mix well. Add a little water if the mixture seems dry.

3 Spoon the mixture into a greased 1-pound loaf tin and bake in a preheated oven 400°F, for about 45 minutes or until the loaf is browned and a sharp knife inserted into the center comes out clean. Serve the loaf in slices with a fresh tomato sauce.

Salads

A salad is much, much more than a tomato and a limp piece of lettuce with a dollop of salad cream. It can be a well-chosen combination of salad vegetables, fruits and pulses, it can be combined with fish or meat, it can feature rice or pasta, it can be simple or more elaborate, it can be a main course or a side dish, and it can be served either warm or cold. Whatever you choose, it should always surprise both palate and eye with contrasting textures, flavors, shapes and colors. Refreshing and nutritious, salads deserve pride of place in every imaginative cook's repertoire.

Zucchini salad with lemon and thyme

Serves 4–6
Preparation: 20 minutes, plus
2 minutes cooking
Carbohydrate: 5 g, Protein: 3 g,
Fat: 12 g, Fiber: 2 g, Calories: 136 kcal,
Sodium: 469 mg (per portion)

What you need:

- 1 pound small zucchini
- about 16 black olives

For the dressing:
- 5 tablespoons extra virgin olive oil
- pared rind of 1 lemon, cut into thin strips
- ½ cup lemon juice
- 1 garlic clove, crushed
- 1 tablespoon roughly chopped fresh thyme
- 1 teaspoon clear honey
- salt and pepper

1 First make the dressing. Place all the ingredients in a screw-top jar. Close the lid tightly and shake to combine.

2 Cut the zucchini in half crossways. Using a sharp knife, cut both ends off each piece of zucchini to a point, 'sharpening' it just as you would do a pencil.

3 Bring a pan of water to a boil. Add the zucchini and cook for 2 minutes. Drain, blot the excess moisture with paper towels and transfer to a bowl. Add the olives.

4 Pour the dressing over the zucchini and toss lightly. Leave until cold before serving.

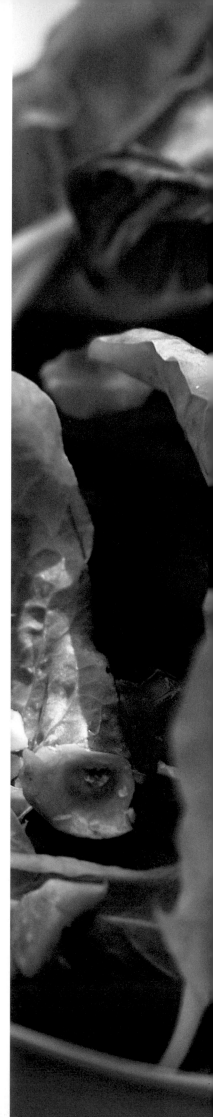

Raw beet and pink grapefruit salad

Serves 4–6
Preparation: 20 minutes
Carbohydrate: 20 g, Protein: 8 g,
Fat: 15 g, Fiber: 7 g, Calories: 238
kcal, Sodium: 112 mg (per portion)

What you need:

- 1½ pounds raw young beets
- 2 pink grapefruit
- ½ cup roasted and coarsely chopped hazelnuts,
- 1 tablespoon raspberry vinegar
- 3 tablespoons hazelnut oil
- 1 garlic clove, crushed
- 1 radicchio, leaves separated
- 8 ounces young spinach leaves
- salt and pepper

1 Peel the beets and cut them into fine julienne strips or grate them finely. Place the julienne strips or grated beets in a salad bowl.

2 Cut a thin slice off the bottom of each grapefruit and place, cut side down, on a cutting board. Cut off the rind in strips, working from the top down. Take care to remove all the white pith. Holding the grapefruit over the salad bowl to catch any juice, cut out the segments with a sharp knife. Add the segments to the bowl. Stir in the hazelnuts and toss lightly.

3 Whisk the raspberry vinegar, hazelnut oil, and garlic in a small bowl; pour over the beet mixture. Add salt and pepper to taste and toss well. Arrange the radicchio and spinach on each plate and spoon over the beet mixture.

Far left: *Zucchini salad with lemon and thyme*
Left: *Raw beet and pink grapefruit salad*

Caesar salad

Serves 4–6
Preparation: 20 minutes
Cooking: about 12 minutes
Carbohydrate: 30 g, Protein: 17 g,
Fat: 40 g, Fiber: 1 g, Calories: 540 kcal,
Sodium: 1379 mg (per portion)

What you need:

- 1 romaine, separated into leaves
- 1 2-ounce can anchovies in olive oil, drained
- 1 small rustic white loaf (uncut)
- ⅓ cup melted butter
- 3 tablespoons freshly grated Parmesan cheese

For the dressing:

- 5 tablespoons mayonnaise
- 4–5 tablespoons water
- 1–2 garlic cloves
- 3 tablespoons finely grated Parmesan cheese
- coarse sea salt and pepper

1 First make the dressing. Put the mayonnaise in a small bowl and stir in enough of the measured water to make a thin, pourable sauce. Crush the garlic to a paste with a little coarse sea salt and add to the mayonnaise with the Parmesan. Stir well. Thin the dressing with a little more water, if necessary, so that the sauce remains pourable. Add pepper to taste and set aside.

2 Tear the romaine leaves into large pieces and place in a large, shallow salad bowl. Snip the anchovies into small pieces and scatter over the lettuce.

3 To make the croûtons, cut the bread into 1¼-inch thick slices. Cut off the crusts and discard. Dip a pastry brush into the melted butter and lightly butter the slices of bread on all sides. Cut the bread into 1¼-inch cubes. Brush a large baking sheet with a little of the butter. Arrange the bread cubes on it in a single layer, brushing the cut sides with any remaining butter. Bake in a preheated oven, 400°F, for 12 minutes, or until crisp and a deep golden color. Watch the croûtons carefully toward the end of the cooking time as they tend to color quickly.

4 To serve, tip the hot croûtons into the salad and quickly drizzle the dressing over the top. Sprinkle the grated Parmesan over and serve at once.

Below: Caesar salad

Variation

Endive and Parmesan salad

Mix together 5 tablespoons mayonnaise, 1 tablespoon chopped fresh parsley, 1 crushed garlic clove and 2 tablespoons grated Parmesan. Stir in water to make a thin, pourable sauce. Season and set aside.

For the croûtons, cut 3 slices of bread, crusts removed, into cubes. Heat 2 tablespoons of olive oil and 2 tablespoons butter until sizzling. Add the cubes and fry, stirring, for 3–4 minutes, until golden. Drain and add salt to taste.

Arrange endive leaves on each plate. Drizzle the dressing over and pile the croûtons on top. Shave some Parmesan over the top and serve.

Radicchio and orange salad with dates and Brie

Serves 4
Preparation: 15 minutes
Carbohydrate: 25 g, Protein: 11 g, Fat: 18 g, Fiber: 3 g, Calories: 304 kcal, Sodium: 519 mg (per portion)

What you need:

- 2 small oranges
- 1 head of radicchio, roughly torn
- 1 bunch of watercress or handful of arugula
- 1⅓ cups pitted and chopped fresh dates
- 6 ounces Brie, rind removed, diced
- 6 tablespoons vinaigrette
- salt and pepper

1 With a zester, carefully remove small strips of rind from 1 of the oranges, then set aside. Using a small, sharp knife, peel the rind and pith from both oranges and slice them thinly.
2 Arrange all the salad ingredients in a large serving bowl or on individual plates and scatter the reserved orange rind over the top. Season with salt and pepper. Drizzle the dressing over the salad just before serving it.

Curly chicory, bacon and hazelnut salad

Serves 4–6
Preparation: 20 minutes
Carbohydrate: 1 g, Protein: 7 g, Fat: 17 g, Fiber: 0 g, Calories: 178 kcal, Sodium: 695 mg (per portion)

What you need:

- 1 large head of curly chicory
- 5 slices of rindless smoked bacon

- salt and pepper
- 6 tablespoons vinaigrette, preferably made with hazelnut oil

1 Tear the curly chicory into large pieces and place in a large salad bowl.
2 Cook the bacon on a rack under a preheated hot broiler for about 3–4 minutes, or until crisp, turning once or twice. Drain the bacon on paper towels, then use scissors to snip into small pieces. Add to the salad and season with salt and pepper to taste.
3 Pour the dressing over the salad. Toss lightly and serve at once with crusty bread.

Cook's Tip

Dates make a delicious addition to the combination of salad leaves, citrus fruit, and Brie. They are also highly nutritious and are full of potassium, calcium, and iron, as well as being high in fiber and low in sodium.

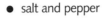

Above: *Radicchio and orange salad with dates and Brie*
Below left: *Curly chicory, bacon and hazelnut salad*

Above: *Chinese duck salad*
Below right: *Warm chorizo salad*
Far right: *Warm lentil salad*
Right: *Warm chicken liver salad with honey and mustard dressing*

Chinese duck salad

Serves 4–6
Preparation: 30 minutes
Cooking: 30 minutes
Carbohydrate: 106 g, Protein: 41 g,
Fat: 15 g, Fiber: 3 g, Calories: 725 kcal,
Sodium: 1328 mg (per portion)

What you need:

- oil, see method
- 8 ounces dry vermicelli
- 8 ounces duck breast
- 6 tablespoons hoisin sauce
- 3 scallions, sliced
- 1-inch piece of fresh ginger root, grated
- ½ head Chinese leaf salad, shredded
- 2 tomatoes, sliced
- 1 carrot, grated
- 4 ounces cooked broccoli florets
- baby corn, cooked and halved

1 Bring at least 2 quarts of water to a boil in a large pan. Add a dash of oil and a generous pinch of salt. Add the pasta, remove from the heat. Cover and let stand for 6 minutes.
2 Meanwhile, brush the duck breast generously with the hoisin sauce. Broil under a high heat for 20 minutes, turning once.
3 Drain the pasta and rinse under cold running water, drain again. Transfer to a salad bowl. Add a little oil and toss, separating any sticky strands. Add the remaining ingredients and mix.
4 Remove the duck from the broiler, cool for 5 minutes, and slice thinly. Add to the salad and toss thoroughly.

Warm chorizo salad

Serves 4
Preparation: 20 minutes
Cooking: 3 minutes
Carbohydrate: 6 g, Protein: 15 g,
Fat: 43 g, Fiber: 1 g, Calories: 465 kcal,
Sodium: 1514 mg (per portion)

What you need:

- about 4 cups bitter salad leaves
- small handful of sage leaves
- 5 tablespoons olive oil
- 10 ounces chorizo sausage, peeled and thinly sliced
- 1 small red onion, thinly sliced
- 1 garlic clove, chopped
- 2 tablespoons red wine vinegar
- salt and pepper

1 Arrange the salad leaves on each plate, or tear into pieces in a large bowl. Add the handful of sage leaves.
2 Heat the oil in a skillet until fairly hot. Add the sliced chorizo and fry over a high heat for 1 minute. Add the onion and garlic, and fry for 1–2 minutes, or until the chorizo is browned. Remove from the heat.
3 Stir the vinegar into the pan and season to taste. Quickly spoon the mixture over the salad and toss lightly. Serve at once.

Warm chicken liver salad with honey and mustard dressing

Serves 4
Preparation: 10 minutes
Cooking: 5–8 minutes
Carbohydrate: 4 g, Protein: 13 g,
Fat: 16 g, Fiber: 1 g, Calories: 208 kcal,
Sodium: 496 mg (per portion)

What you need:

- 2 tablespoons butter
- 8 ounces chicken livers, trimmed, cut into bite-size pieces
- 4 cups mixed salad leaves (radicchio, curly chicory, oak leaf lettuce and arugula)
- salt and pepper

For the dressing:
- 3 tablespoons extra-virgin olive oil
- 1 tablespoon raspberry vinegar
- 2 teaspoons clear honey
- 1 teaspoon coarse-grain mustard
- salt and pepper

1 First make the dressing. Put all the ingredients in a large salad bowl. Whisk with a fork until evenly combined and thickened, then adjust the seasoning to taste. Set aside.

2 Melt the butter in a large skillet over a medium heat until foaming. Add the chicken livers and toss vigorously for about 5–8 minutes until the livers are browned on the outside, but still tinged with pink in the center. Season to taste.

3 Quickly toss the salad leaves in the dressing, then arrange on individual plates. Spoon the chicken livers and cooking juices over the top. Serve immediately with crisp bread.

Warm lentil salad

Serves 4
Preparation: 10 minutes, plus
3–4 hours soaking
Cooking: 45 minutes
Carbohydrate: 53 g, Protein: 32 g,
Fat: 27 g, Fiber: 11 g, Calories: 571
kcal, Sodium: 990 mg (per portion)

What you need:

- 2 cups green lentils, soaked in water for 3–4 hours
- 2 carrots
- 1 onion, peeled
- 1 clove
- 1 bay leaf
- a pinch of dry thyme
- 1 garlic clove, peeled
- 1 leek, thinly sliced
- 1 cup chopped celery
- 1¾ cups diced smoked bacon,
- 1 tablespoon oil
- 1 tablespoon snipped chives

For the vinaigrette:
- scant 1 cup walnut oil
- 6 tablespoons sherry vinegar
- 1 tablespoon Dijon mustard
- salt and pepper

1 Put the lentils in a large pan. Peel a carrot and add to the lentils together with the onion studded with the clove, the bay leaf, thyme, and garlic. Cover with cold water and bring to a boil. Simmer for 30–35 minutes. Discard the vegetables, bay leaf and garlic, then drain the lentils.

2 Slice the remaining carrot thinly and blanch in a pan of lightly salted boiling water with the leek and celery. Drain well.

3 Whisk the vinaigrette ingredients together and fry the bacon until crisp. Stir the vegetables and bacon into the lentils and toss in the vinaigrette. Sprinkle with chives and serve warm.

Three-bean pasta twist salad

Serves 4
Preparation: 20 minutes
Cooking: 12 minutes
Carbohydrate: 93 g, Protein: 27 g, Fat: 8 g, Fiber: 8 g, Calories: 536 kcal, Sodium: 260 mg (per portion)

What you need:

- oil, see method
- 10 ounces dry tricolor pasta twists
- 2 scallions, chopped diagonally
- 1 red bell pepper, cored, deseeded and chopped
- ⅔ cup drained, canned red kidney beans
- ⅔ cup drained, canned pinto beans
- ⅔ cup drained, canned borlotti beans
- scant 1 cup crème fraîche
- 4 tablespoons milk
- 3 tablespoons chopped fresh dill
- salt and pepper

1 Bring at least 2 quarts of water to a boil in a large saucepan. Add a dash of oil and a generous pinch of salt. Cook the pasta for 8–12 minutes, until just tender. Drain well, then rinse under cold running water, and drain again. Transfer to a large salad bowl.

2 Add the scallions, red bell pepper and beans to the pasta. Mix well. Beat the crème fraîche and milk together in a bowl; fold into the salad and season to taste.

3 Fold in the chopped fresh dill and serve at once.

Pasta and avocado salad with tomato dressing

Serves 4
Preparation: 10 minutes, plus 30 minutes standing
Cooking: 10–12 minutes
Carbohydrate: 68 g, Protein: 13 g, Fat: 26 g, Fiber: 6 g, Calories: 540 kcal, Sodium: 215 mg (per portion)

What you need:

- 6 ounces small pasta shells
- 1 pound ripe tomatoes, peeled, deseeded and finely diced
- 6 tablespoons vinaigrette
- 2 ripe avocados
- salt and pepper

1 Bring a large pan of water to a boil. Add the pasta and cook until just tender to the bite. Drain and rinse under cold running water. Drain again and transfer to a large salad bowl.

2 Mix the diced tomatoes and vinaigrette together. Let stand for at least 30 minutes, then add to the pasta and toss thoroughly. Season to taste.

3 Just before serving, halve and pit the avocados. Peel and slice them, then arrange on the pasta.

Lumacone and smoked mackerel salad

Serves 4
Preparation: 20 minutes
Cooking: 12 minutes
Carbohydrate: 62 g, Protein: 20 g, Fat: 23 g, Fiber: 4 g, Calories: 522 kcal, Sodium: 618 mg (per portion)

What you need:

- 10 ounces dried lumacone
- 2 fillets peppered smoked mackerel, skinned and broken into bite-size pieces

- 2 oranges, segmented
- ½ cucumber, chopped
- sprigs of fresh dill, to garnish

For the dressing:

- 1–2 tablespoons whole grain mustard
- 3 tablespoons orange juice
- 1 teaspoon lemon juice
- 3 tablespoons olive oil
- salt and pepper

1 Bring at least 2 quarts of water to a boil in a pan. Add a little oil and a pinch of salt, and then cook the pasta for about 8–12 minutes.

2 Drain and rinse under cold running water. Drain again, transfer to a bowl, and add the mackerel. Mix lightly.

3 Make the dressing. Put the mustard, orange juice, lemon juice, and oil in a screw-top jar. Close tightly and shake well. Season, shake again and pour over the salad.

4 Fold in the orange segments and cucumber. Garnish with dill.

Cook's Tip

For the sweet and sour dressing, cut a scallion into shreds and place in a screw-top jar with 2 plums, diced. Add 5 tablespoons oil, 2 tablespoons sherry vinegar, 2 teaspoons soy sauce, 2 teaspoons tomato paste, ½ crushed garlic clove, ¼ teaspoon light brown sugar, salt and pepper.and shake until combined. Makes about 1½ cups.

Chinese noodle and shrimp salad

Serves 4–6
Preparation: 15 minutes
Cooking: about 6 minutes
Carbohydrate: 39 g, Protein: 18 g, Fat: 16 g, Fiber: 3 g, Calories: 363 kcal, Sodium: 1296 mg (per portion)

What you need:

- 6 ounces Chinese egg noodles
- 6 scallions
- 1 small bunch of radishes, trimmed
- 6 ounces sugar snap peas, topped and tailed
- 1½ cups cooked, shelled shrimp
- 1 quantity sweet and sour dressing (see Cook's Tip)
- salt and pepper

1 Bring a large pan of water to a boil. Add the egg noodles, and cover the pan; then remove from the heat. Let the noodles stand for 5 minutes, or until they are just tender. Drain in a colander and cool under cold running water. Drain again thoroughly and transfer to a bowl.

2 Cut the scallions into short lengths and shred finely. Leave the radishes whole or cut them into slices, as preferred. Add the scallions and the radishes to the noodles in the bowl.

3 Bring a pan of water to a boil. Add the sugar snap peas and blanch for 1 minute. Drain in a colander, and refresh under cold running water; drain again. Add to the salad with the shrimp and season to taste.

4 Just before serving, add the dressing to the salad and toss.

Left: *Lumacone and smoked mackerel salad*
Below: *Chinese noodle and shrimp salad*

Curried chicken salad

Serves 4
Preparation: 20 minutes
*Carbohydrate: 68 g, Protein: 13 g,
Fat: 26 g, Fiber: 6 g, Calories: 540 kcal,
Sodium: 215 mg (per portion)*

What you need:

- 1 small, whole, cooked chicken, about 2½ pounds
- 6 ounces seedless grapes, halved
- about 4 cups mixed salad leaves (e.g. romaine, red oakleaf, corn salad, arugula, curly chicory)
- salt and pepper
- sprigs of fresh cilantro, to garnish

For the dressing:
- 6 tablespoons mayonnaise
- 1 tablespoon medium-hot curry paste
- 1–2 tablespoons mango chutney

1 Skin the chicken and remove all the meat from the carcass. Shred the meat into bite-size pieces and place in a bowl with the grapes. Season to taste.
2 Tear the salad leaves into bite-size pieces and arrange to form a bed on a serving platter or on individual plates.
3 Mix all the dressing ingredi-ents together, adding just enough cold water to give a good thick pouring consistency.
4 Toss the chicken in the dress-ing, until combined. Pile onto the salad with the cilantro.

Smoked chicken, orange and avocado salad

Serves 4–6
Preparation: 30 minutes
*Carbohydrate: 12 g, Protein: 36 g,
Fat: 56 g, Fiber: 5 g, Calories: 690 kcal,
Sodium: 351 mg (per portion)*

What you need:

- 2 pounds smoked chicken
- 3 large oranges
- ½ cup shelled hazelnuts
- 2 tablespoons lemon juice
- 2 teaspoons coarse-grain mustard
- 1 teaspoon clear honey
- scant ½ cup hazelnut oil
- 2 large, ripe avocados
- salt and pepper

1 Remove the meat from the chicken bones and cut into neat, thin slices.
2 Peel and segment 2 oranges, taking care to remove all the pith.
3 Spread the nuts on a baking sheet and toast under a preheated broiler for 5 minutes until browned. Turn into a clean dishcloth and rub off the skins. Chop the nuts.
4 Halve the remaining orange, squeeze the juice and strain into a bowl. Add the lemon juice, mus-tard, honey, and seasoning. Gradually add the oil, beating after each addition until the dressing emulsifies and thickens.
5 Halve, pit and peel the avoca-dos. Slice the avocado flesh lengthways into thin slices.
6 Arrange both the chicken and avocado on a platter. Arrange the orange segments in the center.
7 Mix the dressing, then drizzle over the salad. Sprinkle with the hazelnuts and serve immediately.

Variation

Chicken and grape salad

Cover a chicken with water, 1 onion, studded with 3 cloves, 1 carrot and 1 celery stick, chopped, 1 bunch of tarragon, 1 bay leaf, a few peppercorns and salt. Bring to a boil, cover and simmer until tender. Remove skin, cut the meat into pieces. Reduce the stock by half and reserve. Whip ⅓ cup heavy cream until thick and fold into ⅔ cup mayonnaise. Add the stock, zest and juice of 1 lemon, 1 tablespoon tarragon, season to taste and mix.

Combine the meat with 4 ounces grapes. Spoon over the dressing and mix. Cover and chill for 2 hours, returning to room tempera-ture before serving.

Cook's Tip

For the spicy peanut dressing, heat 2 tablespoons chopped creamed coconut with 4 tablespoons milk for 2 minutes, stirring, until it forms a paste. Purée the mixture with ½ chopped onion, 1 crushed garlic clove, 4 tablespoons smooth peanut butter, 1 teaspoon soft brown sugar, 2 teaspoons soy sauce, ½ teaspoon chili powder, and salt and pepper, until smooth bowl. Cover and set aside. Makes about ¾ cup.

Gado gado with chicken

Serves 4
Preparation: 30 minutes
Carbohydrate: 15 g, Protein: 27 g,
Fat: 17 g, Fiber: 6 g, Calories: 313 kcal,
Sodium: 506 mg (per portion)

What you need:

- 8 ounces carrots, cut into matchsticks
- 6 ounces celery, cut into matchsticks
- 6 ounces leeks, cut into matchsticks
- 4 ounces snow peas
- ½ cucumber, peeled and cut in half lengthways
- 1 cup bean sprouts
- about 6 ounces pak choi
- 2 cooked chicken breasts, skinned and shredded
- 1 quantity spicy peanut dressing (see Cook's Tip)
- salt and pepper
- chopped fresh cilantro, to garnish (optional)

1 Bring a large saucepan of water to a boil. Add the carrot, celery, and leek matchsticks, and blanch for 2 minutes. Drain, and refresh under cold running water, then drain again. Tip into a large mixing bowl.

2 Cut the snow peas in half diagonally. Scoop out the seeds from the cucumber and cut the flesh into neat slices.

3 Add the snow peas, cucumber slices and the bean sprouts to the bowl. Season with salt and pepper to taste, then toss all the vegetables together.

4 Arrange the pak choi leaves on a large serving platter, with the shredded chicken and the tossed vegetables. Spoon the dressing over and garnish with cilantro, if using.

Above left: *Curried chicken salad*
Top: *Smoked chicken, orange and avocado salad*
Above: *Gado Gado with chicken*

Salade Niçoise

Serves 4
Preparation: 20 minutes
Carbohydrate: 13 g, Protein: 31 g,
Fat: 30 g, Fiber: 5 g, Calories: 444 kcal,
Sodium: 1127 mg (per portion)

What you need:

- 1 garlic clove, peeled and bruised
- 1 lettuce
- 4 ounces celery hearts, thinly sliced
- 4 ounces cucumber, peeled and thinly sliced
- 8 ounces small green beans, topped and tailed

- 8 ounces canned artichoke hearts, thinly sliced
- 1 pound tomatoes, peeled, deseeded and quartered
- 1 large green bell pepper, deseeded and sliced
- 1 onion, sliced
- 4 hard-cooked eggs, halved
- ½ cup black olives
- 8 canned anchovy fillets, drained
- 1 8-ounce can tuna in oil, drained

For the dressing:
- 7 tablespoons olive oil
- 4 fresh basil leaves, finely chopped
- salt and pepper

1 Gently rub around the inside of a large salad bowl with the bruised garlic clove. Line the bowl with lettuce leaves. Chop the remaining lettuce leaves roughly and then arrange in the bottom of the salad bowl.

2 In a mixing bowl, combine the celery and cucumber with the green beans and artichoke hearts. Arrange the mixture on top of the lettuce leaves in the salad bowl.

3 Arrange the quartered tomatoes, the sliced bell pepper and onion, eggs, black olives, and anchovies on top of the vegetables in the bowl. Cut the tuna into chunks and place in the bowl.

4 Make the dressing. Mix together the oil and basil, and season with salt and pepper to taste. Pour the dressing over the salad and transfer to individual serving plates.

Monkfish salad with cilantro and mint

Serves 4
Preparation: 15 minutes
Cooking: about 10 minutes
Carbohydrate: 4 g, Protein: 22 g, Fat: 10 g, Fiber: 1 g, Calories: 191 kcal, Sodium: 227 mg (per portion)

What you need:

- 1 pound monkfish, filleted

Variation

Californian potato salad

Boil 1½ pounds baby potatoes until tender. Drain. Broil 6 rindless bacon slices until crisp, then chop. Mix the bacon with the potatoes and add ¼ cup raisins.

For the dressing, mix 4 tablespoons yogurt with 1 teaspoon honey and ½ cup grated blue cheese. Season to taste. Add to the potato mixture and toss to coat. Serve warm or cold.

- 1 14-ounce can pimientos, drained
- 5 tablespoons olive oil
- 1 tablespoon coriander seeds, crushed
- 1 onion, sliced
- 2 garlic cloves, chopped
- 3 tablespoons capers, rinsed and drained
- pared rind of ½ lemon, cut into thin matchsticks
- a few sprigs of cilantro, roughly torn
- a few sprigs of fresh mint leaves, stripped from the stems and roughly torn
- 1 tablespoon balsamic vinegar or lemon juice
- salt and pepper

1 Cut the monkfish fillet into thin slices and set aside.

2 Tip the canned pimientos into a colander and rinse thoroughly under cold running water. Drain well and cut the pimientos into thin strips.

3 Heat the olive oil in a large skillet. Add the crushed coriander seeds and cook over a medium heat for a few seconds. Add the sliced onion and then cook slowly for about 5 minutes, stirring frequently, until the onion has softened but not browned. Add the garlic and cook for about 1 minute longer.

4 Increase the heat to moderately high. Add the monkfish to the skillet and cook, stirring lightly, for about 3–4 minutes, or until the fish is firm and opaque. Lower the heat and stir in the pimiento strips, capers, and strips of lemon rind. Remove the pan from the heat and let cool for a few minutes.

5 Add the cilantro and mint to the pan with the balsamic vinegar or lemon juice. Season to taste with salt and pepper and toss lightly. Serve the monkfish salad warm or let it cool.

Potato salad with salmon and shrimp

Serves 4
Preparation: 20 minutes
Cooking: 15–20 minutes
Carbohydrate: 33 g, Protein: 23 g, Fat: 19 g, Fiber: 3 g, Calories: 388 kcal, Sodium: 1265 mg (per portion)

What you need:

- 1¼ pounds waxy potatoes, scrubbed
- 2 ounces smoked salmon, cut into thin strips
- 2 cups cooked shelled shrimp
- 4 ounces seedless green grapes, halved
- ½ cup pecan nuts
- 1 tablespoon snipped chives
- 1 tablespoon chopped fresh dill, to garnish

For the dressing:

- 1 tablespoons mayonnaise
- 4 tablespoons sour cream
- 1 tablespoon lemon juice
- salt and pepper

1 Cook the potatoes in a saucepan of lightly salted boiling water for about 15–20 minutes until the potatoes are just tender. Drain well. When cool, slice the potatoes into a large salad bowl.

2 Add the smoked salmon, cooked shrimp, grapes, pecans and snipped chives. Mix the salad lightly, using two forks.

3 For the dressing, mix the mayonnaise, sour cream, and lemon juice together in a small bowl. Season to taste and whisk until thoroughly combined. Pour the dressing over the salad. Toss lightly to coat. Sprinkle with dill and serve at once.

Pasta and rice

Pasta and rice are staple ingredients in every cook's kitchen. Their place is a well-deserved one, because there is so much you can do with them. They are perfect for every occasion, whether it's a quick family meal you require, such as Spaghetti bolognese, or a grand dinner party dish like Linguine alla marinara, which is guaranteed to impress even your smartest friends. Add other grains, such as couscous and bulgar wheat, to your supply of staples, and you'll be ready for any culinary experience.

Right: *Lasagne*

Cook's Tip

A lot of traditional Italian recipes for lasagne add a pinch of ground nutmeg to the white sauce. To get the authentic flavor of Italian lasagne, just like mamma used to make, add nutmeg and leave out the cloves. One way of getting rid of any lumps, if you do not manage to achieve a smooth white sauce first-time, is to rub it through a fine strainer.

Lasagne

Serves 4
Preparation: 1 hour
Cooking: 1 hour
*Carbohydrate: 38 g, Protein: 56 g,
Fat: 60 g, Fiber: 3 g, Calories: 902 kcal
Sodium: 1060 mg (per portion)*

What you need:

- 9 dried "no-presoak" lasagne sheets
- ½ cup grated Parmesan cheese
- salt and pepper

For the meat sauce:
- 2 tablespoons olive oil
- 2 onions, finely chopped
- 3 garlic cloves, crushed
- 1 tablespoon dry oregano
- 1 tablespoon dry basil
- 3 tablespoons tomato paste
- 5 cups lean ground beef
- 1 14-ounce can plum tomatoes

For the cheese sauce:
- 4 cloves
- 1 onion, halved
- 2½ cups skimmed milk
- 2 tablespoons butter
- ¼ cup all-purpose flour
- 2 cups grated Cheddar cheese

1 Make the meat sauce. Heat the oil in a large saucepan and fry the onions for 3–5 minutes until

Variations

Lasagne verde

Replace the plain lasagne with the same quantity of lasagne verde (spinach flavoured lasagne). Replace the tomato paste with the same quantity of ready-made pesto or 3 table-spoons of chopped fresh basil. Proceed as for the main recipe.

Chicken lasagne

Replace the minced beef with the same quantity of lean minced chicken. Replace half the milk with natural yogurt when making the cheese sauce. Proceed as for the main recipe.

softened. Add the garlic and fry for 1 minute more, then stir in the herbs, tomato paste and beef. Fry the mixture, stirring constantly, for 5 minutes. Add the tomatoes to the filling with salt and pepper to taste. Stir well. Cover the pan and simmer the meat sauce for 45 minutes, stirring occasionally.

2 Meanwhile infuse the milk for the cheese sauce. Stick the cloves in the onion halves and put them in a small saucepan. Add the milk and bring to just below boiling point. Remove the pan from the heat and set aside for 15 minutes. Remove the onion halves and cloves.

3 Melt the butter in a saucepan. Stir in the flour and cook for 1 minute. Add the milk gradu-ally, whisking or beating the sauce over medium heat until thickened. Add the Cheddar cheese, and stir well until melted; then stir in salt and pepper to taste. Set aside.

4 Grease both the bottom and the sides of an oval or rectangu-lar 2 quart ovenproof dish. Spoon one-third of the meat mix-ture over the bottom. Spread over a quarter of the cheese sauce and cover with 3 sheets of lasagne. Some manufacterers of dried "no-presoak" lasagne sug-gest that you dip the sheets in hot water just before arranging them in the dish. Follow the instruc-tions on the package.

5 Repeat the layering process twice more, finishing with a layer of pasta. Cover with the remain-ing cheese sauce. Sprinkle over the Parmesan. Bake the lasagne in a preheated oven, 375°F , for 1 hour. Serve with a fresh green salad and crusty bread to mop up all the juices.

Chili tagliatelle

Serves 4
Preparation: 10 minutes
Cooking: 4–6 minutes
Carbohydrate: 23 g, Protein: 7 g,
Fat: 18 g, Fiber: 2 g, Calories: 278 kcal,
Sodium: 253 mg (per portion)

What you need:

- 4 tablespoons olive oil
- salt
- 12 ounces fresh tagliatelle verde
- 2 garlic cloves, crushed
- 2 fresh red chilies, deseeded and chopped
- ⅔ cup sliced button mushrooms
- 4 tablespoons balsamic vinegar
- 2 tablespoons orange juice
- 3 tablespoons red pesto
- 1 bunch of scallions, shredded
- ¼ cup chopped toasted hazelnuts, chopped

1 Bring plenty of water to a boil in a saucepan. Add a dash of oil and a pinch of salt. Add the tagliatelle and cook for about 4–6 minutes or until al dente.

2 Meanwhile, heat the remaining oil in a large pan. Add the garlic, chilies and mushrooms, and fry slowly for 2 minutes. Reduce the heat and stir in the remaining ingredients.

3 Drain the pasta well and add it to the garlic and chili mixture, tossing well. Serve at once.

Spaghetti alla bolognese

Serves 4
Preparation: 10 minutes
Cooking: 2½–3 hours
Carbohydrate: 41 g, Protein: 40 g,
Fat: 46 g, Fiber: 3 g, Calories: 747 kcal,
Sodium: 879 mg (per portion)

What you need:

- 1 pound spaghetti
- 1 teaspoon olive oil
- ½ cup grated Parmesan cheese

For the bolognese sauce:
- 4 tablespoons olive oil
- 1 onion, finely chopped
- 3 garlic cloves, crushed
- 4 slices rindless bacon, chopped
- 1 carrot, diced
- 1 celery stalk diced
- 5 cups ground lean beef
- ⅔ cup red wine
- ½ cup milk
- grated nutmeg
- 1 14-ounce can chopped tomatoes
- 1 tablespoon sugar
- 1 teaspoon chopped fresh oregano
- salt and pepper

1 Make the sauce. Heat the oil in a pan and fry the onion, garlic, bacon, carrot, and celery until softened and golden. Add the beef and then cook, stirring occasionally, until browned.

2 Add the red wine and bring to a boil. Reduce the heat slightly and cook over a medium heat until most of the wine has evaporated. Season to taste.

3 Add the milk and a little grated nutmeg, and stir well. Continue cooking until the milk is absorbed by the meat mixture. Add the tomatoes, sugar and oregano. Reduce to a bare simmer and cook, uncovered, for 2–2½ hours until reduced and colored.

Cook's Tip

Deseeding the chilies gives them a milder flavor. Cut the chili in half lengthways with a small, sharp knife, then scrape out the seeds and cut away the fleshy, white 'ribs' Always wash your hands afterward and never let any part of the chili go near your eyes.

Right: *Chili tagliatelle*
Far right: *Pasta with chicken, cream and mushroom sauce*

4 Bring a saucepan of salted water to the boil. Add the spaghetti and oil, and cook until al dente. Drain and season with pepper. Serve with the Bolognese sauce, sprinkled with the Parmesan cheese.

Pasta with chicken, cream and mushroom sauce

Serves 4
Preparation: 30 minutes
Cooking: 30 minutes
Carbohydrate: 79 g, Protein: 37 g,
Fat: 35 g, Fiber: 5 g, Calories: 763 kcal,
Sodium: 394 mg (per portion)

What you need:

- 3 part-boned chicken breasts
- 1 small onion, quartered
- 1 carrot, roughly chopped
- 1 bouquet garni
- a few black peppercorns
- 1¼ cups water
- 2 tablespoons dry sherry (optional)
- ¼ cup butter
- 3 cups thinly sliced button mushrooms
- 2 garlic cloves, crushed
- 1 teaspoon chopped fresh rosemary
- 1 tablespoon extra virgin olive oil
- 12 ounces dry pasta (e.g. farfalle, penne or fusilli)
- 1½ tablespoons all-purpose flour
- ⅔ cup heavy cream
- salt and pepper
- fresh rosemary, to garnish

1 Put the chicken in a saucepan with the onion, carrot, bouquet garni, and peppercorns. Pour in the water, and sherry, if using.

2 Bring to a boil; then lower the heat, cover and poach the chicken for 20 minutes until just tender when pierced.

3 Meanwhile, melt the butter in a separate saucepan. Add the mushrooms, garlic, rosemary, and salt and pepper to taste, and fry over a medium heat, stirring frequently, for about 5 minutes until the juices run. Remove from the heat. With a slotted spoon, transfer the mushrooms to a bowl.

4 Bring a large saucepan of water to a boil. Swirl in the oil and add ½ teaspoon salt. Add the pasta and boil, uncovered, over a medium heat for 10 minutes, or according to package instructions.

5 Meanwhile, lift the chicken out of the poaching liquid, then strain the liquid into a pitcher. Cut the chicken into strips, discarding the skin and bones.

6 Return the mushroom cooking liquid to the heat. Sprinkle in the flour and then cook for 1–2 minutes, stirring. Add the chicken poaching liquid, a little at a time, beating vigorously after each addition.

7 Bring to a boil, stirring. Lower the heat and add the chicken, mushrooms, cream, and seasoning. Stir well, then simmer, over a medium heat, stirring frequently, for 5 minutes until the liquid has thickened.

8 Drain the pasta and turn into a serving bowl. Pour in the sauce and toss to mix well. Serve garnished with the rosemary and with a mixed salad.

Above: *Spaghetti alla bolognese*

Cook's Tip

Use white button mushrooms for this sauce – dark ones will spoil its appearance.

Above: *Chow mein*
Below right: *Stir-fried noodles*

Chow mein

Serves 3–4
Preparation: 20 minutes
Cooking: about 10 minutes
Carbohydrate: 50 g, Protein: 29 g,
Fat: 16 g, Fiber: 3 g, Calories: 449 kcal,
Sodium: 962 mg (per portion)

What you need:

- 2 tablespoons rapeseed oil
- 4 scallions, or 1 onion, thinly sliced
- 1-inch piece of fresh ginger root, crushed
- 1 garlic clove, crushed
- 8 ounces skinless chicken breast cut diagonally in strips
- 1 8-ounce package Chinese egg noodles
- 4 ounces snow peas, topped and tailed, cut crossways if large
- 4 ounces boiled ham, cut into thin strips
- 2–3 tablespoons soy sauce, to taste
- 2 tablespoons rice wine or dry sherry
- 2 teaspoons sesame oil
- 1 teaspoon sugar
- salt and pepper

1 Heat a wok or large, deep skillet over a medium heat until hot. Add the oil and heat until hot but not smoking. Add the scallions or onion, ginger root and garlic, and stir-fry over a low heat for 1–2 minutes until softened but not colored.

2 Add the strips of chicken breast and stir-fry over a medium heat for 3–4 minutes until they all change color on all sides.

3 Meanwhile, put the noodles in a bowl and cover with some boiling water. Let stand.

4 Add the snow peas to the chicken in the wok and stir-fry for 2–3 minutes until the chicken is tender when pierced.

5 Drain the noodles. Add to the wok with the ham, and toss over a high heat until hot. Add the soy sauce, rice wine or sherry, sesame oil, and sugar. Season to taste. Toss everything around until all the ingredients are hot and glistening. Serve immediately.

Farfalle alla Napoletana

Serves 4
Preparation: 15 minutes
Cooking: 21 minutes
Carbohydrate: 83 g, Protein: 14 g,
Fat: 6 g, Fiber: 6 g, Calories: 446 kcal,
Sodium: 306 mg (per portion)

What you need:

- 2 tablespoons olive oil
- 1 onion, chopped
- 2 garlic cloves, crushed
- 2 carrots, finely chopped,

Variations

Bacon and corn farfalle

Make the sauce, as for the main recipe. Five minutes before the end of cooking time, add 1 cup crumbled, broiled rindless bacon slices, with 1⅓ cups sliced mushrooms and ½ cup corn niblets. Serve as in the main recipe.

Cilantro and sun-dried tomato farfalle

Make the sauce as for the main recipe, omitting the carrots and basil. Substitute 8 sliced, sun-dried tomatoes and 4 tablespoons chopped cilantro leaves scattered over the sauce to garnish.

3 Meanwhile, bring at least 2 quarts of water to a boil in a large saucepan. Add a dash of oil and a generous pinch of salt. Cook the pasta for about 8–12 minutes, until al dente.

4 Drain the pasta, tip onto a large serving platter, and season well with pepper. Drizzle with a little more oil if you wish. Pour the tomato sauce over the pasta. Shred the basil leaves and scatter over the sauce to garnish.

Stir-fried noodles

Serves 4
Preparation: 10 minutes
Cooking: 20 minutes
Carbohydrate: 35 g, Protein: 12 g, Fat: 12 g, Fiber: 2 g, Calories: 285 kcal, Sodium: 547 mg (per portion)

What you need:

- 4 tablespoons vegetable oil
- 2 garlic cloves, crushed
- 4 ounces medium-size egg noodles
- 2 teaspoons dark soy sauce
- 1 cup mixed sliced chicken breast, prepared squid and shelled shrimp
- ½ teaspoon black pepper
- 2 tablespoons nam pla (fish sauce)
- 1¾ cup shredded cabbage and broccoli florets
- 1¼ cups chicken stock
- 1 tablespoon cornstarch
- 1 tablespoon salted soybean flavoring
- 2 tablespoons sugar

1 Heat half the oil in a work or large, deep skillet. Add half the garlic and then stir-fry for 1 minute until golden brown. Add the noodles and soy sauce, and cook, stirring constantly, for 3–5 minutes. Transfer to a warm serving dish and keep warm.

2 Heat the remaining oil in the pan and add the rest of the garlic. Stir-fry for 1 minute until golden brown. Add the chicken breast, squid, shrimp, black pepper, and nam pla. Stir-fry for 5 minutes longer.

3 Add the shredded cabbage and the broccoli florets to the meat mixture in the pan and stir-fry for 3 minutes longer.

4 Stir in the chicken stock. Mix the cornstarch with 2 tablespoons of water and stir into the wok. Add the soybean flavoring and sugar, and bring to a boil. Lower the heat and then cook for 3 minutes longer, stirring constantly. Pour the thickened sauce over the noodles and then serve immediately.

blanched
- 2 red bell peppers, cored, deseeded and finely chopped
- 4 large tomatoes, chopped
- ⅔ cup red wine
- 1 14-ounce can chopped tomatoes with herbs
- 12 ounces dry farfalle
- salt and pepper
- 1 bunch of fresh basil, to garnish

1 Heat the oil in a large skillet. Add the chopped onion and garlic, and fry for about 3 minutes until softened but not colored.

2 Add the carrots and red bell peppers to the skillet and fry for 3 minutes longer. Stir in the chopped fresh tomatoes with the red wine and canned tomatoes. Add salt and pepper to taste. Simmer, partially covered, for 15 minutes.

Left: *Farfalle alla Napoletana*

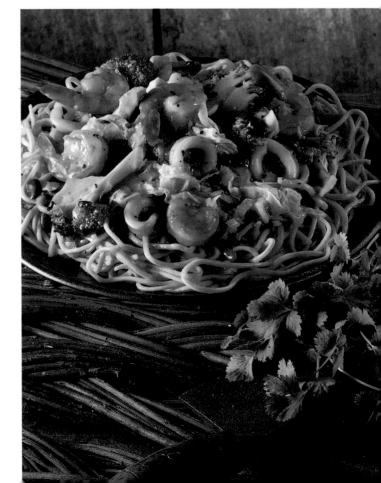

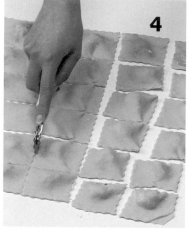

Spinach and ricotta ravioli

Serves 4–6
Preparation: 25 minutes
Cooking: 4–5 minutes
*Carbohydrate: 57 g, Protein: 19 g,
Fat: 21 g, Fiber: 4 g, Calories: 473 kcal,
Sodium: 528 mg (per portion)*

What you need:

- homemade pasta dough made with 2½ cups all-purpose flour

For the filling:

- 8 ounces spinach leaves
- 4 ounces fresh ricotta cheese
- ¼ cup grated Parmesan cheese
- grated nutmeg
- 1 egg, beaten
- salt and pepper

To serve:

- ¼ cup melted butter
- 3–4 fresh sage leaves, torn
- grated Parmesan cheese

1 Make the filling. Wash the spinach leaves and remove the stalks. Put the spinach in a saucepan without any water, cover and cook over very low heat for 5 minutes. Drain well and then place the spinach in a very large colander. Press down firmly with a plate to squeeze out any excess moisture. Roughly chop the spinach.

2 Put the ricotta and Parmesan cheeses in a large bowl and mix in the chopped spinach. Add the grated nutmeg, and salt and pepper to taste, and the beaten egg, mixing well until the mixture is like a paste.

3 Roll out the pasta dough as thinly as possible on a lightly floured surface and cut into 2 equal-size pieces. Put teaspoonfuls of the filling over one piece of pasta at intervals, about 2 inches apart.

4 Cover with the other sheet of pasta and press lightly around each little mound with your fingers. Using a pastry cutter wheel, cut the pasta into squares. Cook the ravioli in lightly boiling water for 4–5 minutes until they rise to the surface. Drain and serve with melted butter, sprinkled with sage and Parmesan cheese.

Cook's Tip

If you want to make this dish even more delicious add some chopped walnut which you can bake in a preheated oven, 350°F, for 10 minutes to crisp up.

Right: *Spinach with ricotta ravioli*

Linguine with mussels and tomato sauce

Serves 4
Preparation: 25 minutes
Cooking: 20 minutes
Carbohydrate: 41 g, Protein: 26 g,
Fat: 11 g, Fiber: 4 g, Calories: 356 kcal,
Sodium: 626 mg (per portion)

What you need:

- 2½ quarts mussels
- 3 tablespoons
  olive oil
- 1 onion, chopped
- 3 garlic cloves, crushed
- 1½ pounds tomatoes, peeled
  and chopped
- 1 pound linguine
- 3 tablespoons chopped
  parsley
- salt and pepper

Below: Linguine with mussels and tomato sauce

1 Prepare the mussels, wash them well and discard any that do not close tightly when tapped sharply against the work surface. Scrub the remaining mussels and remove the beards with a sharp knife. Place in a large saucepan with ½ cup water, cover with a lid and cook over a medium heat for 5–6 minutes until the mussels open, shaking the pan con-

Cook's Tip

Opening mussels either by cooking them or with a sharp knife often kills the mussel. It therefore must be eaten at once. Discard any mussels which are open before you cook them or any which do not open when cooked (see above).

stantly. Drain the mussels and remove their shells, reserving a few still in their shells to use for garnish later.

2 Heat the olive oil in a skillet. Add the onion and garlic. Fry over a medium heat until golden and tender. Add the chopped tomatoes and seasoning to taste, and cook slowly over low heat until the mixture is thickened and reduced.

3 Add the shelled mussels and mix these lightly into the tomato sauce. Simmer the mixture over a low heat for 2–3 minutes, or until the mussels are heated through.

4 Meanwhile, cook the linguine in salted boiling water until al dente. Drain well and toss lightly with the tomato and mussel sauce. Transfer to a serving dish or 4 warm plates. Sprinkle with chopped parsley and garnish with the reserved mussels.

Saffron rice

Serves 4
Preparation: 21 minutes
Cooking: 30–35 minutes
Carbohydrate: 54 g, Protein: 6 g, Fat: 24 g, Fiber: 1 g, Calories: 460 kcal, Sodium: 551 mg (per portion)

What you need:

- ½ teaspoon saffron threads
- 1 tablespoon boiling water
- ¾ cup ghee or butter
- 2 large onions, sliced
- 2 cups Basmati or
  Patna rice
- 1 teaspoon cloves
- 4 cardamoms
- 1 teaspoon salt
- 1 teaspoon black
  pepper
- 3 cups water
- silver leaf (varq), to garnish
  (optional)

water. Let soak overnight. The following day, rinse the kidney beans thoroughly and then drain them well.

2 Put the kidney beans in a large pan and add 3¾ cups boiling water. Cook for about 30 minutes, until the kidney beans are almost tender.

3 Add the coconut milk, thyme, scallions and chili to the saucepan. Season with salt and pepper to taste and bring back to boiling point. Boil rapidly for 5 minutes.

5 Add the rice and stir well. Cover and simmer slowly over a very low heat until the liquid has been absorbed. This will take about 20–25 minutes. If there is any remaining liquid left in the pan, drain the rice and beans. Transfer to a dish and serve hot.

Left: *Saffron rice*
Below: *Rice and beans*

1 Put the saffron threads in a small bowl with the boiling water and let soak for 30 minutes. Melt the ghee or butter in a heavy-bottomed saucepan. Add the onions. Fry slowly for 4–5 minutes until soft.

2 Put the rice in a strainer and wash thoroughly under cold running water to remove any milling and polishing dust. Drain well.

3 Add the rice to the onions in the pan, and stir in the cloves, cardamoms, salt and pepper. Fry for 3 minutes, stirring frequently.

4 Meanwhile, put the measured water in a pan and bring to a boil. Add to the rice, together with the saffron and its soaking liquid. Lower the heat and simmer for 15–20 minutes until the rice is cooked. Drain well and transfer the rice to a serving dish. Serve the rice hot, garnished, if using, with silver leaf.

Rice and beans

Serves 6
Preparation: 5 minutes, plus soaking overnight
Cooking: 55 minutes
Carbohydrate: 95 g, Protein: 16 g, Fat: 4 g, Fiber: 7 g, Calories: 453 kcal, Sodium: 247 mg (per portion)

What you need:

- 1½ cups dry red kidney beans
- 2½ cups coconut milk
- 2 sprigs of fresh thyme
- 2 scallions, finely chopped
- 1 fresh green chili, deseeded and finely chopped
- 2¾ cups long-grain rice
- salt and pepper

1 Put the dry red kidney beans in a large bowl and cover with cold

Variation

Risotto à la piémontaise

Cook as for the recipe for chicken liver risotto but omit the chicken liver, garlic and peas, and add instead ¾ cup grated Parmesan cheese together with 2–3 tablespoons of butter. Add the Parmesan cheese and butter at the same time as you add the peas in the main recipe. You can, if you choose omit the saffron as used in Chicken liver risotto from Risotto à la piémontaise but it does add a delicate and tempting flavor.

Above right: Chicken liver risotto
Above far right: Mushroom risotto

Chicken liver risotto

Serves 4
Preparation: 15–20 minutes
Cooking: 20 minutes
Carbohydrate: 31 g, Protein: 22 g, Fat: 26 g, Fiber: 3 g, Calories: 454 kcal, Sodium: 686 mg (per portion)

What you need:

- 2 tablespoons extra virgin olive oil
- 1 onion, finely chopped
- 8 ounces chicken livers, cores removed, roughly chopped
- 1 garlic clove, crushed
- 1½ cups Italian risotto rice
- ½ cup dry white wine
- about 4½ cups hot chicken stock
- large pinch of saffron threads
- ¾ cup frozen peas or petits pois
- salt and pepper

To finish:

- 6 tablespoons heavy cream
- 2 tablespoons chopped fresh flat leaf parsley (optional)
- about ½ cup grated Parmesan cheese

1 Heat the olive oil in a large flameproof casserole. Add the onion and fry over a low heat, stirring frequently, for 5 minutes until softened but not colored.

2 Add the chicken livers and the crushed garlic. Increase the heat to medium and fry, stirring constantly, for 2–3 minutes, or until the livers change color all over.

3 Add the rice and stir well; then add the white wine and stir until the bubbles subside.

4 Pour in 2½ cups of the hot stock. Add the saffron and salt and pepper to taste and stir well. Bring to a boil, then cover and simmer over a low heat for 10 minutes, stirring occasionally to prevent the rice sticking to the bottom of the pan.

5 Add 1¾ cups of the hot stock to the risotto. Stir well to combine, then add the peas. Cover and simmer for 10 minutes longer, stirring occasionally and adding a little more of the stock if necessary.

6 Remove the pan from the heat and lightly fold in the cream and parsley (if using). Adjust the seasoning to taste. Serve hot, topped with shavings of Parmesan. A crisp green or mixed salad is really the only accompaniment needed for this hearty lunch dish.

Mushroom risotto

Serves 4
Preparation: 15 minutes
Cooking: 30 minutes
Carbohydrate: 43 g, Protein: 14 g, Fat: 35 g, Fiber: 2 g, Calories: 532 kcal, Sodium: 1247 mg (per portion)

What you need:

- ½ cup butter
- 1 onion, finely chopped
- 4 cups thinly sliced mushrooms

Cook's Tip

In a genuine Italian risotto, the liquid is added a little at a time, which means that the cook must stand over the pot for the entire cooking time. This recipe cheats a little, but it is less time-consuming—and it works very well.

- 2½ cups risotto rice, e.g. Arborio
- boiling stock
- ⅛ teaspoon powdered saffron or saffron threads
- ⅓ cup grated Parmesan cheese
- salt and pepper

To serve:
- 2 tablespoons chopped fresh parsley
- freshly grated Parmesan cheese

1 Heat half the butter in a large heavy skillet. Add the onion and fry slowly until it is soft and translucent. Take care that it does not become too colored.

2 Add the sliced mushrooms and cook for 2–3 minutes, stirring occasionally. Add the rice and stir over a moderately low heat until all the grains of rice are glistening and beginning to turn translucent around the edges.

3 Stir in a ladleful of boiling stock and simmer very slowly until it has been absorbed. Continue adding more stock in this way until the rice is cooked and tender, and all the liquid has been absorbed. This will take

about 15–20 minutes. Halfway through cooking, stir in the saffron. Stir frequently to prevent the rice sticking to the bottom of the pan, and season with salt and pepper to taste.

4 When the rice is ready, lighlty mix in the remaining butter and the Parmesan cheese. The risotto should not be too dry–in fact, it should be quite moist. Serve sprinkled with parsley and some more grated Parmesan cheese.

Bell peppers with rice and walnut stuffing

Serves 4
Preparation: 20 minutes
Cooking: 40 minutes
Carbohydrate: 23 g, Protein: 13 g, Fat: 32 g, Fiber: 4 g, Calories: 423 kcal, Sodium: 587 mg (per portion)

What you need:

- 2 tablespoons sunflower oil
- 1 onion, chopped
- 1 large garlic clove, crushed
- ⅓ cup brown rice
- 1 bay leaf
- 2 cups tomato juice
- 1 teaspoon dry basil
- ½ cup grated Cheddar cheese
- 1 cup chopped walnuts
- 4 red or yellow bell peppers, cored, deseeded and cut in half lengthways
- salt and pepper
- shavings of Parmesan cheese, to garnish

1 Heat the oil in a saucepan. Add the onion and garlic, and cook, stirring, for 10 minutes. Add the rice, bay leaf and half the tomato juice. Cover the pan and simmer for 40 minutes, or until the rice is tender. Discard the bay leaf. Add the basil, cheese, and walnuts, and season to taste.

2 Fill the bell peppers with the rice mixture and place in a well-greased casserole dish. Pour the remaining tomato juice all around the bell peppers. Bake in a preheated oven at 350°F, for about 30–40 minutes. Garnish with shavings of Parmesan.

Below: *Bell peppers with rice and walnut stuffing*

Nasi goreng

Serves 4–6
Preparation: 15 minutes
Cooking: about 30 minutes
Carbohydrate: 30 g, Protein: 48 g,
Fat: 13 g, Fiber: 0 g, Calories: 419 kcal,
Sodium: 1539 mg (per portion)

What you need:

- 2 cups long-grain rice
- 2 eggs
- 2 tablespoons
  rapeseed oil
- 1 small onion, finely
  chopped
- 2 garlic cloves, roughly
  chopped
- 1 hot fresh red chili,
  deseeded and roughly
  chopped
- 1 pound skinless chicken
  breast fillets, cut diagonally
  into thin strips
- shelled cooked shrimp
- 2 tablespoons soy sauce, or
  more to taste
- salt and pepper
- scallions, to garnish

1 Rinse the rice and put in a large
saucepan; cover with cold water.
Bring to a boil with 1 teaspoon

Cook's Tip

This famous Indonesian rice
dish can be made with
different meats besides
chicken. Duck or turkey
breasts can be used or pork
or beef, or a mixture of different meats. The authentic
version includes a nugget of
terasi–a dried shrimp paste,
mixed in with the onion,
garlic and chili. It is available
at oriental specialty stores.

salt, and stir well. Lower the heat
and simmer, uncovered, for 20
minutes or until the rice is al
dente. Drain, rinse under cold
running water, and drain again
thoroughly. Set aside to cool.

2 Make an omelette. Beat the
eggs with salt and pepper. Heat
1½ tablespoons of oil in a small
skillet until hot but not smoking.
Pour the eggs over the bottom of
the pan. Lift up the edges and let
the unset egg run underneath.
Cook until the underneath is
golden and the top set. Slide out
of the pan, then roll up carefully
into a cigar shape. Let cool,
seam-side down.

3 Crush the onion, garlic and
chili to a paste, then fry in the
remaining oil in a wok or deep
skillet, for 1–2 minutes until
fragrant. Add the chicken and
stir-fry for 3–4 minutes until it
changes color all over. Add the
shrimp and soy sauce. Stir-fry
until the chicken is tender.

4 Mix the cold rice with the
chicken and shrimp. Toss over a
high heat until the rice is piping
hot. Add salt, pepper, and more
soy sauce to taste.

5 Turn the rice into a serving dish
and garnish with scallions and
the omelet cut into rings.

Chicken couscous

Serves 6–8
Preparation: 40 minutes
Cooking: about 2¾ hours
Carbohydrate: 80 g, Protein: 39 g,
Fat: 22 g, Fiber: 8 g, Calories: 640 kcal,
Sodium: 233 mg (per portion)

What you need:

- ⅔ cup garbanzo beans,
  soaked in cold water
  overnight, then drained
- 2 onions, finely chopped
- 3 garlic cloves, finely chopped
- 2 teaspoons ground coriander
- 2 teaspoons cumin
- 2 teaspoons turmeric
- 2 teaspoons chili powder
- ½ teaspoon ground cinnamon
- 2 tablespoons extra virgin
  olive oil
- 2 tablespoons tomato paste
- 12 skinned and boned
  chicken thighs, cut into large,
  bite-size pieces
- 4 carrots, sliced thickly
- 2 parsnips, sliced thickly
- 2 potatoes, cut into chunks
- ¼ cup butter
- 4 zucchini, thickly sliced
- 2 tablespoons raisins
- 2 cups water
- 2 tablespoons olive oil

- 1 pound ready-prepared "quick" couscous
- a large knob of butter
- harissa sauce, to taste
- salt and pepper
- fresh cilantro, to garnish

1 Simmer the garbanzo beans for 1 hour in a pan, half-covered.
2 Slowly fry the onions, garlic, and ground spices in the oil in the bottom of a couscousière or large pan for 5 minutes until softened.
3 Stir in the tomato paste, drained beans and seasoning. Cover with water and bring to a boil, stirring. Simmer, stirring occasionally, for 1 hour. Top up with water to keep the beans covered. Add the chicken and simmer, covered, for about 20 minutes. Stir occasionally.
4 Add the carrots, parsnips and potatoes and stir. Cover with water and bring to a boil. Cover and cook for 30 minutes or until the chicken and vegetables are tender, adding the zucchini and raisins halfway through.
5 Prepare the couscous. Put the measured water in a saucepan, add the olive oil and 2 teaspoons of salt, and bring to a boil.

Remove from the heat. Stir and pour in the couscous, and let swell for 2 minutes, or according to the package instructions. Add the butter and place over a low heat for 3 minutes, stirring with a fork to separate the grains.
6 Remove the couscous. Check the chicken for seasoning, add the harissa sauce, and stir well.
7 Fork the remaining butter into the couscous. Arrange the couscous in a ring with chicken and vegetables in the center. Garnish with cilantro and serve with some extra harissa sauce separately.

Tabbouleh with raisins, pistachios and cracked pepper

Serves 4
Preparation: 10 minutes, plus 1 hour chilling
Carbohydrate: 64 g, Protein: 10 g, Fat: 38 g, Fiber: 2 g, Calories: 626 kcal, Sodium: 858 mg (per portion)

What you need:

- 2 cups bulgar wheat
- 1 small red onion, finely chopped
- 2 tablespoons chopped fresh cilantro
- 2 tablespoons chopped fresh mint
- ½ cup raisins
- ½ cup extra virgin olive oil
- ¼ cup lemon juice
- 1 tablespoon cracked black pepper
- 2 teaspoons ground coriander
- 1 teaspoon ground cinnamon
- ½ cup chopped pistachio nuts
- ½ cup chopped, pitted black olives
- salt

Above: Tabbouleh with raisins, pistachios and cracked pepper
Below left: Chicken couscous

1 Place the bulgar wheat in a bowl and add plenty of cold water. Set aside the bulgar wheat to soak for 30 minutes, then drain off any remaining water.
2 Mix the bulgar wheat with the red onion, herbs, raisins, olive oil, lemon juice, pepper, and spices, stirring well until all the ingredients are evenly blended. Let the bulgar wheat cool and then chill for about 1 hour in the refrigerator for all the flavors to develop fully.
3 Remove the salad from the refrigerator and then let it return to room temperature. Stir in the nuts and olives, making sure they are evenly distributed. Season with salt and pepper to taste and serve at once.

Vegetables

It wasn't for nothing that your mother told you to eat your greens! But vegetables aren't only good for you, they're also relatively inexpensive, highly versatile, and absolutely delicious–provided, of course, that they are imaginatively cooked. Which is what these recipes are all about: from the humble potato to the glossy eggplant, there are hundreds of exciting and unusual things you can do with them all. Vegetable dishes should never be boring. They should both complement and enhance the meat or fish dish that they are intended to accompany.

Below: *Potato cakes*
Right: *Gratin dauphinois*

Potato cakes

Serves 4
Preparation: 20 minutes
Cooking: 5–10 minutes
Carbohydrate: 49 g, Protein: 12 g, Fat: 16 g, Fiber: 4 g, Calories: 371 kcal, Sodium: 280 mg (per portion)

What you need:

- 2 pounds potatoes
- 3 eggs
- ⅔ cup chopped onions
- 1 tablespoon all-purpose flour
- 1 tablespoon chopped fresh parsley and chives
- 1 garlic clove, crushed
- freshly grated nutmeg
- 6 tablespoons oil
- salt and pepper

1 Grate the potatoes coarsely, using a grater or food processor. Place in a strainer and rinse under cold running water. Drain and transfer the potatoes to a bowl.
2 Add the eggs to the bowl of grated potatoes and mix well. Add the chopped onions, flour, chopped parsley and chives, and the garlic. Season with salt, pepper, and grated nutmeg, then stir the mixture thoroughly.
3 Divide the potato mixture into equal-size portions and, using a spoon, mold them into small cakes.
4 Heat the oil in a skillet. When hot, add the potato cakes and fry until golden brown and crisp on both sides, turning them once during cooking. Serve the potato cakes very hot.

Gratin dauphinois

Serves 4–6
Preparation: 15–20 minutes
Cooking: 1¼–1½ hours
Carbohydrate: 50 g, Protein: 10 g, Fat: 30 g, Fiber: 3 g, Calories: 495 kcal, Sodium: 725 mg (per portion)

What you need:

- 1 garlic clove, cut in half
- ⅓ cup softened butter
- 2 pounds waxy potatoes, peeled and thinly sliced
- freshly grated nutmeg
- 1½ cups hot milk
- 1 cup light cream
- salt and pepper

1 Rub the cut garlic around the inside of a large earthenware baking dish to give flavor to the gratin. Brush the dish thickly with some of the softened butter.
2 Place a layer of the thinly sliced potatoes in the dish and sprinkle with salt, pepper, and nutmeg. Continue layering the potatoes in this way, seasoning each layer.
3 Mix the milk and cream, then pour this mixture over the potatoes, so that they are almost covered by the liquid.
4 Dot the remaining butter over the top, then bake in a preheated oven, 350°F, for 1–1¼ hours, or until tender when pierced with a skewer. Increase the oven heat to 400°F, for the last 15 minutes of cooking time to brown the top layer. Serve hot, straight from the baking dish.

Carrots with ginger and orange butter

Serves 4–6
Preparation: 10 minutes
Cooking: 10–12 minutes
Carbohydrate: 21 g, Protein: 2 g, Fat: 11 g, Fiber: 6 g, Calories:189 kcal, Sodium: 355 mg (per portion)

What you need:

- 2 pounds carrots, sliced, or whole baby carrots
For the ginger and orange butter:
- ¼ cup butter, softened
- 1 teaspoon grated ginger root
- ½ teaspoon grated orange rind
- ½ tablespoon orange juice
- ½ teaspoon clear honey
- 1 tablespoon chopped fresh chervil
- salt and pepper

1 Steam or boil the carrots for 10–12 minutes until tender.

2 Meanwhile, make the ginger and orange butter. Place all the ingredients in a food processor and blend until smooth and evenly combined.

3 Transfer the cooked carrots to a warmed serving dish. Add the butter and toss well together until the carrots are thoroughly coated with the butter; then serve at once.

Roasted fall vegetables with a garlic sauce

Serves 4–6
Preparation: 25 minutes
Cooking: 1¼ hours
Carbohydrate: 49 g, Protein: 8 g, Fat: 13 g, Fiber: 8 g, Calories: 331 kcal, Sodium: 353 mg (per portion)

What you need:

- 1 large head of garlic
- 2 large onions, cut into wedges
- 8 small carrots, quartered
- 8 small parsnips
- 12 small potatoes, halved if large
- 2 heads fennel, thickly sliced
- 4 sprigs of fresh rosemary
- 4 sprigs of fresh thyme
- 6 tablespoons extra virgin olive oil
For the garlic sauce:
- 1 thick slice of day-old bread
- 4 tablespoons milk
- ⅓ cup extra virgin olive oil
- salt and pepper

1 Blanch the head of garlic in boiling, salted water for about 5 minutes. Drain and pat dry on paper towels.

2 Put all the vegetables and herbs in a large roasting pan, placing the garlic in the middle. Season well and stir in the oil to coat the vegetables. Cover the pan with foil and bake in a pre-heated oven, 425°F, for 50 minutes. Remove the foil and bake for 30 minutes longer.

Cook's Tip

Roasting vegetables in a hot oven draws out their natural sweetness and intense flavor. It is important to cut the vegetables into similar-size pieces so they will cook evenly.

3 Remove the garlic. Carefully peel and discard the skin. Mash the garlic flesh with a fork. Put the bread in a bowl. Add the milk and soak for 5 minutes.

4 Place the bread and garlic flesh in a blender and process to form a smooth paste. Gradually blend in the oil, adding a little at a time, until evenly combined, then season to taste.

5 Serve the roasted vegetables accompanied by the garlic sauce to dip.

Roasted Jerusalem artichokes

Serves 4
Preparation: 10 minutes
Cooking: 30 minutes
Carbohydrate: 22 g, Protein: 5 g, Fat: 288 g, Fiber: 7 g, Calories: 2687 kcal, Sodium: 203 mg (per portion)

What you need:

- 1½ pounds Jerusalem artichokes, scrubbed but not peeled
- 4 tablespoons walnut or extra virgin olive oil
- 12 whole garlic cloves
- 1 tablespoon chopped fresh sage leaves
- ¼ cup toasted and chopped walnuts
- salt and pepper

1 Cut any larger artichokes in half so they are all roughly the same size, then blanch in lightly salted water for 5 minutes.

2 Drain well and toss them immediately with the oil, garlic, sage, salt and pepper.

3 Place in a roasting pan and bake in a preheated oven, 400°F, for about 30 minutes, turning occasionally, until they are golden and tender.

4 Transfer the artichokes to a warmed serving dish. Scatter over the chopped walnuts and serve at once.

Cook's Tip

The Jerusalem artichoke is a very underrated vegetable, perhaps due to its anonymity: it could easily be mistaken for just another variety of the potato family. However, it has a flavor all of its own–somewhere between turnip and potato with a nutty, almost peppery taste. When cooking by this method there is no need to peel the artichokes.

Below: *Roasted Jerusalem artichokes*

Variation

Roasted parsnips with thyme butter

Toss ¼ pound baby parsnips with 1 tablespoon olive oil, 1 garlic clove, 2 sprigs of thyme and sea salt. Place in a roasting pan. Bake in a preheated oven at 400°F for 40–45 minutes, stirring occasionally.

Meanwhile, melt ¼ cup butter in a small pan, add 1 tablespoon chopped fresh thyme, 1 teaspoon grated lemon rind, a pinch each of salt and cayenne pepper, and fry slowly for 3–4 minutes until softened.

Remove the parsnips from the oven. Discard the thyme and dot with thyme butter. Toss well and serve at once.

Mixed bean sauté with almonds and chives

Serves 4
Preparation: 10 minutes
Cooking: 6–7 minutes
Carbohydrate: 10 g, Protein: 9 g,
Fat: 1 2 g, Fiber: 6 g, Calories: 177 kcal,
Sodium: 200 mg (per portion)

What you need:

- 1½ pounds mixed beans, trimmed and sliced (e.g. fava beans, runner beans, green beans, snap beans, yellow string beans, etc.)
- 2 tablespoons almond or extra virgin olive oil
- 1 small leek, trimmed, cleaned and sliced
- 2 garlic cloves, sliced
- ½ cup slivered almonds
- 2 tablespoons chopped fresh chives
- salt and pepper

Below: *Mixed bean sauté with almonds and chives*
Above right: *Fried chili cabbage*

1 Blanch all the beans in lightly salted boiling water for 1 minute. Drain, refresh under cold water, and pat dry on paper towels.
2 Heat the oil in a wok or large skillet. Add the leek, garlic, and almonds, and fry slowly for 3 minutes until softened.
3 Add the beans and stir-fry for 3–4 minutes until tender. Add the chives, salt and pepper, and serve.

Fried chili cabbage

Serves 4–6
Preparation: 20 minutes
Cooking: 35 minutes
Carbohydrate: 21 g, Protein: 7 g,
Fat: 39 g, Fiber: 6 g, Calories: 459 kcal,
Sodium: 577 mg (per portion)

What you need:

- ½ cup ghee or butter
- 1 small onion, chopped
- 6 garlic cloves, crushed
- 1 teaspoon white cumin seeds
- 1 teaspoon turmeric
- 1 cabbage, coarsely chopped
- 1 cup chopped potatoes
- ¾ cup shelled peas

- 4 ounces carrots, sliced
- salt
- 8 ounces tomatoes, peeled and sliced
- 1 teaspoon aamchoor (mango powder)
- 1 green chili, chopped
- 1 tablespoon grated ginger root
- 1 teaspoon garam masala
- 1 tablespoon chopped cilantro leaves
- 2 tablespoons melted butter

Cook's Tip

Garam masala is a mixture of spices used in Indian cooking. The ingredients and their proportions vary from one region of India to another, but a typical mixture would probably include black cumin seeds, cloves, cinnamon, cardamom, and peppercorns. You can make up a mixture yourself at home, or you can buy it ready-made in many supermarkets.

1 Melt the ghee or butter in a large saucepan. Fry the onion, garlic, and cumin seeds for about 5 minutes until golden brown. Add the turmeric and shake the pan for a few seconds.

2 Add the chopped cabbage, potatoes, peas, carrots, and salt. Cook, stirring continuously, for 5 minutes. Cover the pan and cook slowly over a low heat for 10 minutes longer.

3 Add the tomatoes, aamchoor (mango powder), the chili, and the ginger root. Stir well, then replace the lid, and continue cooking for 10 minutes longer.

4 Add the garam masala and chopped cilantro and stir well. Heat through over a low heat for about 5 minutes, then serve hot with the melted butter poured over the top.

Morel mushrooms with wild rice

Serves 2
Preparation: 10 minutes
Cooking: 3 minutes
Carbohydrate: 51 g, Protein: 6 g,
Fat: 42 g, Fiber: 0 g, Calories: 627 kcal,
Sodium: 204 mg (per portion)

What you need:

- 5 ounces fresh morel mushrooms, rinsed, trimmed and halved lengthways, or 1½ tablespoons dry morels plus 2 teaspoons dry horn of plenty mushrooms and 4 ounces mixed fresh mushrooms, such as shiitake, yellow and gray oyster, trimmed
- ¾ cup raw wild rice, well rinsed
- ¼ cup butter
- 6 tablespoons heavy cream
- 1 tablespoon brandy
- salt and pepper

1 If you are using the dry mushrooms, soak them in warm water for 20–30 minutes, then drain. Cook the wild rice in a saucepan of salted boiling water for 18–20 minutes until the grains begin to split. Drain well.

2 Meanwhile, melt half of the butter in a heavy-bottomed skillet. Add all of the mushrooms and cook over a moderately high heat for about 2–3 minutes. Season to taste.

3 Add the cream and brandy, and reduce the heat. Continue cooking until the liquid has almost all evaporated. Transfer the mushrooms to a bowl, cover and keep warm.

4 Melt the remaining butter in the pan. Add the wild rice and reheat, stirring to coat well. Season to taste and serve topped with the mushrooms.

Stir-fried garlic mushrooms

Serves 4
Preparation: 5 minutes
Cooking: 5 minutes
Carbohydrate: 5 g, Protein: 2 g,
Fat: 7 g, Fiber: 1 g, Calories: 103 kcal,
Sodium: 258 mg (per portion)

What you need:

- 2 tablespoons olive oil
- 1 tablespoon butter
- 8 ounces mixed mushrooms, such as shiitake and crimini, rinsed, trimmed and thickly sliced

- 3–4 garlic cloves, crushed
- 4 ounces oyster mushrooms, rinsed, trimmed and thickly sliced
- 2–3 tablespoons dry sherry or vermouth
- salt and pepper
- 4 tablespoons chopped fresh parsley

1 Heat a wok or large skillet until hot. Add the oil and butter, and place over a moderate heat until foaming.

2 Add the shiitake and crimini mushrooms, the garlic, salt, and plenty of pepper. Increase the heat to high and stir-fry for about 2 minutes.

3 Add the oyster mushrooms. Sprinkle over the dry sherry or vermouth and stir-fry for 3 minutes longer, or until tender.

4 Taste, and adjust the seasoning. Remove the pan from the heat and stir in the chopped fresh parsley. Serve at once.

Above left: *Morel mushrooms with wild rice*
Below: *Stir-fried garlic mushrooms*

Ratatouille

Serves 6
Preparation: 15 minutes
Cooking: 1¾ hours
Carbohydrate: 12 g, Protein: 4 g,
Fat: 34 g, Fiber: 5 g, Calories: 379 kcal,
Sodium: 350 mg (per portion)

What you need:

- 5 zucchini, peeled and sliced
- 2 eggplants, sliced
- scant 1 cup olive oil
- 3 onions, finely chopped
- 2 large green bell peppers, broiled, peeled and sliced
- 2 pounds tomatoes, peeled and quartered
- 6 garlic cloves, finely chopped
- 1 teaspoon coriander seeds, crushed
- ⅓ cup dry white wine
- salt and pepper
- 1 tablespoon chopped basil
- 2 tablespoons chopped fresh parsley

1 Place the sliced zucchini and eggplants in a colander and lightly salt. Set aside for about 15 minutes to let them drain. Then rinse and pat dry with paper towels.
2 Heat a little of the oil in a large skillet. Add the onions and fry over a low heat for about 15 minutes, until soft and golden, and then transfer to a flameproof casserole.
3 Fry the bell peppers, tomatoes, zucchini and eggplants for 15 minutes each. When cooked, drain and add to the casserole. Replenish the pan with the remaining olive oil as necessary.
4 Mix all the vegetables in the casserole, and add the garlic, coriander and wine. Season to taste, then simmer slowly for about 30 minutes. Add the basil and parsley just before serving.

Okra with chilies

Serves 4
Preparation: 10 minutes
Cooking: 5–10 minutes
Carbohydrate: 8 g, Protein: 5 g,
Fat: 16 g, Fiber: 6 g, Calories: 189 kcal,
Sodium: 217 mg (per portion)

What you need:

- 3 tablespoons ghee or butter
- 1 large onion, sliced
- 3 garlic cloves, sliced
- 1-inch fresh ginger root, peeled and grated
- 2 fresh red chilies, finely chopped
- ½ teaspoon chili powder
- 1 pound okra
- 1 cup water
- salt
- 2 teaspoons unsweetened shredded coconut

1 Melt the ghee or butter in a heavy saucepan. Add the onion, garlic, ginger root, chilies, and chili powder. Fry slowly for about 5 minutes, until softened. Stir occasionally.

2 Top and tail the okra, then add to the pan with the measured water and salt to taste. Bring to a boil. Lower the heat, cover and simmer for 5–10 minutes, until the okra are just tender, but still firm to the bite. Sprinkle with the coconut and serve hot.

Eggplants Sicilian-style

Serves 4
Preparation: 40 minutes
Cooking: 1 hour
Carbohydrate: 7 g, Protein: 6 g,
Fat: 18 g, Fiber: 4 g, Calories: 214 kcal,
Sodium: 2062 mg (per portion)

What you need:

- 3 eggplants, cut into ½-inch dice
- salt
- 1 2-ounce can anchovy fillets
- 1 onion, thinly sliced
- 4 tablespoons olive oil
- 2 celery stalks, diced
- ⅔ cups passata (strained tomatoes)
- 3 tablespoons white wine vinegar
- 1 yellow bell pepper, deseeded and thinly sliced
- 1 red bell pepper, deseeded and thinly sliced
- ⅓ cup chopped capers
- ½ cup pitted and sliced black olives
- ½ cup pitted and sliced green olives
- 2 tablespoons pine nuts
- 2 tablespoons chopped fresh parsley

1 Put the diced eggplant in a colander. Sprinkle with salt and leave for 15–20 minutes to exude the bitter juices. Rinse off the salt under cold running water, then pat dry with paper towels.

2 Soak the anchovies in a little warm water in a bowl to remove some of their saltiness. Remove, pat dry, and cut the anchovies into thin strips. Set aside.

3 Fry the onion in the oil until soft and golden. Add the celery and cook for 2 minutes. Add the eggplant, and cook for 3 minutes until golden, stirring from time to time. Add the passata and cook slowly until absorbed. Add the vinegar and cook for 1 minute. Add the bell peppers, anchovies, capers, and olives, and cook for about 3 minutes.

4 Transfer to an ovenproof dish and bake, covered, in a preheated oven at 350°F, for 40 minutes. Stir in the pine nuts and cook for 20 minutes longer. Serve warm or cold, sprinkled with parsley.

Far left: *Ratatouille*
Left: *Okra with chilies*
Below: *Eggplants Sicilian-style*

Fried mixed vegetables

Serves 4
Preparation: 15 minutes
Cooking: 6–7 minutes
Carbohydrate: 11 g, Protein: 5 g,
Fat: 6 g, Fiber: 4 g, Calories: 116 kcal,
Sodium: 333 mg (per portion)

What you need:

- 4 ounces cabbage
- 4 ounces cauliflower
- 4 ounces broccoli
- 2 carrots
- 4 ounces mushrooms
- 1 onion
- 3 tablespoons vegetable oil
- 1 garlic clove, crushed
- ½ teaspoon black pepper
- 2 tablespoons oyster sauce
- ⅔ cup chicken or vegetable stock
- 1 cup bean sprouts

1 Shred the cabbage; separate the cauliflower florets; and trim and slice the broccoli. Scrape the carrots and cut into matchstick strips. Wipe the mushrooms on paper towel and slice thinly. Peel and coarsely slice the onion into rings.

2 Heat the vegetable oil in a wok or deep skillet. Add the crushed garlic and then stir-fry quickly over a medium heat until softened and golden. Do not let it get too brown.

3 Add the shredded cabbage and cauliflower florets, and a generous grinding of pepper. Stir in the oyster sauce and the chicken or vegetable stock, and then cook, stirring constantly, for 3 minutes.

4 Add the broccoli, carrots, mushrooms, and onion to the pan, together with the bean sprouts. Stir-fry for 2 minutes. Transfer the fried vegetables to a large dish and serve immediately.

Stir-fried greens with turnips

Serves 4
Preparation: 15 minutes
Cooking: 20–23 minutes
Carbohydrate: 15 g, Protein: 6 g,
Fat: 16 g, Fiber: 6 g, Calories: 223 kcal,
Sodium: 39 mg (per portion)

What you need:

- 1 pound greens (see Cook's Tip)
- 4 tablespoons extra virgin olive oil
- 6 ounces baby turnips, sliced
- 4 tablespoons vegetable stock
- 1 teaspoon balsamic vinegar
- 2 garlic cloves, sliced
- 2 teaspoons grated lemon rind
- ⅓ cup raisins
- ⅓ cup toasted pine nuts

1 Trim all the greens and discard the thick central stalks. Shred the green parts thinly and blanch in lightly salted boiling water for 1 minute; then drain and refresh under cold running water, and then pat dry with paper towels.

2 Heat half the oil in a small skillet. Fry the turnips for 5 minutes until lightly golden. Add the stock and vinegar, cover and cook over a low heat for 3 minutes longer.

3 Heat the remaining oil in a wok or large skillet. Add the garlic, lemon rind, raisins, and pine nuts, and stir-fry for 5 minutes longer, or until the greens are tender; then stir in the turnips, together with their juices. Heat through and serve immediately.

Spinach with tomatoes

Serves 4–6
Preparation: 15 minutes
Cooking: 20–25 minutes
Carbohydrate: 12 g, Protein: 10 g, Fat: 47 g, Fiber: 6 g, Calories: 502 kcal, Sodium: 720 mg (per portion)

What you need:

- 2 pounds fresh spinach, washed thoroughly
- ¾ cup ghee or butter
- 2 large onions, thinly sliced
- 2 garlic cloves, thinly sliced or crushed
- 5 ounces fresh ginger root
- 2 teaspoons chili powder
- 2 teaspoons tumeric
- 2 teaspoons garam masala
- 2 teaspoons coriander seeds
- 1 teaspoon cumin seeds
- 1½ teaspoons salt
- 2 teaspoons freshly ground black pepper
- 1 14-ounce can Italian plum tomatoes

1 Shake the washed spinach dry. Remove and discard any thick stalks; then cut the spinach leaves into course strips, about 1 inch wide.

2 Melt the ghee or butter in a large, heavy-bottomed saucepan. Add the onions and garlic. Fry over a medium heat for about 5 minutes until they are golden and soft.

3 Meanwhile, peel the fresh ginger root and cut it into fine strips, about ⅛ inch thick. Add to the saucepan and cook slowly for 5–6 minutes. Stir in the chili powder, turmeric, garam masala, coriander and cumin seeds, with salt and pepper to taste, and cook for 1 minute.

4 Add the spinach and toss well to coat in the spice mixture. Add the tomatoes with their juice and bring to a boil, stirring constantly; then add just enough boiling water to prevent the spinach sticking to the bottom of the saucepan. Simmer for about 5–10 minutes longer, until the spinach and tomatoes are cooked. Serve the spinach with accompaniments such as a curry of fish, chicken or meat, as well as lentils and rice.

Above left: *Fried mixed vegetables*
Far left: *Stir-fried greens with turnips*
Left: *Spinach with tomatoes*

Desserts

The dessert provides the finishing touch to a meal. It is important to plan your menu so that you choose the appropriate dessert for the meal. Try, for example, to balance a rich main course with a light dessert, such as a fruity concoction or a refreshing sorbet. The time of year plays a part, too, in your choice of dessert. The winter months demand something hot, warming and satisfying, while hot summer days call for ice creams, sorbets, and frozen desserts.

Below: *Warm chocolate pots*
Right: *Chocolate tartlets*

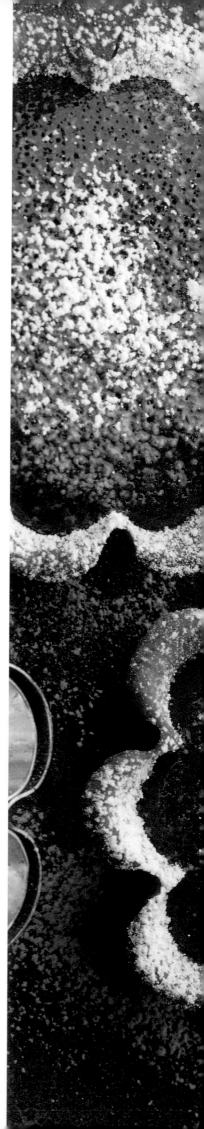

Warm chocolate pots

Serves 8
Preparation: 15 minutes, plus cooling and setting
Carbohydrate: 20 g, Protein: 4 g, Fat: 14 g, Fiber: 0 g, Calories: 223 kcal, Sodium: 28 mg (per portion)

What you need:

- 6 squares dark chocolate, chopped
- 1 cup strong espresso coffee
- 2 tablespoons whiskey
- ¼ cup sugar
- 6 egg yolks
- ¼ cup heavy cream
- grated nutmeg, to decorate

1 Place the chocolate in a small saucepan with the coffee and whiskey. Heat until the chocolate has melted. Add the sugar and stir until dissolved. Remove the pan from the heat.
2 Beat in the egg yolks until thickened. Pour through a fine strainer into 8 espresso cups. Cool and chill until set.
3 Whip the cream until it holds its shape and spoon a little onto each pot. Sprinkle with nutmeg. Pour boiling water into a dish to a depth of ½ inch. Sit the pots in the boiling water for 1 minute, remove and serve.

Chocolate tartlets

Makes 10–11
Preparation: 25 minutes, plus cooling
Cooking: 20 minutes

Carbohydrate: 36 g, Protein: 6 g,
Fat: 30 g, Fiber: 1 g, Calories: 431 kcal,
Sodium: 224 mg (per portion)

What you need:

For the pastry dough:
- 2 cups all-purpose flour
- ½ cup diced chilled butter
- ½ cup superfine sugar
- 1 egg, beaten

For the filling:
- 6 squares dark chocolate, broken into squares
- 2–3 tablespoons water
- 1 tablespoon diced, unsalted butter
- 1 tablespoon brandy
- 3 eggs, separated
- confectioners' sugar, for dusting

1 Place the flour in a bowl. Add the butter and rub in until the mixture resembles bread crumbs. Stir in the sugar; then add the egg and mix to a firm dough, adding a little water if necessary.

2 Knead the dough on a floured surface. Roll out dough and line 8 3-inch deep tartlet pans. Reroll the trimmings and line 2–3 more pans. Fill each with crumpled foil and place on a baking sheet. Bake in a preheated oven, 400°F, for 15 minutes. Remove the foil and bake for 5 minutes more. Cool.

3 Make the filling. Place the chocolate in a bowl. Add the water. Set over a pan of hot water until the chocolate has melted.

4 Remove the bowl and stir in the butter until melted. Add the brandy and the egg yolks. Beat the egg whites until stiff and dry; fold into the chocolate mixture.

5 Spoon the mixture into the pastry cases; let set. Dust with confectioners' sugar before serving.

Peach, apricot and blueberry gratin

Serves 6
Preparation: 10 minutes
Cooking: 5–6 minutes
Carbohydrate: 21 g, Protein: 7 g,
Fat: 7 g, Fiber: 2 g, Calories: 169 kcal,
Sodium: 46 mg (per portion)

What you need:

- 4 firm ripe peaches, halved, pitted and very thinly sliced
- 6 firm ripe apricots, halved, pitted and very thinly sliced
- 1¼ cups blueberries
- 8 ounces mascarpone cheese
- 1 cup Greek-style yogurt
- 3 tablespoons light muscavado sugar
- 1 teaspoon ground cinnamon

Below: *Peach, apricot and blueberry gratin*
Right: *Peach granité*

1 Spoon the peaches and apricots into a shallow flame-proof dish with the blueberries.
2 Beat the mascarpone and yogurt together and spread over the fruit.
3 Combine the sugar and cinnamon. Sprinkle over the gratin to cover the surface and cook under a hot broiler for 5–6 minutes until the sugar is caramelized. Cool for a few minutes and serve.

Variation

Amaretti fruit gratin

Place 1 cup of crumbled amaretti cookies in the bottom of the dish. Add the fruit and 4 tablespoons Kirsch and cook as in the main recipe.

Peach granité

Serves 4
Preparation: 15 minutes, plus cooling and freezing
Cooking: 5 minutes
Carbohydrate: 109 g, Protein: 1 g,
Fat: 0 g, Fiber: 1 g, Calories: 494 kcal,
Sodium: 14 mg (per portion)

What you need:

- 4 ripe but firm peaches
- 1 cup rosé wine
- 1 cup water
- 1 cup superfine sugar
- a pinch of cinnamon
- 4 sprigs of fresh mint, to decorate

For the granité:
- 1 cup rosé wine
- ½ cup fresh orange juice
- ½ cup superfine sugar

1 Blanch the peaches for 30 seconds only in boiling water. Remove with a slotted spoon and let drain. Place under cold running water for a few seconds, to cool them. Cut each in half, peel and remove the pits.

Variation

Poached pears

Replace the 12 figs with 6 firm, ripe pears. Peel the pears and cook them in the syrup for about 40 minutes until cooked through but not mushy. Remove the pears form the syrup and continue as in the main recipe.

2 Put the rosé wine, water, sugar, and cinnamon into a large saucepan and bring to a boil. Add the peach halves and poach slowly for 4–5 minutes. Remove from the heat and let the peach halves cool in the poaching liquid. When cool, transfer them to a plate and reserve the poaching liquid. Carefully, slice the peach halves thinly using a sharp knife.

3 Meanwhile, make the granité. Add the rosé wine, orange juice, and sugar to the cooled, reserved poaching liquid, and then boil the liquid fast to reduce by about one-third. Set to one side and let cool. When cool, pour into a shallow plastic tray and place in the freezer until it is well frozen.

4 Remove the granité from the ice tray with a spoon, scraping it to make it look like shattered glass. Place the peach slices into 4 glass serving glasses or dishes. Pile the granité on top and decorate each with a sprig of mint. Serve immediately.

Poached figs in cassis with cinnamon sauce

Serves 4
Preparation: 10 minutes, plus chilling
Cooking: 10 minutes
Carbohydrate: 23 g, Protein: 5 g, Fat: 4 g, Fiber: 3 g, Calories: 191 kcal, Sodium: 39 mg (per portion)

What you need:

- 1¼ cups red wine
- ⅔ cup cassis
- 2 cinnamon sticks
- 2 strips lemon peel
- 2 strips orange peel
- 1¼ cups water
- 12 large firm ripe figs, washed

For the sauce:

- ⅔ cup Greek-style yogurt
- 2 tablespoons Greek honey
- 1 teaspoon ground cinnamon

1 Place the red wine, cassis, cinnamon sticks, citrus peel, and water in a saucepan and bring to a boil.

2 Add the figs. Cover the pan and simmer slowly for 10 minutes until the figs are dark red and softened. Do not overcook.

3 Remove the figs with a slotted spoon and place in a serving dish. Bring the poaching liquid to a rolling boil and simmer until it is reduced by half, and is thick and syrupy. Pour over the figs and let cool slightly.

4 Meanwhile, combine all the sauce ingredients together and set aside for the flavors to develop. Serve the figs at room temperature with a spoonful of sauce for each serving.

Above left: *Poached figs in cassis with cinnamon sauce*

Cook's Tip

This delicious warm dessert is ideal as a fall dessert. However, to make a cool finish to a summer meal, serve the figs fresh. For each person, simply cut 2 figs in half and serve with the sauce.

Peach tart

Serves 6
Preparation: 25 minutes
Cooking: 50–55 minutes
Carbohydrate: 40 g, Protein: 8 g,
Fat: 19 g, Fiber: 2 g, Calories: 357 kcal,
Sodium: 121 mg (per portion)

What you need:

For the pastry dough:
- 1½ cups all-purpose flour
- ⅓ cup diced chilled butter
- 2 egg yolks

For the filling:
- 2 tablespoons blackberry jelly
- 2 egg whites
- ⅓ cup superfine sugar
- ½ cup ground almonds
- ¼ cup chopped toasted almonds
- a few drops almond extract
- 4 small peaches, halved, pitted and thickly sliced

1 Place the flour in a bowl. Add the butter and rub in with the fingertips until the mixture resembles fine bread crumbs. Stir in the egg yolks and a little cold water if necessary to make a firm dough.

2 Transfer the dough onto a floured surface and knead briefly. Roll out and line a 9-inch deep quiche pan. Chill for 30 minutes, if time permits.

3 Fill the pie shell with a piece of crumpled foil and bake in a preheated oven at 400°F for 15 minutes, then remove the foil and bake the pie shell for 5 minutes longer. Lower the oven temperature to 350°F.

4 Spread the blackberry jelly over the pie shell. In a grease-free bowl, beat the egg whites until stiff and dry. Beat in 1 tablespoon of the sugar, then fold in the remainder with the ground almonds, toasted almonds, and almond extract. Spread the filling over the pie shell.

5 Arrange the peaches over the filling. Bake for 30–35 minutes, or until the filling is set and golden brown. Serve either warm or cold, as you prefer.

Lemon tart

Serves 6–8
Preparation: 15 minutes, plus 30 minutes chilling
Cooking: 30 minutes
Carbohydrate: 70 g, Protein: 13 g,
Fat: 38 g, Fiber: 3 g, Calories: 658 kcal,
Sodium: 340 mg (per portion)

What you need:

- 2 cups all-purpose flour
- pinch of salt
- ½ cup butter
- 1 egg yolk
- 2–3 tablespoons iced water

For the filling:
- grated rind and juice of 3 lemons
- ⅓ cup superfine sugar
- 2 eggs plus 1 egg white
- ⅓ cup heavy cream
- 1 cup ground almonds
- a good pinch of ground cinnamon

For the topping:
- 2 lemons, thinly sliced
- ½ cup superfine sugar

1 Make the pastry. Sift the flour and salt into a bowl and rub in the butter until the mixture resembles fine bread crumbs. Stir in the egg yolk and sufficient iced water to make a soft and pliable dough. Chill in the refrigerator for 30 minutes.

2 Make the filling. Put the lemon rind and juice, and sugar in a mixing bowl. Break in the eggs and add the egg white. Beat well together and then beat in the cream, ground almonds, and cinnamon. The mixture should be thick and smooth.

3 Roll out the dough on a lightly floured surface, and line a 10-inch loose-bottomed quiche pan. Prick the base with a fork and pour in the filling mixture. Bake in a preheated oven at 375°F for 30 minutes, or until it is set and golden, and then set aside to cool.

4 Heat the lemon slices in a little water over a low heat for 10 minutes, or until tender. Remove and drain the lemon slices, keeping about cup of the liquid. Add the sugar and stir over a low heat until dissolved. Bring to a boil. Add the lemon slices and cook rapidly until they are well coated with thick syrup. Remove and use to decorate the tart. Let cool and serve.

Above left: *Peach tart*
Below: *Lemon tart*
Right: *Exotic fruit clafoutis*

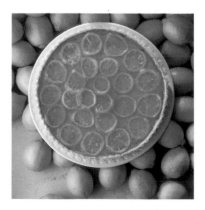

Exotic fruit clafoutis

Serves 4–6
Preparation: 15 minutes
Cooking: 25–30 minutes
Carbohydrate: 35 g, Protein: 9 g,
Fat: 8 g, Fiber: 2 g, Calories: 259 kcal,
Sodium: 207 mg (Per portion)

What you need:

- 8 ounces fresh pineapple
- 8 ounces fresh mango
- 2 tablespoons dark rum
- 3 eggs, beaten
- 3½ tablespoons all-purpose flour
- pinch of salt
- 1¼ cups superfine sugar, plus extra for sprinkling
- 1¼ cups milk
- 1 vanilla bean

1 Peel the fresh pineapple and mango. Cut the flesh into ½-inch chunks. Put the prepared fruit in a bowl and sprinkle with the rum. Set aside while you make the batter.

2 Break the eggs into a bowl and beat lightly together. Sift the flour and salt, and blend well with the beaten eggs. Whisk in the sugar until smooth.

3 Heat the milk with the vanilla bean but do not let boil. Remove from the heat and let infuse for 5 minutes. Remove the vanilla bean and strain into the egg mixture, a little at a time, beating well until it is thoroughly blended. Beat in the rum from the soaked fruit.

4 Arrange the pineapple and mango in a shallow, greased ovenproof dish. Pour the batter mixture over them and bake in a preheated oven at 400°F for 25–30 minutes, until risen and set. Cool slightly and serve warm, sprinkled with superfine sugar.

Strawberry and lychee sorbet

Serves 4
Preparation: 15 minutes, plus freezing
Cooking: 15 minutes
Carbohydrate: 75 g, Protein: 2 g, Fat: 0 g, Fiber: 3 g, Calories: 291 kcal, Sodium: 15 mg (per portion)

What you need:

- 1 14-ounce can lychees in light syrup
- ¾ cup superfine sugar
- ½ cup water
- 1½ pounds strawberries, hulled
- 1 tablespoon lemon juice

Below: Strawberry and lychee sorbet
Above right: Mango ice cream
Right: Apple sorbet

1 Strain the lychee juice into a saucepan. Halve the lychees. Remove the pits and cut away any brown shell that remains. Add the flesh to the pan. Heat through slowly for about 5 minutes and then process in a blender until fairly smooth.

2 Put the sugar and water in a clean pan and heat slowly until the sugar is dissolved. Bring to a boil and simmer for 3 minutes. Remove from the heat and let cool.

3 Process the hulled strawberries in a blender with the lemon juice, adding the cooled sugar and water syrup as you blend. Press through a strainer to remove the seeds and stir into the lychees.

4 Transfer all the mixture to a plastic container and freeze for about 1 hour. Remove from the freezer and beat the mixture to break up all the ice crystals that have formed. Return to the freezer once again, and freeze until it is quite firm.

5 Remove from the freezer about 15 minutes before serving to let the sorbet soften slightly, and serve in scoops.

Mango ice cream

Serves 8
Preparation: 20 minutes, plus 8 hours freezing
Carbohydrate: 14 g, Protein: 4 g, Fat: 40 g, Fiber: 1 g, Calories: 425 kcal, Sodium: 63 mg (per portion)

What you need:

- 1 14-ounce can mango pulp
- 3 tablespoons clear honey
- 2½ cups heavy cream
- ½ cup ground almonds
- 4 egg whites
- a few fresh mint leaves, to decorate

1 Warm the mango pulp in a saucepan over a gentle heat and then stir in the honey until melted. Remove from the heat. Stir in the heavy cream and the ground almonds until they are evenly mixed through. Set aside until cool.

2 Pour the mango ice cream mixture into a freezer container and place in the freezer. Freeze for about 4 hours, or until the mango mixture is just beginning to freeze around the edges and to become slushy.

3 Remove the container from the freezer and transfer the mango ice cream into a bowl. Carefully break up the mixture with a fork.

4 Beat the egg whites in a clean, grease-free bowl until stiff, and then fold them gently into the half-frozen mixture. Return to the freezer container and freeze for 4 hours longer, or until it is solid.

5 Remove from the freezer 20 minutes before serving to soften slightly. Serve in scoops decorated with mint leaves.

Apple sorbet

Serves 4
Preparation: 30 minutes, plus
freezing
Cooking: 10 minutes
Carbohydrate: 24 g, Protein: 2 g,
Fat: 0 g, Fiber: 2 g, Calories: 125 kcal,
Sodium: 36 mg (per portion)

What you need:

- ⅔ cup white wine
- ⅓ cup soft light brown sugar
- a thin strip of lemon rind
- 2 tablespoons lemon juice
- a small piece of fresh ginger
  root, peeled
- 1 pound cooking apples,
  peeled, cored and sliced
- 2 egg whites
- small herb leaves such as
  lemon geranium, to
  decorate

1 Put the wine, sugar, lemon
rind and juice, and ginger root
into a saucepan and stir over a
low heat until the sugar dissolves. Increase the heat and
bring to a boil. Add the apple
slices and poach them for 8–10
minutes, or until soft. Remove
from the heat and let cool.
2 Discard the lemon rind and
ginger root and purée the fruit in
a liquidizer or food processor, or
press through a strainer. Pour
into a freezer container, cover
and freeze for 1 hour.
3 Beat the egg whites until stiff.
Turn the frozen mixture into a
chilled bowl and beat it to break
down the ice crystals. Fold in the
egg whites. Return the mixture to
the freezer for about 3–4 hours,
until firm.
4 To serve, transfer the sorbet
to the refrigerator for 30 minutes. Scoop out and serve decorated with the herb leaves.

Crème caramel

Serves 4–5
Preparation: 15 minutes
Cooking: 45 minutes
Carbohydrate: 32 g, Protein: 12 g,
Fat: 12 g, Fiber: 0 g, Calories: 271 kcal,
Sodium: 155 mg (per portion)

What you need:

- 2 cups milk
- 1 vanilla bean, split in half lengthways
- 4 eggs
- ¼ cup sugar

For the caramel:

- ¼ cup sugar
- 1 tablespoon water
- 1 teaspoon lemon juice

1 Put the milk and vanilla bean in a heavy saucepan and bring to a boil. Remove from the heat and set aside for 5 minutes to infuse. Beat the eggs and sugar together in a bowl until well combined. Remove the vanilla bean and whisk the milk into the egg and sugar mixture.

2 While the milk is infusing, make the caramel. Put the sugar, water, and lemon juice in a small saucepan and cook over a medium heat, stirring well, until the sugar dissolves. Continue cooking slowly and when it turns a rich golden caramel color, remove the pan from the heat immediately.

3 Pour the caramel into 6 small molds or alternatively 1 large Charlotte mold. Rotate the molds quickly so that the caramel coats the bottoms and sides evenly.

4 Press the custard through a fine strainer. Pour into the molds and stand them in a roasting pan half-filled with water (bain-marie). Cook in a preheated oven at 300°F for about 45 minutes, or until set.

5 Let cool, then chill in the refrigerator before unmolding. To unmold, dip the base of the molds into a bowl of hot water for 30 seconds and then invert onto a serving plate.

Below: Crème caramel

Baked lemon and bay custards

Serves 8
Preparation: 5 minutes, plus
2 hours infusing and chilling
Cooking: 55–60 minutes
Carbohydrate: 21 g, Protein: 5 g,
Fat: 13 g, Fiber: 0 g, Calories: 216 kcal,
Sodium: 52 mg (per portion)

What you need:

- 12 bay leaves, bruised
- 2 long strips lemon rind
- ⅔ cup heavy cream
- 4 eggs

Champagne syllabub and strawberries

Serves 4
Preparation: 5–10 minutes, plus
1–2 hours chilling
Carbohydrate: 11 g, Protein: 2 g,
Fat: 36 g, Fiber: 1 g, Calories: 400 kcal,
Sodium: 33 mg (per portion)

What you need:

- ⅔ cup Champagne or dry sparkling wine
- 2 tablespoons superfine sugar
- finely grated rind and juice of ½ lemon
- 1¼ cups heavy cream
- ripe strawberries, to serve

1 Mix the Champagne, sugar, lemon rind and juice together in a large bowl.
2 Add the cream and whisk the mixture until it forms soft peaks.
3 Spoon into glasses and chill for 1–2 hours before serving.
4 Serve with some fresh, ripe strawberries. Best of all, if you can find them when in season, is a mixture of wild and cultivated strawberries.

Above left: *Baked lemon and bay custards*
Below: *Champagne syllabub and strawberries*

- 1 egg yolk
- ⅔ cup superfine sugar
- 6½ tablespoons lemon juice

1 Put the bay leaves, lemon rind and cream in a small saucepan and heat slowly until it reaches boiling point. Remove from the heat and set aside for about 2 hours to infuse.
2 Beat the eggs, egg yolk and sugar together until the mixture is pale and creamy; then whisk in the lemon juice. Press the cream mixture through a fine strainer into the bowl and stir until it is well combined.
3 Divide the custard equally between 8 individual ramekin dishes and place on a baking sheet. Bake in a preheated oven 250°F, for about 50 minutes or until the custards are almost set in the center. Let go cold, and then chill in the refrigerator until required. Return to room temperature before serving.

Cook's Tip

This recipe is a variation of the old classic, lemon tart. Here, the lemon custard is infused with bay leaves, giving it a heady scent. The custard is poured into ramekin dishes and baked in a very low oven: if the oven is too hot the custard will curdle. Check after 40 minutes, the centers should be almost set but still move a little, they will firm up as they cool.

Crêpes Suzette

Serves 6–8
Preparation: 25 minutes
Cooking: 6–8 minutes

*Carbohydrate: 45 g, Protein: 8 g,
Fat: 21 g, Fiber: 1 g, Calories: 415 kcal,
Sodium: 517 mg (per portion)*

What you need:

For the batter:

- 1 cup all-purpose flour
- ¼ teaspoon salt
- 3 eggs
- 2 tablespoons oil
- ¼ cup melted butter
- 1 tablespoon superfine sugar
- 2 teaspoons vanilla sugar
- 1½ cups milk
- 2 tablespoons butter, for frying

For the sauce:

- ½ cup diced, softened butter
- ½ cup superfine sugar
- grated rind and juice of 1 orange
- 6 tablespoons Cointreau or Grand Marnier
- 3 tablespoons brandy

1 Make the batter. Sift the flour and salt into a bowl and make a well in the center. Tip in the eggs, oil, melted butter, and sugars. Blend thoroughly, drawing in the flour from the sides, until the mixture is smooth.

2 Gradually add the milk, a little at a time, beating well between each addition. The batter should be smooth and the consistency of light cream. Add a little more milk if necessary and then let stand for 1 hour.

3 Melt a little of the butter in a small skillet and when it is really hot, ladle some of the batter into the pan. Tilt the pan so that the batter covers the bottom evenly

Left: *Crêpes Suzette*

and fry until golden brown on the underside. Flip the crêpe over, using an egg slice or a spatula, and cook the other side. Carefully slide onto a warm plate and keep warm while you cook the other crêpes.

4 Make the sauce. Put the butter and sugar in a bowl and beat together until smooth and creamy. Beat the orange rind and juice into the creamed mixture, and then beat in 3 tablespoons of the orange liqueur and 1 tablespoon of the brandy.

5 Transfer the orange mixture to a large skillet and heat slowly. When boiling, boil rapidly for 1–2 minutes, and reduce the heat. Add the crêpes, one at a time, folding each one in half and then in half again.

6 Warm the remaining liqueur and brandy in a small pan. Taking great care, set alight and pour the alcohol flaming over the crêpes just before serving, or set alight at the table.

Cook's Tip

Crêpe batter is such a versatile mixture. For instance, adding a splash of alcohol will lift it to new heights. Add 1 tablespoon of dark rum, brandy or apricot brandy to the quantity in this recipe. To enhance this addition, fill each cooked crêpe with a spoonful of lightly whipped cream which has been flavored with the appropriate alcohol and a small amount of sugar. Add 2 tablespoons of alcohol and 2 teaspoons superfine sugar to 1½ cups lightly whipped heavy cream.

Cocktail know-how

As a pre-dinner drink, a reward after a hard day's work, or the basis for a get-together with friends, cocktails are meant to be fun.

● Instant eye-appeal comes from bright colors, a quirky glass, a decoration of fruit–or, for a Bloody Mary, a stalk of celery or a fresh chili on a toothpick.

● Cocktail recipes are usually given in parts or measures: the jigger is a generous measure of about 3 tablespoons–but as long as you keep the proportions right it doesn't matter what measure you use.

● Many cocktails are shaken with ice to cool them, then strained before the ice dilutes the alcohol. A shaker with its own strainer is ideal, but a lidded jar and a small clean strainer will do.

● Ice cubes can be crushed in a food processor, or in a strong polythene bag with a rolling pin.

● Add fizz with soda or sparkling mineral water.

● To sweeten cocktails, make a sugar syrup by boiling 2 parts sugar with 1 part water for 5 minutes. Cool, bottle and keep in the refrigerator. This gives a clearer cocktail than dry sugar.

Far left: *Margarita*
Left: *Sangria*
Below: *Singapore sling*

Margarita

- 2 measures tequila (preferably golden tequila)
- 1 measure triple sec (or other orange liqueur)
- 1½–2 measures fresh lime juice
- 1–2 teaspoons sugar syrup
- salt
- slices of lime and lime leaves, to decorate

Shake the tequila, triple sec, lime juice and sugar syrup with cracked ice–or crushed ice for a frozen margarita.

Rub a slice of lime around the rim of a glass, then dip the glass in a saucer of salt. Pour in the tequila mix and decorate with lime.

Sangria

Serves 6–10
- 1 bottle Spanish red wine
- ¼ cup brandy
- ¼ cup triple sec (or other orange liqueur)
- ⅓ cup lemon juice
- ⅓ cup orange juice
- ¼ cup sugar
- slices of orange and lemon
- soda club

Pour the wine, brandy, orange liqueur, lemon and orange juice, sugar and fruit into a large pitcher, and stir until the sugar dissolves. Add plenty of ice cubes. Pour into glasses and top up with soda.

Singapore sling

- 2 measures gin
- 1 measure cherry brandy
- juice of ½ lemon
- soda club

Shake the gin, cherry brandy, and lemon juice with ice cubes. Strain into a glass over cracked ice. Top up with soda.

Mai tai

- ½ measure triple sec
- 1 measure dark Jamaican rum
- 1 measure light rum
- ½ measure grenadine
- 1 teaspoon sugar
- juice of 1 lime, plus peel to decorate (optional)
- slice of pineapple and cocktail cherry, to decorate

Shake the triple sec, both rums, grenadine, sugar, and lime juice together with ice cubes. Then strain into a glass over cracked ice. Finally, decorate with the lime peel, a slice of pineapple, and a cocktail cherry.

Pineapple cooler

- 3 measures pineapple juice
- 1 measure rum (preferably golden Jamaican rum)
- 1 measure coconut liqueur
- 1 measure orange juice
- slice of pineapple or orange, to decorate

Shake all the ingredients together with ice cubes, then pour into a glass and decorate with a slice of pineapple or orange.

Americano

- 1 measure Campari
- 1 measure sweet vermouth
- soda water
- slice of orange, to decorate

Put plenty of ice cubes in a glass. Add Campari and vermouth. Stir and top up with soda. Decorate with a slice of orange.

Tequila sunrise

- ½ measure grenadine
- 1 measure tequila
- ½ cup orange juice

Half fill a glass with ice cubes. Pour in the grenadine, then the tequila, and then the orange juice.

Cocktail nibbles

Olives and salted nuts are the classic accompaniments to cocktails, but to make your party into an occasion, prepare a selection of snacks. Easy to eat with one hand, crostini are ideal.

Crostini

- French or Italian bread, sliced
- garlic cloves, halved
- extra virgin olive oil

Toast the bread lightly, then rub with the cut side of the garlic and drizzle with olive oil. Serve at once or try one of the following delicious toppings.

Broiled bell peppers and curly chicory

Serves 4
- 1 red and 1 yellow bell pepper, seeded and quartered
- 2 tablespoons hazelnut oil
- 2 garlic cloves, sliced
- grated rind of ½ lemon
- 3 tablespoons golden raisins
- ¼ cup slivered hazelnuts
- 3 cups curly chicory lettuce
- salt and pepper

1 Broil the bell peppers until they are charred and soft. Place in a polythene bag to cool. Peel off the skin and slice the peppers.
2 Heat the oil in a skillet, add

the garlic, rind, golden raisins, nuts and fry slowly for 5 minutes. Add the lettuce and cook over a low heat for 5 minutes. Season well with salt and pepper.
3 Place the lettuce on the toasted bread and top with the broiled, sliced bell peppers.

Mixed mushrooms

Serves 4
- 2 tablespoons dried ceps
- 7 tablespoons boiling water
- 2 tablespoons extra virgin olive oil
- 1 garlic clove, crushed
- 4 cups sliced, mixed fresh mushrooms
- 1 tablespoon chopped fresh thyme
- 1 tablespoon chopped fresh parsley
- grated fresh Parmesan cheese
- salt and pepper

1 Soak the ceps in the boiling water for 20 minutes. Drain, reserving the liquid. Slice the ceps.
2 Heat the oil in a pan. Add the ceps, garlic, mushrooms, and thyme and stir-fry for 3–4 minutes. Add the ceps soaking liquid, cover and cook over a low heat for 5 minutes. Season to taste with salt and pepper.
3 Spoon the mixture onto the toasted bread and top with the parsley and Parmesan.

Eggplant and arugula

Serves 4
- 1 tablespoon cumin seeds
- ⅓ cup extra virgin olive oil
- 1 teaspoon grated lemon rind
- 2 small eggplants, sliced
- 2 cups arugula leaves
- salt and pepper

1 Dry-fry the cumin seeds in a small skillet until they start to pop and give off a rich aroma.

Add all but 1 tablespoon of the oil and the lemon rind. Remove from the heat and let infuse for several hours. Strain the oil.
2 Brush the eggplant slices lightly with the cumin-flavored oil and place under a medium-hot grill for 6–8 minutes, until charred. Turn the eggplants, brush with more oil and broil the other side. Let cool.
3 Place the eggplant slices on the toasted bread and drizzle over a little more cumin oil.
4 Toss the arugula leaves with the reserved olive oil, season and arrange over the eggplants.

Broiled tomato and olive paste

Serves 4
- 2–4 well-flavored ripe but firm tomatoes
- extra virgin olive oil
- 2 tablespoons olive paste
- a few fresh basil leaves
- salt and pepper

1 Depending on their size, cut the tomatoes into wedges or quarters. Drizzle with olive oil and then place the tomatoes under a hot broiler for 5–10 minutes, until tender and beginning to blacken at the edges.
2 Spread the olive paste over the toasted bread and top with the broiled tomato wedges and basil leaves. Season to taste.

Above: Marinated olives are delicious served with cocktails. Buy them from delis or make your own by mixing 1 pound pitted green or black olives with 1 deseeded and chopped red chili, 3 cloves of finely chopped garlic, 1 sprig each of fresh oregano, thyme, and rosemary, and 1 teaspoon each of fennel and cumin seeds. Pack into a screw-top jar and cover with olive oil. Close the jar and leave for at least 3 days, shaking the jar occasionally. Store in a cool, dark place for up to 2 months.
Right: *Crostini with a selection of vegetable toppings. You could also spread crostini with meat or fish pâté.*
Left: *Planter's punch (recipe on previous page)*

Wine

Some of the world's finest—and most expensive—wines are best enjoyed after 30 or more years in the bottle, but the great majority are designed to be drunk young, usually with food. Spirits and liqueurs are too strong or too sweet to make good partners for food, but they too have a big part to play in cooking. In some countries, notably Germany and Belgium, beer plays the same role, being brewed in several styles and drunk as an important part of the meal.

Below: *A table in Provence, where Mediterranean shellfish is accompanied by a glass of good local white wine*

Wine is made in more than 50 countries round the world, from well over 1,000 grape varieties. The choice is much greater than that between red and white. There are many different white wines, including still and sparkling, dry and sweet, light-bodied and full-bodied. Much the same applies to red wines, with a full range of light-, medium- and full-bodied wines.

Which wine with which food?

Many serious words have been written about finding the perfect food and wine partnership, but while it is true that some foods go particularly well with certain wines, there are often other, less obvious possibilities.

In general, simple dishes demand uncomplicated, straightforward wines, while more elaborate dishes ask for the more expensive classics. A richly sauced dish goes well with a wine that has enough natural acidity to cut through the sauce and balance it.

The basic principle of white wine with fish and red wine with meat is a sound one but it is not an exciting one and—as with all the best rules in life—there are many exceptions. Fish is sometimes better accompanied by a rosé wine, and even a red wine can on occasions be better still. The color of the meat is usually best matched by the color of the wine—a full-bodied claret or burgundy with a beef roast, say, a light white wine to complement the light flavors of chicken or turkey, and a full-flavored wine to match the high intensity of goose, duck, and game birds.

How much wine?

Half a bottle of wine per person is a good rule of thumb, but a whole bottle may be a safer estimate as it insures that you will not run short—which is one of the most embarrassing things that can happen to the hosts at a party!

Above all, though, don't worry about it—as long as the food is good and the company excellent, the wine will always slip down with remarkable ease!

Spirits and liqueurs

Spirits are strong drinks, distilled from grains e.g. whiskey, gin, vodka; wine e.g. brandy, Cognac, Armagnac; fruit e.g. fruit brandies and eaux-de-vie such as Kirsch and other things such as rum from sugar cane. Liqueurs are spirits that have been lightly or heavily sweetened, and flavored by the maceration of fruits, herbs or spices; sweeter liqueurs are usually lower in alcohol than spirits, but have a much higher alcohol content than wine. Some of the most widely known spirits and liqueurs are described below, with their percentage of alcohol by volume.

Percentage of alchohol by volume	Description
Advocaat (15–18%)	Yellow liqueur made from egg yolks and brandy
Amaretto (28%)	Amber-colored liqueur made from almonds and apricot kernels
Apricot brandy (21–24%)	Not a brandy, but an amber-colored liqueur
Calvados, applejack (40–45%)	Apple brandies, aged in wood, which gives them an amber color
Cassis (15–25%)	Blackcurrant liqueur
Chartreuse, Izarra (green 50–55%, yellow 40%)	Herbal liqueurs
Crème de cacao (24%)	Brown or clear chocolate-flavored liqueur
Crème de menthe (24–30%)	Bright green or clear peppermint-flavored liqueur
Curaçao (30–40%)	Orange, blue, green or colorless liqueurs made from the rind of bitter oranges. **Triple sec** is a slightly sweeter type of Curaçao; **Cointreau** is the best-known triple sec. **Grand Marnier** is a special orange liqueur in which the orange rind is macerated in genuine French Cognac
Galliano (40%)	Bright yellow, sweetish, herbal liqueur
Kahlúa, Tia Maria (26%)	Brown coffee-flavored liqueurs
Kirsch (43%)	Clear spirit distilled from cherries and their kernels, which give a hint of almond flavor
Maraschino (30%)	Clear cherry liqueur; cherry brandy (22–25%) is also a liqueur, usually deep red
Mirabelle, Quetsch, Slivovitz (43–45%)	Plum brandies
Ouzo, Pernod, pastis (e.g. **Ricard**) (37–45%)	Unsweetened, aniseed or liquorice-flavored spirits; clear, but turn cloudy when water is added
Poire Williams, Williamine (43–45%)	Pear brandies
Southern Comfort (43%)	Amber-colored liqueur based on whiskey, flavored with peaches and other fruit
Tequila (38%)	Clear spirit distilled from a Mexican plant

Cooking with alcohol

Besides flambéeing, alcohol can be put to many good uses in the kitchen. The alcohol evaporates during cooking, leaving the essential flavors of the wine or spirits in the dish. Sherry or brandy add richness to clear soups and creamy shellfish bisques; a wine marinade for meat will tenderize it as well as add flavor; using dry white wine or vermouth in the poaching liquid for fish or chicken forms the basis for a good sauce; red wine is often used to poach pears or peaches; a good cheese fondue contains dry white wine and a dash of Kirsch.

To create an almost-instant sauce for fried fish or meat, first transfer the fish or meat to a warm plate, then pour off excess fat from the pan. Add a little wine, dry vermouth, sherry, Madeira or brandy to the pan, and place over a high heat for a few minutes, stirring constantly to deglaze the pan. Increase the amount of sauce with a little stock or water, bring back to a rapid boil; then, if you like, whisk in a little butter, cream or chopped fresh herbs.

When the alcohol is not cooked, it lends not only flavor, but also a warming kick. Rum-soaked raisins are a good addition to baked apples or cheesecakes; use sherry, brandy or apricot brandy to soak the sponge for trifles; orange liqueurs go particularly well with strawberries and chocolate desserts.

Flambéeing

Setting light to alcohol and pouring it, flaming, over food is the traditional way to serve Christmas pudding, crêpes Suzette, and some savory dishes (brandy over steaks, Pernod over fish). Besides looking spectacular, it imparts the flavor of the spirit at the last minute, while the alcohol burns away.

It is best to use spirits with a high alcohol content, although a flavored liqueur can be mixed with the spirits. The food must be hot, or the flames will die out at once, leaving the alcohol to soak into the food. The spirits should first be heated gently, so that the alcohol begins to evaporate; the spirit can then be ignited with a match and poured, flaming, over the food.

Chilled claret cup

Serves 10–15
Preparation: 5 minutes, plus chilling

What you need:

- 1 bottle young Bordeaux red wine
- ½ bottle ruby port
- ⅔ cup brandy
- 5 tablespoons orange juice
- 3 tablespoons lemon juice
- ⅓ cup confectioners' sugar
- 2 oranges, thinly sliced
- 1 lemon, thinly sliced
- 1½ cups soda or sparkling mineral water
- sprigs of fresh mint, to decorate

Above right: *Mulled wine*
Below: *Chilled claret cup*

1 Put the wine, port, and brandy in the refrigerator and chill for about 2 hours.

2 Then fill a large pitcher with crushed ice; then add the wine, port, and brandy and stir well.

3 Put the orange and lemon juice in a small bowl with the confectioners' sugar and stir until the sugar dissolves. Add to the pitcher with the slices of orange and lemon.

4 Add soda or mineral water and stir. Serve immediately, decorated with a sprig of mint.

Mulled wine

Serves 8–12
Preparation: 20 minutes

What you need:

- 8 cloves
- pinch of ground ginger
- pinch of grated nutmeg
- 2 cinnamon sticks, plus extra to serve (optional)

- 1–2 tablespoons soft brown sugar
- ⅔ cup boiling water
- 1 bottle red wine
- ⅔ cup port

1 Put the spices, sugar and boiling water into a saucepan over a low heat and simmer slowly for 15 minutes.

2 Strain the spiced liquid, add to the wine and heat slowly for 5 minutes, until the liquid is just below simmering point.

3 Add the port and serve the mulled wine hot, in warmed glasses or mugs, with a stick of cinnamon in each.

Variations

Riesling cup

Use a good, fruity dry to medium dry white wine: Riesling is an ideal wine for this.

Chill the bottle of wine, ⅓ cup brandy and ⅓ cup Cointreau for 2 hours, pour the chilled drink over the cubes in a large pitcher and mix well. Still stirring add 2 tablespoons fresh lime juice and 1⅓ cups soda or sparkling mineral water. Add 4 ounces fresh raspberries, 1 peach, peeled, pitted and finely sliced, and a few mint or lemon balm leaves

Baking

There is nothing quite like the satisfaction of baking your own bread. Home-baked bread tastes out of this world, and the aroma it creates in the kitchen is one of the most wonderful smells in the world. Baking bread is not as time-consuming as you might think, particularly if you use all the latest kitchen gadgetry. Get into the habit of making a quick loaf before cooking the dinner, and tomorrow's breakfast will never be the same again!

Millet and cumin loaf

Makes 1 2-pound loaf
Preparation: 15 minutes, plus rising
Cooking: 35 minutes
Carbohydrate: 18 g, Protein: 4 g, Fat: 3 g, Fiber: 1 g, Calories: 109 kcal, Sodium: 218 mg (per slice)

What you need:

- ½ cup millet
- ⅔ cup boiling water
- ½ cup cake compressed yeast
- 2 cups white bread flour, plus extra for dusting
- 1 teaspoon sugar
- ⅔ cup warm water
- 2 cups wholewheat bread flour
- 2 teaspoons sea salt
- 1 teaspoon cumin seeds
- 1 cup grated Cheddar cheese
- vegetable oil, for oiling

1 Soak the millet in the boiling water for 20 minutes. Combine the yeast, 4 tablespoons of the white flour, and the sugar with the warm water in a small bowl and leave in a warm place for 10 minutes till frothy. Drain the millet, reserving any liquid left over.
2 In a large bowl, mix together the remaining white flour with the wholewheat flour, soaked millet, salt, cumin seeds, and cheese. Make a small well in the center and gradually work in the frothed yeast, reserved millet liquid, and enough extra warm water to form a stiff dough.
3 Transfer to a lightly floured surface and knead for 8–10 minutes until smooth and elastic. Place in an oiled bowl, turning once to coat the dough. Cover and leave in a warm place for 1 hour, or until doubled in size.
4 Punch down the dough by kneading gently. Shape into an oval and press into an oiled 2-pound loaf pan. Brush with a little oil and bake in a preheated oven, 450°F, for 35–40 minutes until golden. It should sound hollow when you tap the loaf on the bottom.

Left: *Millet and cumin loaf*

Tomato bread

Makes 2 1-pound loaves
Preparation: 30 minutes, plus
rising
Cooking: 35 minutes
Carbohydrate: 26 g, Protein: 4 g,
Fat: 3 g, Fiber: 1 g, Calories: 137 kcal,
Sodium: 125 mg (per slice)

What you need:

- 4–5 sun-dried tomatoes, very
  finely chopped
- 6 cups bread flour
- 1 teaspoon salt
- 1 teaspoon sugar
- 2 tablespoons butter or
  margarine, or 1 tablespoon
  olive or sunflower oil
- ½ cake compressed yeast, or
  1 package fast-action dry
  yeast

1 Place the sun-dried tomatoes
in a small bowl. Add enough
boiling water to cover and set
aside for 2–3 minutes.

2 Sift the flour and salt into a
large bowl and stir in the sugar.
Rub in the fat or add the oil. If
using compressed yeast, put it
into a separate bowl. If using
fast-action dry yeast, add it to the
flour in the bowl.

3 Drain the sun-dried tomatoes, reserving the soaking liquid
in a measuring pitcher. Make
it up to 2 cups with lukewarm
water. The temperature of the
liquid should be about 110°F.
Cream the compressed yeast and
add the liquid; top with a sprinkling of flour and leave for about
10 minutes, or until the surface is
covered with bubbles. Blend with
the flour. If using fast-action dry
yeast, stir the liquid into the yeast
and flour, and blend to a dough.

4 Transfer the dough onto a
lightly floured surface and knead
thoroughly until the dough is
firm and elastic and no longer
feels sticky. Knead in the
chopped tomatoes.

5 Return the dough to the mixing bowl and cover the bowl with
plastic wrap. Leave in a warm
place for about 1 hour or until
the dough has doubled in bulk.
Then punch down the dough
again and shape it.

6 To make two regular loaves,
grease and warm 2 1-pound loaf
pans. Divide the dough in half.
Press out each half to form a neat
rectangle, the same length and
three times the width of each
pan. Fold the dough to fit the loaf
pans and place it in the pans with
the fold underneath.

7 Alternatively form the dough
into two large sausage shapes
and place on lightly greased baking sheets. Make equally spaced
shallow cuts along the top of
each loaf.

8 Cover the dough lightly and
leave until nearly doubled in
bulk. This will take about 20
minutes or so.

9 Bake the loaves in a preheated
oven, 425°F, for about 35 minutes or until cooked. When they
are cooked, the loaves should
sound hollow when tapped
lightly on the bottom. Finally,
remove loaves from the pans and
let cool on wire racks.

> ### Cook's Tip
>
> If the sides are not as
> crusty as you like, simply
> place on a flat baking
> sheet and return to the
> oven for a few minutes.

Left: *Tomato bread*
Right: *Roquefort bread*

Roquefort bread

Makes 1 1-pound loaf
Preparation: 15 minutes, plus
rising
Cooking: 30 minutes

Carbohydrate: 39 g, Protein: 9 g,
Fat: 7 g, Fiber: 2 g, Calories: 242 kcal,
Sodium: 576 mg (per slice)

What you need:

- 4 cups white bread flour
- 2 teaspoons salt
- 2 tablespoons butter
- 1 package fast-action dry
  yeast
- ⅔ cup lukewarm milk
- 1¼ cups cooked potato,
  pressed through a
  strainer
- 1 cup crumbled Roquefort
  or blue cheese
- beaten egg, to glaze

1 Sift the flour with the salt into
a warmed bowl. Rub in the butter until the mixture resembles
fine bread crumbs. Stir in the
dried yeast.

2 Stir the milk into the potato in
a bowl. Work this mixture into
the flour to make a soft but not
sticky dough. Knead on a floured
board for 5 minutes, then knead
in the crumbled cheese.

3 Grease a 1-pound loaf pan.
Shape the dough to fit the pan, or
shape into a domed round and
place on a greased baking sheet.
Cover with oiled polythene and
let rise in a warm place for 30
minutes, or until the loaf has
doubled in bulk.

4 Brush with beaten egg and
bake in a preheated oven, 400°F,
for 15 minutes. Reduce the heat
to 350°F, and bake for 15 minutes more. Remove the loaf from
the pan and let cool on a wire
rack.

Naan

Makes 6
Preparation: 30 minutes, plus
rising
Cooking: 10 minutes
*Carbohydrate: 67 g, Protein: 10 g,
Fat: 10 g, Fiber: 3 g, Calories: 370 kcal,
Sodium: 725 mg (per ⅙ of a bread)*

What you need:

- ½ cake compressed yeast
- ¼ teaspoon sugar
- 2 tablespoons warm water
- 4 cups self-rising flour
- 1 teaspoon salt
- ⅔ cup tepid milk
- ⅔ cup plain yogurt (at room temperature)
- 2 tablespoons melted butter or cooking oil
- 2–3 tablespoons melted butter
- 1 tablespoon poppy or sesame seeds

1 Put the yeast in a small bowl with sugar and water. Mix well until yeast has dissolved. Leave in a warm place for 15 minutes.
2 Sift the flour and salt into a large bowl. Make a well in the center and add the yeast, milk,

Below: *Naan*
Right: *Soda bread*

yogurt, and fat. Mix well to a smooth dough and knead on a floured surface. Knead for 10 minutes, till smooth and elastic.
3 Place in a bowl, cover with plastic wrap, and let rise in a warm place for 1–1½ hours, or until doubled in size.
4 Transfer to a floured surface and knead for a few minutes; then divide into 6 pieces. Pat or roll each piece into a round.
5 Place on a warmed baking sheet and bake in a preheated oven, 475°F, for 10 minutes. Brush with butter and sprinkle with the poppy or sesame seeds. Serve warm.

Soda bread

Makes 2 1-pound loaves
Preparation: 15 minutes
Cooking: 25–30 minutes
*Carbohydrate: 37 g, Protein: 5 g,
Fat: 3 g, Fiber: 1 g, Calories: 183 kcal,
Sodium: 266 mg (per slice)*

What you need:

- 2 pounds all-purpose flour
- 2 teaspoons salt
- 1 teaspoon baking soda
- 1 teaspoon cream of tartar
- ¼ cup butter or margarine
- 2½ cups buttermilk
- flour for sprinkling

1 Sift the dry ingredients in a mixing bowl and rub in the fat. Add the buttermilk and mix quickly to a soft dough. Transfer to a floured surface, knead and divide in half.
2 Shape into 2 2-inch thick rounds and place on a floured baking sheet. Cut a deep cross on top and sprinkle with flour.
3 Bake in a preheated hot oven, 425°F, for 25–30 minutes. Cool on a wire rack.

Nutrition

Much research has been done in the past few years into the effects of food on health as a result of which some foods which, years ago, were regarded as healthy and energy-giving–whole milk and sugar, for example–are now regarded as things that should be drunk and eaten in moderation. Other foods which were once regarded as fattening–bread and potatoes, for example–are now considered to be healthy and, provided they are not smothered in high-fat additions, unlikely to add to weight.

A balanced diet

So what is the best to develop a balanced diet? First bear in mind that no food is of itself bad for you. The occasional helping of French fries, a packet of chips or a secretly consumed box of chocolates is not going to lead to instant heart disease or cancer, provided that, for most of the time, you eat foods that positively contribute toward health in sensible quantities for your height and weight. Foods are made up of a number of different elements and it is worth knowing more about what these are.

Protein

Protein is found in meat, poultry, fish, eggs, dairy products, beans, legumes, and nuts. Most people need only around ½–¾ cup per day but tend to take in around 50 percent more than that. Protein should make up around 10 percent of your daily food intake in order to insure growth in children and young adults and the maintenance of body tissue at all ages.

Carbohydrates

These come in two forms–both simple and complex.

Simple carbohydrates are the sugars group–dextrose, fructose, glucose, and sucrose–which tend to be added to foods rather than to be eaten alone. Complex carbohydrates are an integral part of starches such as cereals and rice, and are automatically consumed when you eat these foods. Simple carbohydrates provide energy in the form of calories and should be consumed in moderation, if at all.

Complex carbohydrates contain many other nutritional benefits. As long as they are eaten without the addition of simple carbohydrates, they are not, in themselves, fattening.

Fats

Fats are found in oils, nuts, avocados, dairy products, and most processed foods. While a small amount of fat is essential for maintaining a healthy body, most people eat too much. It is estimated that a large proportion of people have a fat intake of around 40 percent. It is interesting to note, too, the success rate of the low-fat diets which have come into fashion in the past decade or so–far more successful than the "starve yourself into slimness" regimes that formerly held sway. Recent nutri-

Good nutrition is about eating the right food to maintain good health. It doesn't necessarily mean avoiding any particular food but it does mean eating more of the foods that do you good and less of the ones that can, in excess, do you harm. Poor nutrition in the western world tends to be the result of over- rather than under-eating. Another contributory factor is the large proportion of processed food in most people's diets–it is estimated that as much as 70 percent of all the food that is eaten in the western world today has been processed.

Below: *a colorful market stall not only looks good–fruit and vegetables also do you good*

tional recommendations suggest that a maximum fat intake should be no more than 35 percent of the diet and that less will do no harm.

Fats consists of units of fatty acid which fall into three types with different chemical structures. All whole fats consist of all three types but in different proportions, some of which are healthier than others.

Saturated fats consist mainly of saturated fatty acids and come in the form of dairy products and meat. They are mainly solid when at room temperature.

Polyunsaturated fats consist mainly of polyunsaturated fatty acids and tend to be liquids such as vegetable oils (though not coconut and palm oils which are saturated fats).

Monounsaturated fats are also found in vegetable oils, notably grapeseed, groundnut and olive, and in avocados.

Evidence shows that eating a lot of saturated fats raises blood cholesterol which, in turn, leads to coronary heart disease (see Cholesterol, below). Polyunsaturated fats help lower cholesterol but not to the degree in which saturated fats raise it.

Less is known about what monounsaturated fats do to cholesterol but looking at Mediterranean diets, which are high in olive oil and where the incidence of heart disease is considerably lower than in other countries, it is likely that they also help to lower cholesterol.

All fats are heavily loaded with calories which is another good reason for cutting down the amount in a diet.

Cholesterol

Cholesterol occurs naturally in the human body and also in some foods, such as eggs, fish, sundries and shellfish. Some cholesterol is essential for good health. Too much leads to a furring up of the arteries (atherosclerosis), which restricts blood flow and leads to coronary heart disease.

People whose doctor's or home tests indicate a high level of cholesterol should avoid foods containing it. Cholesterol level can also be reduced by not getting fat, giving up smoking, and taking plenty of exercise.

Fiber

Dietary fiber is also known as non-starch polysaccharides (NSP) and comes in two forms: soluble and insoluble.

Fiber is found in cereals, fruit and vegetables, and their derivatives such as brown rice, pasta, and whole wheat bread. The soluble variety found in cereals (especially oats) and vegetables (especially dry beans) is thought to help lower cholesterol levels.

Nonsoluble fiber is found also in cereals (especially wheat bran) and vegetables, and absorbs water during the digestion process, creating large soft stools which are easy to pass through the system. Research has shown that apart from the benefits of avoiding constipation and piles, this also reduces the likelihood of bowel cancer.

High-fiber foods are filling and pass through the system easily, so are good for those trying to lose weight.

Sugar

Sugar, like carbohydrates, falls into two groups–intrinsic and extrinsic. Intrinsic sugars are a natural part of foods like fruit, cereals, potatoes, and rice, while extrinsic sugars are not part of cellular structure but exist alone. Examples are glucose, honey, and sucrose. It is extrinsic sugars that lead to tooth decay.

Sugar is not essential for human health. It provides energy in the form of calories but nothing else. Experts recommend consumption of as little extrinsic sugar as possible and certainly no more than around 10 percent of daily food intake (about ¼ cup per day). Doing without it certainly helps to reduce the calories.

Salt

Salt (correct name sodium chloride but usually referred to as sodium) is essential for the health of body cells and occurs naturally in many foods.

Because of the salt added to

Top left: *seafood is full of nutrients*
Above left: *stir-frying uses very little fat*
Right: *sugar has no nutritional benefits*

virtually all processed foods (including some sweet ones) and the salt liberally sprinkled by many people on foods that already contain it, most people consume at least 10 times more salt than their body requires.

Cutting down on salt helps reduce high blood pressure (hypertension), which is a risk factor for coronary heart disease and stroke. If you want to cut down on salt, do not add it at table and avoid salty foods such as bacon and cheese.

Vitamins

Vitamins cannot be synthesized by the body and most must therefore be taken in, on a daily or regular basis, from the diet. The body can store Vitamins A, D, E, K, and B12 but not the rest. Each of the 20 known vitamins performs a different function and is therefore required in different quantities.

Vitamins divide into two types: fat-soluble (main ones A, D, E, and K) and water-soluble (main ones B complex and C).

Fat-soluble vitamins are less affected than the water-soluble type by cooking; water-soluble vitamins tend to leach out into cooking water and be destroyed by heat.

People whose diet is well-balanced should not need to take any of the vitamin supplements that crowd the shelves of health food stores and supermarkets. Too much of some vitamins (notably A, D, E, and K, which are stored in the body and not excreted) can be harmful if toxic levels are reached.

However, if you have been ill, or if your doctor pinpoints a particular deficiency or need, you may need to take certain

Above: carrots are particularly rich in Vitamin A
Right: the humble potato is actually a very good source of Vitamin C

vitamin supplements for a period of time.

Vitamin A

Also known as retinol, this is found mainly in dairy products, such as butter, cheese and milk, sundries (particularly liver), eggs, oily fish, and the substance beta carotene which is found in green, orange, and yellow vegetables, such as spinach and carrots.

Vitamin A is essential for growth, healthy skin and being able to see in poor light.

Vitamin B complex

There are several B vitamins. The best-known of these are probably B1 (thiamin), B2 (riboflavin), and B3 (niacin). They are all discussed in detail below.

Vitamin B1 (thiamin)

This is found in fortified and whole grain cereals, milk, meat (especially pork), nuts, potatoes, and legumes. This vitamin is also present in yeast, yeast extract and wheat germ.

The need for Vitamin B1 is increased when people drink alcohol and caffeine or are on any type of antibiotics and/or the contraceptive pill.

This vitamin is useful because it aids the release of energy from both types of carbohydrate.

Vitamin B2 (riboflavin)

Vitamin B2 is mainly found in cheese, eggs, fortified breakfast cereals, meat, milk, sundries, and yeast extract.

It tends to leach out into cooking water so try to use cooking water in gravy, sauces and soups. Don't leave milk in a glass pitcher as it is also destroyed by ultra-violet light.

Vitamin B2 is essential for growth, healthy eyesight and skin, and for helping release energy from carbohydrates.

Vitamin B3

This is found in most fish, fortified breakfast cereals, meal, sundries and legumes.

It also leaches out into cooking water, so it is therefore a good idea to use it if at all possible when cooking other things. Vitamin B3 assists in the release of energy within the body cells.

Vitamin B5 (pantothenic acid)

This vitamin is present in lots of foods, notably eggs, fish roe, nuts, sundries, legumes, vegetables and yeast.

It is destroyed by cooking above boiling point.

Vitamin B5 helps you produce energy, and also aids other important metabolic tasks.

Vitamin B6 (pyridoxine)

This is present in lots of foods, notably eggs, fish, liver, meat, legumes, vegetables, whole grain cereals, and yeast extract.

Vitamin B6 helps the the body to form new red blood cells and also to utilize proteins. Extra B6 supplements can sometimes help with PMT (premenstrual tension) symptoms.

Vitamin B12 (cobalamin)

This is found only in foods of animal origin such as cheese, eggs, meat, milk, sundries and oily fish. Like other B vitamins, it leaches out into cooking water. It is essential for growth, developing red blood cells, and repairing the nervous system.

People who are following a standard diet will get enough through eating a variety of animal foods. Vegetarians who eat sufficient dairy products should also be all right, but vegans—who don't eat any dairy products—may need to take a supplement.

Biotin

This is a water-soluble member B vitamin without a number. It is found in brown bread and rice, eggs, sundries, oily fish and yeast. Biotin protects bone marrow, hair, and the nervous system.

Folic acid

This is a water-soluble member of the B group, also without a number. It is found in eggs, green leafy vegetables, liver, nuts, legumes, whole wheat cereals, wheat bran and germ, and yeast.

A lack of folic acid can cause anaemia, depression, tiredness, and insomnia. It helps produce red blood cells and amino acids. Pregnant women may need supplements of folic acid to prevent foetal malformation. They may need to take supplements.

Vitamin C

Ascorbic acid is easily lost during cooking, both leaching out into the water and being destroyed by heat. Ideally microwave or steam foods containing Vitamin C to preserve as much of the vitamin as possible. Use any cooking liquid in other ways. Vitamin C is found in fruit and vegetables.

It is vital for growth, development of the collagen essential for strong bones, gums, teeth, and body tissues. It acts as an antioxidant and may help prevent certain illnesses, but there is no firm evidence that it protects against, or cures, colds, and flu.

Vitamin D

Cholecalciferol is found in only a few foods (mainly eggs, liver and oily fish), and most of that stored in the liver is made by the body from sunlight on the skin.

Vitamin D is required for developing healthy bones, general growth, and the absorption of calcium from foods. A lack of vitamin D can cause brittle bones in the elderly and rickets in young children.

Vitamin E

Vitamin E is mainly found in avocados, eggs, nuts, oily fish, all polyunsaturated spreads, spinach, sunflower seeds, and whole grain cereals.

Vitamin E consists of a group of compounds called tocopherols which work as antioxidants at protecting the body from damage by free radicals which can cause cancer.

Vitamin K

Vitamin K is found in alfalfa, cauliflower, cereals, green vegetables, liver, and kelp.

Vitamin K helps in blood clotting and the development of certain proteins. In addition to being present in many foods, it can also be synthesized by bacteria in the gut.

Above: tomatoes are a good source of Vitamin C. Their vitamin content is highest when they are eaten raw

Minerals

Minerals, also known as trace elements, are essential for a number of bodily functions, in particular the development of bones and teeth, regulation of body fluid composition and enzyme control. Minerals come from the soil via animals and plants.

Calcium

Calcium is mainly found in cheese, milk, sardines, white flour (which is fortified with it by law), and yogurt.

Calcium is essential for forming healthy bones and teeth but is not deposited in bones after the age of around 35. It is important to have had a good intake of calcium before this age in order to combat osteoporosis.

Fluoride

Fluoride is mainly found in drinking water which has been fluoridated, also seaweed (though not the chopped cabbage that masquerades as such) and tea.

Fluoride helps build strong bones and teeth and forms some protection against tooth decay. Taken in excessive quantities it can cause erosion of tooth enamel and give a mottled look to teeth.

Iodine

Iodine's richest source is kelp. Other sources include dairy products, fish, milk, and meat.

Iodine is essential for producing thyroid hormones.

Iron

Iron is found in the greatest quantities in liver and red meat although it is also present in eggs, pulses, some vegetables, and whole grain cereals. Vegetarians and vegans need to take particular care that they are getting sufficient iron in their diet as the quantities in the latter group's foods are not as readily absorbed as those from liver and meat.

Iron is a vital component of the haemoglobin in red blood cells that transports oxygen round the body. Anemia is the result of insufficient iron.

Magnesium

Magnesium is found in many foods, notably cocoa, green vegetables, nuts, other vegetables, and whole grain cereals.

Like calcium, magnesium plays an important part in the development of bones and teeth but is also involved in muscle and nerve functions, and the release of energy.

Phosphorus

Phosphorus is found in a wide variety of foods including cheese, eggs, fish, lentils, liver, meat, milk, whole grain cereals, and yeast extract.

Phosphorus is also important for bones and teeth and in the release of energy.

Potassium

Potassium is found in virtually all foods, especially fruit and vegetables, but not in fats, oils or sugar. Bananas are particularly rich in potassium.

Potassium, along with salt, regulates the levels of acidity and alkalinity in the body and controls the balance of water.

A lack of potassium may occur after heavy bouts of diarrhea or vomiting, as well as in people taking diuretics.

Zinc

Zinc is mainly found in cheese, eggs, fish, sundries (notably liver), meat, milk, shellfish (especially oysters), and yogurt.

Zinc plays a major part in the healing of cuts and wounds, and is essential for growth and sexual development.

Calories

Calories are the energy derived from eating foods. The term refers to the amount of heat required to raise the temperature of 1 gram of water by 1°C.

A kilocalorie equals 1000 calories but the word calorie is usually used to describe a kilocalorie. Kilojoule is a term little used in the US although it frequently appears on food labels and is more widely known in continental Europe. One kilocalorie (better known as a calorie) equals 4.183 kilojoules. You can see which measurement is easier to work in!

To lose weight–and bear in mind that many people are overweight–you need to consume fewer calories. Aim for a weight

Below: *fruit is high in fiber and vitamins*
Right: *cheese is rich in Vitamins A, B2, B12, and in calcium and phosphorus*

loss of around 2 pounds a week until you reach your target. Don't crash diet–you'll only put the weight on again quickly, most of what you lose is water. Simply reduce your calorie intake by 500 to 1000 calories a day depending on how many you consume but don't go below about 1200.

When you reach your target, you will need to make permanent changes to your diet to stay there. Reduce your intake of fat and sugar (there's no need to cut them out altogether) and increase your consumption of fresh fruit and vegetables. Fish and poultry (skin removed) are low in calories and lean meat with the fat removed is also very good. Plenty of starchy foods like whole wheat bread, cereals, pasta, and potatoes will fill you up without putting on weight, provided, of course, that you don't dress them with fatty toppings or sauces.

Don't fry foods. Try boiling, broiling, microwaving or steaming, none of which need much, if any, added fat. Use lower fat alternatives where possible; yogurt instead of cream, reduced-fat cheese instead of full-fat cheese, and skimmed or semi-skimmed milk.

Don't deprive yourself of treats you enjoy which are high in calories. Just ration them a little.

And don't make your hosts' lives a misery when you go out for meals. Stick to what guidelines you can and vow to cut out a treat or two over the next couple of days.

Lastly, remember that alcohol is very high in calories. Drink it only in moderation.

Microwave

Think of your microwave as an extra pair of hands in the kitchen. Above all, don't be frightened of it. If you're new to using a microwave and you are nervous of it, begin by using it for simple tasks until you build up your confidence. By using it for the foods that it cooks best, and by pairing it with traditional methods of cooking, you will achieve the best of both worlds. This form of cooking also enables you to reduce the amount of salt, fat, and sugar that you might normally use.

Below: *baking an elaborate cake becomes child's play*
Right: *a microwave turns out a soup in minutes*

Two methods of cooking, steaming and poaching, both of which retain the food's flavor and moisture, give perfect results in the microwave. Fish is particularly suited to these forms of cooking, and vegetables keep their color, flavor, crispness, and a high proportion of their vitamin content. Small quantities of jams and preserves can be cooked quickly; fruit can be poached in minutes; eggs scrambled in no time at all; and porridge can be prepared for breakfast leaving no messy pans.

Roasting needs more attention and you will need to use either a roasting bag, or a microwave roasting rack, and be prepared to baste often during the cooking time. To get the brown finish on a roast, you can add soy sauce, tomato paste, paprika, or even turmeric to the juices, or you can brush the meat or poultry with redcurrant jelly or honey.

A browning dish or skillet will give a broiled appearance to steaks, chops, bacon slices, sausages, kebabs, hamburgers, fish, and poultry pieces. To prevent bacon curling, snip the fatty edge. Sponge cakes cook in a very short time, rise well and stay moist inside, though the outside can harden as the cake cools. Disguise the pale color of microwaved cakes with frosting, or add chocolate, coffee, treacle, brown sugar, ginger or spices to the cake mixture.

Pastry needs to be rolled very thinly to help in crisping, and pastry cases should be baked blind to avoid them being soggy. You will not achieve the golden color of conventionally cooked pastry, but the addition of whole wheat flour to the basic mix will give color. Bread will not be crusty, so only cook rolls and soft breads, and crisp them under the broiler or on a roasting rack.

A combination oven, which offers both microwave and conventional cooking, can be either table-top or built-in and is a good choice for small kitchens.

Techniques

Microwave cooking has its own special methods which you need to employ for total success. They are very simple and extremely easy to follow.

Arranging: any regular-size even food, like tomatoes, etc., should be placed in rings, moving those on the outside to the center during the cooking. Uneven-size food (chops, chicken drumsticks, small fish, etc.) should be placed with their thinner parts toward the center of the dish where they will cook more slowly.

Covering: this traps steam and thereby helps to tenderize food and speed up cooking time. Use an inverted plate, or pierced microwave film to let some steam escape. Foods that splatter, like sausages and bacon, can be covered with paper towels.

Shielding: cover bones that protrude with tiny pieces of foil (shiny side down) topped with microwave film, to prevent them from burning.

Standing: meat roasts, cakes and puddings, should be left to stand, covered, for the time specified in recipes. This is because food continues to cook after it is taken out of the microwave.

Stirring: to distribute heat evenly, food cut into pieces and liquids should be stirred from the outside, where food cooks first, towards the center.

Turning: even ovens fitted with turntables or stirrer blades can still have blind spots where the food might not cook as thoroughly as the rest, so dishes that cannot be stirred, like cakes,

roasts of meat or poultry, should be rotated by a quarter or half turn during cooking.

Chicken stock

Break up a carcass, slice an onion, place in a bowl with bay leaf and mace blade. Cover with boiling water, cook on Full power for 15 minutes. Cool and strain.

Cook's Tip

Do not be frightened of your microwave: make friends with it and you will be richly rewarded.

Fish stock

Put 1 pound fish trimmings in a large bowl with a sliced onion, a carrot, a celery stalk and 2 bay leaves. Pour on 2½ cups of boiling water, then cover the bowl, and cook on Full power for 15 minutes. Cool, strain and use within 24 hours.

Apple sauce

Peel, core and slice 1 pound cooking apples into a bowl. Add ½ cup sugar, cover, and cook on Full power for 7 minutes. Beat in 2 tablespoons butter until smooth. Finally, add 2 tablespoons of chopped fresh herbs, for example thyme, parsley or sage, if you are serving the apple sauce with roast pork.

Béchamel sauce

Place ¼ cup all-purpose flour, a bay leaf and a blade of mace in a large basin. Slowly add 1¼ cups milk, whisking all the time. Season to taste and add 2 tablespoons butter. Cook (whisking twice during the cooking time)

on Full power for 4–5 minutes. Whisk again, then remove the bay leaf and the mace, check the seasoning, and serve.

Fudge sauce

Place 1 cup sugar, ¼ teaspoon salt, contents of a 6-ounce can evaporated milk in a bowl and mix well. Cook on Full power for 5–6 minutes, when the sauce should be boiling fast. Add 2 squares dark chocolate, broken into pieces, 2 tablespoons butter and 1 teaspoon vanilla extract. Stir until chocolate has melted and serve the sauce warm over ice cream.

Fruit poaching syrup

Put ¼ cup sugar, ⅔ cup water and 1 tablespoon lemon juice in a bowl, cover and cook on Full power for about 5–6 minutes, stirring once. Poach any fruit halves in the syrup for 4–5 minutes, stirring once.

Béchamel sauce variations

Cheese: add 1 cup grated Cheddar cheese to the sauce, whisking until it melts. Cook for 1 minute. *Mushroom:* add 3 cups thinly sliced button mushrooms to the sauce and cook for 2 minutes. *Parsley:* chop a handful of fresh parsley and add to the sauce, stir well and serve. *Onion:* finely chop 1 large onion or 2 small onions and cook in 2 tablespoons butter for 5 minutes on Full power. Then add the flour and milk, stir in the bay leaf and mace, and cook as in the main recipe.

Toasted salted almonds

Spread 1 cup almonds (it is not advisable to use a smaller quantity because they will probably scorch) on a flat dish and cook on Full power for 5–7 minutes. As a finishing touch, sprinkle with sea salt. Serve with drinks.

Left: *make Béchamel sauce with absolutey no trace of lumps*

Croûtons

Cube 2 thick slices of bread (you can use white or brown, as you prefer), discarding the crusts. Arrange the cubes of bread in a single layer on paper towels and then cook in the microwave on Full power for 3–4 minutes. Melt 2 tablespoons butter in a medium bowl on Full power for about 20–30 seconds. Add the croûtons and stir until all the butter has been absorbed.

Scrambled eggs

Whisk 4 eggs with 4 tablespoons of milk in a bowl, using a balloon whisk. Season and add 2 tablespoons diced butter. Now cook, whisking every 30 seconds during the cooking time, on Full power for 1½ minutes, until the eggs are light and creamy. The eggs will continue to cook when you take the bowl out of the oven, so it is important that you remove them before they have finished cooking; otherwise you will end up with rubbery-tasting eggs. Serve on hot buttered toast.

Utensil tips

● Container test: to see if something is safe to use, place a tumbler half full of water in it. Cook on Full power for 1 minute. If the water is warm and the container remains cool, then it can be used in the microwave oven.

● For a lighter, less greasy, result when cooking meat in a roasting bag, place the meat on a microwave rack or on an upturned saucer so that it does not sit in the fat as it cooks.

● Keep small rubber bands and use them to secure the neck of roasting bags.

● Pottery that is unglazed and porous tends to overheat and slows down cooking time, so avoid using in the microwave.

● Roasting bags, or boil-in-bags, should be pierced to let any steam escape.

● Round, shallow, straight-sided containers allow quick, even cooking and give the best results.

● Sterilize jars by half filling each one with water and heating until boiling. Remove the hot jars carefully, pour away the water, and drain them upside-down before filling.

● The bigger the dishes used in your microwave, the better. They leave plenty of room for stirring and prevent spillage.

● Utensils can be a choice of ceramics, glass, paper, plastic or wood, so check what you have in your kitchen before being tempted to spend money on something that you may not really need.

● Wood and wicker can be used for warming bread rolls, but make sure metal wire or staples have not been used, and that they are not bonded with glue.

● Vegetables cooked in roasting bags retain flavor and moisture and can easily be stirred or shaken during cooking time. Seal the bags with rubber bands or string, or cut a plastic strip from the top of the bag.

Food tips

● Alcohol for flambéd fruit or puddings can be heated in a pitcher for 15 seconds. Pour the warm alcohol over the pudding immediately and set alight.

● Blanch almonds by heating 1 cup water in a pitcher on Full power for 2½ minutes. Add the almonds, cook for 30 seconds, strain and remove skins.

● Chocolate for decorative piping should be broken into small pieces, put in a bowl and melted on Defrost. Then put it in a baking parchment piping bag and snip off the end.

● Chocolate for sauces can be melted in about 1½–2 minutes. Simply break into small pieces, place in a bowl and then cook on Full power.

● Citrus fruit will yield more juice if you prick the skin and warm it for 15–20 seconds on Full power. Halve and squeeze.

● Clarify crystallized honey by

Warnings

- Microwaves are deflected by metal so you cannot use the following: cast-iron flameproof casseroles, roasting pans, cake and pie pans, china with metallic decoration and lead crystal. Food will not cook in them, and they may damage the magnetron and cause arcing (sparking) which can pit the oven walls.
- Thermometers should never be left in a bowl when cooking jams or preserves.
- Glass tumblers and small dishes can be used, but if they are not designed for the microwave, do not cook food with a high proportion of sugar or fat because it can overheat and make the glass crack.
- Always check foods after the minimum suggested cooking time has elapsed. It is easy to extend the cooking time but impossible to rescue dishes that have been overcooked.
- Plastic wrap designed for the microwave should be used rather than food wrap plastic.
- Never try to hard-cook eggs in the microwave. Pressure inside the shells will make them explode.
- Use only wooden skewers – metal ones can cause arcing (sparking) which will damage the appliance; plastic ones will melt!

placing the open, wide-neck jar of honey in the microwave oven and warm it on Full power for 1–2 minutes.

- If you are entertaining with pasta, it is far easier to cook it ahead, using a conventional method, drain and turn into a bowl. Before you want to eat, dot with butter (do not mix), cover and heat for a few minutes in the microwave. Stir and serve.
- Herbs are good dried in the microwave oven. Rinse ½ cup fresh leaves under cold water, drain and dry. Spread between two pieces of paper towel and cook on Full power for 2 minutes. Remove the top towel and cook for 1–2 minutes longer or until all the moisture has been extracted from the leaves. Crush and store in an airtight container.
- If you like squash, it is useful to know that this vegetable responds particularly well to microwave cookery. First make sure it fits the oven, then slip it in a roasting bag and secure the neck of the bag. Cook a stuffed

4-pound squash on Full power for 10 minutes.

- Meat needs to be evenly marbled with fat to insure even cooking. Boneless, rolled, and carefully tied meat cooks very well in the microwave.
- Pastry can be given an extra touch of color by adding whole wheat flour.
- Peeling tomatoes is easy. Place around the rim of a plate lined with paper towels and heat on Full power for 10–15 seconds. Leave for 5 minutes, slit the skins with a knife, and slip them off.

Above: preserves and jams made easy
Below: *fish is well suited to this method*
Right: *vegetables retain color and flavor*

● All portions need to be evenly cooked, so it is a good idea to place them as far apart as possible in a dish or on a plate, turning and repositioning them several times during the cooking process to ensure even cooking.

● Poultry should be securely trussed to retain its shape whilst cooking in the microwave.

● Rind from oranges and lemons can be saved for flavoring: place it on a glass plate and cook on Full power until all the moisture has evaporated. Cool, then crumble and store in an airtight container until you are ready to use it.

● Salt has a toughening effect on meat, so always add it after your microwave cooking. Use unsalted butter for cooking any meat.

● Scrambling eggs in the microwave works brilliantly, but it is vital to beat or stir the mixture frequently and not overcook it. The eggs should be really very moist when removed from the oven as they will continue to cook for 2–3 minutes.

● Skin surrounding any food must be pierced before microwave cooking, to prevent pressure build-up causing the skin to burst.

● Spices and herbs should be used in moderation, to taste in microwave cooking, because it brings out their flavor.

● Sugar that has hardened is easily softened. Place ¾ cup in a bowl with a chunk of apple, cover and cook on Full power for about 30 seconds. Let stand for 5 minutes.

● Unmold jellies and other molded desserts by placing in the oven on Full power for 30 seconds or so. (Remember not to use metal molds.)

Microwave to freezer to microwave

The modern-day combination of microwave and freezer makes it possible to lead a busy life and still manage to be hospitable! You can cope with unexpected visitors, cook ahead for entertaining, prepare batches of food for the family, and shop ahead for the holidays.

The defrost control on the microwave makes it possible to thaw food automatically by repeatedly giving short bursts of microwave energy followed by rest periods. If your oven is without defrost, this can be achieved by microwaving on Full power for 30-second bursts, with 1½-minute intervals. In this way, you will have even thawing, without the food cooking before the remainder of the food is thawed.

Thawing and freezer tips

● Blanch vegetables in the microwave in preparation for putting them in the freezer.

● Chops and steaks should be separated; fruit and vegetables should be shaken or forked apart; and liquids and dishes such as casseroles and stews should be stirred and broken up at the beginning of thawing.

● Foil freezer containers should not be used in the microwave, so transfer the contents into a suitable dish.

● Freezer- and microwave-proof containers enable you to freeze food that can be later thawed and/or reheated in the microwave, saving you both time and trouble.

● Reheat sliced meat, and vegetables like broccoli and asparagus, in a sauce.

Microwave cooking times fresh vegetables

Fresh vegetables and weight	Preparation	Water to be added	Cooking time
Artichokes 4 medium	Wash and trim	⅔ cup	10–20 minutes
Beets 1 pound	Wash, peel, and cut in half	None	7–8 minutes
Broccoli 8 ounces	Slice into spears	3 tablespoons	4–5 minutes
Brussels sprouts 8 ounces	Trim	3–4 tablespoons	8 minutes
Cabbage 1 pound	Trim and shred	3 tablespoons	7–8 minutes
Carrots 8 ounces	Scrape and slice	2 tablespoons	7 minutes
Cauliflower 1 pound	Trim and cut into florets	4 tablespoons	9–10 minutes
Celery 1 head	Trim and dice	None	10–13 minutes
Corn on the cob (2)	Trim and wash	4 tablespoons	7–8 minutes
Eggplants 1 pound	Peel and dice	2 tablespoons	5–6 minutes
Fava beans 1 pound	Remove from pods and wash	2 tablespoons	7–10 minutes
Fennel 1 pound	Slice	2 tablespoons	9–10 minutes
Leeks 1 pound	Trim and slice	3 tablespoons	7–9 minutes
Mushrooms 4 ounces	Peel or wash whole	2 tablespoons	2½–3 minutes
Onions 8 ounces	Peel and slice	3 tablespoons	4–6 minutes
Parsnips 1 pound	Peel and slice	3 tablespoons	6–8 minutes
Peas 8 ounces	Remove from pods	3 tablespoons	6–8 minutes
Potatoes 1 pound	Peel and cut into even-size pieces	3 tablespoons	6–7 minutes
Potatoes 8–10 ounces	Scrub and prick well	None	9 minutes
Runner beans 8 ounces	String and slice	2 tablespoons	5 minutes
Rutabaga 8 ounces	Peel and dice	None	6–8 minutes
Spinach 8 ounces	Wash and shred	4 tablespoons	7 minutes
Tomatoes 8 ounces	Slice	None	2–3 minutes
Turnips 8 ounces	Peel and dice	2 tablespoons	6–7 minutes
Zucchini 1 pound	Trim, slice and sprinkle with salt	None	7–9 minutes

Microwave cooking times large cuts of meat

Meat and weight	Approx. cooking time	Standing time (wrapped tightly in foil)
Beef 1 pound	Rare: 4–5 minutes Medium: 7 minutes Well done: 9 minutes	20–30 minutes
Lamb 1 pound	7–9 minutes	25–30 minutes
Pork 1 pound	7–9 minutes	20–25 minutes
Ham 1 pound	7 minutes	15–20 minutes
Chicken 1 pound	6–7 minutes	15–20 minutes
Turkey up to 8 pounds	6–7 minutes	25–30 minutes

Microwave cooking times fish

Fish and weight	Approx. cooking time	Standing time (covered)
Cod fillets and steaks 1 pound	4 minutes	5–10 minutes
Flounder, gutted and filleted 1 pound	3 minutes	5–10 minutes
Sole, filleted 1 pound	3–4 minutes	5–10 minutes
Haddock, gutted and filleted 1 pound	3 minutes	5–10 minutes
Mackerel (2), gutted but whole 8 ounces	2 minutes, each side	5–10 minutes
Kipper fillets 8 ounces	3 minutes	5 minutes

Microwave cooking times small cuts of meat

Cut or type of meat and weight	Special points	Approx. cooking time	Standing time
Ground 1 pound	Cook covered	5 minutes	2 minutes
Steak: round or fillet mignon 8 ounces	----	3–4 minutes	2 minutes
Chops, loin: lamb or pork 2 portions 5 ounces each	Cook covered	6 minutes	2 minutes
Tenderloin: lamb or pork 12 ounces	Cook on roasting rack	6 minutes	5 minutes
Breast of lamb 1 pound 4 ounces	Cook on rack	6 minutes	3 minutes
Bacon 8 ounces	Cook on a rack, let fat drain.	4 minutes	2 minutes
Chicken: 2 portions 14 ounces	Cook covered	10 minutes	10–15 minutes
Ham steaks 7 ounces	Cook covered	2½–3 minutes	5 minutes
Ham 1 pound	Slice before cooking	7 minutes	10 minutes
Liver 1 pound	----	4 minutes	5 minutes
Kidneys 2 or 3	----	3–5 minutes	5 minutes

Microwave defrosting times joints of meat

Type	Approx time per 1 pound on LOW setting	Special instructions
Beef		
Boneless (sirloin)	8–10 minutes	Turn over regularly during thawing and rest if the meat shows signs of cooking. Stand for 1 hour.
Joints with bone (rib or beef)	10–12 minutes	Shield bone end with small, smooth pieces of foil and overwrap with microwave film. Turn the meat during thawing. The meat will still be icy in the center but will thaw completely if you leave it to stand for 1 hour.
Ground beef	8–10 minutes	Stand for 10 minutes.
Cubed steak	6–8 minutes	Stand for 10 minutes.
Steak (sirloin, round)	8–10 minutes	Stand for 10 minutes.
Beefburgers		
Regular (2 ounces)	2 burgers: 2 minutes 4 burgers: 2–3 minutes	Can be cooked from frozen, without thawing, if preferred.
Quarter-pounder	2 burgers: 2–3 minutes 4 burgers: 5 minutes	
Burger rolls	2 rolls: 2 minutes	Stand burger rolls for 2 minutes
Pork and Bacon		
Boneless rolled loin or leg	7–8 minutes	As for boneless roasts of beef above. Stand for 1 hour.
With the bone (leg)	7–8 minutes	As for roasts of beef with bone above. Stand for 1 hour.
Tenderloin	8–10 minutes	Stand for 10 minutes.
Chops	8–10 minutes	Separate during thawing and arrange "spoke" fashion. Stand for 10 minutes.
Bacon slices	2 minutes per 8 ounces	Remove from pack; separate after thawing. Stand for 6–8 minutes.
Lamb/Veal		
Boneless rolled loin, leg or shoulder	5–6 minutes	As for boneless roasts of beef above. Stand for 30–45 minutes.
Leg or shoulder with the bone	5–6 minutes	As for roasts of beef with bone above. Stand for 30–45 minutes.
Ground lamb or veal	8–10 minutes	Stand for 10 minutes.
Chops	8–10 minutes	Separate during thawing. Stand for 10 minutes.
Liver	8–10 minutes	Separate during thawing. Stand for 5 minutes.
Kidneys	6–9 minutes	Separate during thawing. Stand for 5 minutes.

Microwave defrosting times fish

Type	Approx time per 1 pound on LOW setting	Special instructions
White fish fillets e.g. cod, flounder, haddock or halibut	3–4 minutes per 1 pound, plus 2–3 minutes	Stand for 5 minutes after each 2–3 minutes.
Oily fish, e.g., whole and gutted mackerel, herring, trout	2–3 minutes per 8 ounces, plus 2–3 minutes	Stand for 5 minutes after each 2–3 minutes and for 5 minutes afterward.
Lobster tails, crab claws, etc	3–4 minutes per 8 ounces, plus 2–3 minutes	As for oily fish above.
Crab meat	2–3 minutes per 8 ounces, plus 2–3 minutes	As for oily fish above.
Shrimp, crayfish	2½ minutes per 4 ounces 3–4 minutes per 8 ounces	Pierce plastic bag, if necessary. Stand for 2 minutes. Separate with a fork after 2 minutes. Stand for 5 minutes, then plunge into cold water and drain.

Microwave defrosting times poultry and game

Type	Approx. time on LOW setting	Special instructions
Whole chicken or duckling	6–8 minutes	Remove giblets. Stand in cold water for 30 minutes.
Whole turkey	10–12 minutes	Remove giblets. Stand in cold water for 2–3 hours.
Chicken pieces	5–7 minutes	Separate during thawing. Stand for 10 minutes
Poussin, grouse, pheasant, pigeon, quail	5–7 minutes	----

Microwave defrosting times baked goods

Type	Quantity	Approx. time on LOW setting	Special instructions
Bread Loaf, whole Loaf, whole	 1 large 1 small	 6–8 minutes 4–6 minutes	 Uncover and place on paper towels. Turn over during thawing. Stand for 5–15 minutes.
Loaf, sliced Loaf, sliced	1 large 1 small	6–8 minutes 4–6 minutes	Defrost in original wrapper but remove any metal tags. Stand for 5–15 minutes.
Slice of bread	¼ inch thick	10–15 seconds	Place on paper towels. Time carefully, stand for 1–2 minutes.
Bread rolls	2 4	15–20 seconds 25–35 seconds	Place on paper towels. Time carefully, stand for 2–3 minutes.
English muffins	2	15–20 seconds	Place on paper towels. Time carefully, stand for 2–3 minutes.
Croissants	2	15–20 seconds	Place on paper towels. Time carefully, stand for 2–3 minutes.

Microwave defrosting times cakes and pastries

Type	Quantity	Approx. time on LOW setting	Special instructions
Cakes	2 small 4 small	30–60 seconds 1–1½ minutes	Place on paper towels. Stand for 5 minutes.
Sponge cake	1 pound	1–1½ minutes	Place on paper towels. Test and turn after 1 min. Stand for 5 minutes.
Jam doughnuts	2 4	45–60 seconds 45–90 seconds	Place on paper towels. Stand for 5 minutes.
Cream doughnuts	2 4	45–60 seconds 1¼–1¾ minutes	Place on paper towels. Check after half the thawing time. Stand for 10 minutes.
Cream éclairs	2 4	45 seconds 1–1½ minutes	Stand for 5–10 minutes. Stand for 15–20 minutes.
Choux buns	4 small	1–1½ minutes	Stand for 20–30 minutes.
Pastry Plain and puff	 8-ounces package 14-ounce package	 1 minute 2 minutes	 Stand for 20 minutes. Stand for 20–30 minutes.

Freezing

Freezing food whether it is fresh or cooked is a wonderful solution for today's busy lives. When you freeze food, do be certain that you prepare and store it correctly so you can be sure that all the ingredients for your meals have retained their original qualities and nutrients.

Cooling

Food must be as cool as possible before being packaged for the freezer, otherwise moisture in the form of steam will be retained. This, and the food's warmth, will cause large ice crystals to form between the food's tissues which will damage them. The best method is to stand pans and dishes of food in bowls of ice cubes or ice-cold water.

Ice glazing

Use for whole fish to protect skin and prevent air getting to the flesh. Open freeze it until solid, then dip quickly in cold water and refreeze. Repeat this process again and again until the ice is about ¼ inch thick, then wrap in a double layer of foil for storing.

Overwrapping

To prevent cross-transference of flavors and odors from one food to another or to give added protection. Wrap the food to be frozen in a double thickness of foil, or with rigid containers, double wrap and seal in a polythene bag.

Interleaving

Separating portions of food so that they freeze individually. Place sheets of plastic wrap or foil between each chop, steak or hamburger, etc., then freeze together in one container or package. Portions can be taken out and the package resealed and stored again.

Open freezing

Keeps individual pieces separate so they do not freeze in a solid mass and protects delicate, decorated and soft-textured foods. Line baking sheets with foil or baking parchment, spread food on top without pieces touching. Freeze until solid, then remove from the baking sheets and pack in bags.

Discoloration

Apples, apricots, peaches, and pears turn brown when cut. Prevent this by adding the juice of 1 lemon to 4½ cups water. Slice the fruit into the solution, leave for 15 minutes, and rinse before puréeing or freezing as slices. For fruit packed in syrup, dissolve ½ teaspoon ascorbic acid powder in 1 tablespooon cold water and add to 2½ cups sugar syrup.

Headspace

The space between the surface of food and the lid of a rigid container. Liquids expand during freezing and will force off a container lid if packed to the brim. Food then becomes exposed to air and will spoil during its freezing time. Roll or crumple baking parchment into small balls and place on top of stews, casseroles, fruit, etc., to keep contents submerged in liquid.

Sugar syrup

To 5 cups water use 1 cup sugar for light syrup; 2 cups for medium; or 4 cups for heavy. Bring the ingredients slowly to a boil; the water must not boil before the sugar dissolves or it may crystallize into lumps. Boil hard for 2 minutes to get a clear syrup and let it cool.

Packaging

Use bags for small fruit and vegetables; rigid containers for food which might be knocked, crushed or broken during storage. To exclude air and cover surfaces, even-shaped and sturdy food can be enclosed in foil or film using the techniques of druggist's and butcher's wrap.

● Druggist's wrap: Place awkwardly shaped food on a large square of foil. Fold over one corner so it covers food. Turn in one side, then the other so food is nearly hidden. Fold foil back on itself and bring fourth corner to top. Press to exclude air.

● Butcher's wrap: Place even-shaped food on a large foil triangle. Lift up the two long sides, bring to the top. With edges meeting, make one sharp fold. Continue to fold foil until it reaches food. This will press out air. Fold in foil at both sides, seal on top with freezer tape.

To blanch vegetables

This is essential to prevent the loss of Vitamin C. Place 8 ounces vegetables in a blanching basket and immerse completely in 4½ quarts boiling water. Return to a boil quickly, then calculate blanching time from moment water reboils. (Blanching times are given on pp 245–246). Plunge basket of vegetables into ice-cold water for same length of time as boiling to prevent more cooking and drain well before packing. Water can be reused 6 or 7 times.

Preparing fruit

● Free flow pack: For soft fruits which make their own juice and can be used partially frozen. The fruit keeps it shape and small amounts can be removed without having to thaw the whole quantity. Open freeze the fruit until frozen solid. Pack in rigid containers or polythene bags.

● Dry sugar pack: For soft, juicy, whole or sliced fruit. The fruit juice combines with sugar to make a natural syrup. Place in a large shallow dish, sprinkle over sugar, and let stand until the fruit juice begins to flow and the sugar dissolves. Allow 2 cups superfine sugar to 4 pounds fruit. Stir fruit lightly until evenly coated with syrup and pack in rigid containers, leaving ½-inch headspace.

● For small quantities: Place fruit in freezer container, sprinkle with sugar, layer with fruit and sugar until full. In thawing, fruit sugar will make its own syrup.

● Packing in sugar syrup: For non-juicy fruits and those which discolor quickly. Use a really light syrup for delicately flavored fruit, medium and heavy for other types of fruit, depending on the fruit's natural sweetness. Make the syrup a day ahead so that it is cold before use. Pack the fruit to be frozen, into rigid containers, pour over the cold syrup covering the fruit but leaving about ½–1-inch headspace. Fruit must be fully submerged in the syrup before freezing; if necessary push several pieces of crumpled baking parchment or wax paper down into the syrup before sealing the container.

● Purée: For well-ripened or slightly damaged fruit. This is a good and really effective method for fruit which might otherwise go to waste. Wash and dry the fruit. Lightly cook all the hard fruits, such as apples, purée and then add the sugar (The quantities to use are: ¼–½ cup sugar per pound fruit). Pack the fruit into rigid containers, leaving ½-inch head space between the purée and the top of the container and seal securely.

A–Z of freezing fruit

	Preparation	Packing	To use
Apples	Peel, core, slice or chop. For purée, cook in the minimum of water with or without sugar. Strain and cool.	Free flow/light syrup/puréed	Thaw in the unopened containers. For pies and tarts thaw enough to separate the slices for stewing. Used for mousses, soufflés and sauces.
Apricots	Wipe and leave whole; peel fruit by plunging it in boiling water for 30 seconds, rub off skins, pit, halve or slice.	Heavy syrup with ascorbic acid/puréed	Thaw in their containers for 3 hours or at room temperature and serve cold. Frozen in syrup: tip into a saucepan and heat gently. Storage: sugar syrup packs–1 year; purée–4 months.
Blackberries	Pick on a dry day for best results. Avoid blackberries with large woody seeds. Wash in ice water. Dry well and remove stalks.	Dry sugar/free flow/light syrup	Thaw in their containers. Use while partially frozen to serve cold or in pies. Frozen in syrup: tip into a saucepan and heat slowly.
Cherries	Red varieties are better for freezing than black. Wash and dry well, remove stalks and pit.	Free flow/medium syrup	Thaw unopened in their containers for 3 hours at room temperature for pies and fruit salads. Tip frozen into a saucepan and heat slowly.
Currants–red, black and white	Remove from stalks, wash, dry well, top and tail and leave whole. If preferred, freeze currants on the stalks which can be removed when thawing. OR Stew in the minimum of water, sweeten to taste. Cool.	Free flow/light syrup/puréed	Thaw unopened in their containers for 3 hours at room temperature for pies and cold desserts. Frozen in syrup: tip into a saucepan and heat slowly.
Damsons	Wash, dry and cut in halves. Remove the pits, which can flavor the fruit.	Syrup/puréed	Thaw unopened in the container for 3 hours at room temperature. Use in jams and pies, or sauces and mousses.
Figs	Wipe, dry and snip off stems. May be peeled or left unpeeled.	Free flow/light syrup	Let stand in wrappings or containers for 1½ hours at room temperature.
Gooseberries	Wash and drain, top and tail, and leave whole.	Medium syrup/puréed and strained	Thaw unopened at room temperature before using in jams and pies. Frozen in syrup, tip into a saucepan and stew slowly. Use partially thawed purée in fools and mousses.
Grapes	Wash and drain, top and tail, and leave whole.	Medium syrup	Thaw unopened in the container for about 2 hours at room temperature. Use while partially frozen for pies and fruit cocktails.
Guavas	Peel, halve and remove seeds, Leave as halves or slice.	Dry sugar/light syrup/puréed	Thaw in their containers to use in pies or flans. Cook from frozen until tender, stirring frequently.
Kiwifruit	Peel carefully and leave whole.	Free flow	Thaw in containers until partially frozen, then slice to serve.
Lemons	Wipe over the fruit and leave whole, or cut into slices, grate peel, or extract juice.	Whole: wrap in a polythene bag. Slices: free flow. Peel: grate before extracting juice, pack in small cartons. Juice: freeze in ice-cube trays. Pack cubes in polythene bags.	Thaw in wrapping for about 3 hours at room temperature and use as required.
Lychees	Choose fresh fruits with a reddish-brown hue. Remove outer husk and squeeze out central pits.	Heavy syrup	Thaw in the refrigerator for 1 hour. Use partially frozen in fruit salads.
Mangoes	Peel and slice the flesh away from the pit.	Medium syrup with lemon juice	Thaw in the container for 1½ hours at room temperature.
Melon	Peel, cut in half and remove the seeds. Slice, cube or cut into balls.	Dry sugar/medium syrup	Thaw unopened in the container for about 3 hours at room temperature. Serve while still frosty.
Nectarines	Peel if liked, halve and pit.	Medium syrup	Thaw in containers in the refrigerator for 3–4 hours.

	Preparation	Packing	To use
Oranges	Scrub skins and dry. Peel, remove pith and cut into segments or slices. Remove membrane and seeds. Leave Sevilles whole (the bitter type used for marmalade).	Light syrup/dry sugar	Thaw sliced fruit in its container for about 3 hours and serve chilled. Use whole fruit frozen for marmalade.
Papayas	Peel, halve and scoop out the seeds. Cut into thin slices.	Medium syrup/puréed with lemon juice	Thaw in their containers for 1–2 hours.
Passionfruit	Choose firm ripe fruits with soft, purple, wrinkled skins. Halve and scoop out the seeds.	Weigh and mix with half its weight of sugar. Stir to dissolve and pack in rigid containers	Thaw in the container for 1½ hours.
Peaches	Peel with a knife or plunge into boiling water for 30 seconds and then into cold water, this will loosen the skin. Cut into halves or slices and remove pit.	Heavy syrup with ascorbic acid or lemon juice	Thaw in the container for about 4 hours. Serve chilled.
Pears	Wash, peel and core. Halve or slice. Best frozen lightly cooked as they tend to lose flavor and crispness if frozen raw.	Poach for 1½ minutes in heavy syrup with ascorbic acid or lemon juice	Thaw in the container for about 4 hours.
Persimmons	Peel and leave whole or slice, removing any seeds.	Whole: wrap in foil. Slices: syrup with a little lemon juice	Thaw in the wrappings or container for 3 hours.
Pineapple	Peel, core and slice or dice.	Medium syrup/dry sugar	Thaw unwrapped in containers for 3 hours. Serve chilled.
Plums	Wash, halve and remove pits.	Free flow/medium syrup	For pies: thaw for about 3 hours before using. Otherwise tip frozen in a pan and heat slowly in their own syrup.
Raspberries	Wash in iced water, gently and leave whole, or strain fruit to a purée.	Free flow/medium syrup/dry sugar	Thaw unopened in containers for 3 hours at room temperature; use just before the fruit has completely thawed.
Rhubarb	Wash firm but tender fruit and cut into required lengths.	Blanch in boiling water for 1 minute. Drain and pack in polythene bags or rigid containers without sugar.	Thaw partially in containers. Frozen fruit: tip enough water just to stop it catching, add sugar to taste and heat slowly.
Strawberries	Remove stalks. Wash in iced water and dry gently on paper towels. Leave whole or purée with sugar to taste. Note: frozen whole strawberries do show a loss of texture and flavor on thawing. They are best used for decoration or in recipes such as fruit salad.	Free flow/dry sugar/medium syrup/puréed	Thaw in containers for about 3 hours at room temperature and use just before fruit has completely thawed.

A–Z of freezing vegetables

	Preparation	Blanching time	Packing	To use
Artichokes, globe	Remove outer leaves, trim and wash.	Up to six at a time – 7 minutes	In polythene bags or rigid containers, leaving ½-in headspace.	Thaw overnight in refrigerator or 4 hours at room temperature. Eat with vinaigrette dressing.
Artichokes, Jerusalem	Only worth freezing as a purée. Scrub, peel, then simmer in water until tender.	Nil	In rigid containers, leaving 1-in headspace. (Storage: 3 months).	Reheat slowly from frozen with a little milk to prevent it catching, or use for soup.
Asparagus	Clean, trim off woody ends. Grade by thickness of stems. Cut to fit container, but don't tie.	Thin – 2 minutes. Medium – 3 minutes Thick – 4 minutes	Pack closely in rigid containers head to tail or tie in bundles and freeze in a polythene bag.	Plunge in boiling water for 5–8 minutes.
Beans, fava	Choose small young beans. Shell and grade into sizes.	2 minutes	Open freeze, then pack into polythene bags.	Plunge into boiling water for 5–10 minutes.

A–Z of freezing vegetables

	Preparation	Blanching time	Packing	To use
Beans, French and runner	Choose young tender stringless beans. Cut off ends and tips, leave whole if small, or cut into 1-inch lengths.	Whole or cut – 2 minutes	Open freeze, then pack into polythene bags.	Plunge in boiling water for 8–10 minutes.
Beets	Choose young beets not more than 3 inches in diameter. Twist off tops leaving about 2 inches attached.	Nil	Peel, dice or slice or leave whole. Pack into polythene bags or rigid cartons (Storage: 6 months).	Thaw in refrigerator and use in salads. To serve cook in boiling water for about 25–45 minutes or until tender.
Broccoli	Choose compact heads, cut off woody stalks and trim to an even length.	Thin stalks–3 minutes Thick stalks–4 minutes	Pack head to tail in polythene bags or rigid containers, or open freeze, then pack as above.	Plunge frozen into boiling water and cook for 5–8 minutes.
Brussels sprouts	Choose small even-size sprouts. Trim off outside leaves.	Small–3 minutes Medium–4 minutes	Open freeze, then pack in polythene bags.	Plunge frozen into boiling water and cook for 5–8 minutes.
Cabbage–red, white	Wash and shred.	1½ minutes	Pack in polythene bags. (Storage: blanched, 1 year; braised, 6 months).	Plunge in boiling water for 3–5 minutes; braise red cabbage, when it can be re-frozen.
Carrots	Choose small young carrots. Scrub and leave whole. If using large carrots, scrape and slice or dice.	Small, whole–5 minutes Diced or sliced–3 minutes	Pack in polythene bags or rigid containers.	Plunge frozen into boiling water and cook for 5–10 minutes.
Cauliflower	Choose compact white cauliflower. Break into florets of an even size not larger than 1 inch across.	3 minutes	Open freeze, then pack in polythene bags (Storage: 6 months).	Plunge frozen into boiling water and cook for 5–8 minutes. Serve with a sauce.
Celeriac	Choose firm, small roots. Peel and wash, then cut into cubes or slices. Alternatively, grate.	1–2 minutes for cubes and slices; 1 minute for grated.	Open freeze, then pack into rigid containers or polythene bags.	Plunge frozen cubes or slices into boiling water for 5 minutes. Toss in butter or a sauce. Use grated from frozen in soups and casseroles or cook as above for 3 minutes.
Celery	Choose tender young stalks. Scrub and cut into even lengths.	Nil	Pack in polythene bags	Do not use raw after freezing. Reheat in the oven or in boiling water for 3–5 minutes.
Corn on the cob	Choose young, tender corn. Remove husk and silk, and grade according to size.	Small–4 minutes. Medium–6 minutes Large–8 minutes	Pack individually in polythene bags, or scrape off kernels, open freeze, then pack as above.	Thaw cobs before cooking, about 4 hours at room temperature. Plunge whole cob into boiling water for 15 minutes, or cook from frozen in boiling water for about 5 minutes.
Eggplants	Wash and cut in ½-inch slices. Blanch immediately to avoid discoloration.	4 minutes.	Open freeze, pack in polythene bag.	Plunge in boiling water for 3–5 minutes.
Endive	Choose firm specimens with tightly packed conical heads. Remove base and any damaged outer leaves	4 minutes	Pack into polythene bags	Plunge into boiling water for 8 minutes. Or thaw in wrappings at room temperature for 2 hours. Squeeze to remove excess moisture then use as required.
Fennel	Choose firm, tight heads with white leaf bases. Trim and scrub the outer leaves. Cut into quarters.	3–5 minutes	Pack into polythene bags.	Plunge into boiling water for 7 minutes. Use from frozen in stews.

	Preparation	Blanching time	Packing	To use
Leeks	Remove outer leaves. Trim ends and wash well.	Nil	Pack in polythene bags (Storage: 6 months).	Plunge from frozen in boiling water for 7–10 minutes.
Mushrooms	Choose fresh cultivated mushrooms. Wash and dry thoroughly. Leave whole if button, or slice.	Do not blanch in water but sauté in butter allowing 6 tablespoons of melted butter to 1 pound mushrooms, for 4–5 minutes	Pack in rigid containers, with cooking liquid. (Storage: raw 1 month; cooked: 3 months.) Open freeze buttons if wished, pack in polythene bags.	Add while frozen to soups. sauces, stews, etc., or if packed in melted butter, reheat slowly in the oven or under a broiler.
Onions	Choose whole small onions or slice or chop larger onions. Open freeze unblanched for short storage: 3 months.	Nil	Pack in polythene bags or rigid containers and over-wrap to prevent cross-flavoring (Storage: 6 months).	Add while frozen to soups, sauces, casseroles and stews.
Parsnips	Choose small young parsnips. Trim and peel. Cut into strips or dice.	2 minutes.	Open freeze, then pack in polythene bags.	Plunge into boiling water for 10 minutes.
Peas	Choose young, sweet tender peas. Pod and sort carefully.	1 minute	Open freeze, then pack in polythene bags or rigid containers.	Plunge into boiling water for 4–7 minutes.
Peppers–red or green bell	Choose firm glossy peppers. Wash, remove seeds and stem, slice or dice.	Nil	Pack in polythene bags or rigid containers.	Plunge frozen into boiling water for 5–10 minutes.
Potatoes–baby boiled	Choose small even-size ones. Scrape or scrub the potatoes. Slightly undercook until just tender.	Nil	Pack in polythene bags or boiling bags (Storage: 3 months).	Plunge into boiling water for 3–5 minutes, or put boiling bag in boiling water, remove from heat and stand for 10 minutes.
Potatoes– French fries	Prepare in the usual way. Deep fry in hot oil 350°F until just tender, not brown. Drain well, cool.	Nil	Open freeze, then pack into polythene bags or rigid containers (Storage: 6 months).	Fry in shallow or deep frying pan; take care as spitting can occur.
Potatoes– mashed	Cook and mash old potatoes in the usual way. Make into croquette potatoes.	Nil	Open freeze, then pack into polythene bags or rigid containers (Storage: 3 months).	Reheat as directed in the recipe used.
Rutabagas	Trim, peel and dice.	3 minutes.	Pack into polythene bags or polythene containers.	Cook from frozen in boiling water for 8–10 minutes or add to soups, stews and casseroles.
Spinach	Choose young, fresh spinach, wash very thoroughly. Quicker to cook first, then freeze as a leaf or as a purée.	Blanch in small quantities only–2 minutes	Pack in polythene bags or rigid containers (Storage: 10 months).	Plunge frozen into boiling water, cook for 2–3 minutes. Drain well and toss in a little butter.
Squash	Peel and remove the seeds. Chop into large pieces.	3 minutes	Pack in polythene bags or rigid containers.	Plunge in boiling water for 3–5 minutes.
Tomatoes	Choose firm tomatoes, peel and leave whole or purée.	Nil	Pack whole peeled tomatoes in polythene bags or rigid containers. Freeze purée in rigid containers.	Not suitable for eating raw as they collapse. Add to stews, soups and casseroles, or fry or broil whole or halved.
Turnips	Choose small turnips. Trim, peel and dice, if large. Or cook and purée.	Small, whole–4 minutes. Diced–2 minutes	Pack in polythene bags. Pack purée in rigid containers.	Cook from frozen in boiling water for 8–10 minutes or add to soups and stews.
Zucchini	Pick even-size young zucchini, cut in half or into ½-inch slices.	1 minute	Open freeze, then pack in polythene bags or rigid containers.	Plunge while frozen into boiling water for 3 minutes or thaw and sauté in butter.

Glossary

Acidulated water Water with added acid, such as lemon juice or vinegar, which prevents discoloration.

Al dente The Italians say that pasta is ready to eat when it is *al dente* which when literally translated means "firm to the bite."

Antipasti Italian hors d'œuvre. The literal Italian translation is "before the meal" and it usually denotes an assortment of cold meats, vegetables and cheeses which are often marinated.

Arborio The Italian rice used in making risotto. It is similar in shape to pudding rice, but never quite softens in the middle.

Au gratin A cheese and bread crumb topping, browned under the broiler.

Bain-marie A large, water-filled pan in which smaller dishes are set for cooking when an indirect, low heat is required.

Bake blind To part-bake an unfilled pie shell by pricking the bottom with a fork, covering with baking parchment or foil, and filling with ceramic or dry beans.

Ballotine Boneless, rolled and stuffed meat, usually poultry, served hot.

Balsamic vinegar Italian vinegar that has been aged for anything up to 20 years in oak casks. It is dark in colour with an intense, slightly sweet flavor.

Barbecue To cook over glowing coals, often of charcoal.

Bard To cover or wrap lean meats in a sheet of fat to prevent drying out.

Baste To spoon pan juices (usually fat-based) over meat or vegetables to moisten during cooking.

Beignets Fritters.

Beurre manié Flour and butter worked into a paste, then used to thicken soups, stew juices, etc.

Beurre noir Butter heated to a light brown color, usually served with fish.

Bind To hold dry ingredients together with egg or liquid.

Bisque Smooth and thickened shellfish soup.

Blanch To immerse food briefly in boiling water to soften, remove skin, par-cook, set a color, or remove a strong taste.

Bouillon Broth or unclarified stock obtained from boiling meat or vegetables.

Bouquet garni Classically made up of a bay leaf, a sprig of thyme and 2–3 sprigs of parsley, which are either bound together with string or tied into a small cheesecloth bag. It is used to flavor almost any savory dish that needs long cooking, and is removed before the dish is served.

Braise To cook food very slowly in a small amount of liquid in a pan or pot with a tight-fitting lid, after initial browning.

Brochette Broiled and served on a skewer.

Buckwheat Small, triangular-shaped grain, milled into either flour or grains.

Bulgar wheat Cracked wheat that has been partially processed. Sometimes sold as cracked wheat, and used extensively in Mid Eastern cooking.

Butterfly To slit a piece of food in half horizontally, almost cutting through so that when opened it resembles butterfly wings. Often used for jumbo shrimp, chops, and thick fillets of fish.

Canapé Small appetizer of pastry, crackers, etc. with a savory topping.

Capers Small buds of a flowering shrub grown in the Mediterranean. As they are normally pickled in brine or salted, they should be washed and dried before use.

Casserole Ovenproof cooking pot with a lid.

Cassis A fruit liqueur or syrup made from blackcurrants.

Cassoulet A classic French dish which consists of Navy beans cooked in a stewpot with pork, other meat and poultry, seasoning, and a gratin topping. Sausages and duck and goose portions are often added.

Caramelize To cook sugar or sugar syrup to the caramel stage. The term is also used when broiling a sugar topping until brown.

Ceps (dried) Dried mushrooms that need reconstituting in boiling water before using. Also known as porcini, which is their Italian name.

Clarify To melt and strain butter of its milk particles and impurities; to clear stocks, etc. by filtering.

Cocotte A small ovenproof dish without a lid.

Compôte Fresh or dried fruit served cold in a syrup.

Consommé Concentrated clear meat or poultry stock.

Coulis A thin liquid purée, usually of fresh or cooked fruit or vegetables, which can be poured.

Court-bouillon Aromatic liquid generally used for poaching fish or shellfish.

Couscous This is actually a type of pasta though it is treated like a grain and is presoaked before cooking to soften it. It is often used in North African or Mid Eastern cooking.

Crackling The crisp cooked

rind of a joint of pork.

Cream To beat fat and sugar together to a pale consistency.

Croustade Small bread cases, brushed with melted butter and baked or deep-fried until crisp.

Croûte A slice of fried or toasted bread on which food is served.

Croûton Small shapes (usually dice) of fried or occasionally toasted bread used as a garnish.

Crudités Raw vegetables such as carrot, cucumber and celery, usually cut into sticks or slices and used with a dipping sauce.

Curdle To cause milk or sauce to separate into solid and liquid. Often used to describe any mixture that separates.

Dariole A small castle-shaped mold, for cakes, mousses, etc.

Deglaze To free congealed cooking juices and sediments from the bottom of a roasting pan by adding water, stock or wine and stirring over heat. The juices may be used to make gravy or added to a sauce.

Degorge To sprinkle with salt or to soak to remove indigestible or strong tasting juices from meat, fish or vegetables.

Degrease To skim grease from the surface of liquid.

Demi-glace A rich brown sauce.

Deviled A food seasoned with a hot-tasting sauce and broiled or fried.

Draw To remove the innards of birds.

Dredge To sprinkle the surface of food with flour, confectioners' sugar, etc.

Dress To pluck, draw and truss poultry or game birds; or to put dressing onto a salad and toss.

Dropping consistency The stage reached when a spoonful of a mixture held upside down will drop off the spoon reluctantly.

Duxelle A stuffing of finely chopped mushrooms, often with shallots or ham.

Empanada A South American pastry turnover stuffed with a mixture of chopped meat, onions, etc.

Emulsion A milky liquid prepared by mixing liquids that are not soluble, such as oil and water or other substances.

En croûte To cook food in a pastry case.

En papillote To cook food enclosed in paper.

Entrée In Europe a dish served before the main course, now often referring to the main course itself.

Escalope A thin slice of meat from the fillet or leg.

Farce Stuffing.

Fines herbes A mixture of finely chopped fresh herbs. Traditionally these are fresh chervil, chives, parsley and tarragon.

Flake To separate cooked meat or fish into very small pieces.

Flamber To pour warmed spirit, often brandy, over food and set it alight.

Florentine A dish that is made with spinach.

Flute To make decorative indentations in the edges of pastry pies.

Fold in To combine two mixtures gently with a metal spoon to retain their lightness.

Freezer burn Appears as brown or grayish-white patches on the surface of frozen food. It is caused by extreme dehydration and is often seen on meat, poultry and fish.

Fumet A strong, well-reduced stock made from fish or meat.

Galantine Boneless, rolled and stuffed meat, usually poultry, served cold.

Galette Any sweet or savory mixture that is shaped in a flat round.

Garam masala A ready-made spice powder made up of several different Indian spices.

Garnish To decorate a savory dish.

Glaze A mixture that is brushed on the surface of food to give color and shine.

Gnocchi These are little Italian dumplings made from mashed potatoes, potato flour, polenta or wheat flour. They are usually poached in boiling water to cook.

Goujons Small strips of meat or fish, coated and then deep-fried.

Hard ball A stage of sugar boiling used in jams, etc.

Hollandaise A rich emulsion sauce made with egg yolks and butter.

Hors d'œuvre The first course or savory morsels served with drinks.

Hull To remove the green calyx from fruit.

Infuse To extract flavor by steeping food in hot liquid.

Jardinière A garnish of neatly cut, separately cooked vegetables.

Julienne Matchstick strips of vegetables, citrus rind or meat, used as a garnish.

Kibbled Coarsely chopped, used particularly for wheat.

Knead To work dough by stretching and folding it to distribute the yeast and give a springy consistency.

Lard To thread strips of fat (usually pork) into lean meat to moisten it.

Lardons Small cooked strips or cubes of pork or bacon fat, used to flavor or garnish a dish.

Legumes The dried seeds of members of the bean and pea family.

Liaison Ingredients used to bind or thicken.

Macédoine A mixture of diced vegetables or fruit.

Macerate To steep raw food, usually fruit, in sugar syrup or alcohol.

Magret A boned breast of duck, presented with the skin and underlying layer of fat attached.

Marinade The liquid in which food is marinated.

Marinate To soak raw food (usually meat, poultry or game) in liquid, often wine or oil, to tenderize and give flavor.

Medallions Small rounds of meat, evenly cut.

Mesclun This is a French salad using wild salad leaves and grasses.

Millet A small pinhead grain with a nutty flavor.

Mirepoix A bed of diced vegetables (usually carrot, onion and celery) on which meat or whole vegetables are braised.

Mole A Mexican chili sauce.

Mousseline Small mounds made from poultry or fish, and served hot or cold.

Niçoise Food cooked or served with tomatoes, garlic, French green beans, anchovies, and olives.

Noisette Boneless rack of lamb, rolled and cut into rounds; surrounded by a thin band of fat.

Panada A thick white sauce used as a base for dishes such as soufflés, etc.

Pan-frying Uses a thick-bottomed heated pan; the food cooks in its own juices.

Parboil To boil until partially cooked.

Pare To peel or trim.

Parmentier Containing potatoes.

Passata Strained tomatoes.

Pâte The French for pastry dough.

Pâté A savory paste of liver, pork, game, etc.

Pâtisserie A French cake store, or sweet cakes and pastry items.

Paupiettes Slices of meat or fish rolled around stuffing.

Poach To cook by simmering very slowly in liquid.

Polenta The Italian name for cornmeal.

Praline Caramelized sugar and browned almonds mixed together.

Prove To put yeast dough to rise before baking.

Punching down To punch or knead air from yeast dough after rising.

Purée Cooked food, mashed or strained until smooth.

Quenelles Light fish or meat dumplings, usually poached.

Ragoût A stew.

Ramekins Small ovenproof dishes, usually made of porcelain.

Reduce To concentrate–or thicken–a liquid, by boiling it rapidly to decrease its volume.

Refresh To rinse freshly cooked food under cold running water or by plunging into ice water to stop the cooking process and to set the color, used particularly for vegetables.

Relax or rest In pastry to let the gluten in the flour contract after rolling out; to let the starch cells in the flour of a batter expand.

Render To melt and strain animal fat.

Roux A basic liaison of melted fat (usually butter) and flour, cooked as a thickening for sauces, soups, etc.

Rub in To mix fat into flour, using the fingertips to give a mixture resembling fine bread crumbs.

Sabayon A frothy sweet sauce of whipped egg yolks, sugar, wine and liqueur.

Salsa In Mexico this usually applies to uncooked sauces served as a dip or accompaniment. Mexican salsas are usually made from chilies and tomatoes; in Italy the term is often used for pasta sauces.

Sauter This method of frying uses very little fat and the food is moved constantly throughout the process to prevent it sticking to the pan and burning.

Scald To heat liquid, usually milk to just below boiling point. Also to rinse with boiling water.

Score To make shallow or deep cuts over the surface of meat or fish before cooking to let the heat penetrate evenly.

Seal or sear Sealing the surface of food, to retain juices, goodness and flavor.

Seasoned flour Flour with salt and pepper added.

Shiitake Oriental mushrooms available both fresh and dried.

Simmer To cook food slowly in liquid at just below boiling point.

Singe To flame plucked poultry quickly to remove all traces of feathers.

Skim To remove any scum or fat from the surface of a liquid with a metal spoon or small ladle.

Spatchcock A chicken or poussin split open with poultry shears and spread out flat before cooking.

Steam To cook food in the steam above boiling water, in a perforated dish or a special steamer.

Steep To soak in warm or cold liquid in order to soften food and draw out strong flavors.

Stew To cook food slowly in a small quantity of liquid in a closed dish or pan in the oven or on the stove top.

Stir-fry An Oriental cooking method in which food is lightly cooked in a little oil over a high heat with constant stirring.

Sundried tomatoes These are a form of preserved tomato. They have a concentrated flavor and are usually preserved in oil.

Suprême A choice piece of meat, usually a breast of poultry, and also a rich, creamy white sauce.

Sweat To soften food, usually vegetables, in a little fat over a very low heat until the juices run.

Tahini paste A purée of sesame seeds plain or toasted, used extensively in Mid Eastern cooking.

Tempura A Japanese style of deep-frying pieces of meat, fish, poultry and vegetables in a light batter. These are then served with a dip of soy sauce.

Terrine A pâté or minced mixture cooked in a loaf-shaped dish.

Timbale A dish cooked in a drum-shaped mold.

Tofu Soybean curd.

Tortillas These are a flat type of bread unique to Mexico and are made from dried cornmeal or from wheat flour. They are the basis for many Mexican dishes such as tacos and enchiladas.

Truss To tie a roast or bird with string before cooking.

Vanilla sugar Superfine sugar flavored with pure vanilla extract. Make by adding a vanilla bean to a jar of superfine sugar.

Vinaigrette A salad dressing made with olive oil and vinegar or lemon juice.

Well The hollow made in a pile or bowl of flour into which liquid, fat, etc. are put prior to mixing.

Zest The thin outer layer of citrus fruit containing the citrus oil.

Index